TO PURGE
THIS LAND
WITH BLOOD

A Biography of John Brown

STEPHEN B. OATES

Second Edition

THE UNIVERSITY OF MASSACHUSETTS PRESS
Amherst

LC 84–2635
ISBN 0–87023–458–7
Library of Congress Cataloging in Publication Data
Oates, Stephen B.
To purge this land with blood

Bibliography: p.
 1. Brown, John, 1800–1859. 2. Abolitionists—United
States—Biography. I. Title.
E451.O17   1984   973.6'8'0924   [B]   84–2635
ISBN 0–87023–458–7 (pbk.)

For my children
Gregory and Stephanie
with my love

CONTENTS

MAPS

Two sections of illustrations follow pages 114 and 178.

PROLOGUE

TO THE SECOND EDITION

He is still one of the most controversial figures in American history—a dedicated emancipationist and friend of the Negro who failed at nearly everything he tried in his pre-Kansas career, who instigated the Pottawatomie massacre in all the hatred and violence of the slavery struggle in Kansas, and who tried to overthrow bondage in the South itself by attacking Harpers Ferry, Virginia, and inciting a slave insurrection. One hundred and twenty-five years after Harpers Ferry, his name can still provoke rancorous debate about his motives and methods, even about his sanity. "When the subject of John Brown comes up," a historian said recently, "we tend to get a little hysterical." With rare exception, those who have dealt with Brown—biographers, novelists, essayists, and professional historians—have been either passionately for or against the man.* Either Brown was *right* or he was *wrong*. Either he was a great and immortal hero who sacrificed his life to free the slaves. Or he was a crazy horse thief, a murderer, a psychopath. For more than a century, American writers—popular and scholarly alike—have engaged in such polemics over whether Brown was right or wrong, hero or villain, saint or madman, that scarcely anyone has taken the time to try to understand him.[1]

---

* There have been exceptions, of course. Jeffery Rossbach's *Ambivalent Conspirators: John Brown, The Secret Six, and A Theory of Slave Violence* (Philadelphia, 1983) is a brilliant and fair-minded analysis of Brown's relationship with his clandestine backers. In addition, Benjamin Quarles, Albert Fried, and Richard O. Boyer have written books sympathetic to Brown. But apart from studies like theirs, the historical literature dealing with Brown is infested with high-voltage polemics. For Brown historiography, see my own work, *Our Fiery Trial: Abraham Lincoln, John Brown, and the Civil War Era* (Amherst, Mass., 1979), pp. 22–51.

In this biography, I have tried to understand John Brown, to help my readers understand him. The narrative voice is empathetic, not worshipful or derogatory. It seeks to make Brown live again, to transport readers back into his life and times, so that they might view his embattled world through his eyes, sense it through his hurts and furies, hear the injunctions of the Old Testament that roared in his ears. That way readers might gain melancholy insight into what made him a revolutionary, what convinced him that only violence could remove the wrong of slavery in his troubled country.

I hope that these pages convey some sense of him as a living man, a complex, polygonal man who defies easy categorization. He could be dictatorial and self-righteous, with an imperious manner that made him intolerant and unappreciative of others, especially his own sons. As a businessman, he could be inept and self-deluded. He could become obsessed with a single idea—now slavery, now land speculation, now a wool crusade in Massachusetts—and pursue his current project with unswerving zeal. Yet he could be kind and gentle, extremely gentle. He could stay up several nights caring for a sick child, or his ailing father, or his afflicted first wife. He could hold children on both knees and sing them the sad, mournful refrains of his favorite hymn, "Blow ye the trumpet, blow." He could stand at the graves of four of his children who had died of dysentery, weeping and praising God in an ecstasy of despair. He could teach his children to fear God and keep the Commandments—and exhibit the most excruciating anxiety when the older ones began questioning the value of religion. All his life he could treat America's "poor, despised Africans" as his equals and detest the way white people oppressed them. He could challenge racial discrimination in Ohio, hide fugitive slaves on the underground railroad, and feel an almost paralyzing bitterness toward bondage itself—that "sum of villainies," that "great sin against God"—and toward all the people in the United States who sought to preserve and perpetuate it. Finally he could become so enraged at his "slave-cursed" land that he could advocate plunging it into a holocaust.

Yes, Brown smoldered over the manifold evils of slavery. He hated that *"hellish"* institution because it was cruelly unjust to Negroes, because it violated God's Commandments and made a mockery of the Declaration of Independence, because it menaced the nuclear family (he had read about the inhuman breakup of slave families), and because it imperiled him personally. He had striven hard to endure his trial on earth and prepare himself for paradise and a union with his God in Heaven. Yet that same God, in a burst of omniscient rage, might well destroy

Brown's slave-owning country and sweep all Americans—Brown and his wife and children included—into the flames of an everlasting Hell.

We will never comprehend what Brown was about unless we take his religious views seriously. From "earliest childhood," he had learned to oppose slavery and to fear an all-wise, just, and all-powerful God, a God who demanded the most exacting obedience from the frail, wretched sinners He placed on trial in this world. For the rest of his life, Brown was a devout Calvinist who believed in foreordination and providential signs, in the wrathful Jehovah of the Old Testament who intervened in human affairs and directed them to suit His own purposes. In this biography, I have given special attention to Brown's intense Calvinist faith because I think it is the key to understanding him, his view of the world, and his final mission against slavery at Harpers Ferry. However difficult it is for people in our secular age to accept Brown's religious notions, he nevertheless thought himself an instrument in the hands of God. As he and his followers descended on Harpers Ferry that rainswept October night in 1859, he saw himself as a full-fledged warrior of the Old Testament. He was "like David of old." He was like Gideon, who, guided by Jehovah Himself, attacked the Medianites and drove them across Jordan. He was like Samson who single-handedly pulled the temple down. As a soldier of the Almighty, called to punish this _"guilty land"_ for the crime of slavery, Brown was certain that God would use him and his raid for His own designs.

Many students of history, reading statements like these, have labeled Brown a religious maniac, ignoring the fact that Abraham Lincoln and Robert E. Lee—to name only two other figures of this extremely religious time—also came to regard themselves as instruments of God. Because the raid failed to incite a slave rebellion, thanks in part to Brown's own faulty planning, other critics have dismissed him as a blundering incompetent as well as a madman. What they overlook is Brown's alternative objective at Harpers Ferry: should the raid fail, he repeatedly argued, it would nevertheless ignite a sectional explosion in which slavery would be destroyed. Though often maligned as a demented dreamer, Brown in one respect was an extremely insightful man: he perceived the depth of southern anxieties about slavery, perceived that all he had to do—being a northerner and an abolitionist—was to step into Dixie with a gun, announce that he was here to free the blacks, and the effect on the South would be cataclysmic.

He was right. As this book attempts to show, Harpers Ferry polarized the country as no other event had done; it set in motion a spiral of accusation and counteraccusation between North and South that bore the country irreversibly toward the Civil War.

Brown's pilgrimage to Harpers Ferry—to the gallows, the beginnings of legend, and the fulfillment of his own prophecy—is a dramatic story, a tragic story. Yet his solution to slavery may offend many of you. As for myself, I am not a violent man but I can appreciate why he could hate a hateful thing like slavery—and why he could think it too embedded in America ever to be dislodged except by violence. Slavery *was* powerfully entrenched there: safeguarded by the Constitution and a web of court decisions and national and state laws, it was booming and expanding in the 1850s, not dying out. In Brown's eyes, it was never going to die out unless he took matters into his own hands. I do not defend his conclusion that only a blowup could get rid of slavery. But I can appreciate how he arrived at that conclusion.

In our own uncertain time, we can learn a great deal from Brown's life, if we avoid glorifying or denigrating him and try to understand the man in the context of his own era. We can learn why, out of the whirlpool of his own agonies and aspirations, Brown became a revolutionary who rejected peaceful alternatives in favor of violent means to remove injustice. And we can learn something about the society that produced him, too. For the United States of his day had institutionalized a monstrous moral contradiction: the existence of slavery in a Republic that claimed to be both Christian and free, a Republic founded on the enlightened ideal that everybody is entitled to life, liberty, and the pursuit of happiness. Unable (or unwilling) to resolve such a contradiction, the country invited a messianic rebel like Brown to appear with his sword.

Stephen B. Oates
Amherst, Massachusetts
The 125th anniversary year of Harpers Ferry

Sometimes there comes a crack in Time itself.
Sometimes the earth is torn by something blind.
Sometimes an image that has stood so long
It seems implanted as the polar star
Is moved against an unfathomed force
That suddenly will not have it any more.
Call it the mores, call it God or Fate,
Call it Mansoul or economic law,
That force exists and moves.
                              And when it moves
It will imploy a hard and actual stone
To batter into bits an actual wall
And change the actual scheme of things.
                              John Brown
Was such a stone—unreasoning as the stone,
Destructive as the stone, and, if you like,
Heroic and devoted as such a stone.
He had no gift for life, no gift to bring
Life but his body and a cutting edge,
But he knew how to die.

                    Stephen Vincent Benét

I John Brown am now quite certain *that the crimes of this* guilty, land: will *never be purged* away; *but with Blood.*

[John Brown, on his way to the gallows]

PART ONE

TRIAL

I

FIRST AWAKENING

〜〰〰〜

SOMETIME IN THE MONTH OF FEBRUARY, 1799, a tanner and shoemaker named Owen Brown moved his family to the small town of Torrington, on the bank of the Naugatuck River in northwestern Connecticut. "Squire Owen," as his friends back in Norfolk called him, was a rawboned man who spoke with an embarrassing stutter and had an emaciated, humorless face that made him look considerably older than his twenty-eight years. His wife Ruth, a prim woman of twenty-seven, sat in the wagon holding their daughter Anna as Owen and Levi Blakeslee, a five-year-old orphan they were keeping, drove the ox team into West Torrington. Presently Owen halted the team in front of a farmhouse he had recently purchased and started unloading their belongings and carrying them inside.

The house itself was a two-story frame building, situated on a hillside that overlooked a thickly wooded valley called Mast Swamp, where smoke from a sawmill curled out of the towering pine trees and fled southward in the wind. A more worldly man might have thought the stark, shutterless house a forbidding place. But for Owen and Ruth it was a symbol of hope—a place where they could start over again, forget their past difficulties, and have more children of their own, especially a son to carry on Owen's name. For Owen himself the farm promised more than that, for here, with Ruth's help and God's mercy, perhaps he would yet learn how to live like a Christian.

Owen was convinced that he had not shown much faithfulness in his short lifetime. From his Calvinist teachings he knew that people

3

were "sinners in the hands of an angry God"—frail, wretched creatures who must nevertheless *try* to overcome the wickedness in themselves, *try* to resist the Devil's temptations, *try* to exhibit Christian
piety if they ever hoped for God to save their miserable souls. That
much Owen had learned from his mother and the Rev. Jeremiah
Hallock, who had taught him long ago that all human destinies were
controlled by an all-wise, just, and all-powerful God. Owen feared
this God to his bones, feared that because of his "bad habits"—especially his vanity—Providence might already have condemned him
to Hell. He prayed constantly for God to pardon him and grant him
salvation. Praying for mercy, Owen understood above all things, was
the only hope for sinners like himself.[1]

2

Owen was born in 1771, in the hamlet of West Simsbury (now
Camden) in northwestern Connecticut. His parents, John and
Hannah Brown, descended from hardworking New England farmers
of Dutch and British ancestry.[2] When Owen came into the world,
the Browns already had seven children and operated a modest farm
which barely provided for them all. Owen was five years old when
the Revolution broke out and his father went off to fight in the
Continental Army—only to die of dysentery, in a barn in New York,
a few weeks after he had left home. It was a tragic blow for Hannah,
who was pregnant with her eleventh child and who did not know
whether she had the strength to carry on alone. The older children,
of course, tried to help, but it was hard without a man. A generous
neighbor sent over his Negro slave to do the plowing. After work the
slave carried Owen on his back, and the boy "fell in love with him."
But calamity shattered Owen's world a second time when the slave
became severely ill with pleurisy and died. Hannah took Owen with
her to attend the Negro's funeral.

Most of the laboring men were off fighting the British now. For
want of help, the Browns lost their crops and became extremely poor.
Hannah "did all that could be expected of a mother," but there was
not enough to eat and every night the children went to bed hungry.
Then came the "dreadful hard winter" of 1778–79 which killed what

remained of the livestock. After that Hannah could not support them all, and gradually the family broke apart.

Owen had to set out on his own when he was twelve. He learned to make shoes, and worked as a cobbler in West Simsbury in the winter and helped his mother in the summer. He also began to "hear preaching" at the West Simsbury Congregational Church. When a relative named Jeremiah Hallock became pastor of the church, Owen lived with him from time to time and received "a great deal of good instruction" regarding his trial on this earth and that sovereign God they all must fear. But in spite of this good instruction, Owen did not believe he was yet "a subject of the work."

In 1787 Owen left the town of his birth and headed for Massachusetts to work as a shoemaker. He wandered from place to place, accumulated a little clothing and money, learned how to be a fair workman, and then returned home to help his mother in the spring of 1788. He was stricken with anguish because of their poverty. He longed to be one of the better sort—one of God's chosen—and could not conceal his envy for the young people of West Simsbury "who had rich parents that dressed their families in gay clothes, gave them plenty of money to spend, and good horses to ride."

Owen went away again, this time to work as a sort of door-to-door cobbler at Norfolk. There he came "under some conviction of sin" (he never explained clearly what he meant, recalling only that he had not lived like a Christian and that his life had been of little worth, "mostly filled up with vanity"). Afraid that God had damned him, he returned to West Simsbury and sought out the Rev. Hallock for counsel. Hallock not only ministered to Owen, offering sound religious guidance and personal advice, but also "hired him out" for a time. Under the minister's powerful influence Owen gained hope that God might yet grant him salvation despite his sins and unworthiness.

The minister also influenced Owen in another way: the youth overheard him and another preacher talking about slavery in Rhode Island, taking pride in the fact that Connecticut had eradicated slavery by gradual-abolition acts in 1784 and 1787. It was a terrible thing, the preachers said, that Rhode Island should perpetuate an institution that was clearly "a great sin" against God. Shortly after that Mr. Hallock showed Owen a sermon by Jonathan Edwards, the son of the more famous Jonathan Edwards of the Great Awakening, pointing out that the younger Edwards had also condemned slavery as a sin against God. A few years later Owen heard a Virginia preacher defend this evil institution in a packed meeting house in Norfolk. The spectacle so repelled Owen that from then on he was an outspoken opponent of slavery.

In the fall of 1790 Owen's life took a revolutionary turn: he met Ruth Mills, a chaste, deeply religious girl "who was the choice of my affections ever after." Her father was a Congregational minister and her mother came from a family of distinguished Congregationalists and Presbyterians.[3] Thus Ruth too was an heir to the Calvinist tradition of an austere, implacable God who demanded the most exacting obedience from the sinful creatures He put on trial in this world. Owen very much admired Ruth's solemn piety and the prominence of her family. Determined to prove himself in their eyes, he worked for two years paying off family debts and accumulating some livestock, until "we appeared to be noticed by the better class of people." Only then did he ask for Ruth's hand. They were married in West Simsbury on February 13, 1793, the same year that George Washington, the Virginia slaveholder, began his second term as President of the young Republic.

Shortly after their marriage Rev. Hallock, feeling "all the anxiety of a parent" that the newlyweds should begin right, gave them "good council" about leading a pious and God-fearing life. This advice had a good effect on Owen; and so did the steady religious influence of Ruth. She assisted him "without the least appearance of usurpation or dictation," Owen recalled, "and if I have been respected in this world, I must ascribe it to her influence more than to any one thing."

Owen was being too modest, for he was an ambitious and hardworking man. He rented a house in West Simsbury, where he sold butter and cheese to supplement what he made as a tanner and shoemaker. No doubt in deference to Ruth, he took in orphan children to live with them, including Levi Blakeslee, then an infant. In June, 1794, Ruth had a son of their own, whom they named Salmon.

While Owen was proud to be a father in his own right, his mind was on other things. A restless, independent man, he wanted to move out of the rented house and buy his own place, to show some evidence of class and respectability. At the encouragement of friends he moved his family to Norfolk, where he not only bought a small farm but sank tanning vats and built up "a small good business" as a cobbler. Business was so good that the young "squire" was able to hire a fore-man for the tannery. But with success came family sorrow: Salmon, "a thrifty forward child," died in 1796 near his second birthday. The following year a second son died at birth, and Ruth and Owen both were tormented with guilt: had God visited such calamity upon them as punishment for some wrong they had committed? Had Owen been too vain? too ambitious? But God soon showed them mercy: Ruth became pregnant again and in 1798 gave birth to Anna, who cheered them both. Shortly afterward Owen and Ruth both made a public profession of religion, which Owen himself had "so poorly manifested" in his life.

Owen was "quick on the move" in those years and by 1799 was ready to leave Norfolk and try his fortunes—and his religious faith—in a new area. Thus when an opportunity came to sell out he did so against the wishes of his friends and moved his family to West Tor-rington, to start over again on another farm.

At first Owen might have thought he had made a wrong move. The tanning business was slow here, and the rocky soil in back of his place was almost impossible to farm. But in other respects he had much to be thankful for: on the 9th of May, 1800, at the dawn of a new century, Ruth presented Owen with a son, whom they named John in honor of Owen's father and grandfather. That November, in the aftermath of a "great awakening" that had swept through the village, the Browns united with the Torrington Congregational Church. Owen was grateful indeed for his membership in the church. His son, unlike himself, would grow up in the House of God.[4]

II

A CALVINIST UPBRINGING

୨ଚ୬୦

JOHN WAS A THIN, SOBER CHILD, the third of six children in the Brown family (including Levi Blakeslee whom Ruth and Owen had adopted). The Browns insisted that John and the other children learn sound religious habits, and their household—always the picture of Calvinist piety—was filled with prayers and Bible readings. In later years John remembered how his father exhorted him "from earliest childhood to 'fear God & keep his commandments.'" His father also taught him and Anna and the other children not to hate Negroes but to be kind to them and oppose their enslavement as a sin against God, as Reverend Hallock and the younger Jonathan Edwards had proclaimed.[1]

Owen also insisted on stringent discipline (something he had never had himself) and more than once, in that farmhouse in West Torrington, John was lashed for some little-boy wrong he had committed. On one occasion his mother caught him stealing three brass pins from a girl who lived with the family; no doubt following Owen's instructions, she let John brood over his sin for a day, then thrashed him soundly. The rod became for him a symbol of the pain and terror—the inevitable doom—that awaited one who strayed from the path of righteousness.

In 1804 Owen was restless again. He had been unable to make a successful business in Torrington, where all the real profits and prestige were in the lumber industry. He decided to move west, as thousands of other New Englanders had done, believing that he might re-establish himself as a squire on the frontier. That fall he visited

Ohio's Western Reserve, where a number of Connecticut pioneers had resettled, and fell in love with that virgin country. He bought a tract of land in Hudson, then hurried back to Torrington to tell his family the news. He had found the settlers around Hudson "middling prosperous" and "mostly united in religious sentiments." He thought he could pick up money surveying, then open his own tannery. Once he became a prominent businessman he could help build up "religion and civil order," doing his part to win the frontier for the Lord.

In June, 1805, the Browns sold their farm in West Torrington and with another family set out for Ohio in wagons drawn by ox teams. It was a magic journey for five-year-old John, a journey full of excitement and mystery, as the small wagon train rolled over southern New York, crossed Pennsylvania, and headed into a wilderness crawling with Indians and "wild beasts" that filled the boy with a breath-taking dread. He was inordinately thrilled when the families encountered packs of rattlesnakes "which were very large" and "which some of the company generally managed to kill." As they pushed on, his father let him help with the teams, and he "learned to think he could accomplish *smart things* in driving the Cows" and "riding the horses." But in late July, all too soon, the wagons rolled into the little Ohio village of Hudson, some twenty-five miles southwest of Cleveland, and one of the few pleasurable events in John's life came to an end.

2

The Browns' first year in Hudson was an extremely difficult one. They shivered through the winter in a drafty log cabin, subsisting on wild game and a few staples borrowed from neighbors. In the spring they cleared some land and planted corn, but blackbirds and squirrels ravaged most of the crop and a summer frost killed the rest.[2]

At last, in their second year in Ohio, Providence seemed to smile on them, Owen recalled. He started surveying lands for new settlers and gradually saved enough money to construct a tannery along with a better house. As "Squire Owen" rose in prominence, missionaries and other important men traveling through the country called on him at Hudson and he became acquainted with "the business men and ministers in all parts of the Western Reserve, and some in Pennsylvania."

With Owen preoccupied with his business and Ruth tending to a wailing new baby boy, seven-year-old John roamed the wild Ohio country at will. He befriended some Seneca Indians who had a camp nearby and even learned "a trifle of their language." He returned from his wilderness expeditions with a pet squirrel named Bob Tail, which he "almost idolized," and other "little earthly treasures." When he lost a yellow marble an Indian boy had given him, he wept intermittently for days. Then, as though Providence were teaching him a lesson that He could take away all that He gives, John's pet squirrel either ran away or was killed. The boy cried again, and mourned over Bob Tail for "a year or two."

"You may laugh," he wrote in later years, referring to himself in the third person, "but these were *sore trials* to John whose earthly treasures were very *few,* & small." There were other trials too. Unable to bear criticism, John developed "a bad & foolish habit"—he started telling lies to "screen himself from blame" and punishment. His inability to take criticism and his compulsion to lie his way out of blame were traits that would grow with him into manhood. As far as his lying was concerned, he frankly admitted that he was obliged to struggle "long in after life" before he could overcome *"so mean* a habit."

When John was eight, tragedy visited the Brown household. On December 9, 1808, after the death of a newborn daughter, John's mother also died.[3] The boy was stricken with grief. Owen suffered, too, but while he and the other children searched for ways to live with Ruth's death, John believed he would never recover from a loss so "complete & permanent." When his father, knowing that he could not raise six children by himself, married a twenty-year-old girl named Sally Root, John refused to adopt her in his feelings and "continued to pine after his own Mother for years."

Grief hardened into bitterness, and John emerged from his season of mourning a resentful and belligerent boy. When he enrolled in the log schoolhouse in Hudson, he had an insatiable appetite for the *"hardest & roughest"* kinds of play. He took grim pride in his ability "to wrestle, & Snow ball, & run, & jump, & knock off old seedy Wool hats." Such aggressiveness greatly impressed Milton Lusk, one of Brown's classmates. In later years Lusk remembered how the boys of the village formed into rival gangs—the "little Federalists" and the "little Democrats"—and fought one another with snowballs. "Brown and I were federalists," Lusk recalled, "as our fathers, Squire Brown and Captain Lusk, were." In one especially bitter engagement the little Democrats (whose fathers supported Jefferson and Madison, the Virginia slaveowners) pelted the Federalists with wet balls, "which were hard and hurt 'masterly.' " John withstood the pelting for a few moments, then charged the Democrats and single-handedly drove them back into the schoolhouse. "He did not seem to be angry," Lusk said, "but there was such force and mastery in what he did, that everything gave way before him."[4]

Unfortunately for John, he did not apply that same determination to his studies. At best he was an indifferent student, caring little for arithmetic or "grammer." But he did acquire some taste for reading, thanks to a friend who induced him to study history and gave him free use of his library. Reading history may not have taught him how to survive "the School of *adversity*" in which he was growing up, but it did keep him "from bad company" and widened the horizons of his mind beyond the little world of Hudson, Ohio.

In time John quit school (he was no "Schollar" anyway), put his books aside, and went to work at his father's tannery. Owen had already taught him to dress his own leather from "Squirrel, Raccoon, Cat, Wolf, or Dog Skins" and to fashion "Whip lashes," which he sold for pocket money. John loved to work with leather and was proud of his ability as a tanner. He also developed a consuming interest in fine cattle, horses, sheep, and swine—an interest that was to last all his life.

When the War of 1812 broke out, Owen became a beef contractor for General William Hull's forces on the Detroit front. John's task was to round up wild steers and other cattle in the forest and drive them, all by himself, over a hundred miles of wilderness to army outposts in Michigan. Barefoot, clad in buckskin pants held up by a leather shoulder strap, John circulated among the soldiers at the army posts, listening to all their war talk. This would have thrilled any ordinary boy. But not John: the soldiers' profanity, mutinous complaints, and lack of discipline repelled the boy. He was back in Hudson when General Hull surrendered Detroit in disgrace, and saw some of Hull's troops who had been paroled wander through Hudson on their way home. Local citizens were extremely apprehensive, for there seemed nothing to stop the British from invading Ohio. No invasion took place, but American troops marching west to meet the British left their sick in Hudson; the townspeople were infected; and there was much illness in John's own family. The whole spectacle of the war in the Northwest so disgusted John with military affairs that he later paid fines like a Quaker to avoid the required militia drills.

As he claimed later, he saw something else during the war that made him understand what his father meant about the evil of slavery. As it happened, John had just completed one of his cattle drives and took lodging with a landlord who owned a slave about John's age. Observing that the Negro was "badly clothed" and "poorly fed," John felt sorry for him. But contrition turned to horror when the master, right in front of John, beat the Negro boy with an iron fire shovel. John returned to Hudson with an unrelenting anguish for the "wretched, hopeless condition" of that *"Fatherless & Motherless"* slave boy. He insisted later—and there seems no reason to dispute him—that the beating he witnessed made him "a most *determined"* foe of slavery from then on.

3

After the war Owen was gone from Hudson much of the time, attending to business matters in other villages in the Reserve. Later he confessed that his long absences had injured his family (including eight additional children by his second wife). His hard work had caused him to be "unfaithful" to his children and he deeply regretted it.[5]

Without firm parental guidance fifteen-year-old John had his troubles. He was arrogant and contentious, told lies, and acquired other "bad habits" he would never talk about. He felt guilty about them and sought escape in hard work at his father's tannery and in the company of older men, around whom he affected a precocious self-assurance. Around girls, however, young Brown was painfully shy, something which deprived him of "a suitable conne[c]ting link between the different sexes"—and which, as he admitted himself, "might under some circumstances have proved his ruin."

He had also become skeptical of religion, but his infidelity did not last long. Lonely, disappointed in love, and troubled with doubts about his "future well being," he returned to the Calvinist faith of his father and "became to some extent a convert to Christianity." Once he had experienced religion, young Brown read his Bible with single-minded determination, accepted its "divine authenticity," and set about committing its "entire contents" to memory. He took pleasure in spicing up his own language with scriptural flourishes and in correcting anybody who quoted wrongly from the Bible.

In the spring of 1816 John made a formal profession of religion and was admitted to membership in his father's church, the Congregational Church of Hudson.[6] Impressed with the preaching he heard, John soon felt that God had called him to the ministry. Toward that end he traveled to Connecticut and called on the Rev. Jeremiah Hallock (the same preacher who had helped Owen in his youth) to inquire how one went about entering the ministry. The minister suggested that Brown prepare for college by studying at Moses Hallock's school in Plainfield, Massachusetts. His school already had a reputation for turning out future ministers—and men of the arts as well. In fact, the poet William Cullen Bryant had been a student there.[7]

Brown thanked Mr. Hallock, and not long after that (it was either late in the summer or early in the autumn of 1816), he and one of his brothers and another Hudson boy named Orson M. Oviatt enrolled in Moses Hallock's school. In sharp contrast to his earlier lethargy as a pupil, Brown set about his studies with a relentless zeal. Such diligence impressed Schoolmaster Hallock, who doubtless expected as much of this "tall, sedate and dignified young man" as the young man expected of himself.[8]

For some reason Brown stayed at the Plainfield school for only a few months, than transferred, with his brother and friend, to Morris Academy in Litchfield, Connecticut, to continue his preparation for the ministry. But all his dreams collapsed when he ran short of funds and developed an inflammation of the eyes, which forced him to abandon his studies and return to Ohio in the early summer of 1817. It seems that Brown accepted his setback with cheerfulness and "true resignation"—he would never question the will of Providence—and arrived in his father's village determined to excel in whatever the Lord had planned for him.[9]

4

For a few months Brown lived at his father's crowded house and toiled hard at the family tannery in Hudson. But young Brown was too independent and too ambitious to work for his father or anybody else. He wanted to be his own boss, to give his own orders. Accordingly, he and his adopted brother, Levi Blakeslee, set up their own tannery outside the village and kept "Bachelors hall" in a log house near the tanning yard. Brown was as fussy as a woman about keeping the place clean; he did all the cooking himself, scrubbed the pots and pans meticulously, sanded and swept the floor, and insisted on scrupulous neatness throughout. As Milton Lusk remembered, Brown was equally fastidious in his personal habits: he was simple but tasteful in his dress and always kept his close-cropped black hair combed straight back.[10] His head was disproportionately small even for his lean, 5-foot 9-inch frame. His eyes—always his most memorable feature—were steel-gray and already had a fierce glare about them. He was such an austere, tense young man, stiff as a New England deacon, utterly humorless, and so fixed in his ways that he would not bend for anybody.

He had no hobbies, no romance, no means of letting off steam. In the evenings and on Sabbath afternoons, when his inflamed eyes permitted it, he continued to read the lives of "great, wise, & good men," memorized their sayings and writings, and grew to dislike vain and frivolous talk as much as he disdained card playing, dancing, and other useless forms of entertainment.

Action, work, tenacity—these made up his motto—and he went about his tasks at the tannery with an electrifying intensity. He also taught himself surveying from a tattered copy of *Flint's Survey*; and old-timers who saw him hurry about the tannery all day and then practice surveying in the evenings remarked that here was a young fellow who was bound to amount to something. Brown confessed that their praise fed his vanity so much that "he came forward to manhood quite full of self conceit . . . notwithstanding his *extreme* bashfulness."

Brown was not jesting. By the time he was twenty he not only regarded himself as an unimpeachable businessman but adopted an imperious attitude toward his employees that must have seemed appallingly pretentious for somebody his age. He gave orders, said a younger brother, like "A King against whom there is no rising up." As Milton Lusk put it, Brown "doted on being the head of the heap, and he was."[11]

He was already a man of strong, uncompromising convictions too. Politically, like his father, he supported John Quincy Adams of Massachusetts, the dogmatic, overbearing Secretary of State, an advocate of the neo-Federalist American system and heir apparent of President Monroe. Theologically Brown was an orthodox nineteenth-century Calvinist who believed in foreordination and providential signs, in the doctrine of election, innate depravity, and in man's total dependence on a sovereign and arbitrary God. He believed, too, that once an individual had "experienced religion" through "God's infinite grace and mercy," then God became for that person a constant, all-powerful, directive presence in his life.[12]

Brown's opposition to slavery also had grown, thanks to the influence of his father and their antislavery business and ministerial friends (the young tanner was living in an "antislavery town," although most people in the Hudson area apparently wanted to colonize all Negroes once slavery was eradicated). As one of Brown's journeymen remembered, Brown "was always of one mind" when the subject of slavery came up. He insisted that slavery was "a great sin against God" and that it was his sworn Christian duty to help slaves escape from the South to Canada and freedom.[13] Brown meant what he said too. Already he had assisted at least one fugitive in his flight to the "North Star" and had made it clear, to anybody who was interested, that he would shelter any other runaways from Kentucky or Virginia who came knocking at his door.[14]

5

Being "the head of the heap" at the tannery was a lonely and time-consuming task, so much so that Brown had no more time to cook or tend his cabin. Eventually he decided to bring in a housekeeper and offered the job to Milton Lusk's mother. She was a widow and as meticulously neat as Brown himself. She also had a nineteen-year-old daughter named Dianthe.

Mrs. Lusk not only accepted the job and moved into Brown's cabin; she brought Dianthe along to help. Brown desired this "remarkably plain" and pious girl from the first, but he was so painfully shy, even around an unintimidating creature like Dianthe, that it took him a while to summon his courage. Finally he made the necessary advances and the two embarked on a prim and laconic courtship. In a few weeks, however, open antagonism broke out between Brown and Dianthe's brother Milton. Milton was extremely fond of his sister ("she was my guiding-star, my guardian angel") and the affection was mutual. A couple of times Dianthe took Milton to a secret place in the woods where she went to pray. But she never took John there, not even during their courtship. After Milton went to work in the village, however, he could get out to the Brown cabin to visit Dianthe and his mother only on Sunday. Brown pronounced this a sacrilege and bristled with hostility the next time his former schoolmate came to the cabin. "Milton," Brown said, "I wish you would not make your visits here on the Sabbath." "John," Milton replied hotly, "I won't come Sunday, nor any other day," and he left in a huff. Not long afterward, "led by his own inclination & *prompted also* by his Father," Brown asked Dianthe to be his wife, and they were married on June 21, 1820, in the church in Hudson. Milton, though, was still so furious at Brown's insolence that he refused to attend the wedding.[15]

Brown admitted that his young wife had "a most powerful and good influence over him" during the early years of their marriage. Her gentle admonitions and fragile sensitiveness forced him to control his "haughty obstinate temper"—at least for a time—and her earnest piety inspired him to be more righteous himself. They always attended church together; and at night, after he came home from the tannery, she read the Bible aloud and sang his favorite hymn, "Blow ye the trumpet, blow." God soon rewarded them for their faithfulness: on July 25, 1821, Dianthe gave birth to their first son, whom Brown christened John Brown, Jr.

Now that Brown had a family he set about, with a clear vision of his place in the world, to make himself a model Christian businessman and community leader. He started teaching Sunday school in Hudson, beseeching his pupils to be honest and always to fear God. He not only made church attendance compulsory for his workers but also required them to come out to his cabin every morning for worship services. He prayed constantly, both at home and at the tannery. James Foreman, one of Brown's journeymen, remarked that "I do not believe he ever eat a meal of even Potatoes & Salt but he asked a blessing and returned thanks."

But should his employees defy him or do something wrong, Brown punished them with an Old Testament vengeance. For example, when a journeyman who had protested against Brown's religious dsicipline was caught pilfering a calfskin, Brown confronted the man so fiercely that he wept "like a child." Brown made him stay on, too, threatening to prosecute him "to the end of the law" if he ran away. Brown then ordered the other employees not to speak to the condemned man under any circumstances. "I think a worse punishment could not have been Set upon a poor human," Foreman recalled, "but it reformed him and he afterwards became a useful man."[16]

Brown took immense pride in his growing reputation as a businessman. As befitted one of his social standing, he joined the Masonic Lodge of Hudson in 1824 and served the following year as a minor officer.[17] He had already purchased several acres of farm land near his tannery; and in 1823–24 he tore the cabin down and constructed a handsome frame house complete with a garden and an orchard. There were other children too. Jason, who was to become an intelligent, sensitive youth, was born on January 19, 1823, and Owen, named after Brown's father, arrived on November 4, 1824.

Brown ruled his growing household with a rod in one hand and the Bible in the other. He insisted that his small sons learn "good order and religious habits" and refused to let them play or to have visitors on the Sabbath. Brown's iron rule, together with the trials of motherhood, evidently took their toll on sensitive Dianthe. Early in their marriage she exhibited signs of serious emotional troubles that not even her faith could assuage. Her distraction disturbed Brown— and it softened him a little too. He prayed for mercy and stayed up nights watching over Dianthe with a gentleness that his children would remember all their lives. But despite his efforts she grew worse. Relatives and friends later claimed that she was mad.[18]

Would moving away from Hudson help her? Brown was ready to sell out anyway and try his luck in a new region, one that he could develop by himself much as Squire Hudson had done here in Ohio. Accordingly, in the fall of 1825, Brown made a trip to Randolph Township in northwestern Pennsylvania, a forested and sparsely settled wilderness where land was selling at remarkably low prices. Brown inspected the timber there, noting the abundance of oak and hemlock, whose bark he could use in tanning. He was so taken with the region that he purchased a 200-acre tract in the northern part of the township, some twelve miles from Meadville, then returned to Ohio to get his family.[19]

Before he moved from Hudson, Brown made a business arrangement with Seth Thompson of Hartford, Ohio. The exact nature of their agreement is not known, but presumably Thompson was to provide Brown with calfskins and purchase assorted leather from him, while Brown was to sell Thompson's cattle to buyers in the East.[20] At any rate, by May, 1826, Brown had sold his place and was ready to go; and with James Foreman, who also wanted to resettle, the young tanner led his family eastward into the Pennsylvania wilderness.

III

SMARTING UNDER THE ROD
OF PROVIDENCE

⧼⧽

Everybody in randolph township was impressed with the new settler from Ohio. In four months, as wolves howled in the distance, he
cleared twenty-five acres of his timbered homestead and constructed
a two-room log house, a large barn (which contained a secret room
for hiding runaway slaves), and an imposing frame and stone tannery complete with eighteen vats. The tannery was the first industry
to come to Randolph Township and John Brown its first entrepreneur. By October 1, 1826, the young businessman had from ten to
fifteen men working for him and had won the admiration of all his
neighbors—especially the Delamaters, who became close friends of
the Brown family.

Once he had his tannery in operation, Brown plunged into a
number of projects to build up the community. He surveyed for
roads, imported the first blooded stock his neighbors had seen, and
helped get a post office established for what was soon called Richmond Township, formed from part of Randolph Township in 1829.
Brown himself served as postmaster of "New Richmond" from January 7, 1828, until May 27, 1835. He also opened a school—the first in
the township—for his sons and the Delamater children. Initially
classes were conducted on a rotating basis, with the children boarding and studying at the Delamater place in the summer and at
Brown's in the winter. As a teacher, Brown insisted on strict religious
instruction, rousing his pupils before daylight to lead them in scriptural recitation and in prayer. But he realized that they needed to

19

know grammar and arithmetic, too, and eventually built a school-house himself and employed a woman to teach there full time.

Brown's neighbors extolled him for his prodigious work in their behalf. Yet they also held him a little in awe. A perfectionist in his business, he refused to sell his sole leather unless it was completely dry, once turning away a customer from another community because Brown had detected a trace of moisture in his stock. But he could be charitable as well as rudely honest. When he learned that a destitute family lived nearby, Brown summoned the husband to his tannery, gave him work for the following summer, and insisted that he take clothes, food, and money in advance. In conversation he quoted the Old Testament "from one end to the other" and occasionally indulged in sarcastic humor. He strove to learn everything he could, readily accepting new information and collecting books for his library, which included the works of Benjamin Franklin, Aesop's *Fables*, and the sermons of the older Jonathan Edwards. Brown enjoyed holding lively discussions with his employees and neighbors, especially around a roaring fireplace during the long winter evenings. He could be domineering (especially when discussions turned on religious matters) and liked to argue others down. Yet he told James Foreman that he despised people who always agreed with him and respected a man only when he had ideas of his own.

On some subjects, however, Brown was completely uncompromising. When a stranger moved into his township, Brown made it a point to call on the newcomer and inquire "whether he was an observer of the Sabbath, opposed to Slavery and a Supporter of the Gospel and common Schools, if So all was right with him, if not he was looked upon by Brown with Suspicion."[1]

Brown was just as unyielding in his politics. Still a firm Adams man, he deeply distrusted Andrew Jackson and Henry Clay—and of course anybody who supported them—because both were slaveholders and both had fought duels. Both were Masons too—and the Masonic Lodge, despite Brown's earlier affiliation with it, was now something he opposed with extreme hostility. In 1826, when William Morgan mysteriously disappeared in New York after threatening to reveal the secrets of Masonry, thousands of Americans were convinced that members of the secret fraternal order had murdered him. After several Masons were tried for Morgan's murder and all but two were acquitted, a great public outcry arose against the secret lodge; by turns it was accused of being immoral, anti-Christian, and sinister. Since Jackson was a Mason, his opponents identified Masonry with the Democrats, and anti-Masonic politicians soon formed a new political party designed to exorcise the "grand kings" of Masonic privilege from the United States government.

Brown was swept up in the anti-Masonic tempest. Obviously a secret order that "sanctioned" murder and harbored slaveholders could not be a Christian institution; and he resolved "to leave, renounce and expose a system so iniquitous and full of damage to the country." Everywhere he went he denounced the lodge "in the hottest kind of language." In 1830 a pro-Mason crowd almost lynched him in nearby Meadville because of his outspoken views. After that, convinced that spies were watching his movements, he bought a gun and learned how to use it.[2] But no harm came to him, and after Andrew Jackson was re-elected President by an impressive margin and Antimasons joined with Clay's National Republicans and Southern slaveholders to form the Whig party, Brown's excitement quickly subsided. He flirted with Whiggery for a time, then lost interest in politics altogether. Convinced that American politics were dominated by proslavery sentiments anyway, he apparently did not vote in another presidential election.[3]

2

Brown always exhibited a puritanical obsession with the wrongs of others, and throughout his residency in New Richmond he waged a one-man campaign against wickedness in any form. Once when a man was arrested for stealing a cow, only to be released when the owner found out how poor he was, Brown was outraged. Stealing a cow was a violation of God's Commandments, Brown reminded the harried constable, and intimidated him so much that he finally arrested the man a second time. But while he was in jail Brown himself provided for the prisoner's family.

Worried that his neighbors might backslide, Brown distributed "good moral books and papers" for them to read and implored them to attend the church of the Independent Presbyterian and Congre-

gational Society at Guy's Mill, some six miles away. Eventually
Brown decided that what the township needed was a church of its
own. On January 1, 1832, he organized an Independent Congregational Society in New Richmond, drawing up the articles of faith
himself. The society held its services on the second floor of Brown's
tannery.[4] Sometimes a minister came to deliver the sermon; on other
mornings Brown gave it himself, preaching from the works of the
older Jonathan Edwards, whose mystical Calvinism, as expressed in
such sermons as "The Eternity of Hell Torments," "The Evil of the
Wicked Contemplated by the Righteous," and "Sinners in the Hands
of an Angry God," had powerfully influenced Brown's own beliefs.
He told his congregation one Sunday: "Is not the reflection that full,
& complete justice will at last be done enough to make the very
Heavens & Earth to tremble?" Before him, on the second floor of his
tannery, sat his employees and their families, the Delamaters, and his
own wife and children. "Providence," Brown went on in his halting
but imperious manner, "unfolds to our darkened minds, Three cardi-
nal traits in the character of the true God, vis Justice, mercy, & love
of propriety." Yet there was one attribute men should have above
all others. "Humility," Brown declared, for "What can so properly
become poor dependent, sinning, & self condemned mortals, like *us*;
as humility?"[5]

He preached about the nature of sin, too, and wrote of how "Our
stupidity ingratitude & disobedience we have great reason to mourn
& repent of." He himself felt that he should expect God's judgments
because His mercies had not awakened more of Brown's "love &
gratitude, & zeal for his honor." In his sermons and his morning
Bible classes Brown drew his scriptural examples largely from the
Old Testament, reminding his listeners how the wrathful Jehovah
of ancient Israel brought famine and pestilence to those who did
not "fear the Lord thy God" and failed to "serve him and swear
by His name." For "the fear of God," as the Preacher taught in
the last chapter of Ecclesiastes, "is the whole duty of man."[6]

3

Brown, like the old Puritans of Massachusetts Bay, regarded marriage
duties—sexual union and childbearing—as commands of God, and

so he and Dianthe continued having children in spite of her emotional troubles. Frederick I was born on January 9, 1827; Ruth, whom Brown named after his mother, on February 18, 1829; and Frederick II on December 31, 1830. As a father, Brown was more strict now than he had been in Ohio. Since (as Jonathan Edwards pointed out) children were not sinless and consequently must be rigidly disciplined, Brown punished his sons with the wrath of a Hebrew patriarch at the slightest breach of good order and religious habits. He was especially determined that they should not tell lies (as he had done as a boy), and his punishments for mendacity, all his children recalled, were "terribly severe." Even if they indulged "in noise" or "other disorderly conduct," Brown's manner of admonition, observed young George B. Delamater, was "like no other man's." He permitted no childish fantasies either. When three-year-old Jason insisted that a dream of his had actually happened, Brown thrashed him terribly, getting tears in his eyes as he did so.

Of course, strict discipline for children was not unusual in the United States in the early nineteenth century. Teachers employed the whip unsparingly. And some men also beat their wives, such as the Methodist class leader and exhorter in New York who, "every other week," applied a horsewhip to his spouse "in order to keep her in subjugation, and because she scolded so much." Brown never beat Dianthe; she would never have scolded him anyway. But he does seem to have taken the rod to his children more frequently and rigorously than most fathers in New Richmond (or anywhere else). And no man could match his "Lyon eye" and fierce "tut, tut!" at the slightest sign of a lie from his children. Sometimes, however, his ferocity had the reverse effect of what he wanted. Ruth recalled that when he accused her of a wrong she did not commit, he looked at her so sternly that she did not dare tell the truth.[7]

When Brown was not punishing his children he was lecturing them to live by the Golden Rule and to abhor all forms of human wickedness—not only lies and disobedience but immorality, laziness, hunting and fishing (which promoted laziness), and slavery. He warned his children: "Remember them that are in bonds as bound with them." He also insisted that his children acquire a plain and practical education, such as he had received in the school of adversity in which he had grown to manhood. Such an education would enable them to transact the common business of life; it would train them to be useful though poor servants of God and to meet the stern realities of their trial in this world. He quoted from *Poor Richard's Almanack*: "A small leak will sink a great ship." "God helps those who help themselves." "God gives all things to industry."

Occasionally the older boys rebelled against "the very strict control and Sunday School rules" imposed on them. Salmon remembered that they used "to carry on pretty high" sometimes, although all that got them was a tongue-lashing from Brown or another whipping. John Jr. said that he rebelled so frequently, and was so irresponsible in his chores at the tannery, that Brown made him keep an account book of the punishment he was due:

> John Jr.
> For disobeying mother ....8 lashes
> " unfaithfulness at work ....3 lashes
> " telling a lie ....8 lashes

When the debits outran the credits, Brown decided that John Jr. was "bankrupt." John Jr. told what happened next: "I then paid about one-third of the debt, reckoned in strokes from a nicely-prepared blue-beech switch, laid on 'masterly.' " Then, to his astonishment, Brown stripped off his shirt, sank to his knees, gave his son the whip, and ordered him to "lay it on." Said John Jr.: "I dared not refuse to obey, but at first I did not strike hard. 'Harder!' he said; 'harder, harder!' until he *received the balance of the account*." John Jr. noticed that "drops of blood showed on his back where the tip end of the tingling beech cut through."

At first John Jr. was mystified as to what his father had meant by such a bizarre act. Later he decided that Brown had intended it as a "practical illustration" of the Doctrine of the Atonement. "I was then too obtuse to perceive how Justice could be satisfied by inflicting penalty upon the back of the innocent instead of the guilty," John Jr. said; "but at that time I had not read the ponderous volumes of Jonathan Edwards's sermons which father owned."[8]

4

The year 1831 was a turning point in Brown's life. In that year his business fortunes began to deteriorate; and for the next four years, as his letters to Seth Thompson reveal, Brown was not only continuously short of money but in debt both to Thompson and to the bank. In April, 1832, he could barely raise the money for a down payment on an ox team.[9] Such financial woes marked the beginning of a leitmotif that was to run through the rest of his life.

He was also sick during much of 1831 and 1832—presumably with the ague, a malarial-type fever attended by fits of shivering and high temperatures—which impeded his work at the tannery and further cost him in profits.[10] There were family tragedies too. Four-year-old Frederick I died on March 31, 1831, and the Browns buried him in a family graveyard near the tannery. As the months passed, the signs multiplied that the Brown family was entering a season of trial. Dianthe, her strength drained away by almost continuous childbirth, developed heart trouble—and then she caught the fever, too, which only compounded her emotional anguish. Then she became pregnant again, and what little strength she had left ebbed away. Brown nursed her as best he could (for he was still sick with the fever), but it was no use. On August 10, 1832, shortly after a newborn son had died, Dianthe "went to her rest."

"We are again smarting under the rod of our Heavenly Father," Brown said in writing his father of Dianthe's death. He was still so sick that he barely had the strength to bury her and the baby in the family graveyard. He felt a deadness inside. "Such is the state of my health," he wrote his business partner, Seth Thompson, " (& of my mind in consequence) for I am unwilling to ascribe it to any other cause that I have felt my loss but very little & can think or write about her or about disposing of my little children with as little emotion as of the most common subject." This frankly surprised him, for "I loved my wife & had lived verry agreeibly with her." In any case, he wanted Thompson to know that sickness and death, not laziness, accounted for his inattention to Thompson's business affairs during the past week.

Still his numbness lingered, making him "more & more unfit for everything."[11] That winter, unable to keep house or care for his five children, he moved in with James Foreman (who had recently married), agreeing to pay him board. But as Brown should have expected, five children were too much for the newly married Foremans, and Brown finally had to hire a housekeeper and move his family back to his own place. The housekeeper was the daughter of

Charles Day, a blacksmith who lived in nearby Troy Township. Presently the housekeeper brought along a younger sister named Mary to do the spinning. Although Mary was only sixteen (half Brown's age), her sturdy features, reticent manner, and steady pace at the spinning wheel caught his eye. One day—to her astonishment —Brown gave her a letter which contained a proposal of marriage. His grim, overbearing manner may have frightened her a little, because it was the next morning before she dared to read the letter; and even then she could not answer his question. Awkwardly, she took a bucket and hurried to the spring for water. Brown followed her there, and when they returned he had his answer. On June 14, 1833, less than a year after Dianthe had died, John Brown and Mary Ann Day were married.

In almost every respect Mary was a better wife for Brown than Dianthe had been. A large-boned girl with wide jaws and black hair, Mary seemed in complete control of her emotions, and she had tremendous physical stamina which enabled her to endure the most rigorous hardships. Moreover, she had been taught since childhood that a woman's task was to bear children, tend her house, and obey her husband. Thus she subordinated herself completely to Brown's will (quite as he expected her to do), enduring his intractable ways with what Robert Penn Warren has called a kind of primitive stoicism.[12] If she was uneducated and slow, she was nevertheless a loyal, self-sacrificing wife whose whole existence was contained in the small confines of her home. And she never complained.

Ten months after they were married, Mary gave Brown a baby girl named Sarah, bringing his total number of children (not counting the two sons who had died) to six. He had a difficult time providing for them all, for his tanning business had declined sharply during the season of illness and death that had just passed. He despaired of paying off his bank debt when it fell due—unless he borrowed money from his friends—because he had been unable to tan much leather or to collect from people who owed him money. "It is a time of General Jackson darkness here about money," he complained to Thompson in March, 1834, probably referring to Jackson's war against the United States Bank and the hard-money schemes advocated by Jacksonians in the Cabinet and the Congress. Somehow Brown raised a little cash, because that November he sent $20 to

Thompson along with some leather. But business prospects remained gloomy indeed, with that hard-money, slaveholding Tennessean in the White House.[13]

5

Although Brown was preoccupied with business and family troubles in New Richmond, he was not unaware of the momentous antislavery developments that had taken place during the past three years. In 1831 an intense young reformer named William Lloyd Garrison, who felt that God was working through him to carry out the "final triumph of righteousness over sin," started publishing the *Liberator* in Boston. In his editorials Garrison focused his moral indignation on the worst evil in American society—human bondage—and shocked Northerners and Southerners alike with his bold, strident assaults on the "conspiracy of silence" that had thus far protected slavery in the United States. In a stunning display of moral outrage, Garrison said things that most slaveowners (and thousands of Northern Negrophobes) could not bear to hear: he asserted that slavery violated the cherished ideals of the Declaration of Independence, that Negroes deserved "life, liberty, and the pursuit of happiness" just like white people, and that the slaves must be immediately and unconditionally emancipated. "*I will be* as harsh as truth, and as uncompromising as justice," Garrison wrote in his manifesto in the very first issue of the *Liberator*. "On this subject, I do not wish to think, or speak, or write, with moderation. . . . I am in earnest—I will not equivocate—I will not excuse—I will not retreat a single inch—AND I WILL BE HEARD."

Ironically, in the summer of 1831, just seven months after Garrison started publishing the *Liberator*, a Negro preacher named Nat Turner—who believed that he was divinely inspired—led a slave insurrection in Southampton County, Virginia. Although the uprising was suppressed, it sent a spasm of fear across the South, and slaveholders inevitably blamed the insurrection on Garrison's newspaper and other antislavery publications—such as David Walker's *Appeal*, which actually called for slaves to revolt. Garrison, of course, emphatically denied Southern charges that he was trying to incite Negro insurrection, and in an editorial in 1833 he sought to clarify his position. "We aim to overthrow slavery in this country," he explained, not only because it made a mockery of Christianity and the American ideal, but because it violated the laws of God and exposed this hypocritical land "to the severest judgments of heaven." But by immediate emancipation Garrison did *not* mean that slaves should be "let loose to roam as vagrants" or that they should be "instantly invested with all political rights and privileges." Nor did Garrison want to send the black man back to Africa—as the American Colonization Society advocated—because banishment was not the Christian solution to the problem of the Negro in American society. What Garrison wanted was to break the chains of the black man, guarantee him the protection of the law, preserve his family, and place him under "benevolent supervision" until he learned religion and became "economically secure," whereupon he was to be assimilated into American society. Garrison declared that he intended to overthrow slavery "not by encouraging rebellion, nor for the free states to interfere, nor by forcing laws on the South which would be despotism—but by pricking the slaveholders' conscience, by setting public sentiment against slavery through means of press and pulpit."

The message was clear enough for anybody who would listen: Garrison's abolitionist crusade was a nonviolent one, a crusade which condemned slavery because it denied God to Negroes and whites alike and which sought to bring the slaveholder, an unregenerate sinner of the most despicable sort, to his knees by the sheer moral force of Garrison's words. Once the Southerners had freed their slaves and repented for their sins, Garrison would have purged the United States of its most shocking evil.[14]

While Garrison preached abolitionism in Boston (and gained an enthusiastic following of male and female reformers, most of them radical perfectionists), a group of wealthy New York philanthropists, among them Arthur and Lewis Tappan, had launched an antislavery movement of their own. They published a number of papers and tracts that called for immediate emancipation, formed local antislavery societies, set up a committee to work for a national antislavery organization, and sought to extend the movement out to Ohio and the Northwestern states, where Evangelical revivalists had converted thousands to Christ in the past two decades. With the Tappans' support, Theodore Dwight Weld—a convert of the celebrated evangelist, Charles Grandison ·Finney—led a group of theology students out to Lane Seminary in Cincinnati, with plans to make the school a center of immediate emancipation that would win all Ohio to the antislavery cause.

In December, 1833, the New York abolitionists joined forces with Garrison and his followers, and together they founded the National Antislavery Society, whose task was to coordinate the work of all abolitionist groups and organizations, to circulate books, sermons, and other antislavery tracts in an effort to convert the entire country to abolitionism. With the formation of the national society, the most intense moral crusade in nineteenth-century America, one that was to haunt the American conscience and arouse latent racism everywhere in the land, was irrevocably under way.[15]

The crusade had already spread to Hudson, Ohio, where Brown's father still lived, and had provoked a tremendous controversy there between the majority of people who supported the American Colonization Society and a zealous, highly articulate minority who subscribed to the doctrines of Garrison. The dispute began when two professors at Western Reserve College in Hudson—Elizur Wright (one of Brown's former schoolmates) and the Rev. Beriah Green, both recent Garrisonian converts—organized a society for "immediate emancipation." They held discussions on slavery in their classrooms, interjected abolitionist discourses into their lectures on moral theology, mathematics, and natural philosophy, and commenced in July, 1832, a scathing attack against the "colonizers" in the columns of the Hudson *Observer and Telegraph*. When the colonizers launched a counterattack in the press and the churches, the controversy became so heated that it split the college and the Hudson Congregational Church into two seemingly irreconcilable factions. Soon the dispute was raging in churches and schools all over Ohio—including Lane Seminary in Cincinnati, where Weld and other zealous students had clashed with conservative authorities and had "seceded" from the seminary in a storm of controversy.

Brown's father was involved in the fight with the colonizers from the outset: as a member of the board of trustees for Western Reserve he enthusiastically supported the anticolonization stand of President Charles B. Storrs, as well as the abolitionist activities of

Wright and Green. But to Owen Brown's dismay, the "conservative" trustees mildly reprimanded the professors, who in the summer of 1833 voluntarily resigned. Not long after that Storrs himself died of tuberculosis. When the college hired a new president who was not so radical in his views, Owen Brown regarded this as a triumph for the colonizers and resigned his post in disgust. Eventually he transferred his support to Oberlin College, a coeducational and coracial school which students and faculty alike were making a center of immediate abolitionism.[16]

Brown, who shared his father's strong antislavery convictions, made several business trips to the Western Reserve in the 1830's. According to family tradition, he first saw the *Liberator* in his father's home sometime in 1833 or 1834, enjoyed Garrison's furious denunciations of slavery, and later took out a subscription for himself. In 1848 Brown hinted that it was Garrison who had initially "converted" him to the abolitionist crusade, with his ringing pronouncements that slaveowners were unregenerate sinners and that slavery itself violated both the Higher Law of God and the principles of the Declaration of Independence (a splendid antislavery argument which Brown himself adopted).[17]

But if Brown responded to Garrison's rhetoric, he never became a Garrisonian disciple or follower. For one thing, Garrison was well on his way toward becoming a radical Christian perfectionist; by 1837, in fact, he was writing in the *Liberator* that the purpose of his movement was not only to liberate the slaves but to emancipate *all men* from the bondage of sin and to create a perfect world "under the dominion of God, the control of an inward spirit, the government of the law of love, and . . . the obedience and liberty of Christ." Brown, for his part, was too orthodox in his religious views ever to endorse such radical perfectionism (eventually he rejected Garrison's nonresistance argument as well). A Unitarian minister later remarked that "John Brown is almost the only radical abolitionist I have ever known who was not more or less radical in religious matters also. His theology was Puritan, like his practice," and it pained him to hear anybody talk about God and man with all the strict teachings of Calvinist theology abandoned. (Brown, of course, was not the only "Old School" abolitionist around in the 1830's—there were Calvinists in Ohio and New England who also opposed slavery.) As a Calvinist,

Brown rejected any notion that man could be perfected. Only God was perfect—man was a frail, dependent, sinning mortal. Moreover, as Brown pointed out to a Methodist preacher he met in Pennsylvania, the Devil would always be present to woo men into sin. And if imperfect human beings expected merciful God to grant them salvation, they must strive both to "show piety" and "do good," constantly struggling to overcome the inherent wickedness in themselves as well as to combat Satan's treacheries from without. And the worst of Satan's evils that must be combated in this country was the "hellish system" of Southern slavery.[18]

In spite of their religious differences, Brown admired Garrison and his fellow reformers and kept apprised of their work as it was reported in the *Liberator* and other newspapers. He knew that they were not only assailing the supporters of colonization but were trying to educate the oppressed and underprivileged free Negroes of the North as well. In Cincinnati, for example, former Lane theology students like Marius Robinson and Augustus Wattles (whom Brown was later to befriend) had set up a school for Negroes; and a girl named Prudence Crandall had attempted to do the same at Canterbury in eastern Connecticut. Miss Crandall, who had operated a female boarding school there, was an avid reader of the *Liberator* whose editorials about the need for Negro schools gave her a marvelous inspiration. With the encouragement of Garrison himself, she opened a school for black girls in April, 1833—and at once caused a racist backlash among the anti-Negro townspeople. They not only boycotted Miss Crandall and her girls but subjected them to insults, dumped filth on the doors and steps of the school, and prevailed on the authorities to invoke an obsolete vagrancy law which made the children liable to fines and whippings "on the naked body" if they did not leave. Finally, the state legislature passed a law prohibiting such schools, and Miss Crandall herself was arrested and put in jail. During the trial the Garrisonians made a martyr of her and launched an intensive campaign against anti-Negro prejudice in the North.

As the abolitionist crusade increased in intensity (and created considerable racial tension in the East as well as the South, a tension reflected in antiabolitionist and anti-Negro riots in New York City and Philadelphia), Brown became convinced in the fall of 1834 that God was about to smash "the house of bondage" and deliver all the slaves to freedom. Back in New Richmond now, he beseeched his neighbors to open their homes to runaway slaves, hundreds of whom would soon be pouring into the North. On November 21 he wrote his brother Frederick, who was living in Hudson, that he had worked out two plans of his own to assist "my poor fellow-men who are in bondage." First, he would adopt a Negro boy and "give him a good education, learn him what we can about the history of the world, about business, about general subjects, and above all, try to teach him the fear of God." If no "Christian slaveholder" would donate a Negro for Brown's experiment, then he and his family were prepared "to submit to considerable privation in order to buy one."

Second, Brown wanted Frederick to help him get "a school a-going here for blacks." Brown claimed to have been contemplating such a project "for years." But more than likely Miss Crandall's school in Connecticut and those in Cincinnati and the Western Reserve, as well as Garrison's own editorials about manual labor schools for Negroes, had given Brown his inspiration. In any case, he believed that the citizens of New Richmond would go along with such a project, for they were considerably less prejudiced against Negroes living in their midst than people in Ohio, with all their "conflicting interests and feelings" over the race issue. Brown was probably referring to Ohio's "black laws," which denied Negro residents full rights as citizens, and to the controversy between colonizers and abolitionists which still raged in the Western Reserve.

At any rate, he thought such a school should be set up for young blacks "whether they are all to be immediately set free or not," because such a school "under God" would do more toward breaking their chains than anything else the Browns could try. He used a little Garrisonian logic to explain what he meant. "If the young blacks of our country could once become enlightened, it would most assuredly operate on slavery like firing powder confined in rock, and all slaveholders know it well. Witness their heaven-daring laws against teaching blacks. If once the Christians in the free States would set to work in earnest in teaching the blacks, the people of the slaveholding States would find themselves constitutionally driven to set about the work of emancipation immediately."

He pointed out that the school could be supported by "a tax in aid of the State school-fund," which Pennsylvania law empowered townships to raise by a vote. If Frederick would gather some "first-rate abolitionist families" in Ohio and move them to New Richmond to implement the project, Brown would pay part of the expenses. "I do honestly believe," he declared, "that our united exertions alone might soon, with the good hand of our God upon us, effect it all."[19]

6

As it turned out, the good hand of God was not upon Brown at all. By the end of 1834 his financial troubles had become a veritable nightmare; he did not have enough money to operate his tannery, let alone to establish a Negro school, and finally he had to abandon his project. By the spring of 1835 money was so tight in northwestern Pennsylvania that Brown found it impossible to sell anything for cash or to collect old debts. Soon he could not even support his family, and looked around for some fast money-making venture. Zenas Kent, a wealthy businessman of Franklin Mills, had been urging Brown to move back to Ohio and form a partnership in the tanning industry. In April Brown decided to take Kent up on his proposition. But he could not afford the move. Swallowing his pride, he wrote Kent and asked for a loan. Brown was on the verge of turning everything he owned into "shingles" and selling them in Ohio, "as one way to realize cash," when $25 from Kent finally arrived.[20] In late May Brown resigned as postmaster of New Richmond, settled his "honorary debts" the best way he could, and took his family back to the Western Reserve, anxious indeed to recoup his fortunes and restore his reputation as a businessman.

IV

OHIO AGAIN

༄༅

SUMMER WEATHER HAD SET IN by the time the Browns relocated in
Franklin Mills, a small village near Hudson in eastern Ohio, and
Brown and fourteen-year-old John Jr. set about constructing a tannery on land owned by Brown's new partner, Zenas Kent. But no
sooner had they completed the building than Kent changed his mind
about a partnership and rented the tannery to his son, Marvin Kent,
who wanted to engage in business by himself.

Of course Brown was disappointed, for he had expected much to
come of his association with a wealthy man like Zenas Kent. But he
soon forgot about the tannery and turned to something far more
promising: a land boom was under way in Ohio in 1835 and everybody was talking about how speculators were making fantastic
sums of money virtually overnight. It was a fact that farms in Portage County (where Franklin Mills was located) had risen from 50
percent to 100 percent in value and that town lots in Akron, Cleveland, and Cuyahoga Falls were selling at unprecedented prices. The
entire nation was caught up in a runaway inflation which the Jackson
Administration failed to check. Money in the form of state bank
notes was plentiful in Ohio, credit was easy, and "everyone seemed
filled with ideas of manifest destiny and permanent prosperity."[1]

Brown soon had such ideas himself; he recouped his fortunes
and, with that reckless, go-ahead spirit which typified the frontier
speculator of his time, he plunged into a vortex of business ventures
that defy clear description. He obtained a subcontract to build a lock
gate on part of the Ohio and Pennsylvania Canal that ran from Akron

34

to Franklin Mills. Then, convinced that Franklin Mills would boom into a great manufacturing center because of the canal, Brown began speculating in land with single-minded zeal. In January, 1836, as the land boom reached spectacular proportions, Brown expanded his working partnership with Seth Thompson to include land speculation; Thompson gave Brown $1,134 on the spot and agreed to put up about $13,000 more as soon as he could borrow the money. Brown himself borrowed an additional $7,000—mostly from Frederick Wadsworth and a wealthy Hudson businessman named Heman Oviatt—and purchased the Haymaker farm and several pieces of adjoining land. Brown called the property "Brown and Thompson's addition to Franklin Village," divided it into lots and put them up for sale.

Brown pored over diagrams of his lots and compiled an impressive list of facts and figures. In April he wrote Thompson that he had sold two lots for $800 and that he was trying "to feel out the public pulse" to decide at what price the other lots would sell. Meanwhile he wanted Thompson to send him all the money he could spare, so that Brown could keep up with land payments—and also purchase a wagon and "a good lively yoke of oxen." Thompson sent him $250 in June, but money had suddenly become so tight (thanks in part to Jackson's controversial Specie Circular) that prospects for land sales in June and July were dim.

Perhaps so in Franklin Mills, but what about in Hudson? Might not sales be more lively among Brown's relatives and acquaintances? Borrowing $350 from his father, Brown purchased a tract of land in Hudson and moved his family there about the middle of July.[2] Then word came that Jackson had signed a law that would distribute surplus treasury funds among the states, the payments to be made in four quarterly installments beginning on January 1, 1837. Ohio, it was estimated, would receive about $2,676,000 all told, and such "fair prospects added substantially to the hope of things."[3] Brown, like many other landholders, was caught up in a new round of speculative fever. Using all his powers of persuasion, which were considerable, Brown convinced Oviatt and several other men to provide security for a $6,000 note to Brown from the Western Reserve Bank—a note he used to buy another farm called Westlands.

At the same time he went in with twenty-one other businessmen from Franklin Mills, Akron, and Ravenna to form a large speculative firm called the Franklin Land Company. Borrowing heavily, Brown's company bought all the water rights and land between the upper and lower villages of Franklin Mills. When the Ohio and Pennsylvania Canal Company agreed to cooperate, Brown and associates laid off a whole new town along Cuyahoga River between the two villages, then stood back and waited for a spectacular boom to begin that would make them all rich men.

But their dreams were shattered when the canal company suddenly refused to stand by its agreement. It drew water from the Cuyahoga River, thus depriving the new townsite of adequate water power and destroying whatever prospects for land sales it might have enjoyed. Brown and his colleagues accused the canal company of doing this deliberately to push Akron at the expense of Franklin Mills, but there was nothing they could do except shake their heads bitterly as interest accumulated on their heavy loans.

For a man who believed in signs and omens, Brown should have expected the worst. After the election of Martin Van Buren, the entire U.S. financial system, plagued by a dizzy credit expansion since Jackson had destroyed the United States Bank, became extremely unstable. Hard money disappeared; credit tightened. Thompson, afraid of an impending crash, wanted to sell out now before it was too late. Brown disagreed. "I do think it is best to sell all out if we can at any thing like a fair rate," Brown wrote him, "but I think the time unfavourable." He was convinced that they could sell at better prices the following year; and nobody could persuade him otherwise. "If we have been crazy in getting in, do try & let exercise a sound mind about the maner of getting out," he admonished Thompson, "let us presume on a merciful Providence (if presumption it be) a little longer. let us try and trust all with a wise and gracious God, & all will be well some way or other."[4]

2

But all was not well. The Panic of 1837, which shook the national economy and caused suffering and distress everywhere, brought all of Brown's castles crashing down on him. He would never fully recover from the wounds sustained in that disaster. His creditors foreclosed on him right and left; former friends and business associates dragged him relentlessly into the Portage County Court of Common Pleas at Ravenna, Ohio, suing him for loans he could not repay, land payments he could not make, contracts he could not fulfill. His father and Seth Thompson suffered their losses quietly, loyal to the end, even though Brown had wanted to hold their property with the incredible belief that, even as prices plummeted downward, they could still sell out to advantage.[5]

Brown had not been dishonest in his manifold speculative ventures—even those who sued him testified to that—but he had certainly been incompetent. He had been negligent, shortsighted, confused, excessively indebted, and unrelentingly stubborn, insisting that he was above reproach in business matters and that anybody who disagreed with him was wrong. As Marvin Kent put it, Brown had "fast, stubborn and strenuous convictions that nothing short of mental rebirth could ever have altered." Of course, Brown was partly a creature of his time—a wild, go-for-broke era when businessmen were hardly noted for their prudence or their restraint. As the Cincinnati *Daily Gazette* said, "Men absolutely became dizzy at the height to which they were elevated—nor paused to reflect—but each urged the other on by example, when suddenly, in 1837, the storm that had been gathering for years, burst with the fury of an avalanche over the whole country" and scores of men who had crowded "too much sail" were wrecked. But even by comparison Brown does seem to have been a bit more reckless and incompetent in business matters than the average Western entrepreneur and speculator, although he would never have admitted that. Even as he sat through more than a dozen lawsuits in the courthouse at Ravenna, he insisted that his *only* error was having done business on credit.[6]

Harried on all sides, Brown blamed much of his troubles on former friends he thought had betrayed him—although he could not prove it—and especially pointed a finger at a one-time business associate named Amos P. Chamberlain.

Brown's feud with Chamberlain grew out of a tangled controversy over the Westlands farm. Initially Brown had received only a penal bond of conveyance for the property and had given the bond to Heman Oviatt as collateral, since Oviatt had provided security for Brown's bank note. When Brown eventually obtained a deed

to the farm, he failed to notify Oviatt. Then he mortgaged Westlands to two men and neglected to tell Oviatt about that either.
Afterwards came the panic and a veritable avalanche of lawsuits, one
of them brought by Daniel C. Gaylord (whom Brown regarded as a
wicked man). Gaylord won a judgment against Brown. To settle it,
the sheriff put the farm up for sale, and Chamberlain bought it.
Chamberlain, a friend of Brown's, probably intended to sell it back
to him when he was solvent again.

Meanwhile Brown had failed to pay off his $6,000 note to the
Western Reserve Bank (the note he had used to purchase Westlands
in the first place), and the bank had sued Oviatt for the full amount.
Oviatt had then demanded Westlands as compensation for his loss,
only to suspect fraud when he found that the farm had been sold to
Chamberlain. Oviatt could not sue Brown, who was "legally safe,"
but he did seek a judgment against Chamberlain, eventually to lose
his case in a bitter legal fight in the Ohio Supreme Court.

Later Oviatt decided that Brown had not deliberately deceived
him but had simply been negligent with the deed and mortgage
to Westlands (which was the truth). Brown had been sick with the
ague, too, which only added to his confusion as he struggled about
in a financial jungle which he never really understood.

Ill, plagued with lawsuits, and financially devastated, Brown
vented his frustrations on Amos Chamberlain. Insisting that Chamberlain had promised to return Westlands to him, Brown refused to
get off the place. When Chamberlain tried to take possession of the
farm, Brown turned him in for trespassing. Then Brown and two of
his sons (John Jr. and Owen) armed themselves with shotguns and
occupied a wind-blown shack, threatening to shoot Chamberlain if he
set foot on the farm again. Chamberlain finally sent out the sheriff,
who arrested the Browns and marched them off to jail in Akron.
After Chamberlain secured the farm, however, he dropped the
charges, and the Browns, defiant to the end, were released.

Not long after that Brown wrote Chamberlain an indignant letter, demanding to know why he had trampled on the rights of an
"old friend" and his "numerous family." Was it because Brown was
poor? Did Chamberlain not remember that Brown owed money to
"honest creditors" like Thompson and Oviatt, whom he could have
paid off through the sale of Westlands? Now, thanks to Chamber-

lain, they were suffering too. "Will God smile on the gains which you may acquire at the expense of suffering families deprived of their honest dues?" Brown did not think so. Furthermore, he accused Chamberlain of circulating "evil reports of me" in order to prevent "the community from inquiring into your motives and conduct." Such wicked tactics, of course, were nothing new. "If it could be made to appear that Naboth the Jezreelite had blasphemed God and the King, then it would be perfectly right for Ahab to possess his vineyard. So reasoned wicked men thousands of years ago." Now, Brown did not want to injure Chamberlain or any of his family, for Brown well remembered "the uniform good understanding" that had existed between them from their youth until "last fall." Therefore Brown was going to offer Chamberlain two alternatives to settle their dispute "once and for all." First, Chamberlain could take "ample security" from Seth Thompson and "release my farm and thereby provide for yourself an honorable and secure retreat out of the strife and perplexity and restore you to peace with your friends and with yourself." Or Chamberlain could submit the matter "to disinterested, discreet, and good men to say what is just and honest between us." If Chamberlain refused either offer, Brown would commence "a tedious distressing, wasteing, and long protracted war" to get his farm.

How Chamberlain reacted to Brown's letter is not known. But he never surrendered the farm; and there is no evidence that Brown ever started a legal war to get it. In any case, as Oswald Garrison Villard has said, the Westlands controversy closed a chapter in Brown's life that left deep and lasting scars on him.[7]

3

Other events Brown witnessed in Ohio were to leave marks on him as well. Since 1834 Ohio abolitionists, inspired by Theodore Dwight Weld and his "Oberlin disciples," had steadily increased their efforts to defeat the colonizers and to convert all Ohio to immediate emancipation; and by 1837–38 the abolitionists seemed well on the road to victory. They had won over most of the churches and many of the newspapers in the Western Reserve, had organized some 200 antislavery societies, and converted some 17,000 people—2,249 of them in Trumbull County alone. The Western Reserve Synod had adopted an emphatic resolution that slavery was "a sin against God; a high-handed trespass on the rights of man; a great physical, political and social evil, which ought to be immediately and universally abandoned." Many liberal Congregationalists, who stressed man's virtue and goodness more than his depravity, actually wanted to withdraw their churches from the Presbytery (Congregationalists and Presbyterians had merged in the celebrated Plan of Union in 1801) thereby freeing themselves from an ecclesiastical organization that included Southern slaveowners. In 1837 dissident Congregationalists got their wish: the Presbyterian General Assembly, striving to hold its Northern and Southern churches together, not only overthrew the Plan of Union but expelled the Western Reserve Synod because of its "loose" New School Congregational doctrines and because it was composed of "ill-mannered fanatics" on the slavery issue.[8]

Even though the abolitionists had made impressive gains in Ohio, there was still much to be done. Hundreds of persons still clung to the old colonization argument that, while the slaves should be liberated, they and all the free blacks of the North should be sent back to Africa "where they belonged." Racist crowds had held anti-abolitionist "meetings" in Cleveland (where 7,500 free Negroes resided). And racial prejudice existed among many professed abolitionists, too, who practiced the hypocrisy of damning slaveowners on the one hand and discriminating against free Negroes on the other. In addition, Ohio's notorious "black laws" remained in operation—laws that relegated more than 10,000 Negro residents to a subservient position in Ohio society. According to these measures, a Negro could not get a job without proof that he was a free man. To live in the state he had to give a bond, underwritten by two good securities, that he would behave himself (anybody who harbored an unregistered Negro, incidentally, was subject to a heavy fine). A Negro enjoyed only limited legal rights, and he could not attend public schools, even though he paid school taxes. Going beyond the law, the white public often excluded Negroes from the better sections of Ohio's cities and sharply disapproved of white people who hired Negro help or who fraternized with blacks.[9]

Already some abolitionists, mostly from Oberlin, had commenced a crusade against such discrimination, and they soon received an ally in the person of John Brown of Hudson. In January, 1837, he left his business troubles and attended a mass meeting of Negroes and abolitionists in Cleveland, a meeting called to consider the expediency of petitioning the state legislature to repeal the black laws. Brown stood before that gathering and gave the blacks a rousing address. It spurred them to action, too, for they not only sent an agent out to gather signatures but appointed a committee of correspondence, of which Brown was a member.[10] But the petitions which Brown's committee and other abolitionist groups circulated around the Reserve failed to impress Ohio's politicians. It would be another twelve years before the legislature, in a fervor of political and antislavery radicalism that had seized the state, repealed the black laws.

Brown was back in Hudson, trying to find his way out of the financial nightmare brought on by the Panic of 1837, when news came of a shocking incident in Illinois. On November 7, at a town called Alton on the Illinois side of the Mississippi, an antislavery newspaperman named Elijah Lovejoy had been murdered by a proslavery mob from Missouri. All across the North abolitionists gathered to hail the slain editor as a martyr and to repeat his eloquent words: "It is because I fear God that I am not afraid of all who oppose me in this city." "Have I not a right to claim the protection of the laws?" In Hudson, Laurens P. Hickok, professor of theology at Western Reserve College and an outspoken abolitionist, summoned a prayer meeting in the Congregational Church to commemorate Lovejoy's martyrdom. Brown and his father were present and heard the professor deliver an impassioned speech. "The crisis has come. The question now before the American citizens is no longer alone, 'Can the slaves be made free?' but, are we free, or are we slaves under Southern mob law?" What could they do against such injustice? "I propose that we take measures to procure another press and another editor," Hickok cried. "If a like fate attends them, send another, till the whole country is aroused; and if you can find no fitter man for the first victim, send me."

According to two reliable witnesses, Brown sat at the back of the room, listening silently to Hickok's stirring words and all the other angry speeches and resolutions against Southern mob law. As the meeting drew to a close, Brown suddenly stood up, raised his right hand, and vowed that here, before God, in this church, in the presence of these witnesses, he would consecrate his life to the destruction of slavery.[11]

4

Contrary to legend, Brown did not drop all his other interests after the Hudson meeting and devote his energies single-mindedly to the overthrow of slavery.[12] On the other hand, the vow was no idle gesture either. He helped his father and Milton Lusk in their fight against the colonizers, who retained a powerful foothold in the Hudson Congregational Church and kept the entire community sharply divided over the whole issue of slavery and the position of the free Negro in American society. Brown's aging father became so angry at the "conservative" clergy that he left the regular church and joined a group of "seceders" who had set up what was called the Free, or Oberlin, Church, which abolitionists at Oberlin enthusiastically supported. Brown did not secede with his father. But if Milton Lusk may be believed, Brown did censure the clergy of the regular Congregational Church for giving in to "the prejudices" of the colonizers.[13] Brown also hid fugitive slaves from Kentucky in open defiance of the law; helped his black neighbors in spite of his own hardships; and lashed out against racial bigotry in the most dramatic way in Franklin Mills, where he moved his family in 1838.

As it happened, Brown united with the Congregational Church in Franklin Mills "by letter" on February 15, 1838, and the next month his wife and three of his sons—John Jr., Jason, and Owen—also joined.[14] That summer an evangelist preacher from Cleveland arrived in town to conduct "a protracted meeting" in the Congregational meeting house (the only one large enough for a revival) and invited Methodists and Episcopalians to attend as well. On the first night of the meeting the Browns sat dutifully in the family pew, listening to the preacher exhort a crowd of mixed faiths. Brown might well have regarded the minister with suspicion, for he apparently leaned toward the popular Evangelicalism of the Methodists. Brown had always steadfastly opposed their doctrines of free will, individual salvation, and perfectionism; in fact, he had once "talked down" a Methodist preacher in New Richmond, refuting his beliefs by posing a series of ambiguous questions about predestination, Satan's presence in the world and his current "State of Sin and rebellion against God," which rendered Satan incapable of "doing good."[15] Brown was also skeptical of the New School doctrines which liberal Congregational ministers—especially the younger ones —were preaching in Ohio and elsewhere in the North. "It tried his soul," a friend said later, "to see the juvenile clerical gentlemen who came into the pulpits" and dared call themselves Congregationalists or Presbyterians—"preachers of the gospel with all the hard applications left out."[16]

At any rate, as the revival in Franklin Mills moved into the second day, people from other towns came to hear the preaching, and so did some of the free Negroes and runaway slaves who lived in the neighborhood. The Negroes, however, had to sit by the door in the back, where the stove rested in the winter. Such discrimination in the House of God made Brown blazing mad: the next night, in a packed meeting house, he defiantly escorted some of the Negroes down to the Brown family pew. The act struck the audience—and the church deacons—like "a bomb shell." The following day the deacons called on Brown to admonish him and labor with him for what he had done. But Brown defied them all, and that night, with the bold audacity of a man who *knows* he is right, Brown took his black brothers straight to his pew.

A year later, after the Browns had again returned to Hudson, they received a letter from one of the deacons of the Franklin Mills Church: the letter announced that "any member being absent a year without reporting him or herself to that church should be cut off." The Browns had been expelled! But not, they believe, because of the reason set forth in the deacon's letter. They were convinced they had been cut off because Brown had seated those Negroes in the family pew (the membership rule, in fact, had been adopted after the Browns had left Franklin Mills). "This was my first taste of the proslavery diabolism that had intrenched itself in the Church," John Jr. said, and he and his brothers "left the church" in disgust and "never belonged to another."[17]

How Brown reacted to the deacon's letter is not recorded. But in view of the kind of man Brown was, it is not difficult to imagine what he said about the Franklin Mills church and all the hypocrisy that continued to infect so-called Christians in his neighborhood—a neighborhood that boasted of its antislavery convictions, its godliness, and its dedication to the freedom and equality of all men. He later transferred his official membership from the Congregational Church in Hudson to that in Richfield, where he had moved to engage in tanning and sheepherding. But evidently he did not attend any church regularly after 1840.[18]

If Brown went his own way as a Christian, he likewise was always a nonconformist as an abolitionist. He never joined any antislavery society or other organized abolitionist group; he argued constantly with his abolitionist "friends" about their religious beliefs, seemingly unaware of the paradox he posed in defending an old-fashioned theology on the one hand and proclaiming radical social views— immediate emancipation and Negro rights—on the other. He kept his own counsel, a long-time friend and business associate remembered, "and always acted upon his own impulses—he would not listen to anybody."[19]

5

Brown did a lot of talking, though, about grand money-making projects that would pay all his debts, restore all his losses. Late in 1838 he embarked on what he believed was just such a venture: he formed a cattle company with Tertius Wadsworth and Joseph Wells of Connecticut, who furnished several thousand dollars for the enterprise (obviously they did not know about Brown's business record in Ohio). In 1838 and 1839 Brown made two cattle drives to Connecticut, trying to sell his stock at various places. But the cattle drives, like everything else he tried, failed to bring any profits. Still, if this were the will of Providence, he was prepared to endure "with cheerfulness and true resignation." He wrote his family from New Hartford: "We must try to trust in Him who is very gracious and full of compassion and of almighty power, for those that do will not be made ashamed." He reminded them that "Ezra the prophet prayed and afflicted himself before God, when himself and the captivity were in a straight," and asked them to join with him under similar circumstances. "Don't get discouraged, any of you, but hope in God, and try all to serve him with a perfect heart."[20]

Brown told them nothing, however, about all the trouble he was in now. He had spent $5,000 of the money Wadsworth and Wells had given him for the cattle company—money that had to be replaced lest Brown be accused of dishonesty. He tried to get a loan from a party in Boston, who evidently promised to send some money in a few weeks. While waiting for the loan to come through Brown met a man named George Kellogg, an agent of the New England Wool Company of Rockville, Connecticut. When Kellogg found out that Brown raised sheep and cattle back in Ohio, he asked Brown to buy some wool for his company and on June 15 sent him $2,800 for that purpose. Predictably Brown regarded the money as an answer to his prayers. He pledged the entire sum to pay his own debts, then returned to Ohio believing that he could redeem the money when the loan from Boston arrived.

But the loan did not materialize, and "in painful anxiety" Brown waited for the inevitable. In August he received a letter from Kellogg, who asked for an accounting of the wool. After a long delay Brown replied: "I have found it hard to take up my pen to record, & to publish, my own shame, & abuse of the confidence of those whom I esteem, & who have treated me as a friend, & as a brother." He confessed straight out what he had done. But he promised to pay the money back, even "if I & my family [have] to work out by the month, & by the day, to make up a full return."[21]

But several months later he wrote Kellogg that he had failed to raise a dollar of what he owed the company. "That means are so limited," Brown explained, "is in consequence of my being left penyless for the time being, by the assignment and disposal of my property with no less than a family of ten to provide for, the sickness of my wife and three of my oldest children since that time, and the most severe pressure generally for want of money ever known in this Country." Yet he remained hopeful "that Devine Providence will yet enable me to make you full amends for all the wrong I have done, and to give you . . . some evidence that the injury I have occasioned was not premeditated and intentional at least."[22]

Fortunately for Brown, the company took him at his word and did not press charges. In the meantime lawsuits continued to pile up against him. Seeking some way out of his financial imbroglio, Brown prevailed on his father for advice. Evidently Owen, who was still a trustee of Oberlin College, told him that a wealthy New York reformer named Gerrit Smith had given the college a thousand acres of land in the Ohio Valley of western Virginia and that the college was looking for somebody to survey the property. Why didn't Brown apply for the job? The more Brown thought about it the more he liked the idea; soon he even had visions of moving his family to western Virginia and starting over again on that virgin frontier, as the agent of the college in charge of settling the area. On April 20, 1840, Brown wrote Oberlin's governing body, the Prudential Committee, and asked that it hire him to survey the lands and determine their boundaries, at a salary of a dollar a day plus "a moderate allowance" for necessary expenses. Frankly, he was not making such a request merely for employment and wages. "If I should settle my family on those lands I believe I could be the means of rendering them a source of allmost immediate income to your institution, and believe the institution can well afford to be quite liberal towards a family like my own who should go to commence a settlement upon them." He remarked that his three oldest sons were "all resolute, energetic, intelligent boys & as I trust of very decided religious character," the kind who would "prove to be valuable members of any community, or faithful and competent agents should they be kneeded."

The committee granted Brown's request, appointing him as an agent of the college and authorizing him "to enter upon, explore and occupy" its Virginia lands. Accordingly, Brown traveled to western Virginia and spent the rest of April and part of May surveying the college property, which lay in a fertile region just south of the Ohio River and some eighty miles west of the Allegheny and Appalachian Mountains. Brown investigated the farming methods of the people in the area (he did not think much of their methods), located a spot on Big Battle Creek "where if it be the will of Providence" he would settle his family, and then returned to Ohio. In July he submitted his reports and surveys to the Oberlin Prudential Committee, which spent some time examining and deliberating over them. Finally, on August 14, the committee obtained authorization from the board of trustees to "convey by deed to Bro. John Brown, of Hudson, One Thousand Acres of Virginia land."

But Brown hesitated in accepting the proposal because he was now negotiating with Heman Oviatt about a partnership in the sheep and tanning business in Richfield. Eventually Brown changed his mind about such a partnership, and on January 21, 1841, he notified the secretary of the college that "I expect Providence willing to accept the proposal of your Board, and that I shall want everything understood and arranged as nearly as may be." Now the Prudential Committee changed *its* mind. Perhaps because the college was having severe financial troubles, too, the committee decided not to give the land to Brown after all and had the secretary withdraw the offer. Brown was extremely unhappy and wrote the school a sharp reply. When he received no answer, he sent a second letter demanding a settlement. At that the college sent him a remittance of $29 "to balance account." And the Oberlin project, like all the others, ended in failure.[23]

6

Trying to scrape out some kind of existence for his family, Brown did some tanning "at the old stand" in Hudson and also talked with Oviatt, Marvin Kent, and others about various projects and loans to pay his debts. At one time Brown was too poor to buy postage for a letter to Seth Thompson. His family scarcely knew where the next meal would come from. And there were additional mouths to feed— Watson, Salmon, Charles, Oliver, and Peter were all born between October, 1835, and mid-December, 1840. The older boys had attended school in Franklin Mills and Hudson for a time, but after the panic all of them except John Jr. apparently dropped out to help Brown do the chores and tan leather.

Of the children only John Jr. and Ruth, a black-haired, temperamental girl, attended school regularly during these years of trial. John Jr., a big, taciturn youth with wide jaws and curly hair, was afraid of his father (all the boys were afraid of him) and always studied hard to live up to Brown's demands and expectations. At the age of nineteen John Jr. got a job teaching district school, but it proved such a thankless and demanding task that he seriously thought about quitting, and apparently wrote his father so. Brown replied: "I think the situation in which you have been placed by Providence at this early period of your life will afford to yourself and others some little test of the sway you may be expected to exert over mind in after life, & I am glad on the whole to have you brought in some measure to the test in your youth. If you cannot now go into a disordered

country school and gain its confidence, & esteem, & reduce it to good
order, & waken up the energies & the verry soul of every rational
being in it yes of every mean ill behaved, ill governed, snotty, boy &
girl that compose it; & secure the good will of the parents, then how
how how are you to stimulate Asses to attempt a passage of the Alps.
If you run with footmen & they should we[a]ry you how should you
contend with horses. If in the land of peace they have wearied you,
then how how how will you do in the swelling of Jordan Shall I
answer the question myself. If any man lack wisdom let him ask of
God who giveth liberally unto all and upbraideth not. Let me say to
you again love them all & commend them, & yourself to the God to
whom Solomon sought in his youth & he shall bring it to pass."[24]

But this time John Jr. did not heed his father's advice: he resigned
his post and in the spring of 1842, with all his belongings in a knap-
sack, he left his father's home and journeyed on foot to Austinburg
in Ashtabula County. There he enrolled at Grand River Institute, a
manual labor school, and pursued a practical course of education of
which his overbearing father could only have approved.[25]

Actually, in his own way Brown was fond of his oldest son, who
bore his name and was a good deal like him in resolution and stub-
bornness. Later Brown sent John Jr. whatever money he could spare.

Meanwhile Brown had been driven to the point of distraction by
all his financial woes. Finally he went to see Heman Oviatt again.
Would Oviatt let Brown tend his sheep flocks and move to his land
in Richfield as they had talked about earlier? Oviatt was a generous
man who had forgiven Brown for his negligence in the Westlands
farm controversy. Knowing how Brown was suffering, Oviatt not only
accepted his proposal but eventually promised to provide Brown
with hides and calfskins to tan into leather. Brown was to return all
leather he made, however, and Oviatt would apply a certain percent-
age of the wholesale value of the leather toward canceling Brown's
debt to him.[26]

In 1842 Brown moved his family to Oviatt's land, where they
lived in an old whitewashed log house, with a creek and a millpond
nearby. The pond had mud turtles in it which the younger boys
caught for Mary's frying pan. As Brown herded Oviatt's sheep he
strove faithfully to pay what he owed to Thompson and the New
England Wool Company. He had already sent the firm a bank draft

for $56.64—a commendable move indeed, since he could easily have used that money for his family.

And still the lawsuits piled up. Haymaker dragged Brown into court, "determined to keep on with his litigation till Death closes his account." Then Wadsworth and Wells sued Brown for a mortgage he had given them against the $5,000 he had spent from the treasury of their cattle company. This suit was the final blow. Faced with a multitude of debts he could never pay, Brown applied for bankruptcy. In the final settlement on September 28, 1842, a federal court took everything he owned except what was essential to live on. He was left with eleven Bibles and Testaments, a volume called *Beauties of the Bible*, another volume entitled *Church Member's Guide*, some furniture and household utensils, certain farm implements, and two mares, two cows, two hogs, three lambs, seven sheep, and nineteen hens. Although the court absolved him of his obligations, Brown promised again, "as Divine Providence shall enable me," to pay the debts he owed to the New England Wool Company and to Heman Oviatt.[27]

Bankruptcy, the climax of his mounting failures, took a terrible toll on Brown's pride. Rejected by the world of business, a failure in the eyes of his enemies as well as his friends, Brown turned increasingly to his family for comfort and security in a hostile world. He was very close to his "affectionate aged, & honored Father" and took care of him with considerable tenderness when he was sick. Also, Brown was more understanding with his children now, no longer thrashing them at the slightest sign of misconduct. He was still extremely strict with them about maintaining good Christian habits and still made them read their Bibles and attend family worship services every Sabbath evening. But there was often a paternalistic tenderness about him, brought on by the hardships they had suffered together over the past six years. Ruth remembered that he showed her "a great deal of tenderness," and that when the children were ill he stayed up at night caring for them. He enjoyed taking the smaller children on his knees and singing Isaac Watts's old hymn, "Blow ye the trumpet, blow."

> Blow ye the trumpet, blow
> Sweet is Thy work, my God, my King.

I'll praise my Maker with my breath.
O, happy is the man who hears.
Why should we start, and fear to die.
With songs and honors sounding loud.
Ah, lovely appearance of death.[28]

Brown said later that in these years of trial he cherished "a steady, strong, desire; *to die*," so that he might be taken from the torments of this life and be united with God in Paradise.[29] But as though by some grisly transmutation of Brown's own longing, death visited his children instead. In September, 1843, an epidemic of dysentery swept through the Brown home, killing four children in succession—Charles, Peter, Sarah, and a newborn son named Austin. Ill himself, Brown buried them side by side, weeping and praising God in an ecstasy of despair. "God has seen fit to visit us with the pestilence," he wrote John Jr., "and Four of our number sleep in the dust, and Four of us that are still living have been more or less unwell but appear to be nearly recovered." It was "a bitter cup" and they had "drunk deeply," but "still the Lord reigneth and blessed be his great and holy name forever." For even "in our sore affliction" Brown took some comfort in the knowledge that the children were with God now. They were in Paradise.[30]

V

SPRINGFIELD CRUSADER

ભ‍જ‍જ‍

IN JANUARY, 1844, Brown called at the home of Simon Perkins, a
wealthy Akron businessman he had recently met. Perkins thought
highly of Brown, and when he learned how destitute Brown and his
family were he agreed to form a partnership in which the two men
would merge their sheep flocks and share profits and losses. Brown
would herd the flocks himself, shear the wool and ship it to market
in the Northeast, and Perkins would provide feed and shelter. He
also agreed to rent Brown a house in Akron at $30 a year.

"I think this is the most comfortable and the most favourable
arrangement of my worldly concerns that I ever had," Brown wrote
John Jr., who was still in school in Austinburg, "& calculated to afford
us more leisure for improvement, by day, & by Night, than any other."
But "I do hope that God has enabled us to make it in mercy to us, &
not that he should send leanness into our soul."[1]

2

That April Brown moved his family (including a new baby girl
named Annie) into their new home, a plain farmhouse across the
road from Perkins' impressive brick mansion, and Brown and his
retinue of sons and sheep dogs went to work with "unrelenting earn-
estness" on Perkins' large sheep farm, located a mile west of Akron
Station. As time passed and Brown's worldly concerns looked increasingly favorable, he thanked God that the days of pestilence and death

really seemed over. He was able to send a few dollars to John Jr. and Ruth, who had also enrolled at the institute in Austinburg, along with stern reminders for them not to "forget *God, & that unchangeing state to* which we are going." But even if conditions were improving Brown still kept the other boys at home so they could help with the chores. Jason and Owen, who had a crippled arm (the result of a childhood injury), actually managed the sheep farm while Brown went up to Cleveland or traveled east to sell wool and buy additional sheep. Frederick, a slow, strapping lad who suffered from chronic headaches, followed after the little boys—Salmon, Watson, and Oliver—as they romped among the herds out in the meadow.

As a sheepman Brown was rough on his flocks, Perkins recalled, but he was "a nice judge of wool" and even contributed articles on the subject to the *Ohio Cultivator* and other journals. He also devised a cure for bots in sheep, which earned him the respect of farmers and other sheepmen in the area.[2]

The wool business, however, was not Brown's only concern while he resided in Akron. He had not forgotten his vow to consecrate his life to the destruction of slavery. Nor had he been impervious to the antislavery fervor that had swept the Reserve in the election of 1840 —and again in the election of 1844—when the Liberty party tried to force the slavery issue into national politics. Despite his personal difficulties, Brown also knew about Joshua ("Old War Horse") Giddings, the irrepressible Ohio congressman who had fought with John Quincy Adams against the infamous "gag rule," which permanently tabled all abolitionist petitions sent to the House of Representatives. In March, 1842, Giddings had emphatically opposed an effort to retrieve some slaves who had mutinied on an American boat and taken it to British-owned Nassau. The House had censured Giddings for his stand, whereupon he had resigned and returned to Ohio, where he had addressed cheering crowds at Cleveland, Ashtabula, Jefferson, and other towns in the Reserve. That May, in a special election called by the governor, Giddings had been re-elected and triumphantly returned to Congress.

Brown admired Giddings—he told him so personally in later years—and made a point to keep up with Giddings' career as it was reported in Ohio newspapers. Brown also kept up with the antislavery campaigns in Ohio itself, where the celebrated "Liberty Men"

—abolitionists like Charles S. S. Griffing and Marius Robinson—helped build the Ohio Underground Railroad into an extensive operation, one that escorted some 2,000 runaways a year over a network of lines that ran from Virginia and Kentucky to various points along Lake Erie, where steamboats carried fugitives to Canada. Brown and his father both were "conductors" on a line that crossed through Akron and Hudson; and if Charles S. S. Griffing may be believed, Brown actually cooperated with the Liberty Men in their slave-running operations. "No one would brave greater perils or incur more risks to lead a black man from slavery to freedom than he," Griffing said. He recalled how Brown would "come in at night with a gang of five or six blacks that he had piloted all the way from the river, hide them away in the stables maybe, or the garret." Should anybody try to take the Negroes into custody, Brown was prepared to fight "like a lion." If he had to he would lay down his life to help fugitives, because "death for a good cause," he told George Delamater, "was glorious."[3]

Some of Brown's friends, recalling his land speculations and his capacity to become greatly excited when his mind fixed on one idea (now the tanning industry, now land speculation, now slavery, now the wool business, now the Underground Railroad), later questioned his emotional stability. But Griffing demurred. "He was eccentric, but not crazy. He had a consuming idea in life, and that was to free the black man. He had no other aim."[4]

Griffing was not altogether correct. Brown had another consuming idea, which late in 1845 or early in 1846 concerned him even more than the plight of the black man. In his travels around Ohio and across New York and Massachusetts, Brown had talked at length with various woolmen and had become convinced that Northeastern wool buyers were perpetrating a great wrong on growers like himself and Simon Perkins. Manufacturers and dealers, he believed, dishonestly graded wool so that they could purchase fine and medium grades at low-grade prices. In his mind the wool growers were being robbed.

There was some truth in what Brown said. Wool growers were not getting a fair price for their better fleece. Worse, the wool market was quite unstable, thanks to the bitter tariff fights in Congress and an impending war with Mexico. Wool growers did need some sort of protection. But it is highly questionable whether wool buyers had formed a conspiracy to keep prices deliberately low, as Brown charged. Nevertheless, once he got that idea into his head there was no getting it out. He addressed various Ohio meetings about how pernicious manufacturers were cheating growers out of money and asserted that he intended to do something about it.

In March, 1846, he went to Perkins with a plan. Let them set up an office in Springfield, Massachusetts, with Perkins supplying the capital and Brown acting as manager. Brown would receive wool from growers in Ohio, Pennsylvania, New York, Vermont, and Virginia who had already approved of his plan. He would sort the wool and sell it by grades, thus compelling manufacturers to pay growers a just price. For his services Brown would charge a commission of 2 cents per pound (later he offered to apply some of his commission toward old debts). He was not going into this project to make money, but to correct a great wrong.

Perkins was not exactly ecstatic about Brown's project. But Brown was so stubborn and so convinced that he was right (and for all Perkins knew maybe he was) that he finally put up the cash, allowing Brown to manage the Springfield agency according to "his own will" and "his own impulses."[5]

In June, 1846, Brown set up the firm of Perkins & Brown in a warehouse in Springfield, a bustling town of 11,000 located on the banks of the Connecticut River in western Massachusetts. Brown's crusading zeal was contagious. Jason came to help; and in July so did John Jr., after he had completed the spring term at the Grand River Institute. The rest of the family, including a new daughter named Amelia, remained at Akron where Perkins and Brown's father could occasionally look in on them. Brown had neglected his family during the past two years, but he had not forgotten them. Once he had his agency established in Springfield he wrote regularly to Mary (who was pregnant for the tenth time). His letters were full of advice and instructions to her and the boys, and he could even be affectionate sometimes. "I do not forget the firm attachment of her who has remained my fast, & faithful affectionate friend, when others said of me (now that he lieth he shall rise no more)." When he thought about all his follies and mistakes and all the hard times she had endured, he was amazed at her constancy. "I really feel notwithstanding I sometimes chide you severely that you ar[e] *really* my better half."

In October, 1846, with Brown, Jason, and John Jr. hard at work in Springfield, calamity again visited the Brown home—Amelia was accidentally scalded to death through some carelessness on Ruth's part. When Brown heard the news he wrote Mary that "This is a bitter cup indeed, but blessed be God: a brighter day shall dawn; & let us not sorrow as those that have no hope. Oh that we that remain, had wisdom wisely to consider; & to keep in view our latter end. Divine Providence seems to lay a heavy burden; & responsibility on you *my dear Mary*; but I trust you will be enabled to bear it in some measure as you ought." He hoped that they would not blame "my dear Ruth" too much for the dreadful trial they were called to suffer. He also regretted that he could not go home to console Mary and the other children. "If I had a right sence of my habitual neglect of my familys Eternal interests; I should probably go crazy. I humbly hope this dreadful afflictive Providence will lead us all more properly to appreciate the amazeing, unforseen, untold, consequences; that hang upon the right or wrong doing of things seemingly of trifling account. Who can tell or comprehend the vast results for good, or for evil; that are to follow the saying of one little word. Evrything worthy of being done at *all*; is worthy of being done in *good earnest*, & in the best possible manner."[6]

Brown had a mission now and not even another death in his family could shake his determination. As large consignments of wool arrived at the Springfield agency (from 50 to 80 bales a day), Brown and Jason worked assiduously to sort and grade the fleece for sale, while John Jr., growing out of his taciturnity as a youth, managed most of the correspondence in a florid writing style and a flair for language he had developed at the Austinburg Institute. Jason soon returned to Ohio. But John Jr. remained to assist his father in what was turning out to be a backbreaking crusade. Yet Brown remained optimistic. "Mary," he wrote in his next letter, "let us try to maintain a cheerful self command while we are tossing up & down, & let our motto still be Action, Action; as we have but one life to live." But in spite of his hard work, events beyond his control—and probably his understanding—were conspiring against him. Congress had recently reduced duties against imported wool in the Walker Tariff, and the price of Saxony fleece, in which Brown was especially interested, fell from 75 cents to 25 cents per pound. To make matters worse, the war with Mexico, which had begun on May 13, caused the wool market to fluctuate wildly. That, and Brown's refusal to adjust his prices once he had fixed them, almost wrecked Perkins & Brown the first year. Although Brown "contracted away" some low-grade fleece in October, "large quantaties" of unsold wool lay in piles on the floor of Perkins & Brown. Anxious wool growers pressed him to adjust his prices to the fluctuating market, but he refused to "sacrifice their wool" and hung on to it with both hands. Brown would have gone down in disaster had not an Englishman on December 21 bought some of his fine wools for export.[7]

Brown returned to Ohio in February, 1847, to attend a national wool convention in Steubenville and win back the confidence of the growers. His speech at the convention about his methods of grading and selling wool impressed everybody. In fact, the convention adopted a resolution which accused the wool buyers of deliberately purchasing all wool at low-grade rates, thus endorsing Brown's Springfield crusade. The convention designated Perkins & Brown as the Eastern depot for Western wool growers—a move supported by the influential *Prairie Farmer*.

It was a great triumph for the crusading shepherd, and he returned to Springfield certain that the "experiment" would succeed. In July, 1847, he moved his wife and most of his children to Springfield, lodging them in a small plain house on Franklin Street around the corner from Perkins & Brown, which was now located in an impressive building "on a prominent busy street" south of the railroad office. In the meantime John Jr. had returned to Austinburg for the spring term of the Grand River Institute. In July he married a girl he had met there named Wealthy Hotchkiss; and shortly after the ceremonies, at his father's earnest summons, he and his bride moved to Springfield, where John Jr. resumed his duties at Brown's agency. Only Ruth and Jason remained in Ohio. Jason, who had married Ellen Sherbondy, wanted to free himself from Brown's influence and make his own way.[8]

Whatever else may be said of Brown, he was a man of prodigious energy. Driving himself from daybreak to dusk, he sorted and graded perhaps 500,000 pounds of wool in 1847. But all his energy and zeal could not compensate for his ineptitude as a businessman. Even with John Jr. around to help, Brown could not keep his accounts straight. He failed to acknowledge letters and wool shipments, and often waited so long to fix his prices that what buyers he might have attracted turned elsewhere. Moreover, he would accept advice from no one, insisting throughout that his methods were irreproachable.[9]

Take the testimony of Aaron Erickson, a veteran wool dealer from western New York. Erickson, who believed the present system of buying wool a fair one, came to see Brown in 1847 to find out whether he was not actually "an unscrupulous sharper, seeking to turn his neighbors credulity to his private gain." Erickson was quite taken aback, for instead of an unscrupulous sharper he found Brown a blunt, simple man who had an "almost childlike ignorance of the great enterprise in which he was embarking." Erickson saw him again that same year, and the more they talked about the wool business the more Erickson questioned Brown's abilities. Showing Erickson how he graded wool (Erickson thought the system was awful), Brown "claimed infallible accuracy in his discrimination, and would hear no opposing argument." When Brown's back was turned, Erickson changed fleece from one pile to another. Then he asked Brown whether some of the wool was not improperly graded. No, Brown said without hesitation, the classifications were absolutely correct.

Later Brown said that his fine wool was among the best in the land and that he had therefore valued it at 50 percent above its market value. At the same time he had fixed the lower grades at about 25 percent below their market value. Erickson was aghast, pointing out that the manufacturers would snap up the underpriced grades immediately. Brown said, "let them take them, they are graded right," and added, "I will make it up in my fine wool, which I am determined shall be appreciated." Erickson left Springfield convinced that Brown was "a victim of his own delusions."[10]

But others who knew him better were more sympathetic. E. C. Leonard, who had an office near Brown's warehouse and visited him frequently, pointed out that Brown strove to be impartial in his wool dealings, "with all the rigor of theory and of his habits of thought." Brown was "a scrupulously honest and upright man,— hard and inflexible, but everybody had just what belonged to him."

Even Leonard had to admit that Brown "was no *trader*," that he had no idea how to sell his wool on the open market. And, just as Erickson had predicted, manufacturers bought up the lower-grade wools at ruinous prices to the growers Brown represented. The finer

wools remained unsold in Brown's lofts. As some growers withdrew
their fleece, Brown blamed the manufacturers for his troubles, accusing them of conspiring to destroy him since he was trying to protect
the wool grower at their expense. But defensive accusations did not
revive his stricken business or pay his bills. As his expenses rose he
fell into his old habits—he borrowed from the bank again.[11]

3

In Springfield Brown began reading a variety of radical abolitionist
publications which the Garrisonians circulated out of Boston, and he
met several immediate abolitionists and "friends of freedom" right
here in town. The Hampden County Antislavery Society, formed
back in 1838, held frequent meetings in the First Congregational
Church on the town square. There Dr. Samuel Osgood, the minister
of the church and an officer of the society, gave lectures on the evils
of slavery to gatherings of clergymen, merchants, professional people, and free Negroes (some 270 of them resided in Springfield at
this time and about 130 more lived elsewhere in the county).
Osgood and other members of the society—black and white alike—
were also conductors on the Connecticut Valley Line of the Underground Railroad, which smuggled fugitives from the South into Vermont and New Hampshire and from there into Canada.[12]

   Brown, a thoroughgoing nonconformist by this time, did not join
the local antislavery society or serve as an actual conductor on the
Underground Railroad. But he did assist fugitives on his own. And
in his spare time away from the wool agency he thought up various
projects to help the black man and the cause of abolition—now an
"African high school" which he wanted George Delamater to establish in Canada, now an abolitionist-sponsored wool exhibit designed
to add luster and respectability to the antislavery cause to which
Brown was now "most thoroughly devoted." Brown was astonish-
ingly secretive about the wool exhibit. While he offered to put up
$1,000 as prize money, he wrote Congressman Joshua Giddings and
asked him to manage the affair, requesting that his own name be
kept *"wholly & absolutely out of sight"* and that the project itself
remain "a most *profound secret"* until Brown could go to Washington to consult with Giddings about it. Brown added in a postscript:

"Mr. H. Clay has been called an *American*. Why may not Abolitionists?" But Brown was so "pinched for money" in his wool business that nothing ever came of the wool exhibit or the African high school.[13]

Still, his enthusiasm for the abolitionist cause remained high. On the prescribed evenings, after a harrowing day at his agency, he even attended antislavery meetings in town, where he befriended a firebrand abolitionist clergyman. Evidently Brown was a little more tolerant of the religious views of other abolitionists than he used to be. He suggested himself that he had spent more time arguing with his antislavery friends about their religious practices than in fighting slavery, their common enemy.

Brown also befriended a number of Negroes in Springfield, some of them runaway slaves. He asked them about their experiences in slavery. He spoke to them about the *Liberator*, which pictured all plantations as dens of cruelty and lechery. And he wanted to know what they thought of racial oppression in the North and the prevailing opinion there that Negroes were passive, feeble-minded "Sambos." Apparently he did not like what the Negroes said about these and other subjects, because in 1847 or early 1848 he took the time to compose a satirical essay called "Sambos Mistakes," in which he posed as a Negro named Sambo who records all the errors and mistaken attitudes of his life, in hopes that his fellow blacks will learn from them. The piece is revealing in more ways than one, for some of the mistakes Brown described were clearly his own. The essay was printed in the *Ram's Horn*, a short-lived abolitionist newspaper published by Negroes in New York.

What were Sambo's follies? To begin with, he had learned to read but, instead of giving his attention "to sacred & profane history" which would have acquainted him with "the true character of God" and with the course of individuals and societies, Sambo had spent all his time devouring "silly novels & other miserable trash such as most of the newspapers of the day & other popular writings are filled with." Sambo had also wasted money on tobacco, thinking that smoking and chewing would make him but little inferior to white men, when Sambo should have applied that money toward a farm, or a library, or toward helping members of his own race. Moreover, Sambo had wasted his time in the Freemasons, Odd Fellows, Sons of Temperance, and "a score of other secret societies instead of seeking the company of intelligent wise & good men." In addition, Sambo had been too inflexible in his opinions and too critical of others; those who did not rise to his standards Sambo would reject entirely, injure their influence, oppose their measures, and glory in their defeats, even if their intentions had been good and their plans well laid. While Sambo had always been "a most zealous Abolitionist," he had been constantly at war with his friends about their religious differences. He would never think of acting with his Quaker friends, who were "the rankest heretiks," or with the Baptists, who "would be in the water," or the Methodists, who "denied the doctrine of Election." But in later years, after he had been enlightened by Garrison and Abby Kelly, Sambo had spent all his force on those who loved the Sabbath, because all seemed to be at stake on that point. Notwithstanding that he had been "unsuccessful" in his efforts, he could claim a "peculiar quick sightedness," for in a second he could see where he missed it.

Brown did not explain what Sambo had missed, but in the climax in the last chapter he provided a few clues. Sambo [Brown wrote] had always sought the favor of white men "by tamely submitting to every species of indignity contempt & wrong insted of nobly resisting their brutal aggressions from principle" and taking his place "as a man" and assuming "the responsibilities of a man a citizen, a husband, a father, a brother, a neighbour, a friend as God requires of every one (if his neighbour will allow him to do it:) ." And what did Sambo, the Negro, get for his submission? The same reward "that the Southern Slaveocrats render the Dough faced Statesmen of the North for being bribed, & browbeat, & fooled & cheated, as the Whigs & Democrats love to be, & think themselves highly honored if they may be allowed to lick up the spittle of a Southerner." But Sambo was uncommonly quicksighted, because he saw in a minute where he had missed it all.[14]

These are suggestive remarks indeed. Was Brown indirectly rejecting the doctrines of nonviolence and moral suasion which the Garrisonians still insisted would eradicate slavery in their time? Action was Brown's motto. Was he contemplating action when he urged Negroes to resist nobly the "brutal aggressions" of white men? Did he have violent thoughts when he recorded his outrage over Negroes timidly submitting to white contempt and "Dough faced" Northerners licking up Southern spit?

There is evidence that Brown did indeed have violent thoughts at this time. He had met several "prominent colored people" in New York State—most notably the Rev. J. W. Loguen of Syracuse and the Rev. Henry Highland Garnet of Troy. The blacks were impressed with Brown—his contempt for slaveholders was nearly as great as their own—and he was just as impressed with them, especially Garnet. Garnet was an outspoken black militant who, at a Negro convention in Buffalo back in 1843, had called on the slaves to rise up in rebellion as Nat Turner had done. "Brethren, arise, arise!" he had cried in his "Address to the Slaves of the United States of America." Strike for your lives and liberty, he exhorted them. Remember that slavery was a curse against Jehovah, that it murdered the sons of black men and prostituted their wives and daughters. "Remember that there can be no redemption of sin without the shedding of blood," he declared and again pleaded with them to "rise up, rise up! Now is the day and the hour. Let every slave throughout the land do this, and the days of slavery are numbered. You cannot be more oppressed than you have been—you cannot suffer greater cruelties than you have already. *Rather die freemen than live to be slaves.*"

It is difficult to say how much Garnet and militants like him influenced Brown. One story says that Brown liked the "Address" so much that he put up the money to have it published in pamphlet form, along with David Walker's *Appeal,* which also called for slaves to revolt.[15] Maybe this is true and maybe it is not. But the fact is that Brown *was* growing increasingly militant in his own denunciations of slavery, and the passage in "Sambos Mistakes" urging slaves to resist their white oppressors sounds almost exactly like something Garnet would say. Moreover, it was not long before Brown himself was quoting from Hebrews 9, that "almost all things are by the law purged with blood; and without shedding of blood is no remission."

Two other Negroes Brown met while he lived in Springfield—Frederick Douglass and Thomas Thomas, who worked as Brown's assistant for a time—later claimed that Brown actually wanted to "interfere" with slavery in the South at this time. Both said that Brown revealed to them a plan he had devised to establish a "Subterranean Pass Way" in the Allegheny Mountains through which he could run Negroes off to the North.

Douglass was an eminent mulatto of Rochester, New York, who had run away from a Maryland plantation, married a free black woman, joined the abolitionist crusade, and lectured to white audiences up and down New England. He suffered "a baptism of fire" at the hands of white racists, who mobbed him, spit in his face, refused him accommodations, and compelled him to ride in "Jim Crow cars," but he kept speaking. Articulate and extremely intelligent, with a handsome shock of hair, Douglass made a lecture tour in England, where funds were raised to buy his freedom, and started publishing an eloquent Negro newspaper at Rochester, New York, called the *North Star.* Douglass had first heard of Brown through Garnet, Loguen, and other black men, who, when they spoke of him, dropped their voices "to a whisper" and what they said made Douglass "very eager to see and know him." Thus when Brown invited him to Springfield to discuss "urgent matters," Douglass took time off from a lecture tour he was conducting in New England and went to meet that "lean, impressive" white man.

Their meeting took place late in November, 1847, in Brown's sparsely furnished home. Douglass shared a spare, simple meal with the Browns, observing that his host "fulfilled St. Paul's idea of the head of the family," as his wife and children spoke to him with a mixture of respect and diffidence. After Mary had cleared away the dishes, Brown brought up the slavery question. With his eyes "full of light and fire," he denounced slavery fiercely and bitterly, insisting that slavery was a state of war and that the slaves had a right to gain their freedom "any way they could." Brown said he had "a plan" and unfolded a map of the United States on the kitchen table. "These mountains," he said, running a trembling finger along the Alleghenies, "are the basis of my plan. God has given the strength of the hills to freedom; they were placed here for emancipation of the negro race; they are full of natural forts, where one man for defense will be equal to a hundred for attack; they are full also of good hiding-places, where large numbers of brave men could be concealed, baffle and elude pursuit for a long time." His object would be to destroy the value of slave property by rendering that property insecure. "My plan, then, is to take at first about twenty-five picked men, and begin on a small scale; supply them arms and ammunition, post them in squads of fives on a line of twenty-five miles, the most persuasive and judicious of whom shall go down to the fields from time to time, as opportunity offers, and induce the slaves to join them, seeking and selecting the most restless and daring." He said he did not intend to incite a full-scale insurrection—that would only defeat his object—but he was "not averse to the shedding of blood," because using guns gave black men "a sense of their manhood." He believed that "No people could have self-respect, or be respected, who would not fight for their freedom."

Douglass, looking at the map, remarked that the Southerners "would employ bloodhounds to hunt you out of the mountains."

"That they might attempt," Brown replied, "but the chances are, we should whip them, and when we should have whipt one squad, they would be careful how they pursued."

They argued about that point for a moment. Then Douglass suggested that they might still be able to convert the slaveholders and abolish slavery by peaceful means. That could never be, Brown retorted, because "he knew their proud hearts and that they would never be induced to give up their slaves, until they felt a big stick about their heads." After further discussion, Douglass conceded that Brown's plan "had much to commend it" and went away certain that he had never been "in the presence of a stronger religious influence" than that of John Brown. After he left Springfield Douglass sent a letter to the *North Star*, in which he remarked that he had had "a private interview" with Brown, who, "though a white gentlemen, is in sympathy, a black man, and as deeply interested in our cause, as though his own soul had been pierced with the iron of slavery."

Douglass visited Brown again late in 1848. And, in the months that followed, his own antislavery utterances "became more and more tinged by the color of this man's strong impressions." The following year Douglass shocked an antislavery audience in Boston's Faneuil Hall when he asserted that he would welcome news of a slave insurrection in the South. At an abolitionist convention at Salem, Ohio, he said he feared that only bloodshed could annihilate slavery now.[16]

And what did Brown think of Douglass? He said he could scarcely restrain his joy at the appearance of men like Douglass—men who "possessed the energy of head and heart to demand freedom for their whole people." The result would be, "must be, the downfall of slavery."[17]

Although Brown did not mention his plan in his correspondence, this may not mean very much—a plan like that was hardly the sort of thing he would discuss in his letters (Brown may have been a lot of things but he was no fool). Sometimes he could be remarkably furtive about his peaceful abolitionist projects—let alone whatever violent ones he was plotting—as was the case with his abolitionist-sponsored wool exhibit. In view of his secretiveness, his hatred of Southern slaveholders, his friendship with militants like Garnet, and his own experiences on the Underground Railroad, there can be almost no doubt that Brown was secretly plotting a slave-running operation like the one Douglass described. Apparently Brown thought his operation would prove more effective than the Underground Railroad because his own plan called for guerrilla skirmishes against the recalcitrant Southerners (always the nonconformist, Brown had even decided against using the lines of the Underground Railroad for his own escape routes).[18] Like all his other plots and projects, however, the "Subterranean Pass Way" scheme never got beyond the planning stage while Brown resided in Springfield. But he continued to pore over his map of the Alleghenies, indulging in fantasies about fighting a guerrilla war there. He also made a careful study of the wars and insurrections recounted in Rollin's *Ancient History, Napoleon and His Marshals,* and *The Life of Oliver Cromwell,* which occupied a place in his Springfield home alongside his Bible. And he studied his Bible, too, especially those Books of the Old Testament that told how Jehovah, in the time of ancient Israel, directed the wholesale slaughter of the enemies of the chosen people.[19]

4

By the spring of 1848 Brown's crusading zeal in the wool business had begun to subside. Unsold wool still lay in huge piles in the lofts and Perkins & Brown was badly in debt. Brown blamed his difficulties on unstable financial conditions in New England and the failure of certain buyers to pay for the wool they had contracted. Everything seemed to be going wrong. Jason was proclaiming some form of "idolatry" out in Ohio. And Frederick was suffering from an affliction diagnosed as "an accumulation of blood on the brain." Although he was under the care of a physician, he still suffered terrible pain—

sometimes so excruciating that it blinded the boy and left him "wild" and "flighty." Brown brooded over Frederick's affliction. Everything he owned and everything he tried seemed to go wrong, as though Providence were indeed punishing him for his own follies. All he could do was reaffirm his faith in God's mercy and justice, "for that was the only hope for us; *Bankrupts*," and look for some way out of his difficulties.[20]

He remembered Gerrit Smith, the wealthy reformer of Peterboro, New York, who had given Oberlin College the land Brown had surveyed in western Virginia in 1840. Brown had heard that Smith had set aside 120,000 acres of land, in the Adirondack Mountains in northeastern New York, for Negro families who wanted to farm and become useful, productive citizens. But the winters were long and bitterly cold in the Adirondacks, and only a few Negro families had settled there, in a small community called North Elba, when Brown took an interest in the area. In April, 1848, Brown journeyed to Smith's white-columned mansion in Peterboro and presented him with a plan. "I am something of a pioneer," Brown explained to the 6-foot, 200-pound landholder; "I grew up among the woods and wild Indians of Ohio, and am used to the climate and the way of life that your colony find so trying. I will take one of your farms myself, clear it up and plant it, and show my colored neighbors how much work should be done; will give them work as I have occasion, look after them in all needful ways, and be a kind of father to them."[21]

Smith liked Brown, a blunt, Bible-quoting Christian who genuinely cared for the black man, and gave his consent to Brown's plan on the spot. Brown found Smith a bland and generous country gentleman who shared his abolitionist convictions even if they disagreed as to methods—Smith was a political abolitionist, one of the leaders of the Liberty party, who believed that slavery could best be eradicated through the political processes. Actually, Smith was a strange, eccentric individual. A hypochondriac, impulsive, almost childlike at times, he was given to unpredictable moods—now melancholy, now irascible, now charming and gregarious. Yet through all his moods he was a dedicated philanthropist, devoting his money and his nervous energy to a host of causes—land reform, education, temperance, and, above all, abolition and the plight of the Negro.

Brown left Peterboro and traveled into the Adirondack Mountains to visit North Elba. Inspecting the scattered Negro farms there, he was immediately taken with the Adirondacks, "where every thing you see reminds one of Omnipotence, and where if you do get your crops cut off once in a while, you will feel your dependence." Brown felt at home in those mountains. Probably he had never felt so much at home anywhere else.[22]

The Negroes, however, were having an extremely difficult time. Nobody had bothered to survey the area, so that the families did not know whether they were located on the right lots or not. Much of the land was difficult to cultivate, too, and some of the Negroes were destitute. Brown "felt deeply" for them (later he sent them ten barrels of pork and flour). As their new leader he hoped to teach these "poor despised Africans" how to farm and better themselves, and he would also teach them to fear God. If it were the will of Providence, he would develop North Elba from the disorganized place it was now into a model Negro community that would stand as an example to the world.[23]

But before he could move to North Elba he had to close his wool business—a herculean task. The wool had to be sold somehow, all his debts had to be paid. He hurried back to Springfield and in January, 1849, offered his fine wool "at Five cents per lb. below our present prices," but nobody took advantage of the offer. Thereupon he raised the price—and sold 37,000 pounds of fine wool, which convinced him that he had been right all along. But he still had over 200,000 pounds of fine wool on hand, and the agency owed a staggering $57,000 to the Cabot Bank alone. As sales fell off again, he turned on the manufacturers and once more accused them of trying to wreck him. Beset on all sides (from wool growers, bankers, dealers, and manufacturers), Brown resorted to a desperate move, one he had been contemplating since late 1846. He decided to ship all his best wool to England and Scotland, where, according to a Scottish wool agent, he could get "about ten cents more per lb." than in the United States. Brown explained his plan to Perkins, pointing out that American manufacturers were deliberately buying fine wool from Europe at prices that were about 75 cents per pound higher than Brown's. The manufacturers were doing this "on purpose to break down *at all events* the price of fine wool here." He added that "I have done all, &

every thing I could consistently do to get off the fine wools, but when I see manufacturers go elsewhere, & pay 25 to 75 per cent more than we ask than buy of us *in order to get back the full control of the market* it looks dark." Evidently Perkins and most of Brown's clients approved of his plan to ship his wool abroad.[24]

As Brown made his preparations, Aaron Erickson came by for another visit. Erickson found him "greatly depressed in spirits" and listened as Brown reiterated his belief that the manufacturers had "combined against him." When Erickson heard that Brown intended to send his best wool to England, he was appalled. Did Brown not know that fine wool was being exported from England despite the tariff and that it was selling at *lower* prices than American wool? Brown denied that and refused to listen, even when Erickson pointed out that he had tried to export wool himself. "Your wool was not graded like mine," Brown snapped. Throwing up his hands, Erickson walked out and never saw Brown again.[25]

In the meantime misfortune continued to afflict Brown's family. Ellen, Brown's most recent child, caught a terrible cold. In April the cold turned to consumption, and the child died in Brown's arms as he walked her back and forth across the bedroom. "He was very calm," said Ruth, who had come to Springfield to help Mary. He "closed her eyes, folded her hands, and laid her in her cradle." But "when she was buried, father broke down completely and sobbed like a child."[26]

5

Although the signs were ominous, Brown would not abandon his plans. In May he moved his family to North Elba, putting them up in a rented farmhouse until he could build a place on their own land —244 acres which Smith had sold the Browns at $1 an acre. Brown spent most of June getting the farm in order and doing what he could for his black neighbors; he not only hired Negro workers (one a runaway slave) but helped straighten out the Negroes' boundary lines and attempted to secure title to some of the farms.[27]

One morning, while Brown was working in the yard around his farm, he saw three strangers emerge from the woods and head his

way. One of them turned out to be Richard Henry Dana, the celebrated author of *Two Years Before the Mast*. Dana explained that he
and his companions had lost their way in the woods and had wandered
through these "barren mountains" all night, until at last they had
come upon Brown's log house, from which they could see towering
White Face Mountain. When Brown heard that they had not eaten
since yesterday morning, he took them in at once, fed them a meal of
venison and speckled brook trout, and insisted that they spend the
night. Dana found Brown "a strong abolitionist and a kind of king"
among the Negroes in the neighborhood. He noted with disapproval
(for he did not believe in social equality for Negroes) that Brown
referred to his black workers as "Mr." and let them eat at the same
table with his family. The family itself, Dana observed, seemed to
consist of an unlimited supply of children, "from a cheerful, nice
healthy woman of twenty or so [Ruth], and a full sized red-haired
son, who seemed to be foreman of the farm [Owen], through every
grade of boy and girl to a couple that could hardly speak plain."[28]

In July, leaving Ruth to care for the family (Mary was sick and
Owen was treating his crippled arm with a galvanic battery), Brown
returned to Springfield, where he and John Jr. completed preparations for the trip abroad. After 200,000 pounds of his best wool had
been shipped, Brown himself boarded a steamer for England on
August 15, convinced to the end that he was going to make a pile of
money and solve all his difficulties, all his woes.

Brown reached London on August 27. But finding that his wool
could not be auctioned until mid-September, he traveled to Paris,
where he sold five bales to "our French friends." They did not buy
any more, however, and Brown moved on to Brussels, where he
tramped over the terrain of the Waterloo battlefield. Then he hurried to Hamburg, no doubt to investigate the wool market there. Back
in London by September 17, he offered his wool to British buyers in
the public auctions. It was a disaster—all he could get for No. 2 wool
was an outrageous 26 cents to 27 cents per pound. He withdrew all
his other wool from the public sales. "I have a great deal of stupid,
obstinate, prejudice, to contend with as well as conflicting interests,
both in their country, & from the United States," he wrote John Jr.
bitterly. "I can only say that I have exerted myself to the utmost: &
that if I cannot effect a better sale of the other wools privately; I shall

start them back." In desperation Brown hurried to Leeds, but prices were no better there. He went to "Wortley, Branley, Bradford & other places," but it was no use. In the end he had to dump most of his wool at ruinous prices. He wrote John Jr. that he had been "in the midst of sickness and death" and that he was coming home.[29]

Before he left, though, he sent a letter of explanation to Simon Perkins. Brown had failed to effect "a *good* sale" of their fleece because of "all the prejudices that exist against American wools that have come to this country." Yet his efforts had not been entirely in vain, he told Perkins. "However much I may be blamed for doing poorly with the wool; I believe the wool business in the [United States] will be permanently helped by the means."[30]

He set sail for home still believing that.

VI

FEELING OUR DEPENDENCE

ﬤﾉﾊﾊﾟﾛ

ALL BROWN'S CLAIMS TO THE CONTRARY, the trip to England was a monumental fiasco. The great irony of it was that a Massachusetts manufacturer who had offered Brown 60 cents per pound for his wool now bought a consignment back at 52 cents per pound—including freight and tariff costs. After all the casualties had been tallied, Brown had lost about $40,000 on the venture, and Perkins & Brown faced certain liquidation. When Aaron Erickson heard the news he was convinced that on the subject of wool Brown was "crazy." But others sympathized with the crusading shepherd who had failed in what they regarded as a just cause. Brown's attorney, a business friend, and a Northampton manufacturer who had bought heavily from him all testified to his integrity and complete honesty, although the attorney thought him an obstinate man who was "peculiar in many of his notions."[1]

Stunned when he realized the dimensions of his failure, Brown admitted that he had to get out or face bankruptcy a second time. In mid-April, 1850, he met Perkins in Burgettstown, Pennsylvania, to discuss how they should close the agency. Perkins was extremely kind, Brown wrote John Jr. "He met a full history of our difficulties, & *probable losses* without a frown on his countenance, or one sylable of reflection, but on the contrary with words of comfort, & encouragement." Even though the wool agency had ended in disaster, Perkins wanted to continue raising sheep with Brown and urged him to return to Akron after his affairs had been settled. When they parted Brown was sure that "Mr. Perkins has in this whole business from first to last set an example worthy of a Philosopher, or of a Christian."[2]

Still, Brown was melancholy. He traveled across Pennsylvania, western Virginia, and Ohio, trying to defend himself and to settle up with his unhappy clients, but to no avail. One grower in New York was going to sue him; so were his creditors and some of his former customers. It was the Ohio nightmare all over again. He returned to North Elba in September, in time to exhibit his prize Devonshire cattle at an Essex County fair. A few days later, on September 26, Ruth married Henry Thompson, whose family operated a farm at North Elba. Although Brown's mind was on his business troubles, he thought Ruth had "done well," because Henry was a hard worker and hated slavery. To get his mind off his burdens Brown did some surveying in the mountains. It helped some. In October, when he set out to close the Springfield agency, he felt "refreshed, & invigorated."[3]

John Jr. had taken his wife back to Ohio, and Brown had to close his business in Springfield by himself. He slaved and brooded over his chaotic accounts and grew melancholy again. "There seems to be a blue vein running through the letter you send to Jason," John Jr. wrote him. "Well, I do not wonder at it. My surprise is that you can bear up under such a complication of misfortunes with anything like the fortitude you do." John Jr. urged him not to despair too much. "It won't pay to worry and sicken and die for a few paltry dollars."

Of course, $40,000 in casualties was hardly "a few paltry dollars." But it was not the money that bothered Brown so much as the failure of his crusade for a just cause—and the loss of face in the eyes of his enemies and his friends. Yet "what burdens me *most of all*," he wrote his sons in Ohio, "*is*; the apprehension that Mr. Perkins expects of me in the way of bringing matters to a close what no living man can possibly bring *about*; in a short time, & that he is getting out of patience, & becoming distrustfull." Was there not some way he could make a lot of money in a hurry and bail himself out of this mess? He thought seriously about entering the wine business, convinced that "unadulterated Domestic Wines" would "command great prices." He also thought about returning to North Elba and the mountains he loved. "*Nothing* but the strong sense of duty, obligation, & propriety, would keep me from laying my bones to rest there," he told his sons; "but I shall cheerfully make that sense my guide; God always helping."[4] But he was not cheerful. He was lonely and restless, and when he left the agency in the evening, after a maddening day with his disorderly accounts, he changed roles from a much-maligned businessman to a lone crusading abolitionist, who strove to protect his Negro friends from the forces of evil gathering across the land.

2

Actually, there was much to crusade about in the fall of 1850. A new fugitive slave law, intended to appease the South as part of the Compromise of 1850, had just gone into effect. Antislavery groups all across the Northeast put up a tremendous public outcry against this "open bribe" to the Slave Power and demanded that Northern authorities refuse to enforce the law. In Congress Joshua Giddings declared that it was the same as "murder" to return fugitives to the South. And Frederick Douglass and other Negro abolitionists spoke out defiantly against the law, for who among them was safe now? Already slaveowners and hired "kidnapers" were invading the North in search of alleged fugitives. What was to stop them from "mistakenly" identifying free Negroes as runaways and carrying them back into slavery as well?

Brown also boiled with indignation. He had visions of slave-catchers, reinforced by constables and federal marshals, marching into Springfield and North Elba (and Hudson, too, and Akron) to carry his Negro friends back into bondage. "It really looks as if God had his hand in this wickedness also," Brown wrote his wife. "I of course keep encouraging my friends to 'trust in God and keep their powder dry' I did so today at thanksgiving meeting publicly."[5]

How did God have His hand in such wickedness? When Brown wrote that, his mind was fixed on the Book of Judges, which told of how Israel, in the generation after Joshua, had forsaken the Lord and how He had punished His sinning flock by turning them over to the wicked Midian for seven years. Then God had called upon Gideon to save Israel. And Gideon had gathered an army of thousands and gone after the Midianites who were massed in the valley north of the wall of Harod. Before the battle the Lord spoke to Gideon, saying that he had too many people with him. When the Lord delivered the Midianites into their hands they might praise themselves and not the Lord. Go to his people, the Lord told Gideon, and say to them, "Whosoever *is* fearful and afraid, let him return and depart early from mount Gilead." And Gideon, telling his people this and imposing additional tests which the Lord had commanded, saw his army of thousands dwindle to a mere three hundred. But with these three hundred, the Lord said, He would save Gideon and deliver the Midianites into his hands. And as the men of Israel blew their trumpets and cried, "The sword of the Lord, and of Gideon," God laid their swords against the host and drove them across Jordan. And two Midianites who had been captured were slain and their heads carried triumphantly back to Gideon on the other side of Jordan. And Gideon, who had many wives and many sons, told the men of Israel that henceforth God would rule over them.

Brown's mind was full of the Book of Judges when he talked with his Negro friends about the fugitive slave law. A runaway had just been captured in New York and "sent off to slavery," and the blacks in Springfield were terrified. Some could not sleep, so afraid were they that slavecatchers and federal marshals would come in the night to arrest them and their wives and children and drag them away in chains. You must not take such evil lying on your backs, Brown told them. He was fighting mad. You must organize yourselves into guerrilla bands and fight this wicked law with the sword. On the evening of January 15, 1851, Brown gathered his black friends around him in Springfield and read them a remarkable document:

WORDS OF ADVICE
Branch of the United States League of Gileadites.
Adopted Jan. 15, 1851, as written and
recommended by John Brown
"Union is Strength"

"Nothing so charms the American people as personal bravery," Brown read from his "Words of Advice." "The trial for life of one bold and to some extent successful man, for defending his rights in good earnest, would arouse more sympathy throughout the nation than the accumulated wrongs and sufferings of more than three millions of our submissive colored population." He told them: "Colored people have ten times the number of fast friends among whites than they suppose, and would have ten times the number they now have were they but half as much in earnest to secure their dearest rights as they are to ape the follies and extravagance of their white neighbors." Think of the money some individuals have spent in your behalf! "Think of the number who have been mobbed and imprisoned on your account! Have any of you seen the Branded Hand? Do you remember the names of Lovejoy and Torrey?"

Now there was the hellish fugitive slave law. He told them they must rally together and oppose it—and all who seek to enforce it—with the sword. "Whosoever is fearful and afraid, let him return and depart early from mount Gilead (Judges, VII. 3; Deut. XX. 8)."

He told them to organize and make their plans, but let them be known to no one but themselves, with the understanding that "all traitors must die."

He told them: "*Do* not delay one moment after you are ready; you will lose all your resolution if you do. Let the first blow be the sign for all to engage; and when engaged do not do your work by halves, but make clean work with your enemies."

He told them: "Be firm, detached, and cool." Above all, "Stand by one another and by your friends, while a drop of blood remains; and be hanged, if you must, but tell no tales out of school. Make no confession." If they all followed this advice, "the desired end may be effectually secured"—"namely, the enjoyment of our inalienable rights."[6]

Forty-four Negro men and women joined Brown's United States League of the Gileadites. There is no evidence that they ever followed Brown's advice and tried to kill any slavecatchers—probably none came to Springfield and the constables there never enforced the law anyway. But the organization of the Gileadites is significant nevertheless. For Brown's "Words of Advice" was a practical application of "Sambos Mistakes." Brown, sounding emphatically like Henry Highland Garnet, was telling Negroes *how* to resist the "brutal aggressions" of Southern slaveholders; he was trying to put into action a fighting doctrine that other militants only talked about. And some of his assertions are remarkably revealing. *When you engage your enemies, make clean work of it. . . . The trial for life of one bold and somewhat successful man, for defending his rights in good earnest, would arouse more sympathy throughout the nation than the suffering of all the slaves.*

These words still rang in his head when he closed the Springfield agency for good and hurried back to North Elba. There he continued his private war against the fugitive slave law, exhorting his black neighbors—a few of them runaways—to resist the law no matter what authority should invade North Elba and try to enforce it. He made his family swear to protect their Negro friends, even if that meant imprisonment—or death. Ruth said that their "faithful boy Cyrus" was a runaway and that Brown "aroused our feelings so that we would *all* have defended him, if the women folks had had to resort to *hot water*."[7]

But no slavecatchers or federal marshals came to North Elba, and worldly concerns soon pressed Brown away from the fugitive slave law. His family had to be provided for. His enemies were fighting to get him into court and sue him for everything he had. He decided to take his family back to Ohio, where his sons could work with Perkins in the sheep business while he went to war in the courts. In March the Browns uprooted themselves again, heading back over the trail to Ohio. Only Ruth, married to Henry Thompson, remained in the Adirondacks, where Brown—a worn-out old man at fifty-one— hoped someday to put his bones to rest.[8]

3

During the next three years Brown traveled back and forth from Ohio to the East, where he struggled to salvage his reputation and his pocketbook. Mary, who had had still another son (Brown's nineteenth child by the two wives), remained in Akron. Owen and Jason worked one of Perkins' farms near Tallmadge; and John Jr., who was thirty now and determined to make his own way, owned his own place in Vernon. He soon became a justice of the peace and even considered going into the wool business for himself. Brown gave him plenty of advice, but undoubtedly John Jr. had seen enough in Springfield to know that he should ignore the old man's suggestions.

Meanwhile Brown suffered through trial after trial at Pittsburgh, at Utica, Vernon, Boston, and New York. One of his most bitterly contested cases involved a suit brought by Henry Warren of Pitts-town, New York. Warren accused Brown of shipping Warren's fleece to the Burlington Mills Manufacturing Company of Vermont, with-out accounting for it. Warren insisted that he should be compensated according to 1847 prices, since that was the year he had shipped his wool to Brown. Brown, challenging Warren on both counts, insisted that his wool had arrived in 1848, not 1847; that since his wool had been graded and put in separate piles with everybody else's fleece, it was impossible to know where the wool had been sold; and that Warren was a scoundrel who was trying to defraud him. The trial opened in Troy in October, 1851, and dragged on into the next year before Brown's lawyer, Whipple Jenkins, won a judgment in Brown's favor. But Warren would not give up. He appealed his case to a higher court which reversed the previous decision and ruled against Brown, who was extremely bitter and claimed that he had been robbed.

In the meantime the Cabot Bank had also won a judgment against him. Shortly after that the Burlington Mills Company sued him in Boston for breach of contract because he had failed to deliver wools the company had ordered. Whipple Jenkins had died and Brown had hired another lawyer, the eminent Joshua V. Spencer of New York. Convinced that Brown did not stand a chance in a trial, Spencer persuaded him to settle out of court on February 3, 1853. But Brown later won a similar case in New York, which convinced him that had his case with Burlington Mills gone to trial he would have won it too.[9]

The lawsuits dragged on disastrously, exhausting what limited funds Brown had left. By 1854 he was back in Ohio and virtually penniless again. On top of his financial troubles, he had been sick with the ague, whose malarial fevers burned away at his strength. At the same time other woes and calamities combined to take their toll as well. Frederick had grown worse. It grieved Brown to see his son "wild" and "flighty" like this, but all he could do was admonish him to "live abstemiously" and let him sit out in the fields, watching over the sheep. Other members of the family were continuously ill, too, first with the measles, then the whooping cough. The whooping cough killed Brown's baby son in May, 1852, shortly after the first trial with Warren. This was the ninth child Brown had lost—two by Dianthe and seven by Mary. And his losses in business were just as painful in their way (by now he had suffered some fifteen business failures in four different states). "My attachments to this world have been very strong," he wrote his daughter Ruth, "and Divine Providence has been cutting me loose, one cord after another; but notwithstanding I have so much to remind me that all ties must *soon* be severed; I am still clinging like those who have hardly taken a single lesson." Yes, he was still clinging, for he believed, as did few other men, that God had placed him on this spinning world as a trial for his soul—to prove finally that John Brown *was* worthy of His Kingdom in Paradise.[10]

His moods alternated between religious exaltation and despair. Yes, he confessed to his children, he was a broken-down old man, plagued with guilts, scarred by his own sins and follies.[11] Yet he still believed in the only true God and the Divine Purpose of His Plans for such unworthy men as himself. But what troubled him more than anything else was that his children no longer believed in Him. All the skepticism, the terrible delusions, that Jason and John Jr. had been proclaiming over the past couple of years—idolatry among his own children! Brown could not bear it. He beseeched them to return to the path of righteousness. He prayed that God open their eyes and show them the error of their ways. He wrote them letters of exhortation. "Some Ten or Twelve years ago, I was cheered with the belief that my elder children had chosen the *Lord*, to be their God; & I valued much on their influence & example in attoning for my deficiency, & bad example with the younger children. But; *where are* we now?" He knew where he had made his mistake; he was laboring to get back on the path of righteousness. But "how to now get on it with my family is beyond my ability to *see*; or my courage to *hope*." "God grant you *thorough* conversion from sin, & full purpose of heart to continue steadfast in his ways through the very *short season* of trial you will have to pass."

But his older children continued to backslide. "My Grey Hairs must go down to the grave in sorrow," he wrote John Jr. from Akron, "unless the 'true God' forgive [my children's] denyal, & rejection of him, & open their eyes." Then to Ruth and Henry: "Why will not my family endeavour to secure his favours, & to effect in the *One only* way a perfect reconciliation?"[12]

John Jr. wrote back, trying to defend his agnostic views. Brown accused him of "sermonizing" and replied with a seven-page exhortation. Now his younger sons had followed the older ones and "thrown off the *old Shackles* entirely." After "thorough and candid investigation," they had discovered the Bible to be "all a fiction." Should he point out that John Jr.'s letter only added to his "pain and sorrow"? Then, with his grammar steadily deteriorating, Brown launched into a veritable storm of quotations from Moses and Joshua, Ruth and Samuel:

The Lord says turn back one's backsliding children. "But they hearkened not, nor inclined their ear, but walked in the counsels & in the immaginations of their evil *heart*, & went *backward*, & not forward."

"The *heart* is deceitful *above all things* & desperately wicked: who can *know it?*" "Thy Prophets have been vain & foolish things for thee; & they have not discovered *thine iniquity.*"

"That the generation to come might *know them* [the words of truth], even the children which should be born, who should arise & declare them to their children: that they might set their *hope in God*, & not forget the works of God; but keep his Commandments: & might not be as their Fathers, a stubborn & rebellious generation; a generation that set *not* their *Heart aright*, & whose spirit was not *stedfast with God.*" "Who is *wise*, & he shall *understand* these things? *prudent* & he shall *know* them? for the ways of the Lord *are* right, & the just *shall walk in them*: but the transgressors *shall fall* therein."

"And many *false* Prophets shall rise, & shall deceive many. And because *iniquity* shall *abound* the *love of many* shall wax *cold.*" But on the last day God would judge those who "rejecteth me, & receiveth not my words." "And I beseech you," said John Brown to his children, "suffer the word of exhortation."[13]

4

Since February, 1853, Brown had wanted to return to North Elba, where everything he saw reminded him of "Omnipotence." But

Simon Perkins seemed so good to him, and so anxious to have him continue in their partnership, that Brown could not "tear away from him." Still, he feared that he might die before he saw North Elba again and that he would be buried here in Ohio and not in the mountains he loved. By 1854 he was too restless to remain in Ohio any longer. He had already asked Henry Thompson to build a house for him at North Elba, even though he might never live to see it.[14] Now, in January, 1854, he dissolved his partnership with Perkins— one that had sustained him for ten years. He and Perkins did not agree over the slavery question anyway, and Mrs. Perkins had made critical remarks about Brown's wool debacle in England that irked the Brown family. Brown still thought highly of "Mr. Perkins," however. And Perkins for his part still thought Brown an honest man, if too impulsive and uncompromising in his views. "I had no controversy with John Brown," Perkins remarked in later years, "for it would have done no good."[15]

As it turned out, Brown did not have the money for an immediate move to North Elba. He rented a farm near Akron, hoping to make enough money to finance a move in the fall. Then he rented two additional farms and set about planting crops on them all with a flash of his old determination.

Though he worked hard in the fields, he remained deeply troubled over all the wickedness that prevailed in the United States. How could he be otherwise when "sects who bear the Christian name" sanctioned "that mother of all abominations—man-stealing"? How could he echo these so-called Christians and "cry peace when there is *no* peace"?[16] "I have thought much of late of the extreme wickedness of persons who use their influence to bring law and order and good government, and courts of justice into disrespect and contempt of mankind," he wrote Frederick Douglass on January 9, 1854, five days after the explosive Kansas-Nebraska bill had been reported in the United States Senate. "What punishment ever inflicted by man or even threatened by God, can be too severe for those whose influence is a thousand times more malignant than the atmosphere of the deadly Upas—for those who hate the right and Most High."

Who were these "malignant spirits"—these "fiends clothed in human form"? They were all the legislators who had voted for the "most abominably wicked and injust" laws that prevailed in this slaveholding land; all the judges who interpreted and the constables and sheriffs and marshals and policemen who enforced these evil enactments; all the proslavery newspaper writers and preachers and "Doctors of Divinity" who defended them with their sanctimonious and sacrilegious declarations which stifled conscience and insulted God Himself. God commanded "That thou shalt not deliver unto his master the servant which is escaped from his master unto thee." And the conscience of every man cried "Amen." But what said the divines? "You must obey the enactments of the United States Congress, even to the violation of conscience, and the trampling under foot of the laws of our final Judge." "Remember them, O my God, because they have defiled the priesthood."

"But I have done. I am too destitute of words to express the tithe of what I feel." Would Douglass "or some friend of God and the right" clothe his words in suitable language and present them to the American people? He wanted to raise the inquiry everywhere. It was time to stop the corruption of "our truly republican and democratic institutions" by wicked proslavery men.

Douglass printed Brown's letter in *Frederick Douglass' Paper*, published in Rochester, New York.[17] But Brown's words did no good. The United States Congress passed the Kansas-Nebraska bill and President Pierce signed it into law on May 30, 1854. The Missouri Compromise line was gone; now the citizens of each territory— including the new territories of Kansas and Nebraska—were to vote on whether to have slavery or not. In the stormy debates over the bill, Salmon P. Chase of Ohio had sent out his inflammatory (but politically shrewd) "Appeal of Independent Democrats," charging that the bill was part of a Southern plot to extend slavery into Kansas and then all the West. William H. Seward of New York had given the South a ringing ultimatum: "Come on, then, gentlemen of the Slave States; since there is no escaping your challenge, I accept it in behalf of the cause of freedom. We will engage in competition for the virgin soil of Kansas, and God give the victory to the side that is stronger in numbers as it is in right."

Newspapers all over the North picked up the chant. Horace Greeley's New York *Tribune*, which Brown subscribed to in the 1850's, launched an editorial crusade against the Kansas-Nebraska Act, warning its readers that a Southern conspiracy was under way to extend human bondage not only into the West but into the North as well. The Slave Power was trying to take over the Union! In a convulsion of fear and moral outrage abolitionists from New England to Ohio clamored for the North to secede rather than remain in a nation dominated by the Slave Power. The abolitionists were not the only ones who were upset. Thousands of Americans, who were content to leave slavery alone in the South, nevertheless did not want it to expand onto their cherished frontier, and they, too, spoke out against the alleged Slave Power conspiracy. As Allan Nevins phrased it, the Kansas-Nebraska Act "had converted more men to intransigent freesoil doctrine in two months than Garrison and [Wendell] Phillips had converted to abolitionism in twenty years."[18]

Brown must have been profoundly disturbed, too, but he said nothing about the Kansas-Nebraska Act in his letters (at least not in those that have survived). In his correspondence he spoke only of his sheep business, his farms, his family (Mary was pregnant again), and the long move he was planning back to North Elba. He recounted his journeys back and forth from Ohio to the Northeast, where he sold wool and bought and sold cattle in an effort to raise some money. He told John Jr. that Frederick had undergone "a most terrible operation for his *breach*; which brought him near the grave," and that Brown had scarcely left his bedside for two weeks. By August 3, however, Frederick appeared to have enjoyed "a radical cure," which relieved Brown on that score. But nothing else cheered him. He complained to Ruth and Henry that "this part of the country is suffering the most dreadful drought ever experienced during this Nineteenth Century." Most of his crops except his hay had burned up under the blazing Ohio skies. Even so he had been "much more highly favored" than his neighbors, who had not even made a hay crop and who were eyeing his fruit (which still might survive) as though they intended to steal it. The more he thought about it, though, the more he regarded the drouth as part of God's plan "to make us feel our dependence." And "we shall probably feel it a little: untill a *favourable* change takes place."[19]

VII

WEST TO THE PROMISED LAND

❧❀❧

THE KANSAS FEVER SPREAD OVER DROUTH-RIDDEN Ohio and the other Northwestern states like an epidemic, charging street-corner conversation with excitement and hyperbole. A land of undulating prairies and forest recesses, of placid streams and fertile valleys, the Kansas Territory had just been opened for settlement by government proclamation, and already scores of pioneers from the Northwest and the border South, in covered wagons and on crowded riverboats, were on their way to that new land of beginning again—126,000 square miles of unclaimed wilderness lying west of Missouri in the very heart of North America.

Yet ominous shadows lay over the trails and rivers leading to the new territory. For the opening of Kansas, after all the antislavery hysteria that had surrounded the Kansas-Nebraska Act, heightened sectional tensions that had already divided the United States into mutually fearful and suspicious halves, and in North and South alike there were voices of violence in the wind. At the border town of Weston in slaveholding Missouri, a pro-Southern lawyer told a cheering crowd on July 4, 1854, that he would hang with his own hands any "free soil" emigrant who came to Kansas. And in the North— in Ohio and Massachusetts especially—emigrant aid societies were feverishly at work recruiting colonists who would go out and fill up Kansas with "free men"—men who hated slavery, who would "drive the hideous thing from the broad and beautiful plains where they go to raise their free homes." The most energetic leader in the save-Kansas movement was Eli Thayer, an educator and businessman of Worcester in central Massachusetts. Convinced that Salmon Chase and Horace Greeley were right, that the Kansas-Nebraska Act was a Southern plot to take over the West, Thayer had formed the Massachusetts Emigrant Aid Society (later reorganized as the New England Emigrant Aid Society) whose task was to help free-soil emigrants settle in Kansas and "vote to make it free." The society also hoped to provide handsome dividends for its stockholders through various speculative and business ventures in the territory. In July, thirty colonists migrated there under the auspices of Thayer's society and built a town called Lawrence on the southern bank of the Kaw River, a town that seemed "a piece of New England set down in the prairie," with brick and stone buildings and a massive "Free State" hotel which could double as a fortress.[1]

In the meantime border Missourians had poured into northeastern Kansas and staked out claims and built their own towns (Leavenworth, Easton, Atchison) along or near the Missouri River, hoping thereby to control settlement and commerce in the territory. Some of these emigrants were hard-working, law-abiding farmers who, like pioneers coming in from the Northwestern states, wanted to start a new life on a virgin frontier. But many others were speculators, Indian traders, cattle dealers, gun vendors, and river-bottom riffraff who had clustered in northwestern Missouri, mostly around outfitting towns like Independence, Weston, and St. Joseph, to make money from rich caravans crossing the Santa Fe Trail and from emigrant trains heading overland to Oregon and California. This "excitable, speculative, greedy element" saw Kansas as a business windfall and went there to make fortunes in land speculation. Thus when they heard the news of Thayer's $5 million New England emigrant aid company they viewed it as an enormous corporate threat to their own business interests and both they and the hard-working farmers (who were suspicious of Yankees anyway) were extremely alarmed when Thayer's colonists arrived. Rumors flew that the Northern company planned to seize Kansas by force and rob border Missourians of a territory they regarded as rightfully theirs, that the Yankee invaders would import rowdy Irishmen and other aliens to carry off slaves from Missouri plantations and would convert Kansas itself into a haven for "runaway niggers" and rabid abolitionists. At once slave-owners and pro-Southern politicians in border Missouri called on their neighbors to occupy Kansas and counter the free-soil peril which the New England Aid Society represented; rabble-rousers

like Benjamin Franklin Stringfellow and Senator David R. Atchison
(who had helped pull the Kansas-Nebraska bill through Congress)
issued violent warnings—"abolitionists" and Northern "free-lovers,"
stay out of Kansas—and vowed to make the territory a gateway for
proslavery expansion to the Pacific.[2]

Threats like that, of course, only confirmed the suspicions of
free-soil Northerners that a Slave Power conspiracy *was* under way to
seize the West, then the whole United States, and the various emigrant aid societies doubled their efforts to send out colonists who
would make Kansas free.

Still, migration to Kansas remained largely spontaneous and peaceful during the late summer and early fall of 1854. Most of the pioneers who went there came from the old Northwestern states—
farmers, artisans, and speculators, doctors, lawyers, and politicians
who hoped to start over again on a "free-soil frontier," and who
settled around the Kaw and Marais des Cygnes rivers, building log-
cabin farms and laying off new towns like Topeka, Big Springs, and
Osawatomie. At the same time Missourians and emigrants from the
border South also moved into eastern Kansas and took claims on
Sugar and Pottawatomie creeks. Although no incidents had occurred
so far, it seemed inevitable that violent confrontations would soon
break out between Northern and Southern settlers—confrontations
over rival townsites, conflicting claims, and the most combustible
issue of all, whether Kansas would be slave or free.

2

As the Kansas fever spread over sun-parched Ohio late that summer,
five of Brown's sons—Owen, Salmon, Frederick, Jason, and John Jr.
—got the westering urge too. If what the promotional literature of
Ohio's emigrant aid societies said was true, Kansas would be a
magnificent country to start over again—if honest, free-soil men could
keep it from the grasp of the South. Samuel Adair, whose wife Florilla
was Brown's half sister, was going out as a missionary and wanted
"good men and true"—men like the Browns—to follow him there.
So, as autumn came on and the drouth showed no signs of ending,
Brown's sons decided to sell out and try their luck as farmers and
stockmen in the Kansas Territory.[3]

Did their father want to go along? Here was an opportunity to resettle in a new land—and, by doing so, to help resist the advance of the Slave Power. Brown seriously thought about migrating to Kansas, then wrote John Jr.: "If you or any of my family are disposed to go to Kansas or Nebraska, with a view to help defeat Satan and his legions in that direction, I have not a word to say; *but I feel committed to operate in another part of the field.* If I were not so committed, I would be on my way this fall."

But the more he thought about Kansas the more he wanted to go. In September, as his sons made their plans, Brown wrote Ruth that he had been hard pressed to take his family to Kansas "as more likely to benefit the colored people *on the whole* than to return with them to N. Elba." He did not know what to do. The Adirondacks still called to him in ways that could not be described. But the call of Kansas—of starting over again on the frontier—was equally strong. What did Ruth and Henry think he should do? Would they ask the Negroes at North Elba what they wished of him? "As I volunteered in their services; they have a right to vote, as to course I should take." He also wrote Frederick Douglass, Gerrit Smith, and other friends in the East for advice. Smith—and probably the others—wanted him to come back to North Elba. In November he more or less made up his mind to do so.[4]

Early that same November Owen, Salmon, and Frederick (who was still weak from his operation) drove a herd of livestock—11 cows and 3 horses—across to Illinois, where they wintered with an uncle. In the spring of 1855 they took their herd westward across the Missouri River and on into eastern Kansas, where they staked out claims on the east side of North Middle Creek, about ten miles northwest of Osawatomie (where Samuel Adair had just settled) and some thirty miles south of Lawrence.[5] Jason and John Jr. were to follow sometime in April, bringing their families out by boat on the Missouri River.

3

During the winter of 1854–55, while Jason and John Jr. sold their farms and prepared to follow their brothers to Kansas, Brown himself journeyed back and forth between Ohio and the Northeast, trying to sell his cattle so that he could finance his move to North Elba. What he planned to do there now is not clear. Perhaps, as he implied in his correspondence with Ruth and Henry, he wanted to start his long-neglected projects to help the Negro families of North Elba. It is possible (as suggested by a letter Salmon wrote him a few months later) that Brown also intended to perfect his Subterranean Pass Way scheme to run slaves out of the Southern mountains, a scheme that might well destroy the Slave Power from within.

But early in 1855 he received "an encouraging word about Kansas from Mr. Adair," got the Kansas fever himself, and decided to go there after all. Exhibiting some of his old optimism and go-ahead spirit, Brown wrote a friend in Connecticut: "Since I last saw you I have undertaken to direct the operations of a Surveying; & exploring party to be employed in Kansas for a considerable length of time; perhaps for some Two or Three years." He would also investigate opportunities for business and land speculation. If conditions were favorable, he could bring his family to the territory, doing his part to win Kansas for God and the Right.[6]

Brown notified Jason and John Jr. about his change of plans, explaining that he would follow them to the territory in the summer or fall. Then he headed for Illinois to find Oliver. Meanwhile Jason and Ellen, with their son Austin, and John Jr., Wealthy, and their son John Brown III (a mentally retarded boy nicknamed "Tonny"), all set out for Kansas by boat; Jason took along his prize grapevines and choice fruit trees to transplant in Kansas soil. The two families took a riverboat down the Ohio and up the Mississippi to St. Louis, where they bought some tents, a plow, and smaller farm implements. In April they headed up the Missouri on a steamer crowded with passengers, "mostly men from the South bound for Kansas." One of them—a Virginian who seemed friendly enough— warned John Jr. that he and his brother were heading for trouble, because proslavery Missourians had organized "Annoyance Associations" to harass free-state settlers and scare them away from the territory. The news infuriated John Jr., who had learned to talk tough from his father, and he vowed that no Missourians were going to scare *him* out of the territory. If any tried, he would draw his sword, "that final arbiter of all the great questions that have stirred mankind," and strike a blow for freedom.

The river journey turned out to be a nightmare. Cholera broke out on the boat, and four-year-old Austin (Jason's child) caught it and died. When the steamer docked at Waverly for repairs, the Browns went ashore during the night, "our lonely way illumined only by the lightning of a furious thunderstorm," and buried Austin near the river. But more bitter luck was to follow. The steamer was gone when they returned; and heartbroken, furious, and weary to the bone, they had to take a stage to Kansas City, right through the heart of proslavery Missouri. They cheered up a little when they crossed into Kansas, headed southwest over a trail surrounded by oceans of grass, and came at last to the settlement of Osawatomie at the confluence of the Marais des Cygnes River and Pottawatomie Creek. It *was* lovely around Osawatomie, with thick stands of timber (mostly oak, cottonwood, sycamore, and black walnut) fringing the river and its tributaries, which meandered off to the south and west. Between the streams lay prairies covered with succulent grasses and sunflowers; the prairies were broken here and there by hills and steep ravines which added a kind of raw beauty to the countryside. The Browns spent some time in Osawatomie with Samuel Adair, who may have told them how gangs of border Missourians had invaded the territory, made violent threats and recriminations against free-soil emigrants, and illegally voted in territorial elections. Jason, a quiet, gentle man who had never had a fistfight and whose conscience (according to Salmon) was "almost abnormal," left no record of what he thought about the Missourians' deeds. But John Jr. did. "If the question of Slavery or no Slavery in Kansas must be settled at the cartridge box, instead of at the ballot box, I pray the day may speedily come."[7]

After a day or so with Adair, the Browns took the Osawatomie wagon road down into the Pottawatomie Creek region, passing cabins here and there in the windy trees. Near Dutch Henry's Crossing they turned northwest onto the California Road (which connected Fort Scott with the Santa Fe Trail) and followed that for some seven miles until they reached their brothers' claims near North Middle Creek.

It was the middle of May now—the climax of the rainy season in eastern Kansas. As Jason and John Jr. staked out their own claims and erected makeshift tents at Brown's Station, thunderstorms raged overhead, showering the Pottawatomie region with some of the heaviest rains "sense Noahs flood," Salmon reported later; "some times it looked as thou the whole territory was agoing to be drownded."[8] With the storms—the pelting rains, fierce lightning, and ear-splitting thunder—came news of man-made violence threatening from border Missouri, news that caused excitement and consternation all along the Pottawatomie. On May 20 John Jr. started a long letter to his father, in which he described the coming violence and everything else he had seen and heard.

4

On May 24, Brown himself wrote his sons from Rockford, Illinois, asking how he should come to Kansas and what necessities they might want him to bring. He also inquired about the prospects for surveying and speculating in land and about the going prices for beans, apples, cornmeal, bacon, horses, and cattle. It took him another month to settle his affairs in Ohio and to make arrangements for the sale of his Devonshire cattle. On June 18 he wrote Ruth that he and the rest of his family (including a new daughter Ellen, his twentieth child by both wives) were on their way to the Adirondacks.[9]

They arrived about a week later and moved into a frame house which Henry Thompson had built on some of Gerrit Smith's land. Evidently Ruth gave her father two or three letters from John Jr. and Salmon (including the one John Jr. had begun on May 20) which she had saved for him. Salmon's letter, dated May 21, mentioned that on the way out "we saw some of the curses of slavery, and they are many." He said that "the boys have their feelings well worked up, so that I think that they will fight." Why were the boys' feelings worked up? What had happened to them? What had they seen? Salmon was exasperatingly reticent. He merely said that "There is a great lack of arms here at Brownsville.* I feel more like fight now, than I ever did before, and would be glad to go to Alabama. I have no doubt of the success of the plan."

Alabama? Plan? Surely Salmon knew about Brown's secret plot to send a small guerrilla force into the mountains of the Deep South to

* The Browns variously called their claims Brownsville, Brown's Station, and Fairfield. I've used Brown's Station for consistency.

run off slaves and was referring to that plan. If so, had Brown discussed it with him before he had departed for Kansas last November? Did Brown have that scheme in mind when he wrote John Jr. that he felt committed to operate against Satan and his legions "*in another part of the field*"?

Salmon went on to say that he intended to return home in the fall, although the others planned to stay. On the whole, he was impressed with Kansas—it "is the greatest country to make money in, that I ever saw"—and wished the entire family could come out with Brown.[10]

John Jr.'s letter told how Austin had died on the way out, described the country and weather, the farming methods and implements the settlers used, and complained about how short they were on money (a leitmotif in the life of all the Browns). Still, "I know of no country where a poor man endowed with a share of common sense & with health, can get a start so easy. If we can succeed in making this a *free* State, a great work will be accomplished for *mankind.*" Then John Jr. came to "the principal subject of this letter," one that was to alter significantly Brown's own reasons for going to the territory. Proslavery Missourians, John Jr. wrote, were attempting to make Kansas a slave state "by means no matter how foul." He repeated what the Virginian on the boat had told him about the "Annoyance Associations" which border Missourians had organized to terrorize free-state settlements in Kansas. Since then John Jr. had learned that "hundreds of thousands" of proslavery men—"desperate" men "armed to the teeth with Revolvers, Bowie Knives, Rifles, & Cannon"—were massing along the border to "fasten slavery on this glorious land" through outright invasion. Every slaveholding state from Virginia to Texas was sending men and money for this odious cause. The free-state people around Osawatomie and Pottawatomie were afraid to resist, exhibiting "the most abject and cowardly spirit, whenever their dearest rights are mocked and trampled down upon." The Missourians, when they heard about such cowardice, boasted "that they could obtain possession of the polls in any of our election precincts without having to fire a gun." (Although John Jr. did not say so, the Missourians *had* taken possession of the polls in Kansas: on March 30 no fewer than 5,000 of them—"enough to kill every God-damned abolitionist in the Territory," screamed Atchison—had poured across the border to vote in the election for a territorial legislature. By using fists and threatening murder, unseating fair judges and counting illegal ballots, the intruders had elected an over-whelmingly proslavery legislature.)

What could be done to stop the proslavery menace? John Jr. wanted to fight. "The Antislavery portion of the inhabitants should *immediately, thoroughly arm and organize themselves in military companies,*" John Jr. wrote his father, repeating virtually the same language Brown had used in organizing the Gileadites in Spring-field and exhorting the blacks to kill anybody who tried to enforce the fugitive slave law. John Jr. went on to say that he and his brothers (except perhaps for Jason) were ready to fight this very moment, but that they were desperately short of guns. Would Brown get some Colt revolvers, Minié rifles, and Bowie knives, and bring them along when he came to Kansas? Maybe he could borrow the money to buy such weapons from Gerrit Smith, "until we can raise enough to refund it from the *Free* soil of Kansas."

In Brown's mind the picture of a massive proslavery army invad-ing Kansas, killing his sons and laying waste to free-state settlements, was far more profoundly evil than the image of slavecatchers swarm-ing into Northern cities in search of Negro runaways, and he "fully resolved to proceed at once to Kansas; & join his Children." With his sons' letters in his pocket he hurried out of the Adirondacks to find Gerrit Smith.[11]

5

Smith was at Syracuse, where a convention of "Radical Political Abolitionists" had been under way since June 26. Frederick Douglass was also present; so were Samuel J. May, Lewis Tappan, and other abolitionists who had long since broken with Garrison because he repudiated the notion that slavery could or should be eradicated by political action (Garrison thought politics was corrupt to the core) and because he insisted that females should occupy powerful posi-tions in the antislavery crusade. The convention had already adopted a "Declaration" calling for the suppression of slavery by the federal government, had resolved to prevent the return of runaway slaves, and pledged over $4,600 for abolitionist activities, when Brown marched into the convention hall on June 28. Standing before the assembled delegates, Brown declared that free-soil forces in Kansas desperately needed men and money—especially money—with which to buy guns and fight the armies of evil now massed along the border. Would the delegates contribute money and weapons so that he could go to Kansas and help his sons fight the battles of freedom? There was a great deal of unrest in the hall; most delegates were more interested in defeating slavery through the political processes than in fighting it in faraway Kansas, although in less than a year many of them would radically change their minds. Douglass and Smith spoke dutifully in Brown's behalf; and Smith himself read John Jr.'s letters "with such effect," Brown observed, "as to draw tears from numerous eyes in the great collection of people present." But Smith's eloquence did not draw much money from their pockets; in all they contributed about $40 to Brown's cause—and Smith tossed in an additional $20. On the whole, though, Brown was satisfied. "I have met with a most welcome reception," he wrote Mary, "and, except by a few sincere, honest, peace-friends a most hearty approval of my intention of arming my sons and other friends in Kansas."[12]

In July he went to Springfield, where he had crusaded for quite another purpose nine years earlier, and purchased a box of firearms and flasks which he shipped to Cleveland. Then he returned to North Elba, where more letters from his sons awaited him. In reply to Brown's letter of May 24, John Jr. wrote detailed instructions on how to get to Kansas and to find their claims, including a diagram of where Brown's Station was located. Brown should come out in "a covered lumber buggy," as travel on the Missouri River was "a horrid business in a low stage of water, which is a considerable portion of the year." Again John Jr. described the weather in Kansas, noting that the rainy season, accompanied by high winds and "tremendous thunder and lightning" storms, lasted six weeks from April into May. In answer to Brown's questions about business prospects, John Jr. regrettably reported that there was "no great demand" for horses or cattle in Kansas and that, "owing to the rapid settlement of the country by squatters, it does not open a good field for speculation."

There was a note from Jason, who explained that he had not felt like writing until now because Austin's death had left him depressed.

Ellen was so lonely and sad that he might have to bring her east in the fall, unless she learned to "enjoy herself better." All in all, he liked Kansas. "It is very rich and beautiful country." But he needed a stove. Would Brown stop in Akron and pick one up for him?

There was also a note from Salmon, who said that Brown should bring pork, meal, and beans, to last until the boys could harvest their crops. He said he needed summer pants and a hat, and added: "There are slaves owned within three miles of us."[13]

Another letter from John Jr. (dated June 29) reported that a convention had met at Lawrence to talk about organizing and arming free-state men into military companies, as John Jr. had advocated all along. They had a few Sharps rifles which "friendly associations" in the East had sent out. Would his father examine some of these weapons? Maybe he could induce "one or more capitalists to furnish means to purchase a number of these, with the revolvers I write you of." "The storm every day thickens," he declared, "its near approach is hourly more clearly seen by all." Now was the time to help in the cause, for he was convinced "that the great drama will open here, when will be presented the great struggle in arms, of Freedom and Despotism in America. Give us the arms, and we are ready for the contest."

In a postscript John Jr. pointed out that "the jobs of surveying the base and meridian lines have all been under contract for some time, and that the work is moving very slowly. Whether you will, in consequence of this, be able to get immediate business or not, I cannot say." In spite of that, he thought that there was still "a great amount of surveying to be done" and that it would "be a good business here many years.[14]

Perhaps Brown was glad to know that he could eventually work as a surveyor. But, other than that, business concerns obviously were the last thing on his highly excitable mind. John Jr.'s moving words—"the storm every day thickens," "now is the time," "the great drama will open here" between "Freedom and Despotism"—thrilled him to his bones, and he was anxious indeed to get out to Kansas before the struggle between Freedom and Despotism began.[15]

His family helped him get ready with stoical resolve. Twenty-year-old Watson would stay behind to manage the farm and look after Mary and the girls. Oliver, who was working in Illinois, would meet the old man in Chicago and accompany him to Kansas. Brown also persuaded Henry Thompson—Ruth's husband—to go along.

Brown left North Elba early in August and traveled to Ohio, where he solicited more money and weapons—including several artillery broadswords—for his *"particular business"* in the territory. Henry joined him later at Hudson. Then they picked up one box of "freight" at Cleveland, another at Chicago, found Oliver, loaded Brown's surveying instruments and all the freight ("Guns Revolvers, Swords, Powder, Caps") into a one-horse wagon and set out for Kansas before the storm broke.[16]

PART TWO

PILGRIMAGE

VIII

THE WICKED SHALL CEASE
FROM TROUBLING

∽∾∽

THE COUNTRYSIDE DID NOT EXCITE HIM as it had his sons. It was Sunday morning, October 7, 1855, and the old man was traveling northwest on the California Road, over a sloping prairie that afforded a view of the Kansas landscape for ten or fifteen miles in nearly every direction. In back of him lay the timber-fringed Pottawatomie, where a number of pioneers (mostly "of the poorer class," he had learned) had settled and built cabins. Ahead he could see steep ravines like scars on the prairie and a line of trees along North Middle Creek where his sons had their claims (he was riding alone now; Henry and Oliver had gone ahead during the night). The area reminded him of the upland portion of Illinois, although he had seen no wet or marshy lands as yet and the region was "better timbered" than he had expected. He did not think Kansas was "the only desirable spot on Earth"—it was windy and bitterly cold on this Sabbath morning—but in the end Kansas would be "a good country," if enough antislavery men came to win it for freedom.

When he arrived at Brown's Station a short while later the old man was shocked at what he found. His "children" were living in makeshift tents, "shivering over their little fires all exposed to the dreadfully cutting Winds." All of them except Wealthy and Tonny were sick with the ague, brought on by exposure and inadequate food. Salmon had almost died of bilious colic. They were all so weak and demoralized that they had not gathered in any of their crops. All they had to eat was ground corn and their cattle and horses roamed loose on the prairie.

John Jr. explained that conditions were similar all over "the more Eastern country." Continuous storms and epidemics of the ague had plagued the settlements there: many pioneers had died; others, sick and disillusioned with frontier life, had left the territory (none of the promotional literature about Kansas had mentioned the howling winds and rainstorms, the epidemics, the shortages of food and medicine). The weather had been so severe these past few days that even the Missouri "border ruffians" and their Kansas allies had been quiet.

Brown set about at once tending his feverish family, while Oliver and Henry unloaded the wagon, stacking blankets, a tent, surveying instruments, and all the "freight"—revolvers, rifles, dirk knives, and those menacing broadswords—inside one of the tents. There was an unexpected item for Jason and Ellen in Brown's cargo—the body of Austin, which Brown had taken up at Waverly on the way out, thinking it would lift their spirits to have Austin buried on their homestead in the free soil of Kansas. Brown's thoughtfulness did cheer them some: Ellen agreed to stay in Kansas; and Jason started talking about fruit trees and his dream of owning a large orchard here one day.[1]

As the Browns huddled around their fires that windy Sabbath, the old man questioned John Jr. about what the settlers in the area were like and what had happened in territorial politics since John Jr. had written last. As a matter of fact, an election for a free-state congressman, as well as for delegates to a constitutional convention to convene at Topeka, was scheduled for next Tuesday—October 9. Free-state citizens in Pottawatomie anticipated trouble at the polls again, perhaps another invasion of Missourians or interference on the part of local proslavery men (even though they were a distinct minority in the Pottawatomie vicinity). Salmon had written that a slaveowner lived not three miles from Brown's Station. There were proslavery men along the Pottawatomie too—men like Allen Wilkinson and William and Dutch Henry Sherman, the latter a giant of a man who stood 6 feet 4 inches without his boots. None of these men actually held slaves themselves, but they hated Negroes, championed the right of white people to own them, defended the proslavery territorial government, wanted Kansas to become a Southern-dominated state, and gave aid and shelter to Missouri intruders who rode through the countryside.

The Sherman brothers, who were natives of Oldenburg, Germany, were bachelors who had squatted on the creek, at the crossing of the California Road, back in 1844 when Kansas was still unorganized territory. They had built a combination store and tavern at the ford (now called Dutch Henry's Crossing), and since then had made a fair living from caravans that rumbled up the road from Fort Scott, on their way to the Oregon Trail along the Kaw River. There was talk that the Shermans occasionally "lifted" cows and horses from emigrant trains that encamped at the crossing. There were also rumors that they were "drunkards" and "profligates" who hated the Indians but "kept" their girls "for criminal purposes." Yet there is no proof that such talk was anything more than malicious free-state gossip.[2]

Allen Wilkinson, his wife Louisa Jane, and their two children had emigrated from Tennessee and built a cabin (which also served as post office) on Mosquito Creek, about a mile north of Dutch Henry's Crossing. Wilkinson had been elected to the proslavery legislature, thanks to more than 150 illegal votes cast by Missouri intruders the previous March, and had become one of the leading champions of that government in the Pottawatomie area. According to free-state gossip, Wilkinson was a violent, abusive man who took sadistic pleasure in beating his wife, a "nice," "fine" Southern woman. However, Mrs. Wilkinson disclaimed this later, insisting that her husband was a law-abiding proslavery man who never beat anybody.[3]

The free-state men of Pottawatomie were not exactly angels either. Some of them—such as Theodore Weiner, who had just come out from St. Louis and opened a store on the California Road, some three miles northwest of the Pottawatomie—were as crude and "low class" as the proslavery settlers were said to be. Salmon recalled that Weiner was "a big, savage, bloodthirsty Austrian" who "could not be kept out of any accessible fight."

Nor were all Northern pioneers in the Pottawatomie-Osawatomie area open-minded humanitarians. Like a majority of free-soil settlers elsewhere in the territory, most of them disliked and resented being called abolitionists and wanted to keep free Negroes out of Kansas as well as the oppressive slavery-plantation system. They wanted to make the territory free all right, but free and white. John Everett of Osawatomie was so disgusted with the anti-Negro prejudice of his free-state neighbors that he later asked his father to send out an extra copy of Harriet Beecher Stowe's *Key to Uncle Tom*. "We could do good by lending it," Everett explained. "They need light on that subject."[4]

Yet the free-state men stood virtually united against the outrageous acts of the proslavery legislature. Meeting at Shawnee Mission in July, the legislature had not only appointed a full slate of proslavery military and civil authorities (the postmaster of one Missouri town, for example, was appointed sheriff of Douglas County, where Lawrence was located), but had also adopted the revised statutes of Missouri as general law. According to these measures, only proslavery men could hold office and only those who recognized the right of slavery could sit on juries. Anybody who asserted that slavery did not exist in Kansas, or denied the right to own slaves, or circulated abolitionist literature, was subject to imprisonment at hard labor for not less than five years. Anybody who assisted runaways was subject to ten years in prison. Anybody who incited a slave insurrection would be hanged.

Governor Andrew H. Reeder, a rotund Pennsylvania Democrat trying to maintain some semblance of justice, argued that the legislature was illegally in session (he had specified that it sit at Pawnee, not Shawnee Mission) and vetoed all its laws. Already proslavery toughs had threatened to kill him for challenging the legislature. The proslavery legislators themselves defiantly passed the laws over his veto, petitioned President Pierce (a Southern sympathizer) to get rid of this troublemaker, and gave a resounding cheer when the chief justice of the territory announced that the legislature *was* sitting legally, no matter what the harried governor said. Finally, President Pierce dismissed Reeder from office, ostensibly because of his land speculations among the Indians, and sent out Wilson Shannon as the new territorial executive. A Cincinnati lawyer and former Democratic governor of Ohio, Shannon was a blustering, tactless man who had no idea how combustible the situation in Kansas had become. Although a majority of citizens there were emphatically free-state, the "dough-faced" governor promptly recognized the Shawnee Mission legislature as legal, befriended the leaders of the proslavery party, and imbibed all their suspicions of the free-state majority.

A proslavery legislature and now a proslavery governor—free-state settlers had taken all they could stand. Already at Pottawatomie, Osawatomie, Lawrence, Topeka, and other communities they had held meetings to protest the misdeeds of the Missourians, whose interference in territorial elections had made a mockery of the electoral process and the whole philosophy of popular sovereignty.[5] Angry free-state leaders—including ex-Governor Reeder—called for a "mass meeting" to assemble at Lawrence on August 14 and challenge the proslavery legislature and its hated "black laws." In reality two conventions met simultaneously in Lawrence in mid-August. Some free-state leaders—among them, Martin F. Conway and Dr. Charles Robinson, the Lawrence agent of the New England Emigrant Aid Society—were conspicuous in both conventions. The first and larger gathering adopted resolutions roundly denouncing the "bogus" legislature and calling for another convention to meet at Big Springs and organize a free-state party. The second of the Lawrence meetings, which John Brown Jr. attended, was a more "radical" one. It called for antislavery men to gather at Topeka on October 19, draft their own constitution, and demand that Kansas be admitted to the Union as a free state. John Jr. himself was a member of the "Committee on Business" which drew up this call. In that position he met several prominent figures in the free-state movement, including Robinson, George Washington Brown, the zealous editor of the Lawrence *Herald of Freedom* (which was subsidized by the New England Emigrant Aid Society), and James Henry Lane, a hatchet-faced political opportunist from Indiana and a man of "infectuous enthusiasm."

On September 5 and 6 free-state delegates met again at Big Springs and there put together a powerful party organization. They adopted a platform which not only repudiated the proslavery legislature and vowed to make Kansas a free state but also—in accordance with the wishes of a majority of their constituents—advocated measures to bar free Negroes from the territory. The convention urged its followers not to participate in the October 1 Congressional election called by the proslavery legislature and set an election on October 9 for a free-state representative, as well as for delegates to attend a constitutional convention at Topeka. The Big Springs convention also set up a "Territorial Executive Committee," of which John Jr. was a member, to count the returns.[6]

John Jr. returned to Brown's Station full of fiery enthusiasm for the free-state cause. On September 14 he came face to face with a proslavery man in Pottawatomie, threw caution to the winds, and declared that "no man had a right to hold a slave in Kansas." Witness that he had broken the law, John Jr. cried, and that he would continue breaking the law whenever he could. "If any officer should attempt to arrest me for a violation of the law, and should put his villainous hands on me," he wrote his stepmother the next day, "I would surely kill him, so help me God." "We shall probably get shot for disobeying their beautiful laws," Wealthy added, "but you might as well die here in a good cause as freeze to death there."[7] A few days later, however, all the storms and illnesses began, taking much of the fight out of the zealous Browns.

Nevertheless, Brown himself was extremely excited by what John Jr. told him that Sunday of October 7. As long as he was alive, none of his sons was going to be shot for breaking the "bogus" laws, nor was any trouble going to take place in the forthcoming free-state elections. On Tuesday Brown accompanied those sons who could walk down to the Pottawatomie precinct, where votes for a free-state congressman and for delegates to the Topeka convention were being cast. The Browns went "powerfully armed," too, but "no enemy appeared." Perhaps the bitter cold kept the Missourians away and the local proslavery partisans around the fires in their cabins. Evidently Brown did not vote. He did not regard himself as a Kansas citizen, for he had not come to settle, and never voted in any election. He stood aside with a basketful of knives and revolvers while those sons who had claims cast their ballots. Then they all went home.

On October 13 Brown wrote Mary for the first time since he had arrived in Kansas. He described the trip out and the trying circumstances in which he had found the children. He sympathized with Mary's hardships in the Adirondacks, but pointed out that Kansas was no paradise either. He declared that, since no invasion had occurred during the Tuesday elections, Missouri seemed about to give up on Kansas. The prospects that the territory would be a free one were "brightening every day." In closing, Brown implored her and the children at North Elba to remain cheerful and trust in God, for He would never forsake those who remained obedient to Him.

"I humbly trust we may be kept & spared; to meet again on Earth; *but if not* let us all endeavor earnestly to secure admission to that Eternal Home where will be no more bitter seperations; 'where the wicked shall cease from troubling; & the weary be at rest.' "[8]

2

Word came to Pottawatomie that portly Andrew Reeder had been elected to Congress as the free-state representative and that a convention had met at Topeka, as scheduled, to write a free-state constitution. Still the Browns had little time to cheer, for October 25 came in with blowing sleet and freezing temperatures and another round of sickness began. Frederick collapsed with a ravaging fever; some of the others also suffered relapses. For a time Brown was the only well man at Brown's Station, and having to care for his family and tend to the homesteads there "prevented my being as active among the emigrants as I intended." Working outside despite the "cutting cold winds, and storms," the old man gathered in the crops, stacked the hay, husked the corn, rounded up the cattle and horses, and cut and stacked logs for a shanty for Jason and Ellen. By November 2 he had completed a crude but sturdy frontier lodging, with chinked and mudded walls, a tent for a roof, and a chimney "far enough along" to keep a fire in it. Ellen was immensely pleased. At last, she wrote Mary, "I can cook a meal without smoking my eyes almost out of my head."

With Salmon helping, Brown next constructed a log cabin for John Jr. in "a low brushy hollow" not far from the creek. When that was finished he wrote Mary that, notwithstanding the "cold stormy weather," he had put Brown's Station in order and that "a tolerable degree of cheerfulness seems to prevail." Obviously "God had not forsaken us; and we get 'day by day our daily bread.' "[9]

Meanwhile the political situation in Kansas had become increasingly combustible. The Topeka convention had finished drafting a free-state constitution and had submitted the document for popular ratification in an election scheduled for December 15. In retaliation against the Topeka movement, proslavery forces had convened at Leavenworth on November 14 and organized a "Law and Order"

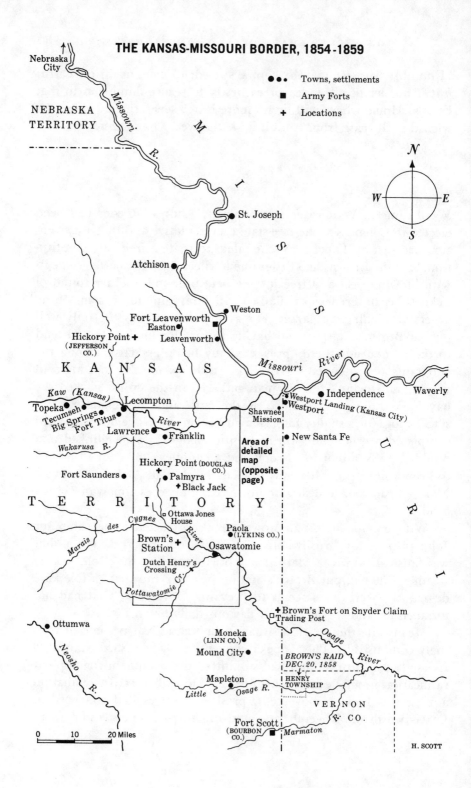

THE KANSAS-MISSOURI BORDER, 1854-1859

• • •   Towns, settlements
■   Army Forts
+   Locations

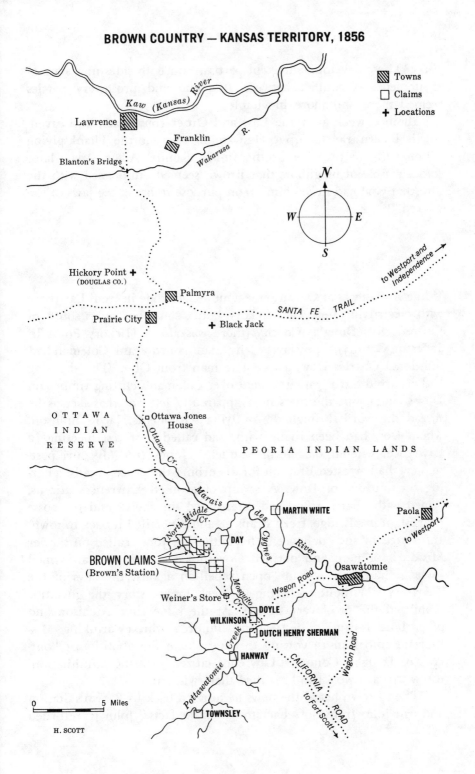

BROWN COUNTRY — KANSAS TERRITORY, 1856

Towns
Claims
Locations

Kaw (Kansas) River

Lawrence

Franklin

Wakarusa R.

Blanton's Bridge

N

W — E

S

Hickory Point
(DOUGLAS CO.)

to Westport and
Independence →

Palmyra

SANTA FE TRAIL

Prairie City

Black Jack

OTTAWA
INDIAN
RESERVE

Ottawa Jones
House

Ottawa Cr.

PEORIA INDIAN LANDS

Marais

North Middle Cr.

des Cygnes

MARTIN WHITE

Paola

to Westport

DAY

River

BROWN CLAIMS
(Brown's Station)

Osawatomie

Weiner's Store

Wagon Road

Mosquito Cr.

DOYLE

WILKINSON

DUTCH HENRY SHERMAN

Pottawatomie Creek

HANWAY

CALIFORNIA ROAD

Wagon Road

to Fort Scott →

0   5 Miles

TOWNSLEY

H. SCOTT

party. These developments kept partisans on both sides in a state of excitement, as conflict between free-state and proslavery parties seemed more and more inevitable.

About a week after the Law and Order convention at Leavenworth, Brown traveled up to Osawatomie to spend the Thanksgiving season with his preacher brother-in-law, Samuel Adair. Adair later told a couple of neighbors that Brown seemed "impressed with the idea that God had raised him up on purpose to break the jaws of the wicked."[10]

3

While Brown was at Osawatomie a messenger rode in from Lawrence with electrifying news: at Hickory Point, some ten miles south of Lawrence, in Douglas County (there was also a Hickory Point in Jefferson County), a proslavery Virginian named Frank Coleman had murdered Charles Dow, a free-state man from Ohio. The shooting had occurred during an argument over Coleman's cutting timber on Dow's claim, but the messenger apparently left out that fact as he spread the word through the outlying settlements. Jacob Branson, whom Dow had been living with, had called a protest meeting in Lawrence; whereupon Sheriff Samuel J. Jones (the Missouri postmaster) had arrested Branson for disturbing the peace, totally ignoring the murder of Dow. A group of aroused Lawrence citizens, armed with Sharps rifles, had intercepted the sheriff and his posse near Blanton's Bridge, freed Branson, and hightailed it back to town. Infuriated by such defiance of his authority, Jones called on border Missouri for help and notified Governor Shannon that an armed force in Lawrence was in "open rebellion against the laws of the Territory." Without bothering to check Jones's story, the governor mobilized the proslavery militia. At the same time Atchison and other border captains led several hundred whiskey-drinking Missourians into Kansas, vowing to exterminate the abolitionist "outlaws of Douglas County." Lawrence citizens, fearing annihilation, threw up earthworks and manned them with rifles.

When Brown heard the news he hurried back to Brown's Station and sent John Jr. by horseback to "learn the facts." John Jr. returned at a gallop. He had met a runner up the road who said over 2,000 Missourians and Kansas militia were massed on the Wakarusa River south of Lawrence and planned to burn the town.[11]

The Browns at once set about packing provisions, running bullets, loading their guns and stacking them and the knives and swords in the wagon. Henry, Jason, and Oliver, who were sick and "wholly unfit fur duty," remained behind with the women. The others set out for Lawrence at five o'clock on Thursday evening (December 6)— Brown driving the wagon, John Jr., Owen, Salmon, and Frederick marching alongside. Except for a brief rest, "The Five" traveled all night to reach the outskirts of Lawrence on the forenoon of the next day. At a bridge south of town they encountered a band of armed Missourians. Moving onto the bridge with knives and revolvers showing in their belts and their rifles leveled, The Five headed relentlessly, defiantly, at the enemy. The Missourians parted, allowing the Browns to pass "without any interruption," said the old man afterwards, "save that of looking very earnestly at us." Brown thought they were cowards.

As the Browns entered Lawrence, companies of grim-faced citizens, carrying their celebrated Sharps rifles, were drilling behind the earthworks; and the streets were teeming with men and wagons. Brown, immeasurably thrilled by all the commotion, halted his wagon in front of the Free-State Hotel, where a Committee of Public Safety, headed by Robinson and Lane, was directing the defense of the town. G. W. Brown, who saw the Browns arrive, was impressed with their armor. "To each of their persons was strapped a short heavy broad sword," the editor observed. "Each was supplied with a goodly number of fire arms, and navy revolvers, and poles were standing endwise around the wagon box with fixed bayonets pointing upwards." They looked "really formidable" and "were received with great eclat."

Editor Brown hurried over to shake hands with John Jr., who then introduced his father and brothers. The editor took the Browns inside the hotel, a large, unfinished stone "fortress," and led them through the crowded dining hall toward the council room on the third floor. The dining hall was buzzing with talk, for yesterday evening the body of a free-state settler named Thomas Barber, murdered by proslavery forces near Lawrence, had been carried into

the hotel and placed in a room there. This morning Barber's wife
and friends had come to see the body; it had been a "Heart-rending"
scene, Brown was told, one "calculated to exasperate the men exceedingly; & one of the sure results of Civil War."

In the council room Editor Brown introduced the old man and his
sons to Robinson and Lane, who pointed out that they were presently
negotiating with Governor Shannon to sign a peace treaty, but that
they welcomed reinforcements nevertheless. In fact, as a reward for
the zeal "the aged gentleman from Essex County" had exhibited "in
the cause of freedom, both before and after his arrival in the Territory," Robinson commissioned the old man a captain in the "First
Brigade of Kansas Volunteers" and gave him command of a small
company called the Liberty Guards. It consisted of Brown's own sons
and fifteen other men, some of whom (William Partridge and H. H.
Williams, for example) were also from Pottawatomie.[12]

According to G. W. Brown, the captain led his sons out to the
earthworks and began causing trouble on the spot. He refused to
take orders from superior officers, told the defenders to use pitch-
forks should the Missourians launch an assault, then called for volunteers to follow him down to the Wakarusa and "make an attack upon
the Pro-slavery forces encamped there." Brown's sons later claimed
that he worked out a plan whereby a column of hand-picked men
was to steal up on the enemy during the night and slaughter them
in their sleep.[13]

However that may be, Brown was unquestionably itching for a
fight—he had not brought those guns and swords along for appearances. But if he did advocate attacking the Missourians (and probably he did), the committee quickly restrained him. So far the
Lawrence defenders had broken no laws and committed no atrocities,
in sharp contrast to the Missourians, who had not only killed
Thomas Barber but had become so drunk and disorderly that even
their officers feared the worst. Such conduct had shocked Governor
Shannon, who called the Missourians an uncontrollable "pack of
hyenas" and who notified Lawrence that he was ready to parley.
Robinson and Lane were not going to let Brown or anybody else
commit a rash act when they were within reach of a tremendous
propaganda victory.

Around noon on Saturday December 8, the governor came to
town and met with Robinson and Lane behind closed doors in the

hotel. The three men drew up a peace treaty whereby the governor denied that he had called on the Missourians for help and agreed to order them home and Robinson and Lane swore that they had no intention of resisting the territorial laws. Then they held an "open-air meeting" outside the hotel, announcing to an anxious crowd (including Brown and his sons) that a peace treaty had been signed. When Robinson remarked that he had nothing more to say, that "they had taken an honorable position," some men expressed misgivings that the truce might not be to their advantage; whereupon Brown himself demanded to know the terms. According to William A. Phillips, an eyewitness, Brown tried to address the crowd, "but a desire was manifested to prevent his speaking." Brown cried out: had they conceded anything to the "bogus" legislature in the treaty? But he was interrupted by angry shouts. Fearing a revolt was under way, the "influential men" assured the crowd that no concessions had been made, that nothing at all had been yielded to the proslavery legislature. "With these assurances," Phillips said, "the people were satisfied and withdrew."

Brown retired, too, persuading himself that as cunning as Robinson and Lane were, they had probably taken advantage of the governor's "cowardice, & Folly" to secure "a written arrangement with him much to their own liking."[14] That Saturday evening, while Shannon and the two free-state leaders were out negotiating with the Missourians near the Wakarusa, Brown supposedly had a long talk with a man named James F. Legate, who had lived in the South for a number of years. According to Legate, Brown asked a number of pointed questions about the slaves. Were they as passive as some people said? Did they have attachments with their masters? Or were they willing to fight for their liberty should the opportunity arise? (Questions like these had probably crossed Brown's mind more than once since he had composed "Sambos Mistakes," studied abolitionist publications, and conceived his Subterranean Pass Way scheme.) Legate did not relate how he answered such questions. But he did claim that he and Brown got into an argument about the nature of prayer. The argument ended, Legate said, when Brown prayed for power to repel the Missourians—those "enemies of God"—and for freedom to triumph all over the earth.[15]

In the meantime Shannon, Robinson, and Lane were still negotiating with Atchison and twelve other Missouri captains at Franklin, about two miles southeast of Lawrence. As night came on and a storm moved in from the north, with sleet and high winds, the Missouri captains, alarmed by the drunken rowdiness of their own men, finally agreed to take them home, and Robinson and Lane returned to Lawrence in triumph.[16]

Free-state men, of course, were proud of their victory, all the more so because the governor now seemed on their side. Brown was proud, too, and chided the Missourians for running off like cowards, leaving "the Free Statemen *organized, & armed; & in full possession* of the Territory." He was grimly humored to learn that, at "a peace gathering" on Sunday evening, Robinson got the governor so drunk that he cheerfully signed away a document which authorized Robinson and Lane to use force the next time the Missourians invaded. When Brown learned the terms of the peace treaty a few days later, he could not say how much truthfulness and sincerity had attended the negotiations. But he did believe that the "Wakarusa War" had been characterized by "a good deal of trickery on the one side and of cowardice, folly, & drunkenness on the other"—not an unfair summation of what had happened.

On December 12 the Liberty Guards formally disbanded and the Browns set out for home with their heavily loaded wagon. Back at Brown's Station the old man was still so excited about the Wakarusa War—his first encounter with the armies of the Slave Power—that he wrote detailed descriptions of all the dramatic events to his wife, his brother-in-law Orson Day, Frederick Douglass, and the editor of the Akron *Summit Beacon*. "I did not see the least sign of cowardice or want of self-possession exhibited by any volunteer of the Eleven companies who constituted the Free State Force," he said in his letter to Mary, "& I never expect again to see an equal number of such well behaved, cool, determined men." Truly, in this heroic struggle between Good and Evil, they had all sustained "the high character of the Revolutionary Fathers."[17]

4

On December 15 Kansas voters not only ratified the Topeka Constitution but also approved a special "Negro Exclusion clause." In the Pottawatomie precinct the constitution passed by 39 to 3; the Negro exclusion clause by 25 to 18. How Brown reacted to the anti-Negro prejudice that prevailed among his free-state neighbors is not recorded. James Redpath, the hyperbolic correspondent for the New York *Tribune* and several other papers and later an enthusiastic admirer of Brown, claimed that such bigotry infuriated the old man. In view of Brown's hostility toward racial discrimination in Ohio, he probably was angry—until he put things in perspective. When compared to the wickedness of the "hellish" proslavery legislature and its Missouri allies, racial prejudice among free-soil pioneers seemed a minor evil indeed. He did not even complain about it in his letters to his wife.[18]

On the contrary, he continued to praise the free-state defenders of Lawrence—"the most intelligent, sober and orderly set of men I have ever seen collected, in equal number, except at religious worship"—and declared that all of them had become so well acquainted and so "strongly knit together" from their mutual experiences in the Wakarusa War that the proslavery forces would never defeat them. And now, with the free-state constitution ratified and elections scheduled in January for a free-state governor and legislature, Brown was hopeful indeed. "What now remains for the Free State men of Kansas," he rejoiced, "is to hold the ground they now possess, *and Kansas is free.*"

Still, he was "exceedingly anxious to learn how matters go off in the States and in Congress this winter," and asked the editor of the Akron *Summit Beacon* to send him an issue of the paper so that he might keep apprised of any new developments in the Slave Power conspiracy.[19]

IX

SIGNS AND PORTENTS

∾⁀ℳℴ

A VERITABLE "SIBERIAN COLD" settled over Kansas that winter, sending temperatures down to 29° below zero. Snow blanketed the prairies and ice formed eighteen inches deep in the ravines and creeks. Trees, frozen with icicles, danced like skeletons in the wind, which blew snow into huge drifts against the Brown shelters on North Middle Creek and into the ravines and across the roads and trails until they were obscured from view. For a time in January, all mail communication was cut off by snowdrifts.

The Browns survived the winter "middling well," although Oliver and Owen were laid up with frozen toes and Frederick suffered a temporary relapse of his old "trouble"—excruciating headaches that left him wild with pain. Brown's father (who was over eighty now) sent $50 to help Brown and the children through the winter, together with letters sympathizing with their Kansas cause and urging them to pray for the salvation of his soul, as he felt he was dying. (On May 8, in fact, he was dead.) [1]

In his letters home Brown mentioned that his father had sent him money and that he made frequent supply trips to Westport, Missouri, to buy pork, flour, and corn. On the frozen streets of Westport Brown defiantly announced that he was a free-state man from Kansas, but nobody paid much attention (likely people thought him a crank). "In this part of the State there seems to be but little feeling on the Slave question," Brown wrote Mary from Westport; "all is very quiet & very little news to be had of any kind." The $50 was soon gone, however, and he had to sell his horse and wagon to make ends meet. Even then the Browns had to subsist largely on "cornmeal Johnnie-cakes" and coffee made from parched corn. They did without meat for months, Salmon recalled, until he captured some quail in a cornfield.[2]

Brown was extremely homesick for North Elba that winter, almost enough to "unMan" him. He had thought about taking a claim near Brown's Station, only to change his mind a second time about settling in Kansas. He was too old and still too attached to the Adirondack Mountains to uproot himself and his wife again. No, he would keep his farm there, those mountains would remain his home. His sons, for their part, could go where they liked—and take his blessings.

Despite the subzero temperatures and blowing snow, the Browns played a conspicuous part in local settlers' meetings held that winter. On January 5, 1856, the old man himself acted as chairman of a convention at Osawatomie, called to nominate candidates for state offices. John Jr. was nominated for the free-state legislature, thus prompting Henry Thompson to remark that "the meeting went off without any excitement and to our satisfaction." Wealthy observed that Brown seemed to enjoy politics and wrote Mary that "he is now situated so as to do a great deal of good; he certainly seems to be a man here who exhibits a great amount of influence and is considered one of the most leading and influential minds about here." She added that "Our men have so much *war* and *elections* to attend to that it seems as though we were a great while getting into a house."[3]

On election day—January 15—the Browns again marched down to the Pottawatomie with a basketful of revolvers and dirk knives, just in case "the legal voters" should need them. But no enemy appeared this time either; and when the returns were announced, Charles Robinson had won the governorship and John Jr. had been elected as a delegate to the Topeka legislature. His victory was quite a triumph for the genuine abolitionists of Pottawatomie—and a mark of how popular tough-talking John Jr. had become among his free-state neighbors.[4]

But the Browns had little time to enjoy their victory. An ominous sequence of events soon convinced them that they had been wrong about the effects of the Wakarusa War and the Topeka movement, that a monstrous conspiracy was still underfoot to force slavery on

Kansas by subterfuge and violence—a conspiracy that in their view involved not only the proslavery territorial legislature and its Missouri and Southern allies, but the Pierce Administration and the United States Army as well.

First, alarming news came to the Pottawatomie that border Missouri was *not* going to give up on Kansas, that proslavery forces planned to incite a "general disturbance" there after the snows melted. No sooner had this intelligence reached Pottawatomie than reports arrived of severe troubles at Leavenworth. Bitter fighting had broken out there during the recent free-state election; two free-soilers had been wounded and one proslavery man had been killed and two others injured. Outraged, the *Kansas Pioneer* of Kickapoo screamed for proslavery men to "Sound the bugle of war over the length and breadth of the land and leave not an Abolitionist in the Territory to relate their treacherous and contaminating deeds. Strike your piercing rifle balls and your glittering steel to their black and poisonous hearts." Proslavery forces captured one "black and poisonous heart" near Leavenworth that very day: the leader of the local free-state men himself, Captain R. P. Brown (no relation to John Brown). They hacked on Brown with knives and a hatchet, tossing him mortally wounded at his cabin door. "Here's Brown," they told his wife, who became hysterical when she saw his mangled body.

"*War! War!*" raged the proslavery press in upholding the murder. "These higher-law men will not be permitted longer to carry on their illegal and high-handed proceedings." "*War! War!*"[5]

"We have just learned of some *new*; & shocking outrages at Leavenworth," Brown wrote his wife on February 1, "& that the Free State people there have fled to Lawrence: which place is again threatened with an attack. *Should* that take place we may soon again be called upon to 'buckle on our Armor'; which by the help of God we will do."[6]

In mid-February the sun broke through the overcast skies, soon melting the snow and thawing the scattered communities into action. In a few days passions were again running high, as the mail routes reopened and news of what had transpired in the East reached free-state settlements. On January 24 President Pierce had delivered a special address to Congress in which he blamed all of Kansas' troubles on the various emigrant aid societies in the East, upheld the bogus

The farmhouse in Torrington, Conn., in which John Brown was born in 1800. *Library of Congress*

Owen Brown, father of John Brown.

John Brown's father, "Squire Owen," in later years. *Library of Congress*

The earliest known photograph of Brown, probably taken at
Springfield in 1846. *Boyd B. Stutler*

Mary Ann Brown with Annie (left) and Sarah (right) about 1851. *Boyd B. Stutler*

John Brown, Jr., from a ferro-
type made in the 1840's while he
was attending the Grand River
Institute in Austinburg, Ohio.
Boyd B. Stutler

Jason Brown, the second son—a kind
and gentle man whose "conscience
was almost abnormal"—from a photograph taken later in California
where he spent the remainder of his
life. *Library of Congress*

Owen Brown, third of Brown's twenty children, who had red hair and a crippled arm. He never married. *Kansas State Historical Society, Topeka*

Watson Brown, who at the age of twenty-four left his wife Belle and their baby son to help Brown "free the slaves." *Kansas State Historical Society, Topeka*

Salmon Brown, who fought with Brown in Kansas but refused to participate in the Virginia scheme. Later he moved to California and Oregon; he committed suicide in 1919. *Boyd B. Stutler*

Oliver Brown, the youngest of Brown's sons who survived childhood, and his wife, Martha, whose parents opposed the marriage because of the Browns' abolitionist militancy. *Boyd B. Stutler*

Henry Thompson,
Ruth Brown's husband,
in later years.
Library of Congress

Annie Brown at
the age of sixteen.
Boyd B. Stutler

Mary in 1860, three years before she moved to California with Salmon and her unmarried daughters. *Boyd B. Stutler*

John Brown's farm at North Elba, N. Y., where his family resided from 1855 until 1863. *Library of Congress*

John Brown in Boston, 1857. This is the famous "mad" photograph which Brown's detractors have often seized upon as evidence that he was a raving maniac. *Boston Athenaeum*

John Brown in Kansas, 1856. *Massachusetts Historical Society, Boston*

John Brown in 1858. *Houghton Library of Harvard University*

Three photographs of Brown about 1857. *Kansas State Historical Society, Topeka*

Samuel Gridley Howe, a physician, well-known educator, and man of romantic causes. *Boyd B. Stutler*

Thomas Wentworth Higginson, Unitarian minister of Worcester, Mass., who asserted that "the worst trait of the American race seems to me this infernal color-phobia." *Boston Athenaeum*

Franklin B. Sanborn, in 1857, a young Concord schoolteacher at the time the conspiracy was formed behind Brown in 1858. *Columbia University Library*

Theodore Parker, perhaps the most eloquent and controversial Unitarian minister of his time, who preached to enthusiastic audiences in the Boston Music Hall. *Boston Public Library*

Gerrit Smith, wealthy landowner and reformer of Peterboro, N. Y., who believed that the United States was "in a state of revolution" and who decided to "go *all* lengths" to support Brown. *Boston Public Library*

George Luther Stearns (from an ambrotype made in 1855), who gave freely to humanitarian causes and became chairman of the Massachusetts Kansas Committee which contributed guns and money to Brown. *Boyd B. Stutler*

legislature, branded the Topeka Constitution as "revolutionary," and warned that organized resistance on the part of free-state Kansans would be regarded as treasonable insurrection."

"We hear that Franklin Pierce means to crush the men of Kansas," Brown wrote his wife on February 20. "I do not know how well he may succeed; but I think he may find his hands full before it is over." With the President openly allied with the proslavery government and border Missouri threatening a war of extermination, could there be any doubt of a general proslavery conspiracy in Kansas? Thus when United States troops turned up in the Pottawatomie vicinity, for the "ostensible purpose of removing *intruders* from certain Indian lands," Brown became quite as alarmed as a Southerner hearing the cry of insurrection on the wind. The old man dispatched a letter forthwith to Congressman Joshua H. Giddings, charging that "the real object" of those troops was to enforce the *"Hellish enactments"* of the proslavery legislature—laws which the Browns had repeatedly broken. Brown was convinced that the next move "of the Administration and its Pro slavery masters" would be to make Pottawatomie citizens submit to "those Infernal enactments" or to "assume what will be termed *treasonable grounds*" by shooting the soldiers. "I ask in the name of Almighty God; I ask in the name of our venerated fore-fathers; I ask in the name of all that good or true men ever hold dear; will Congress suffer us to be driven to such 'dire extremities'? *Will anything be done?*"

Giddings replied that Pierce would not dare use U.S. troops "to shoot the citizens of Kansas," but Brown was never convinced.[7] As he and three of his sons set to work on a cabin for Orson Day (who planned to emigrate from Whitehall, New York, late in the spring), and then took the time to survey the reservation boundaries for the Ottawa Indians, the old man remained alert to any new proslavery threats. And what he heard from border Missouri that windy March only added to his malaise and anger. After the snows had melted wagon trains had started rolling into Kansas once more—most of them from the free states. Viewing this stream of immigration as "an abolitionist invasion," border Missouri called on the Deep South for reinforcements. "Send us help!" cried proslavery leaders. Send men well armed with guns and knives, for "the crisis has arrived. The time has come for action, bold, determined action."[8]

While free-state men lived in constant fear of a Missouri attack and slept with their guns at their sides, the free-state legislature convened at Topeka on March 4, in spite of the President's warning in January, and chose Lane and Reeder as U.S. senators.[9] John Jr. was present as the Pottawatomie delegate and served on two committees, one of them to codify and present "a system of laws" at the next session of the legislature, to begin in July. John Jr. was dismayed, however, when Governor Robinson urged the legislators not to take any action against the federal or the territorial government, but simply to "memorialize" Congress in favor of the free-state cause. A resolution was subsequently passed (with many delegates either absent or voting in abstention) which stated that laws passed by the free-state legislature would not go into effect until after Kansas was admitted as a state. John Jr., refusing to endorse the "moderate" policies of Robinson and Reeder, cast the only negative vote against the resolution and went on record as a "radical" who wanted to put the free-state government into operation and enact a full slate of laws, as though the proslavery territorial government did not exist. However, John Jr. did join with fourteen other delegates in signing a memorial to Congress, which asked that Kansas be admitted as a free state with the Topeka Constitution. James Lane took the memorial with him to Washington.[10]

John Jr. later claimed that Lane, who had also become a radical "in the hysteria of exciting events," initiated him into a secret paramilitary organization called the Kansas Regulators, who vowed to oppose the proslavery government "to the death." However that may be, it is true that John Jr. returned to Brown's Station around March 22 convinced that a nonviolent solution to the slavery question was out of the question and that a great struggle would soon break out in which human bondage would be terminated in this Republic.[11]

In spite of the "wars and rumors of war" that spring, emigration from the free states continued at an unprecedented pace. Lawrence was teeming with new arrivals from Ohio and the Northwestern states, from Massachusetts, Vermont, and New Hampshire; and a number of Northern emigrants, such as James Hanway of Ohio, had just arrived on the Pottawatomie as well. They came well-armed with Sharps rifles too. That was how "we seek communication with

the spirits of 1775–6," John Jr. declared, and urged colonists leaving
Ohio to "come *thoroughly armed*" and "bring plenty of ammunition." If the Slave Power continued "its aggressive acts" against
Kansas, John Jr. warned, speaking for his father as well, "the war-cry
heard upon our plains will reverberate not only through the hemp
and tobacco fields of Missouri but through the 'Rice Swamps,' the
cotton and Sugar plantations of the Sunny South." If "the first act in
the Drama of insane Despotism is to be performed here, you may
look elsewhere for the theatre of other acts."[12]

2

At least one act in that drama was to take place in Pottawatomie.
In early April word came that copies of the proslavery laws were now
circulating among territorial officers and that U.S. district courts
were soon to open their spring terms. The district court session for
Franklin County, where most of the Pottawatomie settlers resided,
was to take place at Dutch Henry's Tavern—a hangout for local
proslavery men—with Judge Sterling G. Cato, a staunch proslavery
man, on the bench. Pottawatomie buzzed with anxious questions:
Would the court enforce the laws? Would offenders be arrested,
imprisoned? Brown himself grew terribly belligerent when he heard
the news. "For once," he wrote his wife, "I have no desire (all things
considered) to have the Slave Power cease its acts of aggression." He
quoted from Deuteronomy, "Their foot shall slide in due time,"
meaning that at His appointed time God would visit sudden and
unexpected destruction on the proslavery forces.[13]

He started to leave Pottawatomie (perhaps to do some more
surveying for the Indians), only to change his mind when a tax
assessor arrived on the creek, announcing that all property would be
assessed and taxed according to the laws. After that a deputy U.S.
marshal came to Pottawatomie and subpoenaed several proslavery
men to sit as jurors in Cato's court. With the proslavery peril actually
threatening Pottawatomie itself, Brown did not go anywhere.[14]

Thirty or forty other free-state men, fearing a general proscription as well as a Missouri invasion, organized a home-defense company called the Pottawatomie Rifles and elected John Jr. captain.

Jason also joined the outfit, no doubt deciding that if he were forced to he would defend his home with a gun.[15]

The old man, utterly incapable of taking orders (especially from his own son), did not join the Rifles, but he was in the thick of the resistance movement nonetheless. On April 16 he attended a settlers' meeting in Osawatomie, called by free-state leaders to decide what they should do if Cato enforced the proslavery laws. In all, twenty-three men (including Samuel Adair and John Jr.) were present, with Oscar V. Dayton acting as secretary and Richard Mendenhall, a Quaker who once had been an Indian missionary, serving as chairman. Martin White, a "free-white-state" settler from Illinois who had a cabin north of the Marais des Cygnes, spoke in favor of peace and submission to the laws. Several men objected angrily, then quieted when Brown got the floor. He declared that he was an abolitionist and that he would rather see the Union drenched in blood than pay taxes to the proslavery government (even though he owned no land and would not have to pay taxes anyway). He swore that he would kill any officer of either the territorial or the United States government who tried to make him obey the laws.

Brown and White's speeches left the meeting sharply divided. Many of the settlers, who did have claims and would have to pay taxes to a government they regarded as illegal, agreed with Brown that forcible resistance was their only course. At that White and other "conservatives" walked out of the meeting. White himself was so appalled at the attitude of the "radicals" that he afterward joined the local proslavery faction, whose views regarding the treatment of Negroes had never been any different from his own.

After the conservative bolt the remaining settlers adopted a set of resolutions which repudiated the proslavery territorial government and warned that any officer who tried to assess and collect taxes or to enforce any of the other "bogus" laws would do so at his peril. A committee was set up to publish the resolutions in the press.[16]

Brown detected the presence of God in these and other developments in the territory. He heard, for example, that a Congressional Committee, headed by William A. Howard of Michigan, had arrived to investigate conditions in Kansas. Brown trusted that much good would grow out of the committee's work (two of its three members were free-soil), "but at all events God will take care of his own cause." At the same time Brown was haunted by a constant ringing in his ears; it was "the despairing cry of millions whose woes none but God knows. Bless the Lord, O my soul, for he hears."[17]

3

All free-state eyes in Pottawatomie were riveted on Dutch Henry's Tavern when Cato opened district court there on April 21. It was an ominous proslavery gathering, with Allen Wilkinson serving as district attorney pro tem and Thomas McMinn as foreman of the grand jury. Most if not all the jurors were proslavery (six had "free-state backgrounds," but presumably had switched their allegiance to the territorial government when "radicals" in the area had threatened to resist the laws with force, and all the jurors had certainly affirmed the right to own slaves in Kansas, as the law prescribed) .[18] Among the jurors were James Harris, who worked for Henry Sherman and lived in one of Sherman's cabins, and James P. Doyle, a poor white from Tennessee who had settled on Mosquito Creek with his wife Mahala, a daughter, and three sons. The Doyles had left Tennessee because they had discovered that slavery was "ruinous to white labor." But when confronted with free-soil Northerners on the Pottawatomie, when brought face to face with genuine abolitionists there like the outspoken Browns, Doyle and his older sons—William and Drury— had joined the Kansas Law and Order party, championed the right to own Negro slaves, and defended the proslavery legislature as staunchly as Wilkinson and the Shermans. Thus when Cato opened court on April 21 the Doyles were more than happy to help the judge uphold the law; and while Doyle himself sat on the grand jury, his oldest son, William, aged twenty-two, served as bailiff.[19]

As the court sat in session that morning the Browns, fortifying themselves in their shanties and cabins near North Middle Creek, were beset with images of gun-bearing deputies coming up the California Road to arrest them for violating the hated laws. Hearing that several free-state men were about to be indicted, the old man allegedly sent Salmon and Henry Thompson "to see," according to Salmon, "if Cato would arrest us." Salmon "did not like it," he confessed later. "I thought father was wild to send us, but he wanted to *hurry up the fight*—always."

If Salmon and Henry went to Dutch Henry's Tavern (as both

claimed later), they soon had company in the form of the Pottawa-tomie Rifles, who came tramping down to the crossing, with Captain John Brown Jr. in the lead, to show Cato and his "proslavery friends" that free-state men here would not be bullied into submission to the "bogus" laws. The old man was with them, as a sort of lone ally. They were not armed, though, having left their weapons at a nearby cabin where the other Browns were standing guard. Should any trouble break out at the crossing, they were to bring the firearms at a run.

John Jr. and an escort went inside the tavern, just as Judge Cato was delivering his charge to the grand jury, with the other officers and the Sherman brothers looking on. John Jr.'s entry created "a lively sensation" in the tavern. But seeing that the intruders were not armed, Judge Cato turned back to the jury and declared that "the laws passed at the Shawnee Mission were to be enforced and recognized as the statutes of Kansas." At that John Jr. went outside and repeated what Cato had said to the Rifles; then he re-entered the tavern and wrote on a slip of paper: Did the judge mean that he would "enforce the acts or laws of the Shawnee Mission, so called"? Cato, "evidently much agitated," glanced over the note, then flung it to the deputy marshal across the table. "The court cannot permit itself to be disturbed by outside issues," the judge snapped. John Jr. promptly led his escort outside, where he announced in a loud voice (for the benefit of those inside) : "The Pottawatomie Rifle Company will meet at the parade ground."

There the Rifles voted to present Cato with the resolutions adopted at the April 16 settlers' meeting. H. H. Williams and "one of the Brown family"—Salmon said it was the old man himself— marched back into the tavern and presented the resolutions to the judge. If Cato tried to enforce the laws he would do so at his "peril." The two free-state men rejoined the Rifles, and all of them tramped off.[20]

Hanway said that the Missouri press later picked up the incident and sensationalized it for propaganda purposes, insisting that "150 abolitionists" had threatened to "exterminate" Cato's court at Potta-watomie and compelled it to flee for safety.[21] Actually, the court appears to have been unimpressed with the free-state resolutions and proceeded with its business in spite of them. While the grand jury did not indict the Browns or any other free-state men who had broken the "black laws," this may not be too significant, since those severe enactments were never really enforced anywhere in the territory. The only persons the jury indicted were Ben Cochran (who had served in Brown's company during the Wakarusa War), for killing two hogs that belonged to Majors & Russell, the large freighting company of the Missouri-Kansas region; sixty-year-old Nelson King, for selling whiskey to the Indians; and David Baldwin, for taking a pot shot at George Wilson, a proslavery probate judge of Anderson County. All three were free-state men, which may well suggest a pro-slavery bias on the part of Cato's court, because free-soilers were not the only ones who had committed crimes in the Pottawatomie area. On the contrary, proslavery men had illegally voted in Pottawatomie elections; others had illegally squatted on the Peoria and Ottawa lands; and still others may have tried to jump free-state claims (the Brown boys themselves had chased away one claim jumper, presumably a proslavery man, in January). Still the court decided not to try any cases this term and the deputy marshal made no attempt to arrest any of the indicted men. So perhaps the free-state resolutions had had some effect after all.

In any event, after the jury made its report at noon on April 22 Cato moved his court into nearby Anderson County, where it opened again on April 28. Among other things the court urged all settlers— even those opposed to the territorial government—to obey the laws until "a majority of them see proper through their legislature to have them altered," and dealt with the tangled problems of conflicting claims and of those who held "more claims than they have any right to hold." The court also indicted another free-state man, named James Townsley, who resided on the North Fork of Pottawatomie Creek (and who was either a member of the Pottawatomie Rifles already or was soon to join), for assault with intent to kill.[22]

4

For the Browns and many other free-state men Cato's court marked the first appearance of the machinery which the proslavery government intended to use "for *crushing us out*." The whole episode heightened tensions in the Pottawatomie-Osawatomie area. To make matters worse, rumors continued that "a distant storm" was gathering, that any day now a Missouri horde would invade Kansas and exterminate "every Goddamned abolitionist in the Territory," as Missouri leaders had threatened to do for months. Brown's half sister, Florilla Adair, wrote "Sister Martha" that Osawatomie was in constant danger of attack and that free-state settlers in the area feared for their lives. "We are constantly exposed and we have almost no protection," she declared. "A few have their guns and revolvers, but as a people and place we are without even these and the place is known and called an *abolitionist nest.*'"[23]

As the rumors and threats increased in intensity, open hostility must have broken out between the Pottawatomie Rifles and the proslavery faction on Pottawatomie Creek—especially Wilkinson, the Shermans, the Doyles, and perhaps Thomas McMinn and George Wilson. Although Mrs. Wilkinson later testified that her husband was an inoffensive man who had taken no active part in the proslavery cause "so as to aggravate the abolitionists," the facts belie her claim—her husband's membership in the hated "bogus" legislature was enough to annoy the abolitionists. Moreover, Wilkinson, the Shermans, the Doyles, McMinn, and Wilson were all connected with Cato's court; and the Doyles in addition were members of the Kansas Law and Order party. They must have been both angry and intimidated when the Pottawatomie Rifles, supported by free-state men in nearby Osawatomie, came out in open resistance against the government which they championed and the legal system with which they were associated. Convinced that they were in the right and perhaps inspired by the bloodthirsty invective of the proslavery press, Wilkinson, the Shermans, and probably the Doyles, too, behaved "obnoxiously" to free-state men and made repeated threats "to shoot & exterminate" them. Samuel Adair, Edward P. Bridgman, and other settlers wrote a month or so later that these men had "thrown out threats & insults" and "acted most outrageously for some time past." James Hanway, a member of the Pottawatomie Rifles, said he heard Dutch Henry boast that he would rather take the life of David Baldwin, a sixty-year-old free-state man indicted by Cato's court, than kill a rattlesnake.[24]

Certainly the more militant free-state men, living in constant fear of proslavery attack, resorted to retaliatory threats and insults (it is inconceivable that with Missouri promising a war of extermination and with the rest of Kansas dividing up into armed camps, proslavery and free-state settlers could continue to live peaceably and amicably together on the Pottawatomie). Still, as the days passed and the Wilkinson-Sherman-Doyle faction did nothing more than talk tough, most free-state men concerned themselves less with the local proslavery threat than with developments around Lecompton and Lawrence and along the Missouri border, where "the distant storm" was gathering. Mutual antagonism between the more belligerent partisans on both sides undoubtedly continued on the Pottawatomie. But all the evidence suggests that, except for John Brown and a few others, the free-state majority—including John Jr.—decided that local proslavery champions were more bluff than fight.[25]

Whether Wilkinson, the Doyles, and their friends were bluffing or whether they actually planned to shoot and burn out their free-state neighbors may never be known. What is known is that Brown himself, in all the tension of those anxious spring days, grew to fear and detest these men, viewing them as part of the whole tapestry of evil which proslavery forces were now weaving over Kansas.[26]

5

There were signs that the long-expected storm was about to break. On the night of April 23 a lone assassin shot and wounded Sheriff Jones outside of Lawrence, after he and a posse of U.S. troops had arrested six free-state citizens for "contempt of court" (they had refused to help Jones apprehend the leader of the Branson rescue party). Although Lawrence citizens publicly condemned the shooting, proslavery forces went berserk. "War to the knife," raged the Atchison *Squatter Sovereign*, "and knife to the hilt. *Jones' Murder Must Be Revenged!*" Of course, Jones had only been wounded, but the proslavery press, exploiting the incident for everything it was worth, ranted about the "murder" for a full two weeks and shrieked for abolitionist blood.

The bloodthirsty headlines had their effect. Boiling with indignation, Atchison and Stringfellow started mobilizing border Missouri. As they did so, drunken proslavery elements in Kansas murdered two free-state men and (for lack of feathers) tarred and cottoned another. Then, on May 2, Jefferson Buford led a battalion of about four hundred armed Southerners into the territory, with banners proclaiming *"The Supremacy of the White Race"* and *"Alabama for Kansas—North of 36° 30'."* Was Buford's column the advance of a massive Southern thrust against Kansas? Was actual war about to commence?[27]

Brown must certainly have thought so when a company of Georgians encamped on the Miama lands near Pottawatomie. There is a much-debated story that he and Salmon, trying to find out what the Southerners were plotting, disguised themselves as government surveyors and pretended to run a line through the enemy camp. The Georgians allegedly declared that, while they had come here to help themselves first and the South second, they still planned to annihilate "those damned Browns" and to stand by Judge Cato "until every damned abolitionist was in hell." Hearing that, the Browns supposedly went home "well served up for future action."[28]

Whether Brown actually visited the Southerners' camp is not that important. In his mind the invaders could only have come to burn and kill—he did not have to talk to them to believe that as an indisputable fact—and there can be little doubt that, gathering his unmarried sons around him on North Middle Creek, he girded himself for war.

He did not have long to wait. On May 8 Judge S. D. Lecompte, trying to crush the free-state movement once and for all, charged a grand jury at Lecompton to indict all members of the Topeka government for "high treason." The jury promptly indicted a number of free-state leaders (including Robinson and Lane), subpoenaed Reeder to testify, and went on to find indictments against the *Herald of Freedom* for seditious language and against the Free-State Hotel in Lawrence as a portholed and parapeted fortress.

It looked as though the long-awaited storm would break over Lawrence. On May 11 Federal Marshal J. B. Donaldson issued a proclamation asserting that a deputy marshal had tried to serve processes on several persons in Lawrence, only to be resisted by a body of disorderly citizens. This assertion was patently false, and so was Donaldson's claim that further resistance in Lawrence was certain. But he used it to justify a general call for all "law-abiding citizens of the Territory" to meet him in Lecompton, where they would form an armed posse to enforce law and order in Lawrence.

Here was the opportunity to wipe out Lawrence, smash free-state resistance, and avenge the shooting of Jones, which the highly agitated proslavery forces had been waiting for. In Missouri companies of militiamen grabbed their guns and whiskey jugs and rode across the border—a "swearing, whiskey-drinking ruffianly horde" who vowed to exterminate those "freedom-shriekers" in Lawrence with chunks of lead. Buford's men headed for Lecompton, too, as eager to fight as the Missourians. Soon large bodies of armed men had gathered at Lecompton "in jubilant encampments," where they played cards, drank, clamored for action, and practiced cavalry charges and infantry attacks.[29]

Already warnings had flashed out of Lawrence, and minutemen companies at Prairie City, Osawatomie, Pottawatomie, and other free-state communities had begun to mobilize. At Pottawatomie John Jr. kept his Rifles on alert, ready to march for Lawrence as soon as he received an official call for help. At Brown's Station the old man organized his unmarried sons and Henry Thompson into "a little company by ourselves" and held them in readiness too.

At last, on May 21, a messenger rode frantically down the California Road bearing the fateful news. "A proslavery army has concentrated outside of Lawrence, and they have cannon! Send help at once!"[30]

X

BLOODY POTTAWATOMIE

❦

WHEN THE LAWRENCE CALL ARRIVED both John Jr. and H. H. Williams spread the alarm along the Pottawatomie. That afternoon (Wednesday, May 21) thirty-four volunteers rendezvoused either at the junction of the Osawatomie and California roads, or at Weiner's store on Mosquito Creek. Minutemen from Osawatomie had planned to march with them, but word now came that the Osawatomie companies had received contradictory reports from Lawrence and had decided to wait for further orders. Too excited to wait themselves, the Pottawatomie Rifles set out for Lawrence at once.

Obviously the Rifles did not believe their proslavery neighbors would do anything violent while the company was gone. The more abusive ones had never carried out their threats to shoot free-state rivals nor had any of them gone up to help the Kansas militia and its Missouri allies destroy Lawrence. If the Rifles regarded the local proslavery faction as a truly dangerous threat, they would never have left their families and the older free-state settlers and marched off on a mission that could well keep them away for days, perhaps weeks. In their eyes the more outspoken proslavery men may have been obnoxious "drunks" and "white trash," but they surely were not vicious enough to attack women and children. Even some of the Browns had to admit that.[1]

While Brown, for his part, despised and distrusted these men, he was far too excited about the Missouri invasion to worry about them now. The great war between right and wrong was about to begin at Lawrence, and Brown would not have missed the opening shots for anything. Leaving Orson Day (who had recently arrived from New York state) to watch over the women and children, the old man and his "little company"—Owen, Salmon, Oliver, Frederick, and Henry Thompson—joined the Pottawatomie Rifles as they moved along the California Road near Middle Creek. Jason was there, too, marching behind Captain John Brown Jr., who led his Rifles on horseback. The fact that Jason was going to fight the Missourians was living testimony to the passions generated by the slavery conflict in Kansas. A man who had never had a fistfight—who had wanted only to plant a large orchard here one day—was marching off to war against his own countrymen.

The volunteers spent the night at Mount Vernon, just north of Middle Creek, and started forward again shortly before daybreak the next morning, Thursday, May 22. At or near the crossing of the Marais des Cygnes, they met a second messenger from Lawrence, who explained breathlessly that free-state leaders had decided not to fight and that the border ruffians were sacking the town without resistance—looting stores, destroying the printing presses, and setting fire to the Free-State Hotel. The men, unable to believe what they heard, were silent for a moment. Then they sent a runner to get the Osawatomie volunteers and hurried on to Ottawa Creek (a tributary of the Marais des Cygnes), where they paused long enough to eat breakfast. As they were eating, a third messenger rode up with more news from Lawrence. He said that the crisis was over, that U.S. troops had taken charge of the ravaged town and that the Missourians were leaving. The volunteers should return to their homes; Lawrence was drastically short of food and anyway there was nothing they could do now.

This news threw the men into considerable confusion. Should they go on anyway? wait here? retreat? John Brown, infuriated because free-state leaders had not put up a fight, exhorted the volunteers to march on at once. John Jr. put it to a vote. The old man helped carry the vote to proceed.

They marched on a few miles, only to receive more inauspicious news: proslavery forces still had control of Blanton's Bridge across the Wakarusa and had reassembled in force at Lecompton. On a motion of James Hanway, the men now voted to encamp near Samuel T. Shore's claim and the townsite of Prairie City (perhaps a half mile south of the Santa Fe Trail) and wait for reinforcements from Osawatomie. Brown, regarding this as a cowardly act, "became considerably excited," Hanway recalled, "and remarked that he would rather be ground in the earth than passively submit to pro-slavery usurpation and wrong." But the Rifles refused to go on without reinforcements and followed John Jr. over to Ottawa Creek where they made camp. Furious at the whole frustrating turn the crisis had taken, Brown ordered his company to encamp as well (they could scarcely attack the invaders by themselves). But the more Brown thought about the sacking of Lawrence and the inexcusable cowardice of free-state leaders there the more "frenzied" he became "at the condition of affairs."[2]

As the hours dragged unbearably by, Brown "turned back to our troubles on the Pottawatomie." And his frenzy subsided into cold, calculating hatred as he bitterly condemned "the slave hounds" on the creek who had supported the "black laws," echoed the threats of the proslavery party, and were as guilty of the sacking of Lawrence as the Missouri mob assembled in Lecompton. With Lawrence in flames, with proslavery columns prowling the territory, and with the Pottawatomie Rifles huddled here in inert confusion, it was up to him—it was up to him and his company—to avenge the proslavery atrocities, to show by actual work that there were two sides to this thing. . . .

Sometime in all the commotion and excitement that prevailed at Ottawa Creek that Thursday night the old man decided what kind of work that should be: a blow against the enemy, their aiders and abettors, who sought to kill and burn out "our suffering people"—a blow delivered in such a frightful and shocking way as to cause "a restraining fear." He called his company about him and revealed the general purpose of his intentions. A "radical retaliatory measure" against their enemies on the Pottawatomie. It would involve "some killing."[3]

2

After daybreak the next morning (Friday, May 23), Jason saw Brown talking with a couple of volunteers around the breakfast campfire. Then Brown walked over to Hanway's mess and told him: "I believe it was well that you moved a reconsideration of the vote yesterday—it was a providential circumstance. I am glad you did it."

Again, "in the gray of the early morning," it is possible that still another messenger from battered Lawrence rode into camp with more maddening news. Salmon Brown, looking back on these events in later years, was confused as to which morning this messenger arrived, but he recalled clearly one of the things he said: Senator Charles Sumner of Massachusetts, an outspoken abolitionist, had been assaulted in the Senate chamber by Preston Brooks of South Carolina. The beating of Sumner had actually taken place early on the previous afternoon (Thursday, May 22); the news presumably had reached Lawrence later the same day; and thus a messenger from the town could certainly have given the news to the Pottawatomie Rifles on Ottawa Creek early on Friday morning. Salmon said that, while everybody in camp was upset about the beatings, he and his father and unmarried brothers "went crazy—*crazy*" when they heard the news. "It seemed to be the finishing, decisive touch."

After breakfast Brown called together a special council of the Rifles or the entire company (it is not clear which). "Something must be done to show these barbarians that we, too, have rights," Brown declared. He called for volunteers who would obey his orders to go with him on a "secret mission." Theodore Weiner, who claimed he'd had angry encounters with the Doyles and Shermans, said he would go. But at that point John Jr. intervened. "Father, I object to any of the men leaving. We are getting up here near the enemy and may need them." Apparently an argument broke out between father and son. Then the old man stomped off with Weiner following. Suddenly apprehensive, John Jr. called out, "Father, be careful and commit no rash act."[4]

Brown sought out James Townsley, the only man in camp with a wagon and team, and told him that trouble was expected on the Pottawatomie. Would Townsley take Brown and his company back to the creek so they could "keep watch of what was going on"? Townsley, who had left a family on the North Fork, said he would be glad to haul them.

Brown then returned to his mess and ordered his company to prepare for action. In all the mounting tension of the last few days his hold over Henry and his unmarried sons had become unbreakable, like a spell. Even Oliver and Frederick, who did not relish the grisly work ahead, obeyed the old man without question. The others, as ready to fight as he was, found something irresistible in his thrilling pronouncements that *they* were in the right, *theirs* was the cause of justice, and that something must be done *now* to uphold that cause.

As Brown set about packing camp kettles and provisions, the boys honed the cutlasses Brown had obtained in Akron to razor-sharp edges. These weapons, with ornamental eagles etched on their blades, had a bizarre history. Originally made as artillery broadswords, they had been sold as surplus property to an Ohio filibustering society called the Grand Eagles, whose members had indulged in fantasies of attacking and conquering Canada. But their plans had never worked out, and when Brown came through Akron, asking for guns and money to defend Kansas from the Slave Power, a member of the defunct society had given the swords to him. Now the Browns were sharpening the cutlasses for purposes which only they and their father knew about.

Eyeing those menacing swords, some of the Rifles decided old Brown meant business and sent James Hanway and another volunteer over to find out what Brown intended to do. He told them that he was going to "regulate matters" on the creek. "Well," said Hanway's companion, "I hope you will act with caution." At that Brown exploded. "Caution, caution, sir. I am eternally tired of hearing that word caution. It is nothing but the word of cowardice."

Meanwhile Hanway had found out from another "one of the eight" the purpose of Brown's mission. "It shocked me," Hanway said later, and he pleaded with his informant to dissuade the old man from his terrible objective; it would only lead to retaliation, a war of reprisal. Pottawatomie would go up in flames.

But nobody could change Brown's mind now. He was as intractable as stone in his conviction that it was his duty to strike back at these "barbarians," to show them—and those cowards in Lawrence as well—that here was one free-state man who was not afraid to fight, who had taken all the proslavery outrages he could stand.

By two o'clock Brown's "Northern Army" was ready for war. Weiner waited on his horse beside the wagon. Brown, wearing his soiled straw hat, a revolver stuck in his belt, climbed into the seat with Townsley; the boys found places among the weapons and camp equipment. Then with Jason, John Jr., and the rest of the Rifles looking on with mixed emotions, Townsley started the team and the little war party headed south toward the Pottawatomie.[5]

3

That evening a company of Osawatomie men reached John Jr.'s camp, reporting that they had passed Brown and some others heading south in a wagon. Brown had told them that he was going on a secret expedition and *"would soon be back"* to accompany the volunteers on to Lawrence. By now John Jr. and the Rifles had turned back to the troubles in the immediate vicinity; and the next morning (Saturday, May 24) all the volunteers moved up to Palmyra on the Santa Fe Trail. They had heard that Governor Robinson had been captured at Westport on his way to the East and that the Missourians were bringing him back to Lecompton. Should they come along the Santa Fe Trail, perhaps the volunteers could make a daring rescue and salvage something out of these frustrating events.

But the volunteers saw not a sign of Robinson, not a single sign. Finally John Jr. and an escort rode into Lawrence to investigate matters there. The captain returned on Sunday morning to report that conditions in town were not so bad as they had feared, although a mob of "400 South Carolinians, Georgians and Border Ruffians," all led by Sheriff Jones, had burned the Free-State Hotel and Governor Robinson's house and destroyed the presses of the *Free State* and the *Herald of Freedom*. What should the volunteers do now? John Jr. wanted to stay in the area. But many others wanted to go home, arguing that "if the Lawrence citizens could not unite in defending themselves against the common enemy, that we could not fight their battles alone." While the volunteers, including another Osawatomie company that had arrived the night before, haggled as to what they should do, John Jr. could not stand the inaction and led a group of men in liberating some slaves from a farm near Palmyra. The act shocked the rest of the volunteers, who did not approve of "slave stealing" and may have feared retaliation from the Missourians. They took the slaves away from John Jr. and had an Osawatomie man return them to the owner (who gave the man a sidesaddle as a reward). This was almost too much for John Jr. His nerves were frayed from a combination of excitement, frustration, lack of sleep, the argument with his father, all the confusion and the worries. Now a majority of his own men—and his friends from Osawatomie—had turned against him. It left him miserably depressed.

As though by some centrifugal force set in motion by the slave-liberation episode, all the volunteers moved about two miles along the Santa Fe Trail, only to find United States troops there under Lieutenant J. R. Church. The lieutenant asked for "Captain Brown." Gloomily John Jr. rode over to talk with Church, who demanded that Captain Brown disperse his men at once. John Jr. said he would not resist a U.S. officer and rode back to tell his volunteers so. He said they should all go home.[6]

Not long after the troops had moved off, a man rode up to the crowd of volunteers, his horse "reeking with sweat," and told them that something terrible had happened on Pottawatomie Creek and that proslavery gangs there were on a rampage.

4

After passing two groups of Osawatomie volunteers, Brown's company had forded North Middle Creek near sundown on Friday, May 23. Somewhere on the road between Owen's claim and Pottawatomie, they spotted a horseback figure in the twilight. Brown stood in the wagon, his gun leveled. "Halt!" he cried. The rider drew rein and in a moment called Brown by name. It was James Blood, a free-state man Brown had met in Lawrence during the Wakarusa War. Drawing alongside the wagon (and glancing furtively at all the rifles, revolvers, and "short, very heavy" broadswords the party had), Blood explained that he had been away in New Hampshire on business, that he had come through Osawatomie, where he had bought a horse, and was now on his way back to Lawrence. Brown told him that the town had been burned by a mob of "border ruffians" and that a number of free-state men had been taken prisoner. As Brown related the news he became "wild and frenzied," denouncing Lawrence for not resisting the invaders and calling free-state leaders "cowards, or worse." The others, Blood observed, "watched with excited eagerness every word and motion of the old man." As Blood started to go, Brown urged him to keep this meeting to himself, "as they were going on a *secret expedition*" and did not want anybody to know they were in the neighborhood.[7]

After Blood had gone, the war party moved down the road to a point near Weiner's store, then turned right and bounced across the prairie until they came to the edge of a stand of timber between two deep ravines. Here, the old man said, they would pitch camp and wait.

After supper Brown told Townsley for the first time how he intended to "regulate matters" on the Pottawatomie: "he proposed to sweep the creek . . . of all the proslavery men on it," Townsley later testified, and wanted Townsley to guide the company into his neighborhood, showing them where all the proslavery men resided. Townsley claimed he "positively refused to do it," because some of his proslavery neighbors were "good men" and others had women-folk who had been kind to his wife. Brown, however, "insisted upon it, but when he found that I would not go he decided to postpone the expedition until the following night. I then wanted to take my team and go home, but he refused to let me do so and said I should remain with them."

Actually, if Salmon and other members of the party may be believed, Brown never intended to "sweep the creek" of all pro-slavery settlers, but planned only to get the "leading, influential" ones, those who "held office" or who had threatened the lives of free-state settlers and given aid and shelter to Missouri intruders. Probably what caused Townsley to become "weak in the knees," as Salmon phrased it, was the way Brown planned to kill these men—to drag them out of their cabins into the blackness of the night and execute them with broadswords. Frederick and Oliver also appear to have balked at such a brutal assassination scheme. But the old man, his eyes shining obstinately, forced them all back to his side with his implacable and domineering will. He spent the rest of that evening and most of Saturday exhorting his men, reminding them what they were duty bound to do. He said it was time to "fight fire with fire," to "strike terror in the hearts of the proslavery people." He said "it was better that a score of bad men should die than that one man who came here to make Kansas a Free State should be driven out." By Saturday evening Weiner, Owen, Salmon, and Henry Thompson were as worked up as he was and anxious to get on with the mission.[8]

At last the sun disappeared over the rim of the prairie. Night came on. About ten o'clock, with a damp wind blowing, the company left camp and headed in a northeasterly direction. They stole across the California Road, made their way to the timber on Mosquito Creek, waded across it at a point "above the residence of the Doyles," and headed for a cabin nearby.* Not a sign of life in the windy shadows. Somebody—probably Brown himself—knocked on the door. In a moment there was a noise from inside—the metallic clank of a rifle barrel being rammed through the chinks of the wall. "We all scattered," Salmon recalled. But Brown regrouped them in the darkness, and they made their way through the crackling underbrush toward the Doyles' place.

It was about eleven o'clock when they reached Doyle's cabin. While Townsley, Frederick, and Weiner stood guard in the road "some distance away," Brown and the others went to summon the Doyles. Suddenly, like visitations of the Devil, two "very savage bulldogs" charged out of the cabin's shadows, barking madly. Townsley and Frederick stabbed one to death with their cutlasses, drove the other howling in terror into the timber.

Brown knocked on the cabin door. Inside a man answered in a distinct Tennessee drawl: Yes, what was it? Brown asked the way to Wilkinson's place. In a moment, old man Doyle opened the door, only to be shoved back as Brown burst into the cabin, declaring that the Northern Army had come and demanding that Doyle and his sons surrender. In a moment the rest of the family appeared in the dimly lit room—Mahala Doyle, a little girl, and three boys. When Brown ordered Doyle and the boys outside, Mrs. Doyle (according to Salmon) started weeping and railing at her husband. "I told you what you were going to get," she cried. "Hush, mother, hush," Doyle said. Then she turned to Brown, begging him at least to spare fourteen-year-old John. Suddenly merciful, Brown granted her wish. Then he shoved Doyle, twenty-year-old Drury, and twenty-two-year-old William—all members of the Law and Order party—out into the windy night.

---

* This may have been the cabin of J. H. Mentzig, who served as a juror on Cato's court.

About a hundred yards down the road Salmon and Owen fell on the Doyles with broadswords. They put up a struggle, striking out, trying to shield themselves from the slashing blades, as they staggered back down the road. But in a few moments the grisly work was done. Doyle and William, mangled and lifeless, lay near one another in the road; Drury, who had tried to run, lay in some grass near a ravine with his head gashed open and his arms cut away. Brown, who must have watched the executions in a kind of trance, now walked over and shot Doyle in the forehead with a revolver, to make certain work of it. The first blood in the slavery struggle on Pottawatomie Creek had been spilled.[9]

The war party then moved south about a half mile to Wilkinson's place. Again a dog "raged and barked furiously" as the Browns roused Wilkinson, asking the way to Dutch Henry's Tavern. There were anxious voices inside. In a moment Wilkinson started telling them the way, but they said "come out and show us." Wilkinson stalled. "Are you a Northern armist?" they demanded, meaning was he opposed to the free-state party. "I am," Wilkinson said through the locked door. Then "you are our prisoner," they declared, and ordered him to open the door. Would they give him time to make a light? Wilkinson asked, again trying to stall. They told him to open the door or they would break it down. When Wilkinson finally let them inside, Brown took him prisoner and confiscated a gun and powder flask. Mrs. Wilkinson, who was sick with measles, pleaded with them to spare her husband. Wilkinson wanted at least to get somebody to stay with her. He promised to be here in the morning if they still wanted him. He was a proud man; he would not run.

"The old man, who seemed to be in command, looked at me," Mrs. Wilkinson later testified, "and then around at the children." He was "a tall, narrow-faced, elderly man," she remembered (she did not know Brown personally), and he wore soiled clothes, a black cravat, and a straw hat. "You have neighbors?" Brown asked Mrs. Wilkinson, probably referring to Thomas McMinn, who lived on the adjoining claim. She replied that she did, but that they were not here and she could not go for them. "It matters not," Brown said, and forced Wilkinson outside in his stocking feet, refusing to let him put on his boots.

Shortly one of the party returned to get Wilkinson's two saddles.

Mrs. Wilkinson asked what they were going to do to her husband; the man replied, "take him a prisoner to the camp." Would one of them stay with her? she asked. He said he would, but "they would not let him." Then he went back outside. After a while Mrs. Wilkinson thought she heard her husband's voice. She went to the door, but "all was quiet." Fearing the worst, she gathered her two children to her and started to cry.

Outside, about 150 yards from the cabin, Wilkinson lay "in some dead brush," where Weiner and Henry Thompson (or possibly "one of the younger Browns") had dragged him after they had slashed his head and side open and slit his throat.[10]

From Wilkinson's place the war party made its way down to James Harris' cabin on Pottawatomie Creek. Harris, who had served as a juror on Cato's court, worked for Henry Sherman and lived in one of his cabins. Ironically, it was after midnight—Sunday, May 25, the Lord's Sabbath—when the party reached Harris' place. While Frederick, Weiner, and Townsley again stood guard outside, Brown and the others broke into the house and woke the inhabitants at sword point. The startled Harris immediately recognized "old man Brown" and his son Owen. They approached the bed where Harris was lying with his wife and child, "and ordered us, together with three other men who were in the same house with me, to surrender," declaring "that the northern army was upon us, and it would be no use for us to resist." One of the men was a traveler named Jerome Glanville, who had stopped for the night. The others were William Sherman and John S. Wightman, who had bought a cow from Dutch Henry and intended to go home the next morning. The Browns confiscated two rifles and a Bowie knife, ransacked the one-room cabin in search of ammunition, then ordered Glanville outside, where they interrogated him at gun point. Evidently they were satisfied with his answers because they let him go back inside. Now it was Harris' turn. "They took me out," Harris testified later, "and asked me if there were any more men about the place." The Browns were referring to Dutch Henry and probably George Wilson, who had allegedly warned free-state settlers on the north and south forks to "clear out" and who was supposed to be staying with the Shermans at this time. Harris said that nobody was here, but the Browns searched the place anyway. "They asked me where Henry Sherman was. . . . I told them that he was out on the plains in search of some cattle which he had lost." Then they asked him the same questions they had doubtlessly posed to Glanville. Had Harris ever aided proslavery men in coming to Kansas? Had he "taken any hand in the last troubles at Lawrence"? Had he ever harmed or intended any harm to the free-state party? Harris must have answered no on all counts because Brown spared his life, too, and sent him back into the cabin. While two of the boys stood guard inside, the old man took William Sherman down to Pottawatomie Creek. There Weiner and Thompson carried out Brown's orders and hacked Sherman to death, throwing his mutilated body into the creek (where Harris found him the next morning with his left hand cut off "except a little piece of skin" and his skull slit open and "some of his brains" washed away).[11]

Confiscating a saddle and a horse of Dutch Henry's (which Harris was keeping), Brown's war party washed their broadswords in the Pottawatomie. Then they returned to their camp in the timber between the two ravines. Just before daybreak Owen came up to Townsley and said: "There shall be no more such work as that."[12]

The old man was silent, transfixed, as the company started back over the California Road that Sunday afternoon, heading for Ottawa Creek to rejoin John Jr.'s command. The enemy had murdered six free-state men since the great struggle had begun in Kansas. Now, in killing five slavery men, Brown and his Northern Army had about evened the score.

XI

WAR HAS COMMENCED

❦

THE MESSENGER WHO RODE UP TO THE VOLUNTEERS, after their encounter with U.S. troops on the Santa Fe Trail that Sunday afternoon, reported what had happened at Pottawatomie Creek in brief but vivid detail: five proslavery men had been "horribly cut and mangled," and their deaths had started a reign of terror on the creek. And, the messenger added, "they said old John Brown did it."

Shocked (but hardly surprised), the volunteers set out for home with visions of their own cabins in flames. On the march they damned the murders as "barbarous & inhuman" and turned against John Jr. and Jason in bitter indignation. In the face of such hostility John Jr. could make no rational response to what had happened. First he said the massacre was "good news." Later he said that he could not justify it, but could not repudiate it either—that there was some excuse for it. He was too emotionally distraught to make any coherent statement.

Jason, too, was extremely upset. "The thought that it might be true, that my father and his company could do such a thing was terrible"—"the most terrible shock that ever happened to my feelings in my life."[1]

By nightfall the men were too exhausted to go any further. They made camp just off the California Road at Ottawa Jones's place (Jones was an Indian who had free-state sentiments and an "excellent white missionary" wife—one reason why some proslavery men disliked him). Around midnight Brown and his band stole into camp with their confiscated horses and supplies. In the darkness the

138

old man met James Hanway and asked where John Jr. was.
Hanway replied that he was "in Jones house." "Any news?" Brown
asked. Hanway repeated what the messenger had said that afternoon.
The old man made an "evasive reply" and went off to find his son.

The next morning, as the volunteers prepared to march, some of
the men "recognized several horses which belonged to the ruffians"
slain at Pottawatomie. This seemed incontestable proof that Brown
and his boys were the guilty ones, and another wave of indignation
spread through camp. When John Jr. was confronted with the evidence, he exhibited "great agitation," George Grant recalled, and
resigned his command. The Rifles promptly elected H. H. Williams
as their new captain and started for the Pottawatomie more as a mob
than a military company. John Jr. and Jason apparently accompanied
the Osawatomie men, although most of them were as bitter about
the murders as the Rifles. The old man and his company traveled by
themselves.[2]

As the crowd spread southward across the prairie, Jason brooded
so much about the murders that he feared he was losing his reason.
Finally, after they crossed North Middle Creek, he could bear it no
longer and went up to his father. "Did you have a hand in the killing?" Jason asked. "I did not do it," the old man said (and strictly
speaking, he had not "killed" anybody, since Doyle was already dead
when Brown shot him), "but I approved of it." "I told him," Jason
said later, "that whoever did it, I thought it was an uncalled for,
wicked act."

"God is my judge," Brown snapped, "we were justified under the
circumstances."

Jason sought out Frederick. Did he know who had done the actual
killing? "Yes, I do, but I can't tell you." Jason asked: "Did you kill
any of them with your own hands?" "No," Frederick replied, tears
streaming down his cheeks, "when I came to see what manner of
work it was, I *could not* do it."

Frederick turned away and followed the old man to the Brown
claims (and on into hiding in the brush). Jason and John Jr. headed
for Osawatomie, where Ellen and Wealthy had gone for safety. The
roads were lined with armed men out searching for "the Browns,"
but miraculously the brothers made it to Osawatomie, only to
meet angry free-state settlers there who accused the brothers of

the murders. At that John Jr. went completely to pieces. First the Pottawatomie Rifles and now his "political friends" at Osawatomie had turned against him—he was "crazed," "deranged" by the time Jason got him to Adair's cabin. But even their uncle seemed hostile, refusing to let them inside for fear of retaliation. Only after Jason swore that he and John Jr. had not committed the murders did Adair open his door. Inside, to Jason's immense relief, were Ellen, Wealthy, and Tonny. Out of concern for their safety, though, Jason remained at Adair's place only one or two nights. Then he set out across the Marais des Cygnes by himself, hoping to find U.S. troops, declare his innocence of the Pottawatomie massacre, and demand protection. In the meantime John Jr., "imagining crowds pursuing him," fled into the timber beyond Adair's cabin and hid in the thickets like a frightened animal.[3]

2

By Tuesday, May 27, a state of intense "fear & excitement" prevailed in southeastern Kansas. Rumors flew that Buford's Southerners were going to kill every free-state settler in the Osawatomie-Pottawatomie area, that mobs of Missourians were going to lay waste to everything. Hoping to ward off a general carnage, settlers without distinction of party held a "conciliation meeting" at Osawatomie that Tuesday and adopted a set of resolutions condemning the murders and pledging mutual cooperation between proslavery and free-state men in bringing the assassins to justice. Although the resolutions did not mention Brown by name, there was little doubt that he, four of his sons, Thompson, Weiner, and Townsley were the guilty ones. H. H. Williams, secretary of the meeting, certainly suspected them; and Dr. Rufus Gilpatrick, a member of the committee that drafted the resolutions, had positively identified Brown as the leader of the executioners, after discovering Wilkinson's body on Sunday morning and talking with Mrs. Wilkinson, who described "the old man" who commanded the party and remembered that he wore a straw hat and black cravat. Gilpatrick knew that Brown habitually wore such a leather necktie. And in any case James Harris had pointed his finger at Brown as indisputably the leader of the midnight murderers.[4]

Although free-state representatives had unanimously endorsed the Osawatomie resolutions, opinion was actually divided about the causes of the assassinations and whether they could be justified or not. Men like Amos Hall, Daniel W. Collis, Edward Bridgman, and John T. Grant emphatically censured the massacre as an inexcusable outrage.[5] But Adair, Hanway, and others, while viewing the murders as a "frightful tragedy," nevertheless thought that the victims had invited trouble with their insults and threats of violence. Hanway, James H. Carruth, and O. C. Brown all thought that a threat the Doyles—and possibly the Shermans "and others"—had made to Squire Morse had actually triggered the murders (although there is no convincing evidence that Brown knew about the incident before he decided to strike his blow). As Hanway wrote in his Memorandum Book about June 1, 1856: "The supposed causes which made the Doyal family the victims, is that the old man & his sons, called on a man who kept a store near Sherman's—and told him to pack up his goods, move off his claim in five days or they would kill him. Morse did not move but is still at home, he was arrested by a body of men & as there was no evidence against him he is at large. Sherman it is said repeatedly threatened to shoot & exterminate free state men, and at the news of the fall of Lawrence raised a red flag: which was said he meant to intimate that war was commenced & he was in for it—Wilkinson appears to have been a very violent & imprudent man making threat of killing & burning & his wife is a fine woman, sick at the time of the murder and told the Dr. that she has frequently urged him to be more quiet—but could not do it—it appears from general opinion that they were extreme men, and very obnoxious to the free-state men." Thus "violence breeds violence," Hanway declared, and went on to place final blame on the proslavery party. "They advocate assassination and now that 5 persons have been murdered on their side perhaps they will learn that such hellish sentiments when carried into effect, will work equally to the destruction of pro-slavery men."[6]

3

In truth the murders did not have that effect at all. The pro-slavery party seemed unanimous in damning this latest "abolitionist" crime and in clamoring for a bloody revenge. "If ever Lynch law was or could be justified," cried one Missouri border captain, who was mobilizing a posse to ride after the killers, "it is in these cases." "WAR! WAR!" raged the Westport *Border Times*. "EIGHT PRO-SLAVERY MEN MURDERED BY THE ABOLITIONISTS IN FRANKLIN COUNTY, K.T." The paper, ignoring its own bloodthirsty threats and all the proslavery atrocities—the murders, beatings, and the sacking of Lawrence—argued that there was only one reason for such hideous butchery: Cato's court was scheduled to open in Lykins County and the victims had been murdered to prevent them from testifying against certain "abolitionists" who were to be charged with treason against the territorial government (although there is no convincing evidence that this had anything to do with the massacre either).[7] All over Kansas and border Missouri the proslavery press reprinted the *Border Times* story under lurid headlines. On June 10 the *Squatter Sovereign* published full front-page reports of the massacre (along with an account of an even worse atrocity which "was forgotten immediately" because it was without political significance: in Buchanan County, Missouri, an entire Mormon family—a man, his wife, and five children—had been "murdered in cold blood, in the dead of night, by five cowardly villains"). The Leavenworth *Herald*, after recounting the Pottawatomie killings and other "Abolitionist Outrages" that followed, issued a declaration of war: "The Abolitionists shoot down our men without provocation, wherever they meet them. Let us retaliate in the same manner—a free fight is all we desire! If murder and assassination is the programme of the day, we are in favor of filling the bill. Let not the knives of the proslavery men be sheathed while there is one Abolitionist in the Territory."[8]

4

When Governor Shannon learned of the massacre, he feared the worst this time. Hoping to prevent civil war from breaking out in southeastern Kansas, he dispatched Captain Thomas J. Woods's regular company to Osawatomie, requested that Colonel Edwin V. Sumner, in command at Fort Leavenworth, send reinforcements to Lawrence, and wrote President Pierce about the murders, remarking that they had "produced an extraordinary state of excitement" in southeastern Kansas. "I hope the offenders may be brought to justice," the governor said; "otherwise, I fear the consequences."

So did Judge Sterling G. Cato, who had just opened district court down in Paola in Lykins County. For a time the town was in such a state of alarm because of the massacre that the court could not continue. Cato himself, hearing of the murders on Monday, talked at length with a militia officer who had actually visited the site of the massacre and then wrote Governor Shannon that the leading suspects were "the Browns and Partridges." In all the confusion Cato set out on his own, taking testimony from James Harris and several members of the Lawrence relief columns (among them Amos Hall, Harvey Jackson, and George Grant), all of whom pointed their fingers at Brown, four of his sons, Thompson, Townsley, and Weiner. Taking matters into his own hands, Cato on May 28 issued warrants for their arrest; two days later the court indicted Brown again, along with John Jr., O. C. Brown (no relation to John Brown), Richard Mendenhall, and six others, for "unlawfully and wickedly" resisting the collection of taxes "in and for the county and Territory." Deputy marshals set out at once to arrest the wanted men.[9]

The officers were soon joined by columns of Missourians, proslavery Kansas militia, and U.S. troops; they arrested a total of fourteen free-state men (although seven were soon released). One band of Missourians, led by Martin White, caught Jason Brown near Ottawa Jones's cabin; they started to kill him on the spot, only to change their minds and turn him over to the authorities in Paola, where feeling was still running so high that a mob almost lynched him. Jason recalled later that he was kept in the same house where Mrs. Doyle and apparently her surviving children were staying. "She said nothing" to Jason. But when she went to Missouri in June she said plenty to a Jackson County justice of the peace, to whom she dictated a shocking eyewitness account of the murder of her husband and older sons. Henry Clay Pate (a captain in the Missouri militia, deputy U.S. marshal, and correspondent of the St. Louis *Missouri Republican*) gave Mrs. Doyle's testimony to the Leavenworth *Herald*, which published it on June 21, 1856. Mrs. Doyle's description of Brown was a scathing indictment: "He said if a man stood between him and what he considered right, he would take his life as coolly as he would eat his breakfast. His actions show what he is.

Always restless, he seems never to sleep. With an eye like a snake, he looks like a demon."[10]

Meanwhile, James Harris and Mrs. Wilkinson (who was on her way back to Tennessee) also gave affidavits about the massacre to the same Jackson County justice of the peace. All the affidavits were later turned over to Mordecai Oliver, a Missouri congressman and a member of the Howard Committee. Oliver included the documents in his "minority Report" on Kansas, which he submitted to Congress that summer. Oliver asserted that John Brown was evidently the leader of the Pottawatomie murderers.[11]

The Northern press had also reported the news of the massacre and some journals (the Chicago *Democratic Press*, for example) had already associated one "Captain Brown" with events that surrounded the killings. But in Washington and all across the North, from Chicago to Boston, the most significant news about Kansas was not the Pottawatomie affair, but the beating of Charles Sumner for his "Crime Against Kansas" speech in the U.S. Senate and the "rape of Lawrence" by a Missouri mob. The latter atrocity riveted the attention of the North on the embattled territory and put "an arsenal of arguments" into the hands of the newly organized Republican party, which intended to make "free soil" and proslavery outrages in Kansas major campaign issues in the forthcoming presidential election of 1856. And in dozens of towns and cities in the North, free-soil leaders were haranguing crowds to donate money and guns for the cause of freedom in Kansas. "The great question now before the people of this country is not the emancipation of the Negro, but the emancipation of the white man," an Ohio politician told a mass meeting in New York on June 9. "The crisis has come. Here are two antagonistic powers about to come into collision—Freedom and Slavery. Which shall be the governing principle of our American institutions?"[12]

5

The crisis had certainly arrived in terror-stricken southeastern Kansas, as columns of Missourians and their Southern allies ransacked the area, plundering homesteads, taking "horses & cattle, and everything else they can lay hold of" as they searched for the Pottawatomie killers. "The War seems to have commenced in real earnest," an Osawatomie minuteman wrote his cousin. Any day now the Missourians were expected to attack the town; "all work is nearly suspended, the women are in constant fear," and reports arrived from all directions of robberies and murders committed by partisans on both sides.[13]

About May 31 a column of Missourians appeared on the Marais des Cygnes and searched the timber near Adair's cabin until they found what they wanted: John Brown Jr., crouching in a ravine in "a wild state." To their credit, the Missourians did not lynch him, but turned him over to Captain Woods, whose company had now arrived in Osawatomie. The soldiers, thinking John Jr. one of the Pottawatomie killers, chained him to a tent pole and beat him with fists and rifle butts until he was "a raving maniac." When Governor Shannon ordered the troops to bring all the arrested men to Tecumseh for examination, John Jr., Jason, H. H. Williams, and four other captives *"were chained two and two,"* reported a *New York Times* correspondent, and "like a gang of slaves they were thus driven on foot the whole distance at the rate of twenty-five miles per day, dragging their chains after them."[14]

At Tecumseh, on June 20, U.S. Commissioner Edward Hoogland held a preliminary hearing to decide whether sufficient evidence existed to hold the seven men for indictment by a grand jury, on a charge of treason for forcibly resisting the territorial laws. Hoogland released Jason and four of the others, but bound Williams and deranged John Jr. over to the U.S. marshal, "on the charge of treason," to await the action of the grand jury scheduled to convene in September. John Jr. remained in custody at or near Lecompton until September 7.[15]

Jason set out for home by way of Big Springs and Lecompton on the Kaw River. At Lawrence he probably heard that, on June 7, 150 "Border Ruffians" had attacked Osawatomie and that many of the settlers, including Ellen and Wealthy, had fled into the blockhouse for protection. Jason traveled on to Brown's Station, only to find everything in ruins: the cabins and shanties had been burned and all the cattle and horses stolen. Melancholy and sick with the ague, Jason tried to make some sort of shelter out of fence rails. But afraid that the Missourians might find and kill him, he fled into the brush after his father, who was "armed to the teeth" and out there somewhere.

By now southeastern Kansas was in complete chaos. Dozens of settlers—proslavery as well as free-state—had fled the region out of fear for their lives. Armed bands of men—one led by John Brown himself—prowled the countryside, shooting at one another and looting enemy stores and homesteads. As Samuel Adair wrote some friends from Osawatomie, the sacking of Lawrence and the assassinations at Pottawatomie had triggered a terrible guerrilla war in southeastern Kansas, one in which "as many pro-slavery men must die as free state men are killed by them." An eye for an eye and a tooth for a tooth—that was the war cry of both sides in Bleeding Kansas—and nobody knew what the end would be.[16]

XII

GOD WILL KEEP AND DELIVER US

⊱✺⊰

BROWN KNEW THAT THE MISSOURIANS would come after him for the executions he had directed on the Pottawatomie. Yet he was not afraid of the consequences of that act, for God would keep and deliver him; God alone was his judge. Now that the work was done, he believed that he had been guided by a just and wrathful God when he and his Northern Army had moved with the inexorability of time itself to mete out a just revenge with their Old Testament swords, to prevent those men from carrying out their threats and treacheries. When questioned about the massacre afterward he was always vague and inconsistent about his own part in it ("I did not kill them, but I approved of it," or "I don't say but what those men were killed by my orders," and "I believe that I did God service in having them killed"). He told a friend that the victims deserved to die because they "had committed murder in their hearts already, according to the Big Book" and later asserted that the killing of those men had been "decreed by Almighty God, ordained from eternity."[1]

On Monday, May 26, Brown and his band (which now included August Bondi) went into hiding on Vine Branch, a mile and a half from North Middle Creek. That afternoon O. A. Carpenter of Prairie City found his way to Brown's camp and told him that proslavery men had commenced a war of reprisal because of the Pottawatomie massacre. In behalf of free-state settlers around Palmyra and Prairie City, Carpenter wanted Brown to take his company into

147

Douglas County where they could help check the Missourians and perhaps make retaliatory raids.

Brown agreed to help and that night, mounted on their confiscated horses, Brown and his band rode up to a secret campsite, which Carpenter had suggested, in a secluded ravine on Ottawa Creek, not far from Palmyra. The next day Brown sent Owen on "a valuable running horse" to get provisions at Osawatomie and to find Jason and John Jr. Owen may also have taken along a herd of stolen horses to sell in Lawrence, provided he could persuade some of the Osawatomie volunteers to help drive the animals.[2]

On May 28—a dry and windy day—two additional volunteers arrived at Camp Brown on Ottawa Creek. One was Charles Kaiser, a native of Bavaria who had fought in the Hungarian Revolution of 1848 and had a badly scarred face (from lance and sword cuts) as a reward for his services. Kaiser, who had a claim nearby, had met Brown during the Wakarusa War, liked the old man, and wanted to fight with him now that war seemed about to begin with the proslavery enemy. Kaiser was a salutary addition to Brown's company, because he injected a touch of humor into their hard and primitive lives at Camp Brown, where they survived mainly on bread and creek water. Kaiser had an endless supply of jokes that made everybody except the old man laugh until tears filled their eyes. The old man, deep in thought, never laughed at all.

The second volunteer was Benjamin Cochran, one of the Pottawatomie Rifles, who brought depressing news for Bondi and Weiner. The Missourians, out hunting the Pottawatomie murderers like wolves, had burned their homesteads and driven off their cattle. Some said Dutch Henry himself had razed Weiner's store—one more reason why they should have killed him on Saturday night along with the others.

Probably that same day Owen returned from his mission to Osawatomie and told Brown that Jason and John Jr. refused to join him here at Camp Brown. John Jr. seemed "quite insane" because of fatigue, anxiety, and constant lack of sleep—and because of the "ungrateful" and "cowardly" conduct of his friends in Osawatomie who threatened to turn him over to "the Bogus men"—and in a wild and frenzied state he had gone into hiding in some timber near Adair's cabin.[3] Perhaps Owen also related that their free-state neighbors had held a conciliation meeting with proslavery men in Osawatomie and had unanimously pledged to bring the Pottawatomie murderers to justice. Cochran, of course, may have told Brown the same thing.

What should they do now? If August Bondi may be believed, Brown told the company around the supper campfire: "If the cowardice and indifference of the free-state people compel us to leave Kansas, what do you say, men, if we start South, for instance to Louisiana, and get up a negro insurrection, and thereby compel them to let go their grip on Kansas?" This sounds perfectly plausible, since Brown's position in Kansas seemed untenable and since he had never really abandoned his old Subterranean Pass Way scheme to oppose slavery in the Southern mountains. As Brown looked from face to face, awaiting a response to his suggestion, Frederick jumped up. "I am ready," he cried. But Bondi shook his head. He had traveled through the South in 1851 and 1852 and was certain that "no baker's dozen could kick up a negro rebellion worth while," because the slaves feared "Judge Lynch" too much to risk it. Kaiser, agreeing with Bondi, argued that they should remain right where they were in Douglas County. He believed that the border ruffians would "wake up the people" and that they would drive the scoundrels from the territory. At present the people were busy planting corn; but when the Missourians attacked and stole their horses they would be infuriated and would join Brown's fight.

Brown, of course, ignored whatever advice his men had to offer. The next day (May 29), while he mulled over what he should do, Captain Samuel T. Shore of Prairie City came out to have a talk. Shore probably told the old man that warrants had been issued for his arrest and that deputy marshals, assisted by Missouri militia and U.S. troops, were out looking for him and his band. Brown, hearing that, remarked that he might have to leave the area after all. But Shore urged him to stay, join up with his Prairie City company, and fight the Missourians together. Brown agreed to think it over and Shore rode back to town.[4]

The following afternoon Frederick brought an unexpected visitor into camp. It was James Redpath, a native of Scotland and a correspondent for various Eastern newspapers, who had ridden into the troubled Pottawatomie region in search of sensational stories for his Northern readers. As Redpath reported the event more than three years later, he had lost his way in the timber along Ottawa Creek, "when, suddenly, I saw a wild-looking man, of fine proportions," with uncombed hair and an unkempt beard. He was armed with revolvers and "a large Arkansas bowie-knife." The man identified himself as Frederick Brown, "the son of John Brown," and said that he had seen Redpath in Lawrence and knew who he was. On the way back to camp Frederick "talked wildly" about the Pottawatomie murders, Redpath recalled. "His family, he said, had been accused of it; he denied it indignantly, with the wild air of a maniac." Although Redpath had a talent for overstatement, there is considerable truth in his description of Frederick, for the Pottawatomie massacre had been a severe emotional shock to him.

Finally, "after many strange turnings" in the timber, Frederick led the correspondent into Camp Brown. Redpath remembered that "near the edge of the creek a dozen horses were tied, all ready saddled for a ride for life, or a hunt after Southern invaders. A dozen rifles and sabres were stacked around the trees. . . . Three or four armed men were lying on red and blue blankets on the grass; and two fine-looking youths"—one was Oliver Brown—"were standing, leaning on their arms, on guard near by." Frederick introduced Redpath to "Old Brown," who stood beside "a great blazing fire with a pot on it." Redpath had heard of Brown since the Wakarusa War, but this was the first time he had met the old man in person. "He was poorly clad," the journalist wrote later, "and his toes protruded from his boots," as he roasted a pig "with his sleeves rolled up." Redpath thought to question Captain Brown about the sacking of Lawrence and the Pottawatomie massacre. "He respectfully but firmly forbade conversation on the Pottawatomie affair," Redpath recalled, and from then on the correspondent categorically insisted that "the Old Hero" had had nothing to do with that atrocity. Brown went on to talk about what constituted a good soldier. "I would rather have smallpox, yellow fever, and cholera all together in my camp, than a man without principles. It's a mistake, sir, that our people make, when they think that bullies are the best fighters, or that they are the men fit to oppose these Southerners. Give me men of good principles; God-fearing men; men who respect themselves; and, with a dozen of them, I will oppose any hundred such men as these Buford ruffians."

Redpath also claimed that he spoke with Brown's men, who remarked that frequently the old man would "retire to the densest solitudes, to wrestle with his God in secret prayer," and that, "after these retirings, he would say that the Lord had directed him in visions what to do." How much of this is true and how much the invention of James Redpath is difficult to say. It is certainly easy to imagine Brown the Calvinist making such remarks (Bondi and another recruit also claimed that Brown told them he had acted "in obedience to the will of God" and entrusted his fate to an all-wise Providence). What is clear is that Redpath's concluding remarks about his visit to Camp Brown, made over three years afterward, when he was assiduously promoting the legend of Brown as an American "warrior-saint," are brilliant examples of pure journalistic propaganda: "I left this sacred spot [Camp Brown] with a far higher respect for the Great Struggle than ever I had felt before, and with a renewed and increased faith in noble and disinterested champions of the right. . . . I went away, thoughtful, and hopeful for the cause; for I had seen, for the first time, the spirit of the Ironsides armed and encamped. And I said, also, and thought, that I had seen the pre-destined leader of the second and the holier American Revolution."[5]

The fact was that Brown was only one of several free-state guerrilla captains—and not even the most important one, because for the most part he stubbornly refused to cooperate with those who formulated free-state strategy and insisted on waging his own private war against the proslavery enemy. But facts aside, Redpath's opinion that Brown was a Cromwellian Ironsides, sent by God to save Kansas for freedom, was precisely the opinion which Brown had of himself.

2

Captain Shore visited Brown twice on May 31, reporting that a large body of Missouri militia had camped on the Santa Fe Trail at Black Jack Springs and that three of the invaders had already broken into a blockhouse at Palmyra, cowing its free-state defenders and capturing their guns. In Brown's mind the Missourians at Black Jack were like the Midianites who had camped near the Wall of Harod. And he was as Gideon who slew the host and drove them across the Jordan. Yes, he told Shore, he would join the Prairie City volunteers tomorrow morning, Sunday, June 1, and together they would ride out to do battle with the enemy.[6]

The next morning Brown and his company arrived in Prairie City just in time to attend church services, held by an itinerant United Brethren preacher in a crowded log building. Suddenly the preaching was punctuated by shouts and gunfire from outside. The congregation rushed out of the building and spotted a group of free-state men standing in the road nearby. They had just captured two Missourians (a third had escaped) who admitted that they had come from the Missouri camp at Black Jack, some three miles to the east. Their commander was Henry Clay Pate, a former student of the University of Virginia and now a captain in the Missouri militia as well as a deputy U.S. marshal. On news of the Pottawatomie massacre Pate had led a column of Missouri troops into Kansas and helped lawmen round up several free-state suspects (including Jason and John Jr.). Brown stepped forward and demanded to know what Pate was doing around Prairie City. The captives replied that Pate had several prisoners with him (among them the father of a couple of Prairie City boys) and that he was out looking for the rest of those "damn Browns." Several Prairie City volunteers wanted to attack Pate at once. But Brown persuaded them to wait until nightfall, when they could steal up on the Missourians and surprise them at dawn.

That night twenty-six volunteers—nine under Brown, fifteen under Shore—left Prairie City and at four o'clock the next morning (June 2) reached a patch of oak trees on a slope north of the enemy camp. They dismounted in the timber, left Frederick to watch the horses, and made their way across the slope, away from the water, just as day was breaking. Suddenly there was a shout, a crack of gunfire. Missouri sentinels! Brown and Shore both led their men forward on the run, Brown's company passing across the front of the enemy camp and taking a position in a nearby ravine, where they opened fire on the Missourians as they scurried about among their tents and covered wagons. Captain Shore tried to flank the enemy on the opposite side, only to encounter a blistering counterfire which threw his command into disorder. From then on everything was pandemonium, every man for himself, as the fighting seemed to give way to indiscriminate shooting in all directions at once. In all the wild gunplay men deserted wholesale on both sides; Brown claimed that all but eight of Shore's company left the battlefield—and three of his men deserted, too, including James Townsley. Shore fought bravely with what men he had—even Brown had to admit that Shore was courageous—but finally he had to fall back. Shore then went for reinforcements, leaving eight of his men to help Brown hold their lines. Meanwhile the Missourians had regrouped in another ravine. Now they opened a veritable barrage of rifle fire on Brown's position, which frightened six volunteers sufficiently that they drew back out of range. The old man crawled on his hands and knees around the ridge and "by the utmost exertion" persuaded the cowards to "make a little show" by shooting the enemy's horses and mules.

At that moment a most extraordinary spectacle occurred which may well have turned the fight in Brown's favor: out of the timber, like some apocalyptic horseman sent by God Himself, charged Frederick Brown on one of the horses, waving his Pottawatomie cutlass over his head and shouting at the top of his lungs: "Father, we have them surrounded and have cut off their communications." Apparently Captain Pate thought the maddened boy was leading a cavalry charge. Frederick soon disappeared in the timber, but Pate was convinced that he "saw reinforcements coming" and raised a white flag. Sending a runner to fetch reinforcements of his own, Pate ordered one of his men out under the truce flag "to gain time, and if possible, have hostilities suspended for a while."

Brown was in no mood to parley. "Are you the captain of that company?" he asked the messenger. When the Missourian shook his head, Brown sent him back with an ultimatum that he would talk only with Captain Pate. In a moment Pate came over under the sanctity of a white flag, announcing that he was a deputy U.S. marshal acting under orders of "the Government" and that he was looking for "certain persons" who had been indicted. . . . Brown cut in on him in a voice cold as death. "I understand exactly what you are, and do not wish to hear any more about it." Brown demanded that Pate surrender unconditionally. "Give me fifteen minutes," Pate pleaded. But the old man drew his revolver and his men lowered their rifles. "You can't do this," Pate protested. "I'm under a white flag; you're violating the articles of war." Brown was unimpressed. "You are my prisoner," he said, pointing his revolver straight at Pate. "I had no alternative," Pate wrote later in his own defense, "but to submit, or run and be shot." Then he added, "Had I known who I was fighting, I would not have trusted to a white flag."

Brown forced him back to his lines with a revolver at his back. "Tell them to lay down their guns," Brown ordered. But Pate refused. Brown put his revolver to Pate's head and gave him exactly "two minutes to make the order." At that (according to Pate) the Missourians laid down their arms to keep Brown from blowing their captain's brains out. Brown's men jabbed the prisoners in line— twenty-five all told—and led them back to their camp. A few moments later a number of free-state reinforcements arrived, among them J. B. Abbott's volunteer company from Lawrence.

The battle of Black Jack was quite a victory for Brown in more ways than one. He had not only killed four Missourians and wounded several others, but had also captured valuable booty in the form of arms, horses, and military stores. Aside from the dozen or so "cowards" who had deserted from his own ranks, all that marred Brown's victory was that Henry Thompson and O. A. Carpenter had been "badly" wounded. Thompson, shot in the side in the middle of the fighting, had made his way back to Carpenter's cabin, where Bondi dressed the wound.

Brown took his prisoners back to Camp Brown on Ottawa Creek. There he and Pate signed an agreement, to be sent out to the authorities, whereby Brown would exchange his prisoners for an equal number of free-state captives. Pate and his lieutenant, W. B. Brocket, would be traded specifically for John Jr. and Jason. "It is agreed that the neutral ground shall be at or near the house of John T. or Ottawa Jones," the document read. "The arms, particularly the side arms, of each one exchanged, are to be returned with the prisoners, also the horses so far as practicable."

Brown was immensely proud of his victory over the Missourians. He wrote his wife that Black Jack was the "first regular battle fought between Free State & pro Slavery men in Kansas. May God still gird our loins & hold our right hands, & to him may we give the glory."[7]

3

First the Pottawatomie massacre, then the victory at Black Jack— Brown was now totally and irrevocably at war with the Slave Power in Kansas. And because in his own mind this was a holy war, waged in the name of God against obstinately wicked men, Brown could justify many acts for the good of the cause: midnight assassination, distortion and secrecy, lies, terrorization, plundering and horse stealing. To the victor belonged the spoils anyway, for as God commanded Moses, as related in the Book of Deuteronomy: "But the women, and the little ones, and the cattle, and all that is in the city, even all the spoil thereof, shalt thou take unto thyself; and thou shalt eat the spoil of thine enemies, which the Lord thy God hath given thee." As one of Brown's new recruits, Luke F. Parsons, phrased it, "a state of war existed and it was quite proper to despoil the enemy."[8] And despoil the enemy they did, throughout the civil war of 1856. On June 3 and 4, for example, Brown's band looted Joab Bernard's store on the California Road near the Franklin-Douglas county line, helping themselves to between $3,000 and $4,000 worth of supplies and several horses and cows. Yet Brown kept none of this plunder for his own personal gain, thus putting to rest the accusation that he was a mere criminal using the free-state cause as a cloak for theft and murder.[9] He mounted his men on some of the horses, sold the others to somebody (possibly Charles Lenhart of Lawrence) near Ottawa Jones's place, and used the money and stolen supplies "for the continuation of the struggle."[10]

Shortly after the battle of Black Jack, a loquacious young man named John E. Cook, a one-time law clerk from Connecticut and probably a member of Charles Lenhart's guerrilla company operating out of Lawrence, came to Camp Brown and talked with the old man about some unknown mission against the enemy. On June 5, with Cook still in camp, a column of 50 United States cavalrymen converged on Ottawa Creek, throwing Brown's command into pandemonium. The old man himself went out and tried to make terms with the officers—Colonel Edwin Sumner and Major John Sedgwick. Sumner informed Brown that he was under orders from the President as well as Governor Shannon to disperse all armed bands he could find in southeastern Kansas and that he would not bargain "with lawless and armed men." At that the colonel led his troops into Brown's camp, liberated Pate and the other prisoners, forced Brown to return their weapons, and ordered him to disband his company at once. Brown tried to argue, pointing out that he and Pate had signed an agreement that the Missourians would be exchanged for an equal number of free-state captives, including Brown's two sons. But the colonel was adamant and finally Brown gave in—he could scarcely do anything else, surrounded as he was by 50 U.S. troops. Bitterly he watched the soldiers and Pate's Missourians ride away. Sumner had not only spoiled Brown's victory at Black Jack but had provided further proof, as far as Brown was concerned, of the "cruel & unjust course of the administration & its tools throughout this whole Kansas difficulty."

Yet Sumner had not arrested Brown, although the colonel must have known that warrants had been issued for the old man. In his report Sumner stated that he had heard that armed bands were prowling around Palmyra and had taken two companies to investigate. He came upon Brown's band, broke it up, and then met a column of some 250 Missourians (who had come to rescue Pate) and ordered them out of the territory. His purpose was not to arrest anybody but to disband proslavery and free-state companies alike and to restore order to southeastern Kansas. He gave no further explanation as to why he had not arrested Brown. Perhaps he believed that he did not have the authority, since he had no warrants with him. Perhaps he thought that apprehending Brown would only cause retaliatory uprisings by other free-state partisans. A man of mild free-state sympathies, he may have been unhappy that free-state settlers accused him of siding with the South and thus elected to interpret his orders in the narrowest possible manner and to break up Brown's company rather than arrest them. Still, as James Malin has pointed out, the colonel's actions remain an enigma, and so do those of other federal authorities in Kansas who had "reasonable grounds" to bring Brown to trial for the Pottawatomie massacre, but never really tried.[11]

In any case, once the troops had gone, Brown ordered his men to break camp. As they set about packing their equipment, Salmon accidentally shot himself and had to be carried to Carpenter's cabin, where one of Brown's cousins took care of him. Brown led the rest of his men to another hideout nearby. On June 8 he sent Bondi to Osawatomie to find out what had happened to Jason and John Jr. Two days later Bondi reported that the brothers were prisoners in a U.S. cavalry camp where they were being "kept in Irons." The Brown women were staying with a neighbor named David Garrison.

Brown called a war council and told his men they had to separate. Thompson, still nursing his side, returned to Carpenter's house to mend. Bondi and Weiner set out for Fort Leavenworth (where Bondi remained while Weiner, claiming to have business in Louisiana, headed for St. Louis). Brown and his other sons moved to another secret camp somewhere in the brush. There, for the next twenty days, they hid from "our enemies," as Brown wrote his wife, "like David of old," finding "our dwelling with the serpants of the Rock, & wild beasts of the wilderness."[12]

4

While Brown hid in the brush, unbridled guerrilla war raged in the territory, and neither Shannon nor the U.S. Army could check it. In all directions partisan bands on both sides burned cabins, attacked settlements, and stole horses and supplies. In an effort to terrorize and starve out their free-state enemies, proslavery forces "blockaded" Topeka and Lawrence and embarked on what seemed a program of encirclement and strangulation, building forts and blockhouses in a wide-swinging arc around the major free-state settlements. Meanwhile armed Missourians guarded all routes into the territory, confiscated guns and supplies shipped out the Missouri River, and turned back all river passengers with free-soil leanings. In the midst of this "reign of terror" much confusion prevailed in free-state ranks and different factions often worked at cross-purposes. Robinson and other leaders were still in prison, although Robinson himself managed to work out a system of vigilance committees while he was in custody— a system which several antislavery communities put into operation late in July. At the same time a Kansas Central Committee in Lawrence attempted to coordinate reprisal military operations against proslavery forces in the area; and other free-state partisans plotted various schemes to liberate Robinson and the other "treason prisoners." But with all the confusion of planning and counsel, the only real hope for ultimate free-soil victory seemed to depend on aid from the North.

And the North was quite prepared to help. From Iowa to New England, free-soil crowds held mass meetings to condemn proslavery terrorism in Kansas and to pledge money and start armed emigrants for the territory. In Boston Samuel Cabot and Amos A. Lawrence, principal stockholder in the New England Emigrant Aid Society, shipped $4,000 worth of Sharps rifles to free-soil Kansans (the Missourians intercepted them, however). In the meantime James Lane had embarked on a spectacular speaking tour, exhorting Northerners everywhere he went to send money and guns to his free-soil colleagues in Kansas. In Chicago Lane recruited a company of armed emigrants and vowed to blaze a new trail to the territory through Iowa and Nebraska—a plan openly supported by the governors of Ohio and Iowa and wildly cheered back in Topeka. At Buffalo a National Kansas-Aid Committee was organized, with auxiliaries in virtually every Northern State except Massachusetts (which had a flourishing state committtee of its own) all dedicated to the task of raising money and supplies for the cause of freedom in Kansas.[13]

Did Brown, still hiding in the brush south of Lawrence, know what was going on? He wrote Mary that "we are not disheartened," even though "we are nearly destitute of food, Clothing, & money" and "Owen & Oliver are down with fever." For "God who had not given us over to the will of our enemies but has moreover delivered them into our hands; will we humbly trust still keep & deliver us." He gave Mary a brief and somewhat inaccurate sketch of Black Jack (remarking, as a sort of parenthetical aside, that "some murders had been committed at the time Lawrence was sacked"); he also reported that John Jr. had been brought to trial before "a bogus court" but that he did not know the results. He told Mary that "if under God this letter reaches you so that it can be read, I wish it at once carefully copied in Ink & a coppy of it sent to Gerrit Smith. I know of no other way to get these facts, & our situation before the world."[14]

Was Brown contemplating some plan to expand his war against his pro-slavery enemies, one that would involve Smith and other wealthy abolitionists in the East? Had he heard about all the money and guns which free-soil Northerners were pledging for the defense of Kansas?

One thing he heard for certain: Colonel Sumner, under orders from Secretary of War Jefferson Davis, planned to break up the free-state legislature when it convened in Topeka on Independence Day. Perhaps it was this news that jolted Brown into action, because on July 1 he and his "little party"—which included Jason now—left their hideout and marched into Lawrence. There the old man penned a reply to Pate's account of the Black Jack engagement, published first in the St. Louis *Republican* and reprinted in the New York *Tribune*, which accused Brown of violating the articles of war—and also called him the Pottawatomie murderer. Brown, ignoring the latter accusation, insisted in his version that he had defeated Pate in a fair and proper manner, then sent the account to the New York *Tribune*, which published it on July 11. The next day Brown called on William A. Phillips, a correspondent for the *Tribune*, and Phillips agreed to accompany Brown to Topeka, where free-state men and U.S. troops were congregating for an Independence Day showdown. On the way Brown talked about politics. He said that the free-state party was run by "broken-down politicians" from the East who would "rather pass resolutions than act" and who "criticized all who did real work"—such as Brown did. That was why Brown had broken with the free-state party and undertaken his own independent war against the proslavery forces. Anyway he was not "in the habit of subjecting himself to the orders of anybody. He intended to aid the general result, but in his own way." Then he broke into a furious denunciation of slavery—that "sin against God," that "sum of villanies"—and asserted that if the American people did not destroy it, human freedom and republican government would "soon be empty names in these United States."

Phillips was most impressed with Brown, although he thought the old man something of an enigma with his inflexible belief that "men were nothing, principles everything." And in a book published in Boston later that year, entitled *The Conquest of Kansas by Missouri and Her Allies*, Phillips described Brown as a courageous, Bible-quoting soldier fighting in his own way to make Kansas free—"a strange, resolute, repulsive, iron-willed, inexorable old man" whom the Missourians both hated and feared.[15]

When the party reached the outskirts of Topeka the next day, Brown for some reason refused to go into town. He and his boys went to a farm nearby and remained there while Sumner broke up the free-state legislature on July 4. Although Brown did not know it at the time, Sumner issued a proclamation in which he declared that this was "the most disagreeable duty of my whole life"—a statement that earned him the respect of almost everybody in Topeka that day. That remark, together with a reference to Missouri interferences he had made in a report to Washington, also cost Sumner his job. Evidently believing the colonel was sympathetic to the "Abolitionists," Jefferson Davis, the Secretary of War, relieved him of his command.

Brown had nothing to do with events in Topeka on Independence Day. On July 5 he and his sons returned to their camp somewhere near Ottawa Creek. There the old man took care of Owen, who was sick and as thin as "a skeleton," while the others moaned and complained. They wanted to go home. They had had their fill of fighting the Lord's war out here in the brush, of living on bread and creek water, of aching with the fever and hurting from their wounds in the hot, cramped, fly-infested Carpenter house. They wanted to go home.

About mid-July Brown decided to leave Kansas himself and wrote John Jr., in prison at Lecompton, about his plans. "Am very glad that you have started," John Jr. replied, "as all things considered I am convinced you can be of more use where you contemplate going than here."[16] Evidently John Jr. had largely recovered from his emotional collapse (which he not only had blamed on "troubles in the Territory," but may also have attributed to the domineering obstinacy of his father—although the present letter was conciliatory enough). Obviously Brown was up to something. But whatever his plans were he did not reveal to anybody except perhaps John Jr. and Owen. Late in July he loaded his sick and wounded boys in an ox wagon and headed for Nebraska, only to be overtaken by a party of free-state volunteers under Captain Samuel Walker, a small and slightly crippled Midwesterner who had a frenzied hatred of slaveholders. Walker recognized the "thin, wrinkled & weatherbeaten" old man who drove the ox team—for Brown had earned something of a reputation as a gun-happy nonconformist in the free-state cause. Walker explained that they were on their way to Nebraska City, too, one of the major stations on the "Lane Trail" which Kansas emigrants had recently opened through Iowa and Nebraska. Lane himself was supposed to be there at the head of his much-trumpeted "Army of the North"—a caravan of some 400 colonists, most of them sent out under the auspices of the newly formed National Kansas

Committee. Word was out that Governor Shannon had ordered U.S. troops to intercept the armed train once it crossed into Kansas, and free-state leaders had sent Walker to escort Lane across the Nebraska line. (Actually, all this was probably unnecessary, for General Persifor E. Smith, who had replaced Colonel Sumner, had refused to carry out Shannon's order; and in any case two agents of the National Kansas Committee—Thaddeus Hyatt and Dr. Samuel Gridley Howe —had visited the emigrant camp, deposed the "impetuous," "trouble-making" Lane, and urged the caravan to enter Kansas peacefully as ordinary emigrants.) [17]

Brown followed Walker to Nebraska City, where he had a long talk with Lane, Walker, and one "Captain Whipple," a strapping fellow whose real name was Aaron D. Stevens and who commanded the caravan's military escort. Apparently Walker and Lane had received reports that Lawrence planned to launch attacks against proslavery outposts at New Georgia and other places. They intended to return to Lawrence at once. Brown now changed his mind about going on (his motives are not clear) and he and Frederick rode back to Kansas with Lane, Walker, and about thirty others, ahead of the wagon train. Henry Thompson and Brown's other sons took the ox wagon and went on to Iowa (where Owen mysteriously remained while the others headed for Ohio and North Elba). On August 10 Brown left the free-state column and alone headed for Topeka. There Brown wrote Jason (who had returned to Osawatomie) that "God still *lives*; & 'blessed be his great & holy name.' The boys may go on farther East; & may hold on for me to join them."[18] *Now* what did he have in mind? There is strong evidence that Brown wanted to liberate John Jr. from the prison camp at Lecompton. If so, perhaps he intended to return to the East after that and recruit an armed company of his own.

His whereabouts during the next six days are not known. But, contrary to reports in the Missouri press, Brown did not participate in the campaigns that occurred between August 8 and 16, when free-state forces from Lawrence raided proslavery strongholds at New Georgia, Franklin, Fort Saunders, Treadwell, and Fort Titus, once more plunging the smouldering border into "a raging fury." On or around August 17 Brown turned up in Topeka again, where he apparently received a letter from John Jr. advising against a rescue attempt. John Jr. had reason to believe that the grand jury might release him—or that, at the very least, he might be sent to the United States for trial. One way or the other he hoped to return to the States, because only by leaving the territory could he fully recover from his emotional troubles.[19]

A day or two later Brown himself left for Lawrence on an unknown mission.

XIII

JOHN BROWN OF OSAWATOMIE

∽☙∾

ON AUGUST 20 C. G. ALLEN, A CHRISTIAN MINISTER from Cottonwood Springs, noticed Brown buying some mules from a well-known horse and mule dealer in Lawrence. Allen had heard a great deal about Brown, but on this day he saw "nothing remarkable in his appearance that impressed me."[1] Actually, had Allen been an old friend he would have been shocked at how much Brown had aged since he had taken to the brush after the Pottawatomie massacre. All the hardship and privation he had endured in the field had left him stooped and emaciated, so that he looked ten years older than his fifty-six years. A daguerreotype taken of him at about this time shows him dressed in his old black suit, with a high collar around his scraggly neck. The face in this photograph is a drawn, unhappy one, with a pair of eyes fixed on some imaginary enemy in the camera lens. Brown's eyes have an unsettling glare in them—the eyes of a man who (as Leonard Ehrlich phrased it) could believe that "Right is everything, God is a god of wrath," and take five men from their beds and kill them.[2]

On August 22, somewhere in or near Lawrence, Brown put into operation one of several schemes he had been plotting during the summer: he organized a company of "Kansas Regulars" and initiated seven recruits who would fight for "the Free State cause" as a trained and disciplined force. The mules Brown had purchased in Lawrence were to serve as mounts and pack animals for the outfit. In the induction ceremony Commander Brown swore in his recruits on the basis of a "Covenant" he had drafted sometime during the past week or so. Among other things, the recruits pledged "their word and sacred honor" to fight "for the maintenance of the rights and liberties of the Free State citizens of Kansas." They also agreed to obey the "*by Laws of this association*," which consisted of twenty-three articles of war. Article 1 provided that all officers, except the commander, would be elected. Article 5 declared that property taken "by honorable warfare from the enemy" would go to the company "for the common benefit, or be placed in the hands of responsible agents for sale." Other articles counseled against using "intoxicating liquors," engaging in disorderly charges or retreats in battle, and firing "guns pistols or caps, or boisterous talking while in camp." Article 20 stated that prisoners would not be put to death or subjected to "corporeal punishment" without an impartial trial.[3]

These "by laws" were tantamount to an official declaration of war against proslavery forces in Kansas, and the commander had an immediate opportunity to put them into action. That same day Lawrence volunteers (the Rev. Allen among them) were mobilizing to go to the defense of Osawatomie, which expected a Missouri retaliation for the free-state raids of August 8–16. Brown decided to go along, despite the fact that his Osawatomie neighbors had turned against him and his sons because of his work on the Pottawatomie. On the afternoon of August 22 Brown and his company joined one of two Lawrence contingents and headed for Osawatomie by way of Franklin, passing deserted homesteads and fire-scarred chimneys along the way—evidence of the civil war which the sacking of Lawrence and the Pottawatomie murders had precipitated in southeastern Kansas.

Brown found Osawatomie deserted except for a handful of armed defenders under Dr. William W. Updegraff, who had fortified themselves in the town's twin blockhouses. Jason was still there, and he and another man agreed to ride with Brown after he arrived in town. On August 24 an armed party, composed mainly of Iowans mounted on "captured pro-slavery horses," also volunteered to fight with Captain Brown. Their leader was a New Yorker named James H. Holmes, who had led a raid against Martin White's place on the night of August 12–13 and run off some of his horses. Holmes, a student of agricultural chemistry, had originally come to Kansas to join a vegetarian colony on the Neosho River. But finding that the colony had broken up, he had gone to Lawrence, joined an armed company, participated in the raid on New Georgia, and eventually assumed command of a band of Iowans. In joining forces with Brown in Osawatomie, Holmes apparently retained direct control of his own men, agreeing merely to cooperate with Brown in raiding proslavery settlements and dividing the spoils.

By now three more companies under captains Samuel T. Shore, James B. Cline, and Samuel Anderson had also arrived in Osawatomie. Meeting in a council of war on August 25, the captains discussed what they should do once the Missourians attacked. Allen reported that Brown took a leading part in these deliberations, arguing that, since natural defenses were superior to man-made ones, they should make the Marais des Cygnes their first line of defense, the blockhouses their second. In the end, though, the other captains decided not to defend the town, since most of its inhabitants had gone.

Brown walked out of the meeting and left town without a word. According to Allen, the old man returned that evening "looking very good natured." Jocularly he asked some men whether they wanted any proslavery beef. He said he had some "that was number one. That he had been out that day collecting taxes." Later Allen learned that Brown had "taken some fine cattle from the plantation of an anonymous Border Ruffian."[4]

Brown learned that the other captains had gone after a column of Missourians reported to be advancing up the California Road from Fort Scott. The commander rounded up his men and rode after the free-state forces at a killing pace. He overtook them on August 26, only to find that they had already whipped the Missourian main body, having surprised and routed them in their camp on the California Road where it crossed the south fork of South Middle Creek. Brown, surveying their spoils, remarked that his allies had made "a pretty good haul." Then he asked if there were any other "ruffians" in the area. George Partridge told him that some of the invaders had ransacked the Pottawatomie settlement, captured him, brought him here to the main camp, and then had ridden away to plunder other homesteads. Brown wanted to ride after them at once and called for volunteers. Partridge officially joined Brown's company and twenty-four others offered to go along.

Brown's column rode all evening and all night around the Pottawatomie region, passing near the cabins of the very men Brown had slain last May. Apparently the old man lost his way in the timber and ravines south of the Pottawatomie, thought he found the enemy's trail in the unfamiliar country, and rode hard until at last he came upon what seemed to be their secret camp on the bank of some stream. He prepared his men for a surprise attack—only to discover that he had circled back to South Middle Creek and that he was about to annihilate Cline, Anderson, and Shore.

Unshaken by this near disaster, the captains decided to raid proslavery settlements along Sugar Creek, where Cline himself had a claim. They paroled their prisoners, vowing to kill them if they invaded Kansas again, and then headed into Sugar Creek country. They attacked and pillaged the homesteads of numerous slavery men there—among them John E. Brown, the notorious proslavery sheriff of Linn County, and P. F. E. Means, whose court had tried Cline for horse stealing. According to two eyewitnesses, Brown prevented Cline from burning Means's place to the ground. Sheer destructive vindictiveness had no place in Brown's holy war against the Slave Power.

Their booty amounted to 75 head of cattle, several horses, and other property. It appears that Shore thought enough work had been done for one day and returned to camp with his company. Cline and Brown continued the raid, confiscating more cattle and horses at other proslavery homesteads. They returned to South Middle Creek the next day, and there the companies divided up their spoils and set out independently for Osawatomie.[5]

Brown arrived in town on Friday afternoon, August 29, driving 150 head of cattle. Richard Mendenhall, a Quaker who lived nearby and had presided over the stormy settlers' meeting back in April, saw Brown's column and went over to have a look. "I playfully asked him where he got those cattle," Mendenhall recalled. "He replied, with a characteristic shake of the head, that they were good Free-State cattle now." Brown drove his herd across the Marais des Cygnes and on to his campsite on the Crane Ranch.[6]

Either before or just after the Sugar Creek raid, Brown received a letter from Ruth, written on July 20 at North Elba. She said that everybody there was extremely upset about the civil war in Kansas and all the suffering and privation which Brown and the boys had endured. She related that the family subscribed to the New York

Weekly Times and had read that John Jr. had been driven insane because of the "inhuman treatment" he had received at the hands of the U.S. troops. "Oh! my poor afflicted brother, what will become of him? Will it injure his reason for life? We hope not, but have great anxiety for him, and we sympathize most deeply with Wealthy." She went on to thank God that "my dear husband" and Salmon had not been killed and that Brown too had been spared (the *Times* at first reported that he had also fallen into the hands of the Missourians). Then, referring to Brown's letter of June 24 and 26 (in which he had deliberately misrepresented events that followed the Pottawatomie massacre), Ruth remarked that Brown "must have had very exciting times" in the battle of Black Jack—a statement unintentionally ironic. A few lines later she said: "Gerrit Smith has had his name put down for ten thousand dollars towards starting a company of one thousand men to Kansas."[7] *One thousand men? Ten thousand dollars?* One can imagine what went through Brown's mind when he read that. If *he* had that kind of money and that kind of manpower, could he not wage a truly great war against Satan's legions in Kansas?

On the same day that Brown returned from the Sugar Creek expedition, he inducted two new recruits into his Kansas Regulars, one of them a "Surgeon." That night, on the other side of the Marais des Cygnes, a mail carrier hurried into Osawatomie and warned both Holmes and Updegraff that a large force of Missourians was advancing against the town. The breathless man explained that he had been held captive in New Santa Fe for ten days and had barely escaped in time to warn Osawatomie of the coming invasion. Both Holmes and Updegraff were too tired to do anything about this report that night (probably they did not believe it) and went back to sleep. At the Crane Ranch on the other side of the river, Brown and his men also bedded down for the night.

2

As it turned out, what the mail carrier said was true: another Missouri invasion was under way, thanks to a rapid-fire sequence of events that had begun on August 18 (while Brown was somewhere in or around Topeka). On that day Wilson Shannon resigned as governor of Kansas because he believed the civil war was out of control. President Pierce, however, refused Shannon's resignation and fired him. The President named John W. Geary as the new governor. A native Pennsylvanian who stood 6 feet 5 inches, who had fought in the Mexican War and served as mayor of San Francisco, Geary was an honest, tough, forthright man—precisely the kind of chief executive Bleeding Kansas needed.

But until Geary arrived Daniel Woodson, the proslavery lieutenant governor, would have to serve as acting chief executive. Determined to avenge the "invasion" of free-soil caravans and the free-state raids of August 8–16, Woodson on August 25 proclaimed that Lane and his cohorts had started an "insurrection" and called out the militia to put it down. Again, Woodson's proclamation was exactly what border Missourians had been waiting for. Some 480 of them, under Major General David R. Atchison and Brigadier General John W. Reid of the Missouri militia, assembled at New Santa Fe, and on August 26 (when Brown and his associates were raiding Sugar Creek) the Missourians invaded Kansas once more. Three days later Reid took 250 men and a six-pound field piece and left the Missouri main column to burn out that "abolitionist nest" in Osawatomie.

When free-state leaders at Lawrence heard reports that another Missouri invasion was under way, they sent Frederick Brown and four other messengers to retrieve the relief columns that had gone to Osawatomie. The messengers arrived there on August 29 and at once set out for Lawrence with the armed companies. Frederick started back, too, but feeling ill he decided to spend the night at a friend's cabin near Adair's place. He would go back to Lawrence the next day.

That very night Reid passed south of Osawatomie, turned and rode up the main road or "public highway" from Pottawatomie, so that anybody who saw his column might think it another relief company from Lawrence. Martin White, hoping to retrieve some of the cattle free-state men had stolen from him, joined the Missourians as they advanced on Osawatomie early that Saturday morning, August 30. At daybreak White and an advance scout rode up to the outskirts of the settlement to reconnoiter. At the same time Frederick Brown emerged from his friend's cabin and walked down the road toward

Adair's house (he had promised to take a batch of Adair's letters to Lawrence), only to stop when he saw the horsemen in the dim morning light. "Good morning," Frederick called out. Then he spotted Martin White. "I think I know you." White replied, "I know you, & we are foes," and promptly shot Frederick through the heart.

Adair and David Garrison both heard the shot and ran out of their cabins just as White's party rode away. They hurried over to Frederick, but he was already dead. While Garrison ran for a neighbor's house (only to be shot to death himself), Adair returned to his cabin on the run, sent his fourteen-year-old boy to spread the alarm in town, and fled into the brush to save his life. In Osawatomie, shouting men ran toward the blockhouses with whatever weapons they could find. One of them splashed across the river to summon Brown.[8]

The old man and "12 or 15 new recruits" were preparing breakfast when the messenger ran into camp yelling that the Missourians were attacking the town and that Frederick and David Garrison had already been killed. "Men, *come on!*" Brown cried, grabbed his gun, and hurried into town, his men following in pairs and groups.

Osawatomie was in a state of panic when Brown arrived. But as if by a miracle the Missourians did not follow up their initial advantage and attack the town while everything was pandemonium; instead they dallied around the bridge, possibly to have breakfast before they burned the settlement. Meanwhile Brown had persuaded Updegraff and Cline to take their men into the timber along the river, where they had a better chance of defending themselves against enemy artillery.[9]

They took up a position in the trees just northwest of town (Brown acting more or less as over-all commander of the thirty-odd defenders) and watched with knots in their stomachs as the Missourians wheeled off the road and charged down the hill with their guns blazing. Firing desperately from the timber, the free-state force managed to check the Missouri charge. But the enemy quickly dismounted, regrouped, and brought the cannon into action, blasting the trees with volleys of grapeshot.

Brown ran back and forth in the timber, exhorting his men to fire low and hold their positions, but his voice was lost in the noise of the gunfire and cannonade. After about twenty minutes of fighting

Cline, almost out of ammunition, saw a party of Missourians attempting to flank him and sensibly ordered his men to retire across the ford. Brown, however, refused to retreat, holding stubbornly to what was now an untenable position. His men fought bravely, shooting at the figures they saw running toward them and ducking as grapeshot crashed into the trees overhead, showering them with twigs and leaves. Presently the enemy overran the ford and cut off any chance for Brown to retire in an orderly manner. Only when the Missourians threatened to engulf them did he allow his men to fall back step by step along the riverbank. Suddenly the old man staggered—struck in the back by a partially spent blast of grapeshot. Luckily for him he was not seriously injured (later he claimed that God had saved his life).

As the Missourians swarmed after them, Holmes and several others waded into the river and tried to swim for their lives. The Missourians opened fire on them, killing George Partridge and capturing four others (including Brown's trusted friend, Charles Kaiser). With rifle balls striking the water all around him, Holmes dived and swam underwater until he was out of rifle range. In the meantime Brown, Jason, and three or four others ran further down the river, then waded across where the water was relatively shallow. To George Grant, the old man looked a "queer figure, in a broad straw hat and a white linen duster, his old coattails floating outspread upon the water and a revolver held high in each hand, over his head."

While the others scattered into the timber Brown and Jason set out alone, looking for a ford where they could cross the Marais des Cygnes and go to Adair's cabin, perhaps to find Frederick. As they emerged from the trees at one spot Jason pointed at a column of smoke rising over the trees. The Missourians were burning Osawatomie! Brown could hear their shouts and gunfire as they rode through the smoking settlement looting buildings and herding off the very cattle which free-state forces had stolen during the past few days.

"God sees it," Brown said, as he and Jason watched Osawatomie smoke and blaze against the Kansas sky. Yes, God saw it, the old man said with tears in his fierce gray eyes: the homes of free-state Christians going up in flames; the body of his own son lying in the dirt with a proslavery bullet through his heart. Brown stood there trembling with grief and rage. "I have only a short time to live—only one death to die," he told Jason, "and I will die fighting for this cause. There will be no more peace in this land until slavery is done for. I will give them something else to do than to extend slave territory. I will carry this war into Africa."[10]

3

Brown's movements in the weeks that followed the Osawatomie disaster are filled with mystery. From all appearances he was deeply absorbed in his own thoughts during that time, largely oblivious to what was going on around him, perhaps preoccupied with some retaliatory blow against the enemy that would avenge the battle of Osawatomie and the death of his son. He did not even have the presence of mind to bury Frederick after the battle, but merely took the boy's cap and disappeared in the brush, leaving others to dig his grave.

Later Brown claimed that he hid out at a nearby farm for a few days, then took Jason and a sick recruit—Luke Parsons—up to Ottawa Jones's place, only to find his cabin in ruins. On the evening after the Osawatomie battle, other Missouri contingents had looted and burned Jones's homestead and that of another free-soil man near Prairie City, "within hearing distance" of the relief columns riding from Osawatomie back to Lawrence. The invaders had not only robbed Mrs. Jones (a New England white woman married to an Indian) of all her valuables but had partially slit the throat of a sick man who was staying with them and thrown him over the bank of Ottawa Creek.[11]

From Jones's place Brown took Parsons to a secret camp somewhere near Lawrence (where Jason joined them later). On September 7 Brown rode into town on a gray horse, with his gun across his saddle and a dazed expression on his face. The old man was well known in Lawrence and as he moved down the street men cheered "as loudly as if the President had come to town, but John Brown seemed not to hear it and paid not the slightest attention." Somebody told him that a war council headed by Jim Lane and James A. Harvey was then in session and was planning a raid against proslavery strongholds around Leavenworth. But Brown was not interested in either accompanying or leading the raid, and rode on.[12]

Later that same day, however, Brown went out to Harvey's camp and told him: "I want some of your men to go & assist me in repelling the outrages of the Border Ruffians. I have suffered from Free State men every indignity that they could heap upon me, yet I am determined to serve throughout the war." But Harvey "talked rather discouragingly"—that is, he probably pointed out that Lawrence might soon be attacked by the Missourians, or even occupied by U.S. troops, and that he wanted to keep all his men around the town. C. G. Allen, lying ill in a nearby tent, overheard what Brown said next. "Well, you can think about it & give me an answer after awhile." In a moment somebody reported that Lane was giving speeches in Lawrence and that certain persons wanted Brown to come in and say a few words. Brown snapped, "I would not come if Gen. Lane himself should send for me," and walked off in a huff. Allen later claimed that he heard some people say they thought Brown was "insane" after the battle of Osawatomie.[13]

Brown may not have been "insane" but something was obviously weighing on his mind as he went about town that day. Somehow he found time to dash off a short letter to Mary, in which he notified her of Frederick's death without a trace of emotion. Perhaps he regarded that event, however tragic to him personally, as a providential sign showing him what must be done. He grandly asserted that in the battle of Osawatomie "we killed & wounded from 70 to 80 of the enemy *as they say*." (While this was an exaggeration of about ten times the number of casualties Reid had sustained, Reid was just as inaccurate, reporting that he had "killed about thirty" abolitionists including Old Brown himself.) Brown also wrote that he had been slightly injured, but that " 'Hitherto the Lord hath helped me,' notwithstanding my afflictions." At the same time, "in great haste, in the midst of constant interruptions," he prepared an account of "the Fight of Osawatomie" for the press—an obvious move to gain publicity for himself in Eastern newspapers. Not insignificantly, he was soon referring to himself as "John Brown of Osawatomie."[14]

For several days Brown came and went, his mind busy with plots. Certainly he was on the verge of something big during these mid-September days. E. A. Coleman later claimed that Brown came to his house near Lawrence and told him and his wife that God had used him "as an instrument for killing men" and would use him "to kill a great many more." Others heard Brown say that he had his mission just as Christ did—that God had appointed him "a special angel of death" to destroy slavery with the sword.[15]

If so, he had to have an army of loyal, God-fearing men, and as he came and went in Lawrence between September 8 and 16 he inducted seven more recruits into his regular company—among them sixteen-year-old William H. Leeman of Maine. On September 10 Brown met briefly with John Jr., who had been released from prison on $1,000 bail. Then the old man disappeared again, probably returning to his secret camp somewhere near Lawrence.

4

Plenty of dramatic events were going on around Brown during those tense fall days. On September 9 Governor Geary arrived in the territory and issued a public statement from Lecompton: "Men of the North—men of the South—of the East and of the West in Kansas. . . . Will you not suspend fratricidal strife? Will you not cease to regard each other as enemies, and look upon one another as the children of a common mother, and come and reason together?" He vowed to put an end to all guerrilla warfare, whether carried out by proslavery or free-state marauders, and to be an impartial but firm and resolute governor. He seemed in earnest, too, for in his first proclamation he disbanded the proslavery Kansas militia (a move that alarmed proslavery officials in Washington) and called for the formation of a new militia force composed of bona fide settlers. Moreover, on September 10 (the day Brown met with John Jr.), Robinson and the other prisoners charged with treason were set free and returned to Lawrence in triumph, something which heartened free-state men all over the territory. "Wednesday was indeed a glorious day for Kansas," the newspaper correspondent Richard J. Hinton recorded in his journal. Everybody in town turned out to receive Robinson and his colleagues and "in the evening a large meeting was held and speeches made." But the excitement quickly subsided when reports arrived that proslavery gangs had been prowling around Lawrence. Ignoring the governor's proclamation, Colonel Harvey raided Easton, Alexandria, and other towns near Leavenworth, returning to

Lawrence on Friday morning with a number of horses, guns, and other confiscated supplies. Hinton, watching Harvey's men ride jubilantly down the street with a captured enemy flag, wrote in his journal: "Glory God is on our side."

So, it seemed, was Governor Geary. Trying to ward off any further guerrilla action, Geary came to Lawrence on Saturday morning with some 200 troops under Lieutenant Colonel Philip St. George Cooke. First the governor held a conference with Robinson and "other principal men," then addressed a large crowd in an open-air meeting. Geary promised to protect the lives and property of the citizens of Lawrence and hoped that in return they would give him their support. He acknowledged that the proslavery laws were "obnoxious" to free-soilers, promised "that he would see justice done" if free-soilers would refrain from violence, and said that if they "were in any danger to let him know." Then he and the troops headed back for Lecompton. Robinson, for his part, was somewhat dubious about Geary's true intentions, but agreed to see the "farce" through.

Sometime that Saturday Robinson sent a puzzling note to "Captain Brown," still hiding somewhere outside of town. "Governor Geary has been here and talks very well," the note read. "There will be no attempt to arrest any one for a few days, and I think no attempt to arrest you is contemplated by him. . . . If convenient, can you not come to town and see us? I will then tell you all that the governor said and talk of some other matters."

On the back of the note was a message from John Jr.: "I am inclined to the belief that unless something unusual shall turn up within a few days, you had better return home, as I have no doubt an attempt will be made to arrest you, as well as Lane, whom Geary says he is under obligations to arrest. His plan, no doubt, will be to get the assistance of Free-State men to aid in making arrests. Don't allow yourself to be trapped in that way. Captain Walker thinks of going East *via* Nebraska soon. I do hope you will go with him, for I am sure that you will be no more likely to be let alone than Lane. *Don't go into that secret refugee plan as talked of by Robinson, I beg of you.*"

Secret refugee plan? John Jr. did not explain what he meant, but it is possible (as James Malin has conjectured) that the plan was

connected with proposals certain Eastern militants had made—that if
the federal government failed to protect free-soilers in Kansas, then
the Northern states should send armed units to the Territory. In any
case, Brown ignored John Jr.'s warning and decided to go into
Lawrence and talk with Robinson the next day.[16]

Meanwhile reports had arrived that the Missourians were assem-
bling in large numbers at Franklin. Were they going to attack
Lawrence? Or were they after James Lane, who was besieging a
proslavery fort at Hickory Point in Jefferson County, north of
Lawrence? Harvey, convinced that they were after Lane, led a force
of about 200 men out to reinforce him, only to find that the
"General" had abandoned the siege and mysteriously disappeared
(he was fleeing to Nebraska so that U.S. authorities could not arrest
him). Harvey then attacked Hickory Point, but the next day United
States troops out looking for Captain "Whipple" caught and captured Harvey's force (although the colonel himself managed to
escape).

That same Sunday Lawrence received ominous intelligence that
an army of Missourians was marching on the town. Robinson and
other "leading citizens" sent a messenger to summon Geary and the
U.S. Army and then held a meeting in a large stone building to plan
the defense of the town. Brown walked in on the meeting early that
Sunday afternoon, accompanied by the abolitionist correspondent,
Richard J. Hinton. Brown listened impatiently to all the talk, then
he went out to the forts and bunkers where some 300 armed citizens
were scanning the timber along the Kaw. Presently a column of about
200 Missourians—the advance guard of a larger force—emerged from
the trees and headed toward town. At once a contingent of free-state
men moved out to skirmish with the invaders on the prairie. Brown,
watching the engagement from a round fort on the edge of town,
told a group of men that if they fired low when the Missourians
charged they could easily whip them. But the Missourians soon withdrew. And Brown himself left the earthworks and went back into
town.[17]

Sometime that day Brown met with Robinson, talked with him
about those "other matters" he had mentioned in his note, and
persuaded him to write a couple of letters in Brown's behalf. In the
first letter Robinson declared that, "so far as I have been informed"

(he had been in prison since late May and probably knew very little about Brown's connection with the Pottawatomie massacre and his work in the guerrilla war that followed), Brown's course "has been such as to merit the highest praise for every patriot, and I cheerfully accord to you my heartfelt thanks for your prompt, efficient, and timely action against the invaders of our rights and the murderers of our citizens. History will give your name a proud place on her pages, and posterity will pay your heroism in the cause of God and humanity." In the second document, addressed "TO THE SETTLERS OF KANSAS," Robinson wrote: "If possible, please render Captain John Brown all the assistance he may require in defending Kansas from invaders and outlaws." Signed: "C. Robinson." With these two "letters of introduction" stuffed in his pocket (for perhaps they were all he had really come to town for), Brown did next to nothing in defense of Lawrence during the next twenty-four hours.[18]

Actually he did not have to, because the U.S. Army intervened and prevented the Missouri main body—some 2,700 strong—from doing any violence to Lawrence. The first troops under Lieutenant Colonel Joseph E. Johnston reached the town at 9 P.M. Sunday night and took up a position on Mount Oread just as the Missouri army was massing along the Wakarusa. The next morning Geary and Cooke rode into Lawrence, conferred with Johnston, then hurried down to Franklin to talk with Atchison, Reid, Stringfellow, and the other Missouri captains. The governor warned them that another sacking of Lawrence would recoil upon the proslavery cause, for it might ruin Democratic chances in the forthcoming presidential election, which pitted "dough-faced" Democrat James Buchanan against John Charles Frémont, candidate of the newly formed Republican party. Again the Missouri captains grudgingly acquiesced and led their unhappy men home. Thereupon Geary and Cooke returned to Lawrence, where the governor assured the citizens that he intended to maintain permanent law and order. To prove it, he proceeded to execute evenhanded justice, as authorities under his direction arrested and jailed numerous free-state "trouble-makers" and issued warrants for John H. Stringfellow and other proslavery rowdies and freebooters as well. In time Geary would almost completely pacify Kansas, and thus bring an end to a civil war that had claimed nearly 200 lives and cost some $2 million in destroyed property.

It is possible that Geary ordered the arrest of Brown, too, and that this was why the old man vanished from Lawrence and turned up in Osawatomie a few days later. Since things were rather quiet in Kansas now (and since Brown was certain that U.S. troops were looking for him), he decided to leave the territory and launch a fund-raising campaign in the East for an extraordinary new scheme he had been mulling over in his mind. The letters from Robinson and his own accounts of Black Jack and Osawatomie would get him started with "all the right people," especially in Boston. He left his volunteer-regular company under James H. Holmes with orders "to carry the war into Africa" (which they did by raiding Missouri later that year). As Brown prepared to leave Osawatomie he fell ill with a severe case of dysentery which in turn brought on a "Chill fever." Still ill in late September, he took John Jr., Jason, and their families to hide with a friend near Lawrence, hoping to elude whatever troops and lawmen were on his trail. The friend was Augustus Wattles, a former student of Lane Seminary and a devoted abolition-ist who had once operated a school for Negroes back in Cincinnati. Wattles was now an associate editor of the Lawrence *Herald of Freedom.*[19]

Early in October Brown started the womenfolk for Ohio "by way of the River," then set out for Nebraska with John Jr., Jason, and Owen (who had returned to Kansas sometime earlier). As the party headed across Nebraska, Iowa, and the Northwestern states, the sick old man lay on a bed inside the wagon, his feverish mind filled with visions of a guerrilla force—more or less like that associated with his old Subterranean Pass Way scheme—fighting in mountain passes and ravines for the liberation of the slaves. On the trail he started writing in a notebook the name of anybody (militant Negroes, "military" abolitionists) who might help in his new enterprise. He left Owen at Tabor in Iowa (henceforth Brown's secret headquarters), just missed Salmon and Watson who were going out to Kansas to kill Frederick's murderer, and stopped in Chicago to meet some officers of the National Kansas Committee. He returned to Iowa long enough to find Salmon and Owen and then hurried back to Ohio, where Jason and John Jr. had already gone to meet their families. In Ohio Brown visited Governor Salmon P. Chase, who wrote a letter of introduc-tion for him. Then the old man caught a train for New York state and Boston, on what could well be the greatest mission of his life.[20]

Jeremiah Anderson, a native of Indiana and a member of James Montgomery's free-state company before joining Brown in Kansas. *Library of Congress*

John A. Copeland, a Negro college student from Oberlin who went to Harpers Ferry because he wanted "to liberate a few of my poor and oppressed people." *Library of Congress*

Osborn P. Anderson, one of Brown's Negro recruits from Canada. *Library of Congress*

John E. Cook, an effervescent and impulsive young man who had a way with women ("mothers as well as maidens") and a rage for talking. *Library of Congress*

Barclay Coppoc, from a Quaker family of Springdale, Iowa, who joined Brown's company in 1858. *Library of Congress*

Shields Green, nicknamed "Emperor," an ex-slave and friend of Frederick Douglass, who introduced him to Brown in 1858. *Boyd B. Stutler*

Edwin Coppoc, brother of Barclay, twenty-four years old at the time of the raid. *Library of Congress*

Albert Hazlett, "a good-sized, fine looking fellow, overflowing with good nature and social feelings," who joined Brown's company in Kansas in 1858. *Library of Congress*

John Henry Kagi, Brown's articulate and noble-minded Secretary of War. *Kansas State Historical Society, Topeka*

William H. Leeman, twenty, the youngest of the raiders. *Kansas State Historical Society, Topeka*

Lewis Leary, mulatto, an uncle of John A. Copeland, who left a wife and child at Oberlin in order to join Brown "at Harper's Ferry, in Virginia." *Kansas State Historical Society, Topeka*

Francis Jackson Meriam, twenty-one at the time of the raid. Frail, one-eyed nephew of Francis Jackson, a well-known abolitionist. *Library of Congress*

Aaron D. Stevens, a strapping fellow with "black, brooding" eyes, who regarded slavery as such a shocking social wrong that he was ready to incite a revolution to get rid of it. *Library of Congress*

Dangerfield Newby, the oldest raider at forty-eight, a mulatto ex-slave (his white father had set him and his brothers and sisters free) who hoped to liberate his wife and his own children from a plantation at Brentville, Va. *Library of Congress*

Stewart Taylor, a Canadian and a spiritualist who, according to Annie, was "nearer a born crank than any other man in the company." *Library of Congress*

Dauphin Thompson, twenty-one years old at the time of the raid, brother of William and Henry Thompson (Ruth's husband) and youngest of a family of eighteen children residing at North Elba. *Library of Congress*

William Thompson, Dauphin Thompson's older brother, twenty-six at the time of the raid. Annie described him as being "an easy-going, good-natured person who enjoyed telling funny stories." He was "kind-hearted and generous to a fault." *Library of Congress*

Charles Plummer Tidd, a hot-tempered recruit from Maine who 'was a fine singer and of strong family affections.'

Richard Realf, an Englishman and published poet who enlisted in Brown's company in 1858. *Library of Congress*

George P. Gill, Secretary of Treasury of Brown's "Provisional Government" who had worked on a whaling ship in the Pacific before he went to Kansas and became involved with Brown. *Library of Congress*

Frederick Douglass, one of Brown's closest friends and among the leading Negroes of his generation. *Kansas State Historical Society, Topeka*

Hugh Forbes, the mysterious "colonel" and drillmaster whom Brown enlisted in New York in 1857. *Library of Congress*

James Henry Lane, a hatchet-faced Indianan of "infectuous enthusiasm" who became one of the chief free-state. guerrilla captains in Bleeding Kansas. *Kansas State Historical Society, Topeka*

James Redpath, hyperbolic free-state newspaper correspondent who wrote the first legend-building biography of Brown. *Kansas State Historical Society, Topeka*

PART THREE

PROPHECY

XIV

FOR THE CAUSE OF LIBERTY

ᘓᗯᘔ

IT WAS JUST AFTER THE NEW YEAR, 1857, when Brown stepped off the train at Boston and called on Franklin B. Sanborn at the headquarters of the Massachusetts State Kansas Committee on snow-covered School Street. Sanborn was a twenty-five-year-old schoolteacher from nearby Concord, who had taken a leave of absence for the winter so that he could devote full time to his duties as committee secretary in Boston. Some of the most influential militant abolitionists in Massachusetts were members of that committee, and Brown needed their support —their contacts and their money—if his great new mission against proslavery forces was to succeed. He hoped young Sanborn could be persuaded to introduce him to the Boston committeemen and any other wealthy reformers who might help in his cause.

Brown had learned about Sanborn from his former brother-in-law, whom the old man had just visited in Springfield. A romantic idealist and very impressionable, Sanborn had graduated from Harvard only two years before and with Emerson's help had opened a school in Concord, where he had attached himself to the town's celebrated intellectual community. Although he was a generation behind the literary gentlemen of Concord, Sanborn "made up in enthusiasm for what he lacked in experience" and later wrote a procession of worshipful biographies of Emerson, Thoreau, Bronson Alcott, and other men he idolized. By the time he was twenty-five, Sanborn had become a sort of intellectual apprentice among Concord's literati: he had long discussions with Emerson, accompanied Thoreau and William Ellery Channing on their nature walks, visited

181

the Hawthornes, and wrote a column of "literary chit-chat" for the Springfield *Republican*.[1] He had grown up on a farm near Hampton Falls, a gangly and bookish farm youth who loved to read about the exploits of great men. At the age of twelve he had already mastered the Bible and Plutarch's *Lives*, studied Greek, and collected with his own money all the Waverley novels of Sir Walter Scott and the complete works of Lord Byron. He spent many an exciting afternoon in the library of his Calvinist grandfather, absorbed in books about the bloody heroics of the leaders of the Scottish Reformation. Precocious in religious matters, too, he had proclaimed himself a Universalist "at the mature age of nine." As he grew older he shifted to Unitarianism and became an ardent admirer of James Freeman Clarke, Thomas Wentworth Higginson, and Theodore Parker, all outspoken Unitarian ministers and abolitionists. Sanborn championed immediate emancipation, too, and believed without question in the alleged Slave Power conspiracy, thanks to the high-powered abolitionist writings he studied in the *National Era* and Horace Greeley's New York *Tribune*.

In his late teens he fell in love with an older girl named Ariana Walker, whose family was considerably richer than his own. Ariana had high hopes for her tall, bookish suitor whose delicate good looks reminded her of "the early portrait of Raphael." At her encouragement Sanborn attended Phillips Exeter Academy and then went to Harvard. They wrote one another moving love letters and made plans for marriage. But at Harvard he received the news that Ariana was dying of some neurological disease from which she had suffered since childhood. Sanborn married her literally on her deathbed (she was buried eight days later), treasured her letters for the rest of his life, and became something of a tragic celebrity in Boston Brahmin society because of his "romantic engagement, marriage and bereavement." Graduating from Harvard shortly after Ariana's death, he moved out to Concord, rented a room in Ellery Channing's home, and secured Emerson's support for his school, which Emerson's children attended.[2]

When civil war broke out in Kansas, Sanborn joined the Kansas aid movement, passed through "all the grades of the Kansas committees," and even made a trip west to inspect the emigrant route through Iowa. He had just begun his duties as secretary of the Massachusetts Kansas Committee when Brown came to see him in Boston shortly after the New Year, 1857. The old man presented him with glowing letters of introduction—two from Charles Robinson, another from Governor Salmon P. Chase of Ohio, and still another from Sanborn's former brother-in-law, George Walker, who had known Brown as a wool merchant in Springfield. Brown came directly to the point about what he wanted of Sanborn. He had heard that anti-slavery and free-soil circles in New England had been aroused by the border ruffian atrocities reported in the Northern press and that various state and local Kansas aid societies had assiduously collected guns, money, and supplies for free-state settlers in the territory. He knew that the Garrisonians had stridently demanded disunion to separate the North from the Slave Power and that other abolitionists —Gerrit Smith and Thomas Wentworth Higginson—had even argued that Northern states should send armed columns out to protect free-soil Kansans if the federal government refused to do so. Anti-slavery groups in Massachusetts, Connecticut, and New York had contributed thousands of dollars to the save-Kansas movement, and Brown had a plan for the defense of the territory that should appeal to them. He explained that he was already recruiting a volunteer-regular company and working out a general defense of Kansas that would involve vigilance units to patrol the border and home guard outfits to protect free-state communities (a plan he may have borrowed from Robinson). But he needed 200 Sharps rifles and $30,000 to carry on his work and wanted Sanborn to help him get the guns and money. He could introduce Brown to the rest of the committee and other friends of Kansas in Boston and assist him in setting up speaking engagements in Massachusetts, Connecticut, and New York.[3]

Young Sanborn was swept off his feet. He had heard about Brown before—the hero of the battle of Black Jack, the defender of Osawatomie—and here he was, sitting right in front of Sanborn in Boston. In Sanborn's romantic vision Brown was like some fantastic border hero straight out of a Scott novel, with his "tall, slender, and commanding figure," his "military bearing," his "singular blending of the soldier and the deacon," and his fire-and-brimstone Calvinism —all of which reminded Sanborn of Oliver Cromwell.

Of course Sanborn would help Brown raise money for his work

in Kansas. Over the next couple of days they held a series of intense private discussions about the civil war in Kansas and Brown's own role in the fighting there. As a result of their talks Sanborn concluded that Brown was not only an expert in military matters but practically single-handed had prevented the Missourians from taking over the territory. The more he got to know Brown the more he found something irresistible in the violence that surrounded the old man, in the visionary look in his "piercing gray" eyes, and in the unyielding tone in his slow, "masculine, deep and metallic" voice. How could anybody refuse to help a warrior "of the unmixed Puritan breed" like Captain Brown? How could anybody resist a man so "conscious of a work laid upon him, and confident that he could accomplish it?" How could *Sanborn* resist such a man?[4]

On January 5 Sanborn wrote his friend Wentworth Higginson of Worcester: " 'Old Brown' of Kansas is now in Boston with one of his sons, working for an object in which you will heartily sympathize—raising and arming a company of men for the future protection of Kansas." Could Higginson come to Boston and meet Brown? If not, could he indicate when he would be in Worcester so Brown could visit him there? Sanborn added, with considerable understatement: "I like the man from what I have seen and his deeds ought to bear witness for him."[5]

Sanborn also took Brown to meet forty-seven-year-old Theodore Parker, the most eloquent and controversial Unitarian minister of his day. His radical sermons called for a new theology, a science of religion that interpreted facts in accordance with human experience and the immanence of God in nature. Sermons like that sounded atheistic to even the broadest of Unitarians, and the result was that all regular pulpits had been closed to him. So he had opened his own "church" in the Boston Music Hall, where he preached every Sunday to enthusiastic audiences—mostly young admirers like Franklin Sanborn—who appreciated his wit, his erudition, and his moral outrage over slavery, intemperance, wars, the mistreatment of criminals and the insane, and all the religious hypocrisies of their time. Brown had heard Parker preach before, back in 1853, and while they "were worlds apart in theology," Brown respected Parker's "deep piety, popular eloquence, and devotion to liberty."

Parker gloried in a feeling of martyrdom (as Brown would do

later), declaring that he was prepared to endure controversy and
ostracism because "the Father is with me." A man of prodigious
learning (he had mastered nineteen or twenty languages), Parker
was dogmatic and supremely egotistical—traits which prompted Julia
Ward Howe to remark that if he became Catholic "the world would
have two Popes instead of one." As late as 1842 Parker had opposed
the abolitionists—he thought them too fanatical—and even refused to
read one of their petitions in his church. But the "Slave Power conspiracies" that allegedly lay behind the annexation of Texas, the
Mexican War, and the fugitive slave law had made him a radical
"disunion abolitionist" like his friend Higginson. Parker had always
detested slavery anyway. Although he believed that the black man
was inferior to the whites "in general intellectual power," he
remained convinced that slavery was an egregious violation of God's
Higher Law—an evil that not even Negroes should tolerate. In 1850
he had felt like "a Hebrew prophet" after delivering a fiery speech
against the fugitive slave law, and in that same year had cried: "God
forgive us our cowardice if we let it come to this, that three million of
human beings . . . degraded by us, must wade through slaughter to
their inalienable rights." Parker marveled at the thunder and lightning in his own speeches, and when Brown came to meet him in the
Music Hall that January and made the same kind of bloody prophecies, Parker was very much taken with the old man. The minister
especially enjoyed Brown's prediction that civil war would break out
again in Kansas, expressed an interest in his work, and offered to
hold a reception for him at his Boston home.[6]

Several prominent Bostonians came to meet "the famous Kansas
chieftain" at Parker's house. Among them was William Lloyd Garrison, a bald, bespectacled man who looked more like a scholar
than the crusading editor of the *Liberator*. Garrison remained
convinced that he was God's chosen instrument for eradicating
slavery, not by violence but by nonresistance and moral suasion
(even though he had confused his position with his frequent and
strident outcries for disunion). Although the abolitionist crusade
had long since divided into a number of squabbling factions, some
demanding political action, others advocating violent interference
with slavery in the West, Garrison still regarded himself as the leader
of the true abolitionists, still argued that his methods of nonviolent,

nonpolitical protest were the only right ones. Inevitably the reception at Parker's home turned into a dramatic confrontation between Garrison and Brown, who not only disagreed as to methods but also represented two fundamentally different religious approaches to abolitionism—Garrison's based in large part on radical perfectionist doctrine and the pacifist teachings of Christ, Brown's on the grim injunctions of Calvinist theology and Old Testament justice. Surrounded by a small group of "interested listeners," the two men of God argued about peace and nonresistance, "Brown quoting the Old Testament against Garrison's citations from the New, and Parker from time to time injecting a bit of Lexington into the controversy." Brown scorned Garrison's "milk-and-water" pacifism and never took the celebrated crusader into his confidence. And what did Garrison think of Brown? Actually, in spite of their differences, Garrison was rather impressed with that "tall, spare, farmer-like man, with head disproportionately small, and that inflexible mouth."[7]

It is significant that, although Brown actually stood about five-feet-nine, almost everybody he met in Boston saw him as a "tall" man.

2

The signs were propitious indeed. Parker was willing to endorse Brown's Kansas work and Sanborn was lining up support among the other friends of freedom in Boston. On January 7 Brown himself called on Amos A. Lawrence, the principal benefactor for the New England Emigrant Aid Society and a rich Boston reformer after whom the town of Lawrence had been named. They had a long talk about the Kansas difficulties, and Lawrence (who knew nothing about Brown's part in the Pottawatomie massacre—nobody in Boston knew anything about that) was most impressed with Brown's plans to defend the territory. Lawrence thought "the old partisan hero" a temperate and pious man, yet "a dreadful foe" when aroused. Dubbing him "the Miles Standish of Kansas," Lawrence pledged $1,000 a year, "for the purpose of supporting John Brown's family and keeping the proposed company in the field," until Kansas entered the Union as a free state.[8]

Meanwhile Sanborn had arranged interviews for Brown with Dr. Samuel Gridley Howe, George Luther Stearns, and other members of the Massachusetts Kansas Committee. They all listened intently as the old man gave his grim appraisal of the situation in Kansas. He denounced Governor Geary as a tool of the proslavery Administration and argued that he had not "*saved* Lawrence, as he boasts of doing in his message to the bogus Legislature!" Brown had written an account of "the Lawrence Foray," pointing out that he was there during the last Missouri invasion and saw the whole thing. He insisted that Geary "*did not on that memorable occasion* get a single soldier on the ground until after the enemy had retreated back to Franklin." This was patently false, but that did not bother Brown, for anything he said in his private war against slavery was justifiable. And so he could argue (and probably believe) that the United States government had spent half a million dollars trying "to harass poor Free-State settlers in Kansas, and to violate all law, and *all right, moral and constitutional,* for the *sole and only purpose* of forcing slavery upon that Territory. I challenge this whole nation to prove before God or mankind the contrary. Who paid this money to enslave the settlers of Kansas and worry them out? I say nothing in this estimate of the money wasted by Congress in the management of this horrible, tyrannical, and damnable affair."[9] What was going to happen next in Kansas? Brown was certain that the Missourians would attack again in the spring. Thus it was imperative that the Massachusetts Committee give him all the guns and money it could spare, so that he could put his plan of defense into operation as quickly as possible.

Dr. Howe did not fully agree with what Brown said about Geary. But the doctor admired Brown's pugnacity and said he wanted to help. The two became immediate friends. A dashing adventurer with an insatiable love for romantic causes, Howe had fought in the Greek Revolution against Turkey, had been knighted by the king as a "Chevalier of the Order of St. Savior" (whence came his nickname "Chev"), and had aided the Polish rebels in their insurrection against Russia. Driven by a passion to correct social wrongs at home, too, Howe had pioneered educational reforms for the blind, the insane, and the feeble-minded. He and his wife, plump and round-faced Julia Ward Howe, were both militant abolitionists and uncompromising foes of the Slave Power (Howe had actually visited the South in 1841 and 1842, had witnessed some of the evils of slavery at first hand, and had been "terribly upset" at what he had seen in a Negro section of a New Orleans prison). By the time Brown met him, Howe had helped a score of runaways through Boston (where he and Parker had organized vigilance committees in open defiance of the federal government) and had joined both the Massachusetts and National Kansas committees. In the summer of 1856 he had visited the Kansas-Nebraska border as an agent of the National Committee. And since Geary had become governor, he had tried his best to assess conditions in Kansas realistically. As 1857 opened and peace continued there, the doctor wondered whether Geary was not actually a man of his word: he was maintaining strict law and order in the territory and did not seem really hostile to the free-state cause. The territory was presently caught up in a land boom ("Land! Land! is the cry," an agent of the National Committee wrote from Lawrence), and Howe may have invested there himself. Believing that free-state forces were on the verge of victory, Howe had urged a Boston relief committee to discontinue operations and announce that Kansas had no more need of contributions. Yet he did think that the Massachusetts legislature should follow that of Vermont and appropriate up to $200,000 for relief; and he was more than ready to give money and guns to Brown, too, just in case the spirited warrior with the "flashing eyes" was right in his predictions that Missouri would strike again in the spring.[10]

George Luther Stearns, the chairman of the Massachusetts Committee, agreed with Howe. A big, solemn merchant who suffered from chronic bronchitis and wore a long beard to protect his chest, Stearns owned a linseed oil mill, cleared from $15,000 to $20,000 a year in profits, and lived in a luxurious Tudor-style mansion in suburban Medford. Although he was a self-made Yankee businessman, having worked his way up from a clerk in his uncle's store, Stearns gave his money cheerfully to benevolent causes, dined with his good friend Charles Sumner at the "Bird Club" (an antislavery group, of which Howe was a member, that met weekly at the Parker House in Boston), helped set up a fugitive slave as a barber in Harvard Square, and freely opened his purse—and persuaded his customers and business colleagues to give as well—to the Massachusetts Kansas Committee. When Sanborn first introduced him to

Brown, they met "like the iron and the magnet," and from then on Stearns was one of Brown's most dedicated and industrious supporters. Although contributions had fallen off sharply since hostilities in Kansas had ceased, Stearns pressed the Massachusetts Committee to help Brown and openly praised him for his "sagacity, courage, and stern integrity."

On January 7 the Massachusetts Committee, accepting without question Brown's claim that he wanted aid only "for the defense of Kansas," voted to make him their agent and gave him 200 Sharps rifles and several boxes of caps and cartridges, which the committee had stored in the Rev. John Todd's cellar at Tabor in Iowa. In addition they authorized Brown to draw on the committee treasurer for "not less" than $500 to cover his expenses. Later the committee voted to let him sell 100 rifles to free-soilers in Kansas and give the proceeds to suffering families there; and it also gave him $500 more so that he could return to the territory with the guns he had collected. Stearns personally authorized Brown to buy 200 revolvers from the Massachusetts Arms Company and later paid the $1,300 bill out of his own pocket.[11]

On January 9 Wentworth Higginson, who himself had just returned from Kansas and was now organizing a disunion convention to convene at Worcester, came to Boston and had a talk with Brown. Higginson was thirty-four years old, a tall, belligerent clergyman who liked "to pitch right into people and show them how foolish they are thinking and acting." Although he was now one of the angriest and most outspoken abolitionists in New England, Higginson had been a shy and introspective youth. He, too, had grown up in a world of books, had entered Harvard at the age of thirteen and graduated in the class of 1841. At Harvard, he befriended Theodore Parker and Samuel Longfellow, younger brother of the poet and a truly "beautiful soul." A physical fitness enthusiast, Higginson ran everywhere, did calisthenics, and played something comparable to touch football. He taught for a time in Samuel Weld's school for boys, then felt the call to preach and entered Harvard Divinity School. There he formed "a romantic attachment" with "a brilliant youth" named William Hurlbert, whom he loved "out of the depths of my heart." But bored with the rigid curriculum, Higginson quit school and became an intellectual recluse in a Boston boardinghouse.

He soon abandoned his "mere intellectual" life for an active Christian one of "Love and Spiritual Trust," finished Divinity School, and plunged into a stormy career as a Unitarian minister and crusading reformer. He proclaimed himself "a disunion abolitionist" at twenty-two, helped runaways on the Underground Railroad, asserted that "the worst trait of the American race seems to me this infernal colorphobia," ran for Congress as a Free-Soil candidate, campaigned for temperance and woman's rights, and married his second cousin Mary Elizabeth Channing, a highly intellectual but sickly woman who was an invalid during most of their married life. In 1847 he began preaching in the First Religious Society of Newburyport, where he outraged his conservative congregation (including racist sea captains) with his radical antislavery sermons. Later he moved to the Free Church of Worcester, where there were "radicals of all descriptions" who enjoyed Higginson's angry denunciations of slavery and the Slave Power. In 1851 he launched a public crusade against the fugitive slave law (that "most cruel and unrighteous bill") and in 1854 led a mob that broke into the Boston courthouse in an abortive attempt to liberate a runaway named Anthony Burns. Several policemen attacked the would-be liberators, and in the melee Higginson received a cut on the chin—a "battle wound" that was to leave a conspicuous scar. In all his zealous work he still found time to write loving letters to his friend Hurlbert, as was the custom among male friends in that Victorian era. When civil war erupted in Kansas, Higginson joined both the Massachusetts and National Kansas committees. In the summer and fall of 1856 he made a tour of the smoldering border country, visited Lawrence shortly after Brown had left for Osawatomie, and saw a slave market in St. Louis that made him sick to his stomach. He wrote in his journal: "My hope is that the contest may be at once transferred to more favorable soil, Nebraska or Iowa, and result in the disruption of the Union, for I am sure the disease is too deep for cure without amputation." He hurried back to Worcester and with over eighty other men issued a call for a Massachusetts Disunion Convention to convene at Worcester on January 15.[12]

Higginson did not record how he reacted to Brown in their meeting in Boston on January 9. He merely noted in his journal that Brown was raising means for the defense of Kansas. Higginson then returned to Worcester, where the disunion convention took place as scheduled and resulted in a call for a national convention to meet in the summer. After the Worcester convention, Higginson received an urgent plea from Sanborn in Brown's behalf. "Can anything be done for the good old man in Worcester County among your friends?" Higginson, who may have seen Brown again by this time, approved of the old man's efforts to raise money in Worcester and apparently did what he could to help. Not quite so captivated by Brown's "flashing eyes" as his colleagues in Boston, Higginson nevertheless admired Brown's "puritan virtues" and enjoyed his conspiratorial air. And who knew but what "the Ethan Allen of Kansas" might not be the man to provoke a major conflict on the Kansas-Nebraska border that would lead to disunion? When the chaplain of the Massachusetts legislature wrote that "I expect to serve in Capt. John Brown's company in the next Kansas war, which I hope is inevitable and near at hand," Higginson was so excited that he resigned his pastorate in order to lecture, write, and promote the cause of disunion full time. Because of "the present condition of the country . . . which is likely to exist for several years," he said, "there will be an increasing demand on me from outside."[13]

3

The more they talked about Kansas, the South, and the plight of the Negro in the United States, the more entranced George Luther Stearns became with Captain Brown. On January 11, after Higginson had gone back to Worcester, Stearns took Brown out to his landscaped mansion and introduced him to his sons and his wife, Mary. Mary was a quarrelsome and high-minded woman who scolded Stearns for working too hard and entertaining too little, but who shared his humanitarian interests and his abolitionism. Mary took to Brown even more zealously than her husband had done; she could scarcely keep her eyes off him that evening, as he entertained the boys with a blow-by-blow account of his victory at Black Jack. He also told how the border ruffians had murdered free-state settlers and remarked that at this very moment fatherless children were crying from hunger in numerous cabins in the territory. Brown's descriptions moved twelve-year-old Henry so much that he gave the old man his own savings in order to relieve some suffering child in Kansas.

Then he asked: "Captain Brown, will you sometime write me a letter, and tell me what sort of little boy you were?" Brown smiled and said that he was very busy with his work now, but that he would when he had the time.[14]

So far Brown's visit to Boston had been a resounding success (thanks in no small part to Franklin Sanborn), and the old man was anxious to get on the lecture circuit. He still had to raise about $30,000 for the kind of activities he was now plotting against the proslavery enemy (activities on a far larger scale—and in a different direction—than any of his new friends realized). Before he left Boston, however, Brown wanted to meet one more abolitionist celebrity—Charles Sumner, who had almost been beaten to death in the Senate chamber on the same day that Lawrence had been sacked. Visiting Sumner's home, Brown asked to see the coat the senator had worn when Brooks of South Carolina had accosted him. Sumner, still recuperating from the assault, limped painfully to the closet and handed the coat to Brown. It was stiff from dried blood. Examining it closely, the old man said nothing, but "his lips compressed and his eyes shown like polished steel."[15]

A few days later, Brown joined Sanborn, and together they took a train to New York, where the National Kansas Committee planned to hold its annual meeting in the Astor House.

4

Appearing before the committee on January 24, Brown declared that he wanted all the guns it had and $1,174 worth of military supplies for his company of "mounted rangers," who supposedly would operate on the Kansas border. Sanborn proposed that the committee not only grant Brown's request, but pledge him from $5,000 to $10,000 as well. At that several Western delegates led by Henry B. Hurd of Chicago objected strenuously, because they thought the old man too violent and unpredictable to be trusted. The discussion was a heated one; in the midst of it Hurd turned to Brown and asked him bluntly: "If you get the arms and money you desire, will you invade Missouri or any slave territory?" Brown refused to be rattled. "I am no adventurer," he replied. "You all know me. You are acquainted with my history. You know what I have done in Kansas. I do not expose my plans. No one knows them but myself, except perhaps one. I will not be interrogated; if you wish to give me anything I want you to give it freely. I have no other purpose but to serve the cause of liberty."

It was a persuasive performance. The "more radical eastern members" carried a vote to transfer what guns the committee possessed to the Massachusetts Kansas Committee (which would, of course, place them in Brown's hands), to give him supplies for 100 men, and to raise $5,000 for his Kansas project. Brown told the committee's Chicago agent to send the supplies to "Jonas Jones" in Tabor. Then he shook hands with young Sanborn (who was going back to Concord) and set out for Peterboro, New York, to see his old friend Gerrit Smith.[16]

5

Brown, of course, had every reason to believe that Smith would give him a small fortune to carry on his war against slavery. In all the antislavery excitement that surrounded the Missouri invasions of Kansas, Smith had become an outspoken militant; he had declared, for example, that "there are instances in which the shedding of blood is unavoidable" and that "nothing short of an army of freedom in Kansas can save Kansas and the nation" and had pledged $10,000 to start an armed company toward the territory, as Ruth had written Brown back in July. Surely this rich abolitionist, whose annual income from all his landholdings was seldom under $60,000, would donate thousands of dollars to Brown's Kansas operations.

But Brown was to be extremely disappointed. Visiting Smith's white-columned mansion early in February, he found Smith totally unresponsive. Smith said that he had pledged $1,000 a year to the National Kansas Committee and that his subscription had caused him considerable embarrassment. He did not elucidate and Brown did not press him for an explanation. Concealing his disappointment, he asked Smith for a list of his North Elba lands, adding that his sons might want to buy some property there one day.[17]

From Peterboro Brown hurried up to North Elba for a brief visit with his family. He had not seen his farm or Mary and the girls in a year and a half—had not even taken the time to visit them last December, on his way to Massachusetts by way of Rochester (where he had called on Frederick Douglass) and Peterboro. The past two winters had been hard on Mary and the girls; while there had been enough to eat, they had not had the money for proper clothes, and Mary had been forced to ask Brown's father for money before he died. Yes, the long cold winters had been difficult without Brown. Yet Mary did not complain. She understood how important his work was to him and was fully prepared to sacrifice for it.

With snow blanketing the fields and mountains around the farmhouse, the Browns enjoyed a partial family reunion, including Owen, Oliver, and Watson, who had returned east with Brown or shortly after him. Ruth and Henry called. They were living on a nearby farm, Ruth knowing little if anything about Henry's connection with the Pottawatomie massacre. Evidently the Thompsons were disappointed because Brown had not paid Henry for building the Browns' frame farmhouse; the old man promised to settle the debt when he could. That evening, with an icy wind pressing against the windows, the Browns enjoyed a family dinner together. Then they retired to the living room, where they talked around a roaring fire. Brown summoned little Ellen—who was just over two now—to come and sit on his knee; he wanted to sing to her. But she drew away in fear of this strange man, with his set mouth and burning eyes, whom she could not remember. Brown told thirteen-year-old Annie to sit with Ellen and comfort the child. Annie obeyed; and with her on one knee and Ellen on the other, Brown started singing the sad and melancholy refrains of his favorite hymn, "Blow ye the trumpet, blow."[18]

6

Anxious to get on with his work, Brown spent only a day or so with his family, then set out for Boston. There, on February 18, he began his fund-raising campaign in earnest, appearing before a joint committee of the Massachusetts legislature on federal relations to urge the appropriation of $100,000 for the defense of Kansas. The address was Sanborn's idea; he and the other members of the Massachusetts Committee had beseeched the legislature to make this appropriation because "the rights and interests of Massachusetts have suffered gross outrage in Kansas" and because Massachusetts emigrants there needed relief. Sanborn introduced Brown as a descendant of a *Mayflower* pilgrim and a spiritual heir of the soldiers of the Revolution. Then he turned the meeting over to "Captain Brown of Osawatomie" who read from a prepared speech. Brown described in detail his own experiences in the Kansas troubles, recounted all the murders and atrocities which the proslavery party had perpetrated there, denounced Governor Geary's pacification program, and asserted that the federal government was "wholly on the side of slavery." The territory needed that $100,000 appropriation, he told the committee; and it needed men—"good men, industrious and honest, who respect themselves, and act only from principle, from the dictates of conscience; men who fear God too much to fear anything human." One senator remarked that things were quiet in Kansas at this time; what danger did Brown foresee? "Whenever we heard last year that the people of the North were doing anything for us," Brown replied, "we were encouraged and strengthened to keep up for the contest. At present there is not much danger of an invasion from Missouri. God protects us in winter; but when the grass gets high enough to feed the horses of the Border Ruffians we may have trouble, and should be prepared for the worst." But despite his vivid descriptions and his prediction that violence would break out anew on the Kansas prairies, the committee remained damnably unimpressed. And in the end the Massachusetts legislature appropriated not a dollar for Kansas, not a single dollar.[19]

But Brown was undaunted. He rode slow, rattling trains all over New England and New York, speaking before antislavery and free-soil audiences in Worcester, Springfield, New Haven, New York, Syracuse, and several towns in Connecticut. Everywhere he went he pleaded for guns and money for the defense of Kansas, accused Geary of complicity with the slavery party, and made prophecies of death and destruction if free-state settlers in Kansas were not protected. On the train between cities he wrote down the names of black men (Dr. James N. Gloucester of Brooklyn, for example) who might help in his cause and kept a list of subscriptions. As he crisscrossed the state of Massachusetts, he finally stopped in Concord, where Sanborn had been trying to get him to attend "a tea party" since late February.[20] Sanborn, tall, ivory cheeked, and bubbling with enthusiasm, met Brown at the depot and took him over to Mrs. Thoreau's house, where he lunched with Thoreau and other boarders. Later Emerson called on an errand and stayed to chat with the famous Captain Brown for a good part of the afternoon. Thoreau and Emerson were both impressed and invited Brown to spend nights with each of them.

That evening Sanborn escorted Brown down to the Town House where over a hundred citizens had gathered to hear Brown's Kansas address. The place was ablaze with lanterns and warmed by a large stove in the middle of the hall. Again Sanborn made a glowing introduction, then Brown began to speak in his slow, imperious tone. Once more he branded the federal government as a tool of the Slave Power, recounted his own sufferings in Bleeding Kansas, and told how U.S. troops there had arrested and *"most barbarously"* marched two of his sons in chains all the way from Osawatomie to Tecumseh. And *"here is the chain,"* he said, "with which one of them was confined, after the cruelty, sufferings, and anxiety he underwent had rendered him a maniac—yes, a maniac." He held up the chain for everybody in the Town House to see. Then he described how the Missourians had murdered innocent God-fearing people and had shot his own son Frederick to death. He declared that proslavery killers like them "had a right to be hung"—a statement that pleased Emerson and Thoreau, who exchanged appreciative nods, and that brought murmurs of approval from the others. Brown did not, of course, mention the murders he had instigated on the Pottawatomie (in fact, he had flatly denied having any connection with the slayings when Sanborn had brought them up earlier). Nor did he say anything about the reprisal raids which free-state forces had made against proslavery strongholds. He blamed all the troubles in the territory on the proslavery government, on the Missourians, on Governor Geary, and contended again that what Kansas needed was men who would fight for their rights—and it needed money, too, a great deal of money. He went on, "without ever giving the least vent to his pent-up fire," Thoreau observed, to speak of his family sufferings: how his wife and daughters were living in near destitution in North

Elba while he and his sons were fighting God's war against an institution of the Devil and the forces of evil that sought to spread it. His vow that he and his remaining sons would never stop fighting until the war was won brought enthusiastic applause from the townspeople, who pledged a modest sum of money and filed out into the chill night convinced that Brown was "the rarest of heroes," as Emerson put it, "a true idealist, with no by-ends of his own." Emerson himself asked that a small subscription he had made to the lyceum be given to Brown instead. Thoreau also "subscribed a trifle," because he "had so much confidence in the man—that he would do right."

But Brown's talk about defending Kansas from the Slave Power was a blind for something far larger, and Emerson especially should have detected it. For in a conversation they had in Emerson's home Brown made a telling remark: he said that he believed in two things —the Bible and the Declaration of Independence—and that it was "better that a whole generation of men, women and children should pass away by a violent death than that a word of either should be violated in this country." Emerson reflected on that for a moment (quite obviously the Bible and the Declaration had been repeatedly violated in this country). Finally Emerson nodded his approval: he thought the old man was speaking symbolically, as Emerson liked to do himself. But Brown meant every word he said, as much as he had ever meant anything in his life.[21]

7

Back on the train again, heading across Massachusetts, the snow-covered landscape receding in the windows of the coach, Brown studied his notebooks and lists of subscriptions. So far all his speeches had netted him only a few hundred dollars in actual cash. A lot of people had promised to pay him something later on—his suitcase was full of such pledges—but subscriptions were of little use to him unless they were paid. And how did he know they would be for certain? In Boston, where he had impressed everybody in January, only Amos Lawrence had given him any cash—and that a trifling $70 for "your own personal use" and "not for the cause in any other way than that."[22] Something was fundamentally wrong, because the events of the past few weeks should have moved New Englanders to shower him with thousands of dollars for his Kansas crusade. For example: Governor Geary had visited the White House in Washington, only to be severely criticized by President Pierce for his charges against the proslavery party and his arrests of numerous Missouri trouble-makers. Indignant at such treatment, Geary announced that he would not violate his own sense of justice and give in to the interests of the slave party. In a storm of controversy he resigned on March 4—the same day that "dough-faced" James Buchanan of Pennsylvania was inaugurated as the new President. Ironically on that same day Brown published in the New York *Tribune* a moving appeal "TO THE FRIENDS OF FREEDOM," urging "all honest lovers *of Liberty and Human Rights, both male and female,* to hold up my hands by contributions and pecuniary aid, either as counties, cities, towns, villages, societies, churches or individuals." Predictably the new President proved that he was no "lover of liberty and human rights." He appointed Robert J. Walker, a Democrat from Mississippi, as the new governor of Kansas. And then Buchanan endorsed the proslavery government there and urged that Kansas be admitted to the Union as a slave state! In the meantime the United States Supreme Court on March 6 had handed down the Dred Scott decision, in which the high tribunal ruled that Congress could not prohibit slavery in the territories and that Negroes could never be citizens of the United States. From an antislavery view this was a monstrous violation of the Higher Law and the Declaration of Independence—and incontestible proof that the Supreme Court, like the Administration, the Congress, and the U.S. Army, was a tool of the Slave Power. All across the North, antislavery circles put up a tremendous public outcry against the decision; Garrisonians and anti-Garrisonians alike chanted for disunion. Yet in all the widespread consternation over the Dred Scott case and the fate of Kansas, Brown could raise only a few hundred paltry dollars for "the struggle of liberty" in the territory, and it distressed him. It left him sullen and bitter. What was wrong with these people? What was he to make of the signs?

Sanborn was disappointed, too, and wrote Brown from Concord on March 9: "I regret that so little has been done by individuals here to aid you in the plans you have in view, but like all the friends of Kansas you suffer from the false confidence of the public."[23]

Although Sanborn did not say so, Brown was also handicapped by the generally unstable financial conditions that prevailed in the Northeast in the spring of 1857. In fact, the country was heading pell-mell for another disastrous panic like the one that had ruined Brown in 1837, thanks to excessive railroad building, business bubbles, overextended credit, inflationary state bank notes, wild speculation in real estate, and other economic ills and malpractices. In such unfavorable circumstances no crusader could expect to raise much cash for any kind of cause.

Truculent and invincibly determined, Brown stormed into Connecticut during the second week in March, but he did no better in his native state: in three successive lectures in Hartford, Canton, and Collinsville he collected a measly $80. Still, his Connecticut tour was not without accomplishment. At Canton he visited the graves of his grandparents and managed to obtain Grandfather John Brown's old gravestone, "to be faced and inscribed in memory of our poor Fredk who sleeps in Kansas" and sent to the Brown farm at North Elba. "I value the old relic," he wrote John Jr., "much the more for its age, & homeliness; & it is of sufficient size to contain more *brief* inscriptions. One hundred years from 1856 should it then be in the possession of the same posterity: it will be a great curiosity."

In a drugstore at Collinsville, on the morning after his Kansas lecture, Brown met a man named Charles Blair, who was forge-master for the Collins Company, one of the nation's foremost manufacturers of edged tools. Brown showed him and a few others a Bowie knife he had captured from Pate at Black Jack. "If I had a lot of these blades fastened to poles about six feet long, they would make good weapons for our freestate settlers to keep in their cabins." He turned to Blair. "You're a forge-master. You can make good edge tools. What would you charge to make five hundred or a thousand of these pikes?" Blair thought for a moment. "Well, I could probably make you five hundred at a dollar and a quarter apiece, or a thousand at a dollar apiece." Brown said, "I want them made," and followed Blair to his shop to discuss terms. Later Brown signed a contract, agreeing to make a down payment of $500 with a promise of an additional $450 when the pikes were delivered.[24]

After Brown had gone, Blair might well have wondered what the old man really had in mind. Brown had implied during their conversations that Kansas was full of revolvers and Sharps rifles. What could settlers skilled in the use of firearms want with a thousand pikes? Also, why should Brown want a Connecticut forge-master to make them when a blacksmith in Iowa or Kansas could do it just as well?

8

Back in New York in March, Brown held a series of meetings with an English adventurer named Hugh Forbes at his quarters on Broadway Street. Forbes was about forty-five (twelve years younger than Brown); he had been a Viennese silk merchant, had fought with Garibaldi in the abortive Italian Revolution of 1848, and had written a two-volume manual on military tactics. After coming to the United States he had taken on the editorship of an Italian-language newspaper called the *European,* become fascinated with the abolition and disunion movements, and attended the Worcester Disunion Convention, where he had met Higginson. At present Forbes was barely making ends meet as a fencing master and a reporter and translator for the New York *Tribune.* In love with conspiracy and eager for a better-paying job (he claimed he had a wife and children to provide for back in Paris), Forbes listened with uninhibited enthusiasm as Brown discussed guerrilla warfare, described his own work on the Kansas border, and invited Forbes to join his regular company as a military instructor at $100 a month. Forbes said he refused to enlist *"merely* to get Kansas *for free white people."* Brown assured him that he and "the leading minds among his associates" shared his views— and evidently explained that his secret plans called for something more than mere defensive operations in the territory. Brown was plotting offensive guerrilla warfare against the South itself, perhaps an expanded version of his old Subterranean Pass Way scheme. He might commence operations on the Kansas-Missouri border and then drive eastward into the Southern Appalachians. If things proved unfavorable for him in Kansas, he might return to the East and strike directly at Virginia. The result could well be the liberation of the slaves.

Intrigued (for was this not a chance for him to become "the

Garibaldi of a revolution against slavery"?), Forbes joined Brown's
company, agreeing to serve as drillmaster and to provide a handbook
of tactics, based on an earlier work, to be entitled *Manual of the
Patriotic Volunteer*. Brown ordered the drillmaster to meet him
later in Iowa, then set out for Massachusetts again. Later Brown
authorized Forbes to draw on a friend at Hartford for a $600 advance.
Forbes got the money within a month.[25]

In late March Brown met Sanborn in New York and they made a
flying trip to Easton, Pennsylvania, to see ex-Governor Andrew
Reeder. They pleaded with him to return to Kansas and take the
free-state leadership away from Charles Robinson, who was too
moderate and "had lost the confidence of many men, there and in
the East." Brown boldly offered to serve as commander of field
forces in partisan warfare. Although Reeder declined their offer,
Brown told Sanborn that he would push ahead with his plans anyway.
Sanborn later wrote Higginson that the old warrior intended to
launch some mysterious "union splitting" operation on the Missouri
border.[26]

9

Back in Springfield, Brown received a letter from Mary, who
reported that his sons—except for Owen—had decided not to fight
any more, in Kansas or anywhere else. Incensed, Brown wrote Mary
from his room at the Massasoit House: "I have only to say as regards
the resolution of the boys to 'learn, & practice war no more'; that it
was not at my solicitation that they engaged in it at the first: & that
while I may perhaps feel no more love of the business than they do;
still I think there may be *possibly* in their day that which is more to
be demanded."[27]

Shortly after that another discouraging letter arrived; it was from
Henry B. Hurd, secretary of the National Kansas Committee, notify-
ing Brown that because of "the present state of the public feeling,
evinced by the almost total cessation of contributions," the committee
was virtually bankrupt and could not send him any of the money it
had promised.[28]

On April 3, back in Boston again, Brown wrote a friend that he planned to head west soon—and to go "with a *sad heart*," too, since he had "failed to secure even the means of equiping; to say nothing of feeding men." He was tired of giving speeches and pleading for money anyway; he felt like "a beggar" and it was humiliating. He was especially disgusted with the National Kansas Committee, from which he could expect nothing "but bad faith." The only men he could depend on were Amos Lawrence, Franklin Sanborn, George Stearns, and a few others who had promised to raise a subscription for his family.

Such cynicism was not entirely merited, because some $13,000 worth of military stores had been pledged to him—not enough to carry his war into the South itself but a considerable contribution nonetheless. He was as truculent and spirited as ever when he wrote Augustus Wattles and James H. Holmes a few days later. He praised God that in his absence "the free-State men of Kansas" had not polluted themselves "by the *foul and loathesome* embrace of the *old rotten whore*. I have been trembling *all along* lest they might *back down* from the *high and holy ground* they *had* taken." He sent his "most cordial and earnest salutation to *every one of the chosen*," and declared that his efforts in the Northeast had not been without success. He hoped to hear from them later at Tabor. He signed the letter "Nelson Hawkins," an alias he would use for over a year.[29]

While at Boston Brown received alarming intelligence from Jason in Ohio: a deputy U.S. marshal had just passed through Cleveland on his way east to arrest Brown. Vowing that no "U.S. Hound" was going to get him, Brown persuaded Thomas B. Russell, an abolitionist judge of the Superior Court of Massachusetts, to hide him in his house until "the track was cold." While Mrs. Russell looked on "stiff from fright," the old man produced "a long, evil-looking knife," two shorter blades, and two revolvers, and declared that he would hate to soil her carpet but that he would not be taken alive. He stayed a week in the Russells' home, barricaded inside a bedroom on the third floor. He came downstairs only for meals, where he persisted "in gravely mentioning . . . unspeakable articles upon which he said he had lived—joints and toes of creatures that surely no human being ever tasted." Still, Mrs. Russell found much in Brown that she admired: his lack of "pretentiousness," his stubborn honesty, his concern for the slaves, his forcefulness, and his bizarre laughter when he thought something ludicrous: "he made not the slightest sound, not even a whisper or an intake of breath," she recalled; "but he shook all over and laughed violently. It was the most curious thing imaginable to see him, in utter silence, rock and quake with mirth."[30]

But such laughter was rare. Back in his upstairs bedroom, with furniture stacked against the door, he brooded over the records he had kept of his subscriptions and donations: he had been promised a miserly $3,000 in cash for his military operations (but had received only about $1,000, if that much) and some $13,000 worth of guns and supplies from the Massachusetts Committee. He had collected a few rifles here and there; and Stearns had agreed to pay for 200 revolvers which the Massachusetts Arms Company would later ship to Iowa. But this was nowhere near enough guns or money to put his secret schemes into operation, and his moods alternated between sullen disappointment and outright hostility toward the people of New England. At one point, he recalled, he had been so pressed for money that he had tried to sell a captured sword to H. N. Rust, writing him that "I am literally driven to beg: which is very humiliating." Indignant, defiant toward everybody, he sat down in his locked and shade-drawn bedroom and composed a statement to all New England, entitled "Old Browns Farewell to the Plymouth Rocks, Bunker Hill Monuments, Charter Oaks, and Uncle Thoms Cabbins." Old Brown "has left for Kansas," the statement read. "Has been trying since he came out of the territory to secure an outfit or in other words; the means of arming and thoroughly equipping his regular Minuet men, who are mixed up *with the people* of Kansas, and *he leaves* the States, *with a feeling of deepest sadness*: that after having exhausted his own small means and *with his family and his brave men*; suffered hunger, cold, nakedness, *and some* of them sickness, wounds, imprisonment in *irons*; with extreme cruel treatment, *and others death*: that . . . after all this; in order to sustain a cause which every citizen of this 'glorious Republic,' is under equal moral obligation to do: *and for the neglect of which, he will be held accountable by God*: a cause in which every man, woman, and child; of the entire *human family* has a *deep* and *awful* interest; that when no *wages* are asked; or expected; he cannot secure, amidst all the wealth, luxury, and extravagance of this 'Heaven exalted,' people; even the necessary supplies of the common soldier. How are the mighty fallen."[31]

There was not a word in the Farewell about the subscription Lawrence and his friends were raising for Brown's family, not a word about the military supplies which his Boston friends had given him, not a word about the gifts of money (however small) he had received through the mail from well-wishing strangers. He drafted several copies of the Farewell, gave one to the Russells and sent others out to his friends (the Stearnses, Parker, and others). Then he fell ill with a ravaging attack of the ague, while a chill easterly storm settled over the city, to last several days. At Brown's summons, Mary Stearns came to see him and to discuss his Farewell. She was so moved by that document and Brown's own "moral magnetism" that, returning to Medford, she urged her husband to sell their carriage and horses (later she claimed she wanted to sell their entire estate) and give the money to Brown "for his sublime purpose." Despite its obvious omissions and exaggerations, Stearns also had been moved by the Farewell and promptly sent Brown a letter authorizing him to draw on Stearns "at sight" for $7,000, to be used in outfitting Brown's company "in the defense of Kansas." Such generosity inspired Theodore Parker and Wendell Phillips (the celebrated Garrisonian abolitionist) to remark that Stearns's "*name* had been written in the Lambs Book of life." And Brown wholeheartedly agreed.[32]

Although still in feeble health and still concerned about that U.S. marshal, the old man was too restless to remain with the Russells any longer. One night in mid-April he slipped out and caught a late train for upper New York. On the way he wrote John Jr. that he had secured "the assistance, & instruction; of a distinguished Scotch officer; & *author* quite popular *in this country*. I am quite sanguine of my success in the matter. My collections I may safely put down at $13000, & think I have got matters in such a train that it will soon reach $30,000" (obviously he was in better spirits now—the estimate was an exaggeration of about $7,000). He went on to say that "I have had a good deal of discouragement; & *have often* felt quite depressed; *but 'hither to God hath helped me.'* About the *last* of last Week, I gave vent to those feelings in a short piece (which you may yet see in the prints,) headed Old Browns, Farewell." He remarked that Lawrence and his brother had started a subscription "for my Wife, & little Girls in my *absence*; *& in case I never return to them.*" He warned John Jr. to say nothing about "these things." He mentioned that a "U.S. Hound" had been on his track, but that the papers had reported that Brown had returned to Kansas last week, so

he thought he would not "be delivered into the hands of the wicked."
With a pair of revolvers Howe had given him, three experimental
guns from Eli Thayer, and a rifle from the Worcester Manufacturing
Company, Brown went back to North Elba, where he rested his fever-
wasted body for a week or so. Then defiance rose in him again and
in mid-May he and Owen left the Adirondacks and turned west
"with Irons *in* rather than *uppon* our hands."[33]

XV

RAILROAD BUSINESS
ON AN EXTENDED SCALE

❦

BROWN, GOING BY THE NAME OF NELSON HAWKINS, was plagued with
the fever again as he and Owen made their way into Ohio. Late in
May they stopped in Hudson and stayed there for some time, so that
Brown could rest with his relatives. He may have contacted John Jr.,
who had written him from Lindenville, Ohio, a month ago: "It
seems as though if you return to Kansas this Spring I should never
see you again. But I will not look on the dark side. You have gone
safely through a thousand perils and hairbreadth escapes." Evidently
Brown had already confided his great new enterprise to his son, for
John Jr. added in the same letter: "Do you not intend to visit Canada
before long? That school can be established there, if not elsewhere."[1]

At Hudson Brown wrote flurries of letters to abolitionists from
Ohio to Connecticut beseeching them to help "the cause of freedom"
in Kansas: he wrote Salmon P. Chase (who had given him $25 last
winter); he wrote "the friends of New Haven," asking where the
money was they had promised him. He wrote Hugh Forbes who
seemed to be dallying in New York to meet him at the Bennet
House in Cleveland on June 17 "without fail," then asked a friend
in New York named Joseph Bryant to check on Forbes and demand
that he return that $600 advance if he was not coming west at once
(Bryant replied that the "Colonel" was acting in good faith and
would be along when his manual on tactics was completed). In the
meantime Brown wrote his wife and daughters that "if I should
never return, it is my particular request that no other monument be

used to keep me in remembrance than the same plain one that records the death of my grandfather and son; and that a short story like those already on it, be told of John Brown the fifth." He added that he was still troubled with the ague and "much confused in mind," so that he could not remember what else he wished to write. He recalled what he wanted to tell his friends in Kansas, however, and wrote them to contact his volunteers and "in the most QUIET WAY" to meet him at Tabor in Iowa. "I have some very important matters to confer with some of you about. Let there be *no words* about it."[2]

In mid-June he felt well enough to travel and set out for Chicago and Milwaukee to find Gerrit Smith, who had come west to attend antislavery meetings and urge Illinois and Wisconsin to continue their opposition to the fugitive slave law. Perhaps because of the Dred Scott decision and President Buchanan's support of the proslavery government in Kansas, Smith was more enthusiastic about Brown's work now than he had been in February, and when they met in Chicago on or about June 20 Smith gave his "old friend" $350 for his operations in the territory. Brown also explained that he owed the Thompsons some money for the farmhouse Henry had built for him at North Elba and that "they were disappointed" because Brown had not paid them. Would Smith help him settle that debt? Smith gladly gave his "dear friend" another $110, and Brown headed back to Ohio with his "head, & hands both so full" he could scarcely conceal his excitement.

What Brown and Smith said about Kansas in their Chicago meeting is not known, but a letter Smith sent to Thaddeus Hyatt in July might give one an idea. "We must not," Smith asserted, "shrink from fighting for Liberty—and if Federal troops fight against her, we must fight against them." Brown, of course, was highly encouraged by Smith's renewed pugnacity; and he was equally enthusiastic about the way Illinois and Wisconsin were flouting the federal government and refusing to obey the fugitive slave law. "*These are good beginnings,*" he wrote Mary, "and the End is by-and-by."[3]

On June 29 he was back in Cleveland. There he recorded in his notebook: "Wrote Joseph Bryant Col Forbes and D Lee Child; all that I leave here Cleveland this day for Tabor, Iowa; & advise Forbes, & Child, to call on Jonas Jones." Sometime that day Brown and

Owen rode out of Cleveland in a wagon drawn by three mules, heading westward "as fast as Providence intends."[4]

2

They crossed into Iowa in a few days and on July 15 came to a place called Red Rock. In camp that evening Brown sat down and wrote young Henry Stearns an autobiographical letter entitled "A boy named John," thus fulfilling a promise he had made the previous January. The story of John, the old man recorded, "will be mainly a narration of follies & errors; which it is hoped *you may avoid.*" It was also designed in part to convince George Luther Stearns that Brown was an honest man who was not afraid to admit his mistakes and who was now ready to die in this holy war against slavery and the "Slave Power." So, the old man wrote, "there is one thing connected" with the story of John "which will be calculated to encourage any young person to perservering effort; & that is the degree of success *in accomplishing his objects* which to a great extent marked the course of this boy throughout my entire acquaintance with him. . . ."

Referring to himself in the third person, Brown recounted his austere and desolate childhood in Connecticut and Ohio. He confessed that John had told lies to escape punishment and had been "fond of the hardest & *roughest* kind of play." He told how John had lost his mother, had grown up "in the School of adversity" on the Ohio frontier, had learned to read history and to avoid "bad company" and frivolous entertainment (dancing, card playing, courting), and had sworn "*Eternal war* with slavery" when he had seen a wicked landlord beat a slave boy with an iron fire shovel. At sixteen John "became to some extent a convert to Christianity & ever after a firm believer in the divine authenticity of the Bible." Now, some of the things Brown had related to young Henry had a purpose: "& I would like to know that you had selected those out; & adopted them as part of your own plan of life; & I wish you to have some *deffinite plan.* Many seem to have none: & others never stick to any that they do form. This was not the case with John. He followed up with *tenacity* whatever he set about so long as it answered his general purpose: & hence he rarely failed in some good degree to effect the things he undertook. This was so much the case that he *habitually expected to succeed* in his undertakings. With this feeling *should be coupled*; the consciousness that our plans are right in themselves."

John was too vain and imperious at times, but then he met and married Dianthe Lusk, "*a remarkably plain*; but neat industrious & economical girl; of excellent character; earnest piety; & good practical common sense," who, "by her mild, frank, & *more than all* else: by her very consistent conduct; acquired; & ever while she lived maintained a most powerful; and good influence over him," without arousing "his haughty obstinate temper." As for his work, "John began early in life to discover a great liking to fine Cattle, Horses, Sheep; Swine; & as soon as circumstances would enable him he began to be a practical *Shepherd*: it being a *calling* for which in *early life* he had a kind of *enthusiastic longing*: together with the idea that as a business it bid fair to afford him the means of carrying out his greatest or principle object."

The old man did not explain what that object was, allowing the Stearnses to draw their own conclusions. Nor did he relate any of his failures in business, now as a tanner, now in land speculation, now as a wool grower and merchant, which had ended in lawsuits and bankruptcy. In concluding the story of John he merely stated that "if I believed it would be worth the trouble; or afford much interest to any good feeling person; I might be tempted to tell you something of his course in after life; or manhood. I do not say that I *will do it*." And except for a fragmentary account of his experiences in Kansas, "watered by the blood and tears" of his family, Brown never wrote a word about those years of trial between 1831 and 1856, when God had made him feel his dependence in the hardest of ways, until at long last "*a favourable* change" had taken place.[5]

In several respects "A Boy Named John" is the most revealing document Brown ever wrote. Not only does it afford rare insight into his childhood and early youth; but certain passages in it, with italicized words like *accomplishing his objects, eternal war with slavery, definite plan, habitually expected to succeed, calling,* and *enthusiastic longing,* together with the allusion to "his greatest or principle object" and the assertion "that our plans are right in themselves," suggest what was now uppermost in his mind.

3

When Brown arrived in Tabor on August 7, he expected to find thousands of dollars from his friends in the East. Again they had disappointed him, for all Brown had received was $110 from E. B. Whitman, the Lawrence agent of the Massachusetts Kansas Committee. The next day Brown wrote a note to George Stearns (attached to the story of John) complaining bitterly about how his friends had failed him, but vowing that he would never give up.

Sanborn wrote back that "Mr. Stearns received your letter with your account of a boy named John. I hope you will continue the history for many of your friends here are anxious to have your story told, and I as much as any." Sanborn for his part was "pained" that they had not helped Brown enough and promised to send whatever money he could raise personally.

But in another matter Sanborn had good news to report: Lawrence and Stearns had raised a subscription of $1,000 to complete the purchase of Brown's and Henry Thompson's farms at North Elba, just as the old man had requested. As the agent of the subscribers, Sanborn had personally inspected the two farms and had told Mrs. Brown that she would never again have to worry about a place to live. Then he had given the subscription to Gerrit Smith (who owned the land the farms were on) and sent the deed and contract back to North Elba.

Brown was genuinely grateful for what Stearns, Lawrence, and the other subscribers had done for his family. He wrote Sanborn and thanked him "for going to look after" Mary and the girls "& *cheer them* in their homely condition." He asked that "God reward you all a thousand fold."[6]

In the meantime Brown and Owen had set up headquarters in Jonas Jones's house in Tabor and taken inventory of all the guns and supplies in his cellar. By his own reckoning, Brown's arsenal consisted of 1 field piece, 70 to 75 old damaged rifles and muskets, 12 old sabers, 2 pistols from Howe, 3 or 4 guns made "for experiment" by Eli Thayer and a rifle from the Worcester Manufacturing Company, and "a few Revolvers commun Guns, & Sabres" left over from the Kansas campaigns, not counting the 200 revolvers which the Massachusetts Arms Company had shipped to "J. B. care Dr. Jesse Bowen, Iowa City, Iowa."

On August 9 Forbes finally arrived in Tabor, after what seemed to Brown a series of alarming and inexcusable delays. Forbes, however, insisted that he had been faithfully at work, condensing his two-volume manual on military tactics and trying to care for his family, to whom he had sent $120 of the $600 advance from Brown. On his way to Iowa Forbes had prevailed on Gerrit Smith for an additional $150, most of it to pay for the printing of Forbes's manual. Smith gave the money happily, writing Hyatt that Forbes would "prove very useful in our sacred work in Kansas."[7]

Not long after "Colonel" Forbes arrived in Tabor, friction broke out between him and "Captain" Brown. Both were obstinate, independent men, oblivious to advice, deaf to criticism, and convinced of their unchallengeable expertise in military matters. The trouble began when Forbes presented Brown, who was supposed to be the commander of this enterprise, with a plan to overthrow slavery in the South (a plan that appears to have been a revision of Brown's own Subterranean Pass Way scheme). Forbes explained that "with carefully selected colored and white persons" they could muster along the Northern slave frontier (Virginia and Maryland specifically) and there instigate a series of slave stampedes, running Negroes into Canada so rapidly that pursuit would be hopeless and loss of life negligible. Inciting an average of one or two stampedes per week, they would render slave property untenable and gradually push the "Slave frontier" southward, producing such excitement and hysteria that the "proslaveryites" would commit "stupid blunders."

Brown categorically rejected the drillmaster's proposal, asserting that he had his own plan for the destruction of slavery that he had been working on for "many years." With 25 to 50 well-armed men—"colored and white mixed"—and with a quantity of spare arms and the pikes which Blair was making in Connecticut, Brown intended *"to beat up a slave quarter in Virginia."* But Forbes objected at once, contending that unless the slaves were warned and agitated beforehand (and he did not see how they could be agitated beforehand), the blacks would not respond. Brown replied that he was certain of a response. Evidently his discussions with Negroes like Garnet and Douglass—and his study of the *Liberator* and other abolitionist publications—had convinced him that slaves all over the South were seething with hatred for their white masters and were on the verge of mutiny. He calculated that between 200 and 500 slaves would swarm to his standard the first night. While selected parties beat up other slave quarters, Brown himself would take 80 to 100 men and "make a dash" against Harpers Ferry, where a federal armory and arsenal were located. He would destroy what arms he could not carry off and move swiftly into the mountains, where slaves from Virginia and Maryland would join him. If U.S. troops gave chase, he could easily maintain himself in the Alleghenies. In the meantime his "New England partisans" would call a Northern Convention (perhaps like the disunion convention that had met in Worcester in January) and "*overthrow the pro-Slavery Administration.*"

Again Forbes dissented. For one thing, since slaves were deficient in education and experience, any insurrection such as Brown envisioned would either be "a flash in the pan" or would "leap out of control," degenerating into anarchy and spreading hysteria among the slaves themselves, who then would "assuredly be suppressed." As for Brown's dream of a Northern Convention, Forbes considered that a "total fallacy," because Brown's "New England friends would not have the courage to show themselves, as long as the issue was doubtful." Brown then argued that foreign intervention was not impossible.

Forbes claimed that he and Brown haggled for days over their rival plans, until Brown "acquiesced or feigned to acquiesce" in a compromise project called "the Well-Matured Plan." Later Forbes insisted that he had been the very picture of trust and innocence in the matter, that he had abandoned his original scheme (which he still preferred) and agreed to the compromise project "to secure mutual cooperation," although he had insisted—and Brown had finally agreed—that they should set up a Committee of Management to direct their enterprise. But Forbes was not quite so innocent as he claimed. From all appearances he thought himself far superior to Brown as a military commander and hoped to lead the entire operation himself, perhaps through the Committee of Management. He denied this emphatically in 1858, but at the same time he remarked that Brown, "with his bigoted mind and limited instruction," was incapable of directing the project, although he "might have been useful in some capacity" had he been a truthful man.[8]

For now, though, an uneasy truce existed between the two as they went about their respective duties in Tabor. Forbes made plans for a military school to train Brown's recruits once they arrived from Kansas. Then, to keep busy, he drilled Owen outside Jones's house and led him in target practice; he also composed a tract, "The Duty of a Soldier," exhorting U.S. troops to stop being "vile living machines" who supported "Wrong against Right" and henceforth to give their allegiance to the free-state cause.[9] Meanwhile Brown himself set about studying partisan warfare on his own, reading about the slave insurrection that had taken place on Haiti in the late 1790's and about Mina's guerrilla operations in the Spanish mountains during the Napoleonic Wars. As he read he made the following entry in his private notebook:

Geurrilla warfare See Life of Lord Wellington Page 71 to Page 75 (Mina) See also Page 102 some *valuable hints* in *Same Book*. See also Page 196 some most important instructions to officers See also Same Book Page 235 these words deep and narrow defile where 300 men would Suffice to check an *army*. See also Page 236 on top of Page

The book Brown referred to was Joachim Hayward Stocqueler's two-volume biography of Wellington. The "most important instructions to officers" pertained to discipline and cooking; and page 235 contained a description of the broken, mountainous topography of Spain at the time of the Napoleonic Wars.

Brown also spent countless hours poring over maps of the Southern states. As he did so he made another telling entry in his notebook.

Fayettville North Carolina
Head of navigation on Cape Fear
River
    Alleghany Pa Pittsburg
    Frankford [?] Pa Bridesburg
    Pikesville Maryland Pikeville
    Augusta Georgia Augusta
    St. Louis Missouri
    Baton Rouge Louisiana
    Mount Vernon Allabama
    Charlestown South Carolina

Washington D C
Little Rock Arkansas
San Antonio Texas
Apalachicola at Chattahoochee
& St Augustine Florida

Like Harpers Ferry, Pittsburgh and all the Southern towns on
Brown's list contained federal forts or arsenals, whose arms and
military stores would prove indispensable to Brown's guerrilla force.
It is obvious from the list that Brown intended to operate not just in
the Appalachian Mountains but all across the Deep South from
Florida to Texas.[10]

4

Brown had already hinted to his Eastern friends that he had something large in mind. He wrote Stearns that he needed from
$500 to $1,000 at once *"for secret service & no questions asked."*
He said that, since nothing exciting was happening in Kansas at
present, "our next advices may entirely change the aspect of things.
I hope the friends of Freedom will respond to my call: & 'prove me
now herewith.' "

He had hoped that his friends in Kansas would rally to his call as
well. But he was disappointed again. Since Kansas was quiet now,
many of his friends had decided that further military operations
were needless and had laid down their arms. Holmes, for example,
was plowing at Emporia. Many of the other "chosen" had taken jobs,
and Conway and Phillips were "talking politics."[11]

Politically, a great deal had transpired in Kansas while Brown
had been in the East. Robert Walker had arrived and assumed his
duties as the new governor. But to everybody's surprise, the Mississippian strove to conduct a scrupulously fair and nonpartisan government. Walker's policy infuriated proslavery men both in Kansas
and in Washington, for they were powerfully determined to force
slavery on Kansas by whatever means (in fact, proslavery delegates
were already drafting a constitution at Lecompton that would bring
Kansas into the Union as a slave state) . President Buchanan, roundly

criticized by Southerners in Washington because of Walker's "duplicity," pressed the governor to abandon his policy. But Walker held firm, vowing that the forthcoming election for a new territorial legislature and United States congressman, scheduled for October 5, would take place without fraud or "outside interference." Hearing statements like that, most free-state settlers had closed ranks behind Charles Robinson and other advocates of peace and promised to overwhelm the proslavery enemy at the polls.

Because the peace party was in the ascendancy, Brown was not sure what to do about Kansas. All his Eastern friends expected him to make some sort of military maneuver there, despite his hints that he was contemplating a move in another direction. At one point he thought he might return to Ohio and the East in the autumn. Then he decided to stay in Tabor, perhaps hoping that some outrage would occur in the October 5 election that would give him an excuse to attack the enemy in Kansas, or maybe even invade border Missouri. That would certainly impress his Eastern friends and possibly make them more amenable to the grand scheme, when the time came to reveal it. He wrote Adair to send him a full account of Kansas affairs. In the meantime James H. Lane, who wanted to continue guerrilla warfare in the territory, urged Brown to come to Kansas at once— and to bring all his guns and supplies. Cunningly the old man replied that ten industrious men with "$150 in cash" might persuade him to leave Tabor.[12]

By September Brown was so short of funds that he could scarcely pay his food bill. Sanborn, always Brown's most sympathetic and ardent supporter, tried to help, but all he could send for Brown's expenses and "secret service operations" was a trifling $75.68. Sanborn doubted that any more money could be raised because of the severe panic that had stricken the nation in August. "There has been no such pressure since 1837," Sanborn wrote gloomily, "if things were as bad then."[13]

To complicate his troubles, Brown had the ague again. As he waited in Tabor, trying to restore his health, hoping that money would arrive from some other industrious supporter or that conditions might radically change in Kansas, not certain what he should do at present, Thomas Wentworth Higginson, the fiery disunionist, wrote Sanborn and wanted to know what the devil Brown was waiting for. Why did he not strike a blow on the Kansas border? What had he done with all the guns the Kansas committees had entrusted to him? Sanborn replied that Higginson did not understand Brown's circumstances. "He is ready for a revolution as any other man, and is now on the borders of Kansas, safe from arrest but prepared for action, but he needs money for his present expenses, and *active* support. I believe he is the best Disunion champion you can find, and with his hundred men, when he is put where he can raise them and drill them (for he has an expert drill officer with him) will do more to split the Union than a list of 50,000 names for your Convention—good as that is." Sanborn was most disappointed that "the friends of Kansas" looked "with strange apathy" upon Brown's work—work which had "all the elements of success" and "a radical purpose." Sanborn did not explain what that purpose was, but he was probably referring to some military operation on the Missouri border, one that would possibly draw the fight into Nebraska or Iowa, as Higginson wanted, and fan the flames of disunion. Sanborn did not know about Brown's Virginia plan at this time. He went on to exhort Higginson: "If you can do anything for Brown *now*, in God's name do it—and the ill result of the new policy in Kansas may be prevented."[14]

But Higginson, impatient as he was for Brown to light a fire in Kansas that would blow the sections apart, had no money to send him and neither did anybody else. Eventually a local Kansas committee in Massachusetts sent him $72.68, but that was hardly enough to pay his board bill. On October 1 Brown wrote Sanborn that he was destitute because the Massachusetts Committee had failed to send the balance of the $500 it had promised to get him back to the territory. He said he had a lot of damaged old guns and sabers, but was drastically short of saddlebags, knapsacks, and holsters. And nobody had done anything about "the *secret service* I wrote about" either. In that regard he dropped a hint to Sanborn that was as subtle as a stab in the chest: he said he had paid $550 on a contract for 1,000 pikes, "as a cheap but effectual weapon to place in the [hands] of entirely unskillful, & unpracticed men."

The days passed and still no money was forthcoming. Angrily Brown wrote Whitman in Lawrence and demanded "what money you have for me—*not papers*." But Whitman was "penniless" because of the panic and could not send a dollar more of the $500 the Massachusetts Committee had promised Brown.[15]

As Brown and Whitman exchanged letters, Kansas voters went to the polls in the crucial elections of October 5. When all the votes had been tallied, the free-state party had won an overwhelming victory, having elected a free-state man to Congress and won thirty-three of fifty-two seats in the new legislature. Governor Walker, true to his promise, had set aside fraudulent returns and reported that there had been no charges of Missouri interference. When the news reached the East, Brown's friends were divided as to what should be done about Kansas now. Sanborn was dubious that ultimate victory could be won at the polls. Howe rather doubted that the Missourians had surrendered Kansas, but he thought that Brown should be extremely cautious. "Dont attack them," Howe wrote the old man in November, "but if they attack you 'Give them Jessie' & Fremont too; you know how to do it." But Stearns, who remained solvent in spite of the panic, apparently believed that Kansas could now be made a free state through the electoral process and decided to withdraw his support from Brown. "I gave J. B. authority to draw on me for money in a certain contingency," Stearns wrote Whitman. "That contingency has not occurred, and I now believe it would be very unwise to attempt to establish order by *force*, I should not be willing to have any of my funds used for that purpose." Later Stearns sent a similar letter to Brown, instructing him not to draw a dollar of the $7,000 Stearns had pledged to him last April.[16]

If Brown was disappointed in his New England friends, Colonel Forbes was furious with them. His salary was supposed to come out of their pledges to Brown; and when they failed to send what they had promised, Forbes regarded it as a deliberate and malicious attempt to wrong him personally. Because of their "breach of faith," Brown had been able to pay him only $60 in the past three months, and he had a wife and children "starving to death" in Paris. The idea that his children "were being killed by slow torture through the culpability of the humanitarians" was more than Forbes could bear (if there was any truth to his family troubles at all) . "You are guilty of perfidy and barbarity, to which may be added stupidity," he wrote a shocked Howe later. "You must be worse than insane—you must be depraved."

He had his suspicions about Brown too. Where were all the recruits he was to train for their Well-Matured Plan? In 1858 he claimed that only one man came to Tabor (no names were mentioned) and that he was an unscrupulous scoundrel who had joined the company only for loot and plunder. Forbes said that he "remonstrated" against Brown for enlisting such "highly objectionable hands" and that they continued to argue over the projected campaign (if there was ever going to be any campaign). By mid autumn, Forbes had convinced himself that Brown had never abandoned that "crude" project to beat up a slave revolt in Virginia, that everything he said about the Committee of Management and the Compromise Project was a lie.[17] But since the details of the Well-Matured Plan are not known, it is impossible to say whether Brown had deliberately deceived Forbes or whether all Forbes's suspicions were the product of his own imagination.

While Forbes fumed and fussed, Brown received auspicious signs from Kansas: Adair sent him $100 from Osawatomie, and Whitman and Lane sent him another $150 by C. P. Tidd, with instructions for Brown to bring his guns to Lawrence. On November 2 Brown set out for Kansas "to see how the land lies." Much to Lane's disappointment, however, the old man shrewdly left the arms hidden in Tabor.[18]

Tidd and a grumbling Forbes went with Brown. At Nebraska City, however, Forbes mysteriously left Brown's party and hurried back east.

5

Around November 5 Brown reached Whitman's place near Lawrence and asked for money and supplies. As it turned out, Whitman had just received $500 from Stearns for Brown's "personal and family needs," and although it was against his better judgment, Whitman gave Brown the money along with some tents. Brown then sent for John E. Cook, the young man he had met after the battle of Black Jack, and told Cook that he wanted "to organize a company for the purpose of putting a stop to the aggressions of the pro Slavery men." Did Cook want to enlist? Did he know of any other reliable young

men who would be interested? Cook was proud to join such a
company and believed Richard Realf, Luke Parsons, and Richard J.
Hinton would want to enlist as well. Cook then returned to Lawrence
and Brown left Whitman's place for an unknown destination, refusing to tell Whitman or anybody else "where he was going or where
he could be found."

Several days later Brown met Cook and Luke Parsons at a place
near Lawrence, then rejoined them later in Topeka. There he
enlisted three other young men in his new company—John Henry
Kagi, Aaron D. Stevens, and Charles Moffett, all of them veteran
guerrilla fighters. On November 16 Brown wrote Stearns that he had
never intended to draw on that $7,000 pledge "unless driven to the
last extremity," nor had he wanted Stearns to give him "the secret
service money I asked for." He said that "I mean to be busily; but
very quietly engaged in perfecting my arrangements during the
winter." That same day he wrote John Jr. that "we have now *full*
command of Ship & freight: & expect to commence steering it in the
proper direction Tomorrow."[19]

6

Around a campfire that night, on the prairie northeast of Topeka,
Brown gave his new recruits a hint of what was ahead of them. A cold
November wind howled out of the night as Brown piled wood on the
smoking embers. All four men sat near, their bedrolls affording
partial shelter from the cold, as they strained to hear what the old
man was saying. Occasionally Cook asked questions with the breathless enthusiasm of a young boy, although he was actually twenty-
seven. A former student at Yale and a one-time clerk in a New York
law office, Cook loved to "talk and rattle on about himself." Fresh-
faced and blue-eyed, he had a way with women—"mothers as well as
maidens"—who were irresistibly attracted to his swagger, his boyish
good looks, and his "long silken blonde hair" that "curled carelessly
about his neck." Next to Cook sat Moffett, a drifter from Iowa, and
Aaron D. Stevens, the mysterious "Captain Whipple" Brown had met
at Nebraska City in 1856. Stevens was a tall, hulking man with an
explosive temper and "black, brooding eyes." A native of Connecti-

cut, he had run away from home to fight in the Mexican War when he was sixteen. After the war he had almost killed an officer in a drunken brawl in Taos, New Mexico, and had been thrown into Fort Leavenworth on a commuted death sentence. He managed to escape early in 1856, hid among the Delaware Indians for a time, and then joined the free-state forces under an assumed name. In battle Stevens fought with uninhibited fury and used a saber with deadly skill. He was something of a minstrel, too, and liked to sing "Just as I am" and "Come to Me" in his rich baritone voice. A man of powerful convictions, he had rejected Christianity ("the Christian religion never looked consistent to me") and become a spiritualist who believed in "the great Bible of Nature." He also believed in the free-state and abolitionist causes and once thundered at a Kansas sheriff: "We are in the right, and will resist the universe."

Next to Stevens sat John Henry Kagi, an articulate and highly intelligent young schoolteacher who carried a satchelful of lectures, essays, and old school compositions wherever he went. A native of Ohio, he had attended an academy in Virginia and taught school there for a couple of years. An outspoken opponent of slavery, he finally left the queen of the slave states and returned to Ohio, where he taught school, wrote essays on subjects like "the alleged law of vibration," and studied law, mathematics, and logic. He also attended the country lyceum and became a skilled debater. He identified strongly with Ohio's free-soil sentiments, and when civil war broke out in Kansas in the summer of 1856 he went there as a correspondent for various newspapers, only to become involved in the fighting himself. He served for a time in Stevens' company, then went to Lecompton to cover the proslavery constitutional convention as a free-state reporter. He was arrested and jailed for four months. Later, in a scuffle at Tecumseh, Kagi shot and killed a man from Alabama who had tried to murder him with a bludgeon. Despite what his enemies claimed, Kagi was no gun-happy adventurer. Although he regarded God and religion as "useless problems," he was an intensely moral and idealistic young man who considered slavery a shocking social evil and whose hatred of that institution was as deeply principled as it was implacable.[20]

Kagi and the other recruits all spoke to Brown with deep respect, for they regarded him as a brave and high-minded warrior who would lay down his life to save Kansas from the Slave Power. But they wanted to know what specific plans he had made. They all knew he had other recruits. Where was it he wanted them to serve?

But Brown, in the glare of the fire, would only say that they were going to Ohio to drill, since Kansas was quiet now and it was too cold to do much campaigning out here. His sons, together with C. P. Tidd, William Leeman, and a couple of others, would go along. Then he gave Cook a draft for $82.68 and said, "Get that cashed in Lawrence tomorrow. We'll meet again at Tabor in Iowa. Then I'll tell you what we are going to do. If you want hard fighting you'll get plenty of it."

At Tabor, Brown gathered nine recruits around him, including Owen, Tidd, a runaway slave named Richard Richardson, and an Englishman named Richard Realf. With a look of grim determination Brown told them, "Our ultimate destination is Virginia."[21]

7

At first Cook, Parsons, and possibly Richard Realf were opposed to "troubling Israel" in Virginia, as Brown phrased it, for they had joined his company to fight in Kansas, not in the South. And anyway what did he mean by "troubling Israel"? But Brown stated only that they were going "to make an incursion into the Southern states, somewhere in the mountainous regions of the Blue Ridge and the Alleghenies," hinting at some large slave-running operation. Cook, however, continued to object, and warm words passed between him and Captain Brown. Finally Cook and the other dissidents agreed to go along, because the other recruits pressed them to do so and they did not have the money to return to Kansas anyway. But all the wrangling with Cook left the old man bristling with irritation. "Father used harsh words several times," Owen recorded in his diary on December 3, and two days later: "Father starts an outrageous jawing" about something Owen failed to do as they prepared to leave Tabor "perhaps for the last time."

On December 5 they collected all the guns and supplies and set out for Ohio, where they were to establish another training school and Forbes was supposed to rejoin them. On the trail, at cold, wet, snowy encampments, Brown gradually revealed some of the details of their "incursion into Virginia." He said that "God had created him to be the deliverer of the slaves the same as Moses had delivered the children of Israel." Kagi, Stevens, and Owen (who was an agnostic) cared little for such "Bible talk," but they respected Brown and listened with rising excitement when he spoke of the "possibility of effecting a successful insurrection in the mountains." Realf said that some of the boys were against the idea, but that the more adventurous ones were for it enthusiastically. Realf, a twenty-three-year-old Englishman who had published poetry, written for Eastern newspapers, and ridden with Jim Lane, thought "a mountainous country is a very fine country for an insurrection." And Stevens, Kagi, Leeman, and Tidd (a quick-tempered youth from Palermo, Maine) were intrigued with the prospects of fighting proslavery forces in the South itself. Think of what the newspapers would say about them! Think of the fame, the glory! But glory and reputation were not the only things these young men thought about as they listened to their grizzled commander, who told them—and the more reluctant ones— that to risk their lives for the liberation of the black man was the most noble thing they could do. Kagi and the others agreed. For whatever else may be said of them, they, too, regarded the black man as a human being who had a right to be free and were prepared to spill Southern blood to break his chains, if that was what it took. Brown, of course, argued that it would take that and more to destroy slavery in the United States. Eventually he won even the reluctant ones to his side with his intensity, his fierce courage, and his unshakable confidence that what he planned to do was *right*. Before December passed they had all pledged to *"stand by the work"*—even if Brown still was vague about specifics—and to put their lives, and their destinies, in his hands.

Owen chronicled what they talked about at other encampments on the trail across Iowa. *December 7*: "Snowy night discussed warmly the present wrong theory of war and the moral right to kill those who forcibly enslave their fellows, and readily take the life of the oppressed to perpetuate the wrong upon them and their posterity. Talk about the inconsistency of the Slave-holder mingling in breed etc. with the Africans at the same time calling them brutes. . . ."

December 8: "Hot discussion upon the Bible and war . . . talked

about polygamy, infedility, etc.; interruptions, swearing. . . . Warm
argument upon the effect of the abolition of Slavery upon the Southern States, Northern States, commerce and manufactures, also upon
the British Provinces and the civilized world; whence came our civilization and origin? Talk about prejudices against color: question
proposed for debate—greatest general, Washington or Napoleon?"
While they discussed racial prejudice and generalship, they applied
a soothing ointment to their bodies to cure "the itch and the lice."
At one point a gust of wind blew snow in on their beds and guns.
They could hear prairie wolves howling somewhere in the frozen
night.[22]

8

By the time they reached Springdale, Iowa, a Quaker community
situated near Iowa City, Brown was short of funds again. He canceled
his plans to train the boys in Ohio and made arrangements to board
them in Springdale for the winter while he returned to the East. Just
before he left, he took Kagi aside and asked him about Harpers Ferry
Kagi knew the area and thought it a good place to begin the
work. Parsons, one of the reluctant recruits, claimed that Brown
mentioned Harpers Ferry to him, too, and assured him that all they
were going to do was help the slaves defend themselves or escape to
Canada. On January 15, leaving Stevens to drill the men with wooden
swords and Kagi to lead discussions about their "adventures and
plans," Brown set out alone for Ohio.

On January 21 he stopped in Lindenville, Ohio, to talk over
urgent business with John Jr. It seems that Hugh Forbes had written
Brown a violent and abusive letter, insisting that the old man had
deceived him and making vague threats to get his due. Henceforth
Brown thought it best to communicate with Forbes through "a third
person," lest he reveal Brown's whereabouts to the authorities. Brown
also persuaded John Jr., despite the fact that he was still emotionally
troubled because of his Kansas experience, to act as a special intelligence agent for the Virginia project. Then Brown left Ohio and
headed for Rochester, New York, to see his old friend, Frederick
Douglass.[23]

9

Brown reached Douglass' home on January 28 and hid there for nearly a month while he perfected his Virginia plan. Brown had visited Douglass on several occasions since their initial meeting in Springfield in 1847, and each time they had spent the night discussing Brown's old Subterranean Pass Way scheme, with various frills and embellishments. Brown had visited him briefly in December, 1856, and several times in the following spring had asked Douglass for help in getting up lectures and soliciting aid for his work. Now, in the 1858 visit, Brown unfolded, probably for the first time, a second version of his old plan to operate in the Southern mountains. Douglass recalled that "the horrors" Brown intended to visit upon the South in this revised plan made the Negro leader shudder, but it was "the shudder one feels at the execution of a murderer." However, as a former slave and a fugitive, Douglass detected several defects in Brown's scheme and warned him of the hazards that awaited him and his guerrilla army in such a perilous enterprise. But Brown characteristically did more talking than listening; he was obsessed with his plan: it was the first thing he talked about in the morning and the last thing at night, Douglass recalled, "until I confess it began to be something of a bore to me." Even so, Douglass did agree to help his old friend. He introduced him to a potential recruit, a good friend and a fellow ex-slave named Shields Green. Douglass also said he would assist Brown in raising money and recruits among the Northeast's black communities. There were some 128,000 Negroes living in New York, New Jersey, and Pennsylvania at this time and another 23,000 in New England. Brown hoped to persuade a substantial portion of them to enlist in his guerrilla force or to give him material support.

During the days, alone in his bedroom, Brown drew up and revised a Provisional Constitution that would create a new state in the Southern mountains after he had invaded them. Forbes's prediction that a slave insurrection would either be "a flash in the pan" or would degenerate into complete chaos had worried Brown; and to avoid "anarchy and confusion," as he explained to Douglass, he had decided that "there should be a regularly constituted government" to direct the course and shape of the revolution.[24]

When Brown was not working on his Constitution, he was writing letters to his sons, to his wife and daughters, to Sanborn, Higginson, and his Boston friends, and to anybody else who might help in the cause. "I am (praised be God!) once more in York State," he wrote Mary on January 30. But he was on such an important mission that he did not know whether he could see her or not, even though he wanted to very much. "But, courage, courage, courage!—the great work of my life . . . I may yet see accomplished (God helping), and be permitted to return and 'rest at evening.' " Then he addressed his daughter Ruth, urging her to "let Henry go 'to school.' " Brown would rather have Henry now "for another term" than a hundred "average scholars." He had an important (but not dangerous) place for Henry in school, just as he had for Salmon, Oliver, and Watson. But he cautioned her not to "noise it about" that he was in these parts, and told her to write her reply to "N. Hawkins, care of Frederick Douglass."[25]

Then he sent letters to Howe and Higginson, Stearns, Smith, Sanborn, and Parker, announcing that he was now perfecting "BY FAR the most *important* undertaking of my whole life" and that he needed from $500 to $800 within the next sixty days. In his letter to Higginson he remarked that "I have been told that you are both a true *man*; & a true *abolitionist* '& I partly believe' the whole story." As for the money he needed, he said he had written Parker, Stearns, and Sanborn about the matter, "but do not know as either Mr. Stearns, or Mr. Sanborn, are abolitionists. I suppose they are." A remarkable statement in view of all the help Sanborn had given him over the past year. Brown went on to ask that Higginson raise among his friends at Worcester "some part" of the money Brown needed, but that Higginson keep this communication "*strictly confidential*" and "write Nelson Hawkins care of Wm Watkins Rochester."[26]

While Brown awaited replies to his letters he turned back to the trouble with Forbes. Sanborn had written Brown on January 12 that "Col F" had sent him an "exceedingly abusive" letter in which he "calls one a cheat and accuses one of lying and other iniquities—you know that I am not guilty of these things—why will you not write and tell him so?" In fact Forbes had written "passionate and denunciatory letters" to Howe and Charles Sumner as well, accusing them of wronging him personally and holding them responsible "for the termination of his engagement with Brown; by which, he said, he had been reduced to poverty, and his family in Paris, deprived of pecuniary aid from him, had suffered great hardship." Sanborn, absolutely mystified by all this, forwarded Forbes's letter to Parker on January 15, noting that "if it were not for the wife and children, who are undoubtedly in suffering, the man might be hanged for all me,—for his whole style towards me is a combination of insult and lunacy. But I fear there was such an agreement between him and Brown, though Brown has told me nothing of it; and if so, he has a claim upon somebody, though not particularly upon us. Is there anything that can be done for him? I have written to Brown inquiring about the matter."[27]

In response, Brown wrote John Jr. to send Forbes "a sharp but well-merited rebuke." Tell him, Brown said, that he had not been "positively engaged" for one year (Brown "will not accept it well to be asked or told to state what he considers an *untruth*") . Remind him also that he had already received $600 "or six months' pay" for the care of his family and that he was to receive $100 a month only as long as he continued in Brown's service. And warn him that John Brown did not take well to *"highly offensive and insulting"* letters either to himself or to his friends. If this rebuke shut him up, then John Jr. was to send him $45. "I am anxious to understand him fully before we go any further," Brown concluded. But for the next month or so Forbes was mysteriously quiet.[28]

In another letter to John Jr., Brown said he wanted his son to make a slow trip through Pennsylvania, getting acquainted with people "of the right stripe" at Bedford, Chambersburg, Gettysburg, and Uniontown. In the meantime replies were coming in from Smith and some of Brown's other friends. Smith was definitely interested in Brown's "undertaking" and invited him out to Peterboro to discuss it. Stearns replied that he was under no obligation to Brown (as Stearns had explained earlier), but that he would not object to talking with Brown in Boston. Higginson answered that "I am always ready to invest in treason, but at present have none to invest. As for my friends, those who are able are not quite willing, and those who are willing are at present bankrupt." He went on to inquire whether Brown's undertaking was related to the "underground railroad" business.

"Rail Road business on a *somewhat extended* scale; is the *identical* object for which I am trying to get means," Brown replied. "I have been connected with that business *as commonly conducted* from my boyhood: & *never* let an opportunity slip. I have been operating to some purpose *the past season*; but I now have a measure on *foot* that I feel *sure* would awaken in you something more than a *common interest*: if you could understand it." Brown said he had written "my friends" Stearns and Sanborn, inviting them out to Peterboro "for consultation." Could Higginson come along too?[29]

Higginson, corresponding with Sanborn and Stearns, decided not to go to Peterboro, in part because Brown's plans were too vague. Sanborn and Stearns then urged Brown to come to Boston and talk there. But the old man refused, insisting that somebody would surely recognize him, that he must keep his presence in the East a secret.

Stearns and Parker, like Higginson, decided against consulting with Brown at this point. Sanborn, however, was still vacillating; at the same time that Brown had written him Sanborn had received a letter from "one of our Kansas correspondents" that Brown had disappeared from the territory and that "some thought him insane." Sanborn, of course, believed the latter allegation was "not so." But Brown's disappearance from Kansas and Iowa and the intimations of Forbes puzzled Sanborn. Was Brown planning something that would involve the slaves? An insurrection on the Kansas border or "in some inland part of Missouri"?

While Sanborn was vacillating he received a letter from Edwin Morton, a former classmate who was staying with Gerrit Smith. Morton reported that Brown had written Smith, too, and that "This is news,—he 'expects to overthrow slavery' in a large part of the country." On February 19 Morton wrote again, informing Sanborn that Brown was now in Peterboro and wanted a message sent to Sanborn. "He said it is not possible for him to go East under the circumstances. He would very much like to see you. He is pleased to find Mr. Smith more in harmony with his general plan than he thought he might be." When Sanborn read that he packed his bags and set out for Peterboro.[30]

In the meantime Brown wrote John Jr. in jubilation that Smith
and his wife were more than merely in harmony with his plan; they
were "ready to go in for a share in the *whole trade*." He added: "I
seem to be almost marvelously helped: & *to his name* be the praise."[31]

XVI

THE CONSPIRACY BEGINS

IT WAS THE EVENING OF FEBRUARY 22, in a bedroom on the third floor
of Smith's mansion in Peterboro. Brown walked up and down the
room, speaking earnestly to Sanborn and Morton. It was too late to
settle the slave question through politics or conventions or any other
peaceful means, Brown was saying. There was no recourse left to the
black man but in God and a massive slave uprising in which the
blood of slaveholders would be spilled. This was a terrible thing, but
slavery was a terrible wrong, the same as murder, and the unrepentant Southerners deserved to be violently punished for their sins. It
was God's will, Brown continued, that *he* should incite this insurrection—by a forced march on Virginia, the queen of the slave states,
with a guerrilla contingent he was already raising. And even if the
insurrection failed—although he was confident that it would not—
it would nevertheless congeal Northern hatred of slavery and thus
provoke a crisis, perhaps a civil war, in which the North would break
the black man's chains on the battlefield. He went on to show them
his Provisional Constitution, which would create a new government
for the territory he conquered, to consist of a Commander-in-Chief
of the Army, a President and Vice-President, a Supreme Court, and
a one-house Congress. After they had examined the forty-eight articles
of this remarkable document, Brown declared that he must have at
least $800 if his war for slave liberation was to succeed. Smith was
prepared to help. What about Sanborn and Morton? What about
the other Massachusetts friends?

"It is an amazing proposition," Sanborn said at last. But even as he said so he was beset with doubts: the plot itself was simply fantastic, desperate in character, inadequately planned . . . and what would the result be for certain?

Brown was unmoved. He insisted that only through insurrection and war could this "slave-cursed Republic be restored to the principles of the Declaration of Independence" and announced that he was prepared to die to bring that about. Sanborn thought these were noble sentiments indeed, but the methods Brown proposed seemed to invite certain failure; and Sanborn and Morton both urged "all the objections that would naturally occur to persons desiring the end he was seeking, but distrusting the slender means and the unpropitious time." Brown refused to listen. He gesticulated, "If God be for us, who can be against us?" and vowed that he would carry on without their support if they had no faith in him. He "left us," Sanborn recalled, "only the alternatives of betrayal, desertion, or support."

They renewed the discussion the next day, but nothing they said could dissuade Brown from his "fixed purpose." Late that afternoon Smith and Sanborn went for a walk, leaving Brown at home by the fire, arguing points of theology with another house guest, Charles Stuart. Stuart was a retired antislavery evangelist, one of Charles Grandison Finney's original "holy band" and a close friend and mentor of Theodore Dwight Weld. The son of a British army officer, he had fought with Wellington in Spain and served with the East India Company forces for thirteen years before he retired and came to America. He had met Brown once before, in the summer of 1855, and had given him $5 for his family in Kansas. There is no evidence that Brown sought Stuart's advice about the Virginia plan.

The sun was just setting behind the "snowy hills" as Smith and Sanborn strolled through the woods and fields, exchanging views on their old warrior and his incredible, yet bold and compelling plot. Although Sanborn still had reservations about Brown's plan of operations, he was irresistibly drawn to the idea of the United States passing through the ordeal of war, of an unrepentant South in flames, in order that the slavery curse might be removed at last. What was it he had said about Brown, in his lecture at Concord the previous March? *If this nation was to have a war over slavery, then the forces of freedom would need men like John Brown.* Now, as he walked with Smith, Sanborn felt "one-half inclined" to support Brown's scheme, for even if he failed to incite an insurrection, might he not bring on the greater war for slave liberation, as he said himself?[1]

Smith was ready for war, too. "Much as I abhor war," he had written of the Kansas troubles in 1856, "I nevertheless believe, that there are instances when the shedding of blood is unavoidable," and he had been prepared to fight the federal government (that friend of the "Missouri Ruffians") to save Kansas for liberty. "We are in a state of revolution," he had written Governor Ryland Fletcher of Vermont, in which only violent resistance could block the relentless advance of the Slave Power in the United States. "Hitherto," he had written the Syracuse *Journal*, "I have opposed the bloody abolition of slavery. But now, when it begins to march its conquering bands into the Free States, I and ten thousand other peace men are not only ready to have it repulsed with violence, but pursued even unto death, with violence."

And now John Brown was mobilizing a force of men to pursue slavery into the South itself, to destroy that institution in a violent insurrection, and Smith was ready to "go *all* lengths" to support him.[2]

"You see how it is," Smith said, turning to Sanborn, "our dear friend has made up his mind to this course, and cannot be turned from it. We cannot give him up to die alone; we must support him. I will raise so many hundred dollars for him; you must lay the case before your friends in Massachusetts, and ask them to do as much. I can see no other way."[3]

Sanborn agreed, and set out for Boston the next day, February 24, to arrange a meeting between Brown and his Massachusetts friends. After Sanborn had gone, Brown wrote him a warm letter and thanked him for feeling "½ inclined to make this common cause with me. I *greatly rejoice at this*; for I believe when you come to look at the *ample field* I labour in: & the rich harvest which (not only this entire country, but) the whole world during the present & future generations may *reap* from its successful cultivation: you will feel that you are out of your element until you find you are in it; an entire unit." But what an inconceivable amount of good Sanborn could contribute with his counsel, his example, and his natural ability for active service. As for himself, "I have only had *this one* opportunity in a life of nearly sixty years" and "I might not again have another equal opportunity. God has honored but comparatively *a very small* part of mankind with any possible chance for such mighty & soul satisfying rewards. But my dear friend if you should make up your mind to do so I trust it will be wholly from the promptings of your own spirit; after having *thoroughly counted* the cost. I would *flatter no man* into such a measure if I could do it ever so easily. *I expect nothing* but to endure *hardship*: but I expect to effect a mighty conquest even though it be like the last victory of Sampson. I felt for a number of years *in earlier life*: a steady, strong desire: to *die*: but since I saw my prospect of becoming a 'reaper' in the *great* harvest I have not only felt quite willing to *live*: but have enjoyed life much; & am now rather anxious to live for *a few* years more."[4]

2

By the time Sanborn arrived in Boston he had apparently made up his mind to support Brown all the way. On February 25 he "communicated the enterprise" to Higginson and Parker and later contacted Howe as well. At Parker's recommendation, they invited Brown to visit Boston secretly so they could discuss his intriguing "experiment." Stearns also expressed an interest, because recent developments in the slavery controversy had convinced him that slavery could not be defeated at the ballot box, in Kansas or anywhere else.

On February 26, after all the melodramatic gestures at keeping his whereabouts a secret, Brown caught a train for New York. He went out to Brooklyn the next day and called on Dr. J. N. Gloucester and his wife, a wealthy Negro couple whom Brown had visited in the spring of 1857 and in whom he had confided his plans to "deliver the slave." Now Brown revealed his plans in full and the Gloucesters, marveling at Brown's spirit, promised to help him raise money and enlist support among New York City's 15,000 black residents. In March Gloucester wrote him that "Every true Son of God and man" should "in the language of that noble *Patriot* of his Country (Patrick Henry) now use those means—that God and nature has placed within our power" to work for Brown's cause. For it was designed not only to liberate "the abject slave," but to free all "those Colored men, north and south—who are but virtually *slaves*—there is in truth no black man, north, or south of mason and Dixon line—a *freeman*—whatever be his wealth, Position—or worth." Such universal injustice to blacks in this country was the result of one overriding evil—the "*hellish system*" of Southern slavery. Gloucester hoped that all Negroes would join Brown "in holy Energy—and Combat—against the *all Damnable* foe."⁵

Brown also contacted J. W. Loguen, a black pastor of Syracuse who had once told William Lloyd Garrison that "my hands will fight a slave holder—which I suppose the LIBERATOR and some of its good friends would not do." Loguen wholeheartedly approved of Brown's plot and agreed to recruit blacks in his area "who would go to war."

"I find much more earnest feeling among the colored people than ever before," Brown wrote his wife, "but that is by no means unusual. On the whole the language of Providence to me would certainly seem to say try on."⁶ Although Brown did not say so, the anger of black men like Gloucester and Loguen must have strengthened his belief that Southern Negroes, too, were seething with hatred for slaveholders and would swarm to his banners once the invasion began.

3

Brown arrived in Boston on March 4 and took a room in the American House on Hanover Street. There, during the next few days, his five Massachusetts supporters—Higginson, the angry Worcester clergyman; Parker, the blood-and-thunder Unitarian; Stearns, the bearded merchant; Sanborn, the young schoolteacher; and Howe, the dashing educator and social reformer—all came to hear the details of Brown's grand scheme.

Presenting them with the same argument he had given Smith and Sanborn earlier, Brown declared that he was an instrument in God's hands to invade the South and uproot its "evil institution." His conviction that he was an agent of God, that a sovereign and wrathful Lord was working through him to punish sinful men, was of course an outgrowth of his absorption with the Old Testament and his intense Calvinist faith. Apparently Brown did not tell his five supporters that he planned to launch his attack at Harpers Ferry, but there can be little doubt that Virginia came up in their discussions. According to one contemporary writer, Brown told them that if the insurrection began and held its ground even for a few days, "the whole country from the Potomac to Savannah would be ablaze."

They were all enthusiastic about the proposal—more so than Brown had probably anticipated. Higginson himself had long advocated disunion to rid the United States of the slavery sickness and had predicted that a revolution was coming. Parker had preached violent resistance, too, and Howe had declared that "some move of actual force" should be made against slavery. Stearns and Sanborn, who were gentler men, nevertheless hated the injustice of slavery so passionately that they, too, were prepared to destroy it with aggressive violence, if that was the only alternative.[7]

And for all of them, that March of 1858, violence seemed indeed the only solution to the slave problem in their troubled times. The South was not going to repent and free the slaves, thereby removing an institution which they and all other abolitionists regarded as an abominable violation of America's most cherished ideals of liberty and justice for all. On the contrary, Southerners adamantly defended slavery as a positive good, claiming that it was justified by history, condoned by the Bible, and ordained by God from the beginning of time. They argued that "niggers" were subhuman anyway and belonged in chains as naturally as cattle in pens. And in the abolitionist publications which Brown and his friends had read, all planters were portrayed as beady-eyed, Heaven-flouting Simon Legrees who not only beat their slaves with savage glee but raped Negro girls in a frenzy of lust. These were the ogres now in power in Dixie—the Simon Legrees. These were the devils trying to graft slavery forever on the tormented face of this Republic. These were the "thieves and murderers" John Brown of Osawatomie proposed to exterminate by revolution or civil war.

Of course, all slaveowners were not grotesque monsters like those described in the abolitionist literature which Brown and his colleagues had studied. There were some cruel and sadistic slaveholders, to be sure, and there were some who fit the opposite stereotype, fostered by pro-Southern writers, of the planter as a benign, God-fearing man who loved his Negroes like his own children. But a vast

majority of the South's 46,000 planters (the other five and a half
million Southern whites were mostly nonslaveholding farmers) fell
somewhere between the two extremes. As Kenneth M. Stampp has
observed, these men did not use the whip because they were sadists;
they used it—or the threat of it—to make their slaves "stand in fear,"
to force them to work and prevent them from running away or
striking back. Without the whip—the symbol of the master's authority—the slavery-plantation system would have disintegrated. Moreover, many slaveowners were aware of the discrepancy between
Jeffersonian liberalism and human bondage, felt guilty about it,
and secretly regarded as an abomination an institution they publicly
defended. Yet they could not eradicate slavery themselves and resolve
their dilemma because they could not bear the thought of what
three and a half million free blacks would do to the South's racist
and class-conscious social order. Nor could they or their nonslaveholding neighbors stand criticism by fire-and-brimstone Northern crusaders. As several historians have argued, the abolitionist
cry of sinner! had aroused the slaveowner's deepest guilt; and he
had responded with uncompromising defenses of slavery that helped
to ease his own conscience. In his "twistings and turnings on the rack
of slavery," he saw abolitionist conspiracies everywhere—in Kansas,
New England, Washington, and the Northwest, where antislavery
groups had invoked state rights to defy his cherished fugitive slave
law. And the slaveowner lived in mortal terror of the very thing John
Brown planned to visit upon him—another Nat Turner insurrection.
An insurrection incited by "abolitionist agitators and Yankee fanatics." An insurrection in which, in the dark of some malignant night,
insurgent Negroes would break into the slaveowner's home and ax him
and his wife, sons, and daughters to death. And so he and his fellow
Southerners had formed militia and vigilante units all over the South
to put down any such uprising; and they had threatened to whip or
hang any "nigger" who even talked disobedience. And yet slaveowners could tell themselves and the rest of the world that their
Negroes were too happy, too docile, and too ignorant ever to dream
of turning against their affectionate masters. And yet, fearing an
abolitionist take-over of the federal government that would result in
forced emancipation at bayonet point, social chaos, and miscegena-
tion, slaveowners demanded that the gag rule against abolitionist

petitions be resurrected, that sedition laws be passed prohibiting criticism of slavery, that even more stringent fugitive slave laws be enacted, that slavery be legalized in the territories, that Kansas be admitted as a slave state, that the Dred Scott decision be rigorously enforced, and that the U.S. Constitution always be construed as guaranteeing the right to own slaves—thus convincing men like Brown and his six abolitionist friends that Southerners *were* involved in a Slave Power conspiracy after all.[8]

For they had no idea what private travail lay behind the Old South's ringing defenses of slavery in 1858. All they knew was that the South not only was justifying slavery in the name of God and civilization but was attempting to force slavery on Kansas and the rest of the predominantly free-soil West, through what seemed to them a program of invasion, terrorization by atrocity, bloodshed, fraud, and subterfuge. And while Southerners were a minority in the United States, they dominated the crucial branches of the federal government—the Presidency, the Senate, and the Supreme Court—and were using these agencies to perpetuate slavery in the laws and legal decisions of the United States and to extend it all over the West —and maybe the North as well.

In fact, at the very time the secret discussions with Brown were taking place in Boston the proslavery Buchanan Administration and the proslavery Senate were attempting to stamp slavery on the soil of Kansas (the first stage of the great conspiracy), despite the overwhelming evidence that most settlers there were free-state. On February 2, the same day that Brown had initially written his abolitionist friends from Rochester, President Buchanan had called on Congress to admit Kansas into the Union as a slave state, on the basis of the Lecompton Constitution. Although that document was plainly "a swindle and a fraud," the Administration-controlled Senate was certain to follow the instructions of Buchanan and his Southern-dominated Cabinet. The controversy had become so bitter that Senator Stephen A. Douglas, the chief architect of the Kansas-Nebraska Act, had broken with the Administration because of the "Lecompton swindle" and the House, controlled by the free states, was certain to reject it or at least demand a compromise. Knowing so, many Southern leaders—and a number of Southern newspapers— were threatening violence if Kansas were not admitted to the Union as the sixteenth slave state. Thus, from an antislavery view, the Lecompton controversy proved that the South was more determined than ever to undermine the democratic process not only to win Kansas and to dominate the Union but to destroy personal and civil liberties and even republican government itself.

This is not to say that all abolitionists (a small minority of the Northern population anyway) were prepared to attack the South in order to block the alleged Slave Power conspiracy and preserve republican government. On the contrary, most antislavery groups were still desperately searching for some solution to the Southern problem short of war. But Higginson, Parker, Howe, Sanborn, and Stearns believed that all peaceful alternatives had failed and that only revolution was left. For them, the time had come when only war upon the South itself could destroy the Slave Power conspiracy, eradicate slavery, and restore their nation to God and the ideals of Jefferson's Declaration.

The courage of Brown himself—his willingness to die for a noble cause, his unbending conviction that he was an instrument of God and that under God he would succeed—also accounts for the enthusiasm with which these men embraced his plot. In Sanborn's vision, Brown loomed up as a Puritan warrior who had "inherited from deacons and Captains of Connecticut 'the sword of the Lord and of Gideon.' " For Howe, Brown was "Coleridge's Ancient Mariner . . . come to life." Higginson, who would never forget "the signs of fire" in Brown's "thin, worn, resolute face," thought the old warrior "a high-minded, unselfish, belated Covenanter; a man whom Sir Walter Scott might have drawn." Stearns believed him "a Cromwellian Ironside introduced in the nineteenth century for a special purpose." It was "to take up the work of the English Puritans where it had ended with the death of Cromwell—the work of social regeneration."

One or two of them, however, may have doubted the soundness of Brown's actual plan of invasion. Since Howe had fought in Greece, they regarded him as an expert on guerrilla warfare and looked to him for his opinion. Although Howe questioned how Brown would recross the Potomac in case of emergency, he thought the scheme on the whole was a feasible one. He had seen Turkish armies defeated in the mountains of Greece by small guerrilla bands and believed the same could be done against Southerners in the Alleghenies. But Brown's friends would probably have supported him anyway. "Without accepting Brown's plans as reasonable," Sanborn declared, "we were prepared to second them merely because they were his." That may have been another way of saying that, even if Brown failed to incite a slave insurrection, the invasion (as Brown himself had explained) would nevertheless ignite a powder keg that might explode into civil war in which slavery would be destroyed. And civil war was something which Parker, Higginson, and a few other abolitionists—Wendell Phillips, for example—had been wishfully predicting for years.[9]

Although Brown's friends still did not know the exact spot where he planned to "raise the mill," they formed a secret Committee of Six—including Gerrit Smith—to advise the old man and to raise $1,000 for his "experiment," Smith, when he was apprised of the meetings with Brown in Boston, was ecstatic about the prospects. On March 25 he wrote Joshua Giddings with cheerful abandon: "The slave will be delivered by the shedding of blood, and the signs are multiplying that his deliverence is at hand."[10]

4

How would the North react to the revolution once it was under way? Surely the Secret Six did not anticipate any massive Northern support for the invasion but counted on the shock value Brown's attack would have on sectional tensions that already existed. As a matter of fact, countless thousands of Northerners would have been horrified at what Brown planned to do, for they regarded slavery as a local problem which Southerners should solve by themselves; and they had a profound respect for Southern property rights too. Maybe most Northerners thought the institution of slavery was unjust and immoral and wanted passionately to keep that institution out of the territories lest their own freedoms somehow be imperiled. And maybe they viewed the typical Southerner as an arrogant, violent-talking slaveowner undoubtedly trying to control the central government to protect his own interests. Yet they would never wish on him the kind of Negro war which Brown was plotting. In fact, a huge majority of Northerners were as virulently racist as Southerners themselves, regarding the Negro as an offensive and inferior brute who should be segregated into ghettos or, better yet, shipped back to Africa where he belonged. Not only did most Northerners fervently support "black laws" that discriminated against free Negroes in virtually every Northern state outside of New England, but they grimaced at the possibility that abolition might result in thousands of Southern blacks flooding into the free states. Most whites in the Northwestern states—where opposition to slavery in the territories, the fugitive slave law, and the Dred Scott decision was strongest— were Negrophobes to the core and made it emphatically clear that they did not want slaves or free blacks living next door to them. These paradoxical sentiments about slavery and the Negro were reflected in the Republican party itself—a coalition of ex-Whigs like Thurlow Weed and Abraham Lincoln; of racist free-soilers, indus- trialists, and small farmers; and of political abolitionists like Chase and Sumner. The party officially advocated a hands-off policy regarding slavery in the South, arguing that neither the Northern states nor the federal government had any constitutional authority to meddle with the peculiar institution where it already existed. But the party strove mightily to prohibit slavery in the territories, because if slavery were not stopped somewhere, as Lincoln put it, then the common white man of the North (with whom Lincoln consistently identified) would end up in chains as well, just as Southern extremists like George Fitzhugh' advocated. Yet Lincoln clearly spoke for a majority of Northerners when he declared that, while Southern slavery was wrong and must be kept out of the West, it could be legally abolished only by Southerners themselves. He hoped that by restricting its growth, the wasteful plantation-slavery system would die out (by 1890? 1900?) for lack of new soil. Then the freed slaves would be colonized in Africa. Obviously nobody with such sentiments as these would approve the black revolution which Brown and the Six intended to stir up in the South.[11]

But might not the North be involuntarily sucked into the con- flagration once Brown had it roaring in Virginia? Sectional hostilities over Kansas, the fugitive slave law, and an upsurge of abolitionism (thanks to religious revivals now sweeping the North) were already at a combustible state; and Southerners themselves, growing increasingly alarmed as the abolitionists continued their moral attack, tended more than ever to see all Northerners as finger-pointing William Lloyd Garrisons who wanted to incite the slaves to revolt. Thus any move such as Brown and the Six were plotting would undoubtedly cause a massive convulsion in the South; and so who knew what the result would be for certain? A successful uprising in all the chaos and hysteria? Or a civil war in which the whole nation would go up in flames?

But the success of the experiment depended on how much support Brown could secure in the next sixty days. He was well aware that he could not expect many abolitionists to go along with him, because most of them, no matter how committed they were to Negro freedom, were not prepared to fight for it—at least not yet. Garrison and his nonviolent followers certainly were not. A number of other abolitionists—Chase and Joshua Giddings, to name only two—still sought a political solution to the slavery problem. And still others—mostly evangelists like George Barrell Cheever—hoped to overthrow the peculiar institution by converting Northerners to Evangelical Christianity and the antislavery faith. Many veteran abolitionists—Garrisonians and anti-Garrisonians alike—agreed that the only solution to the Slave Power conspiracy was disunion, although they conceded that disunion would not help the slave much. A few individuals like Wendell Phillips talked about civil war just as the Secret Six did, but Brown believed men such as Phillips were more talk than fight. In fact, when Sanborn asked if Phillips should be included in the conspiracy, Brown replied, "I have noticed that men who have the gift of eloquence. Such as our friend has, seldom are men of action; now it is men of action I wish to consult; and so you need say nothing to Wendell Phillips."[12]

The kind of men he wanted were angry young whites in the mold of John Henry Kagi and Negro militants like Loguen and Douglass. He believed he could raise a veritable army of Negroes (after all, 151,000 of them resided in the Northeast at that time), and it was for this purpose that he left Boston and hurried back to Philadelphia, where John Jr. joined him in mid-March. There Brown held conferences with several Negro leaders—the Rev. Stephen Smith, William Still, Frederick Douglass, and Brown's old friend and fellow revolutionary, Henry Highland Garnet, who was preaching fiery sermons to his black congregation in New York City. Brown left Philadelphia fully expecting these men to raise money and Negro recruits for the coming revolution.[13]

Then he traveled to North Elba, to enlist his other sons and Henry Thompson in the cause. Ruth, however, was reluctant to let Henry "go to school"—and Henry himself had doubts. "I cannot bear the thought of Henry leaving me again," Ruth had written her father; "yet I know I am selfish. When I think of my poor despised sisters, that are deprived of brother husband and children, I feel deeply for them; and were it not for my little children, I would go almost anywhere with Henry, if by going I could do them any good." Brown argued with her and with Henry, Watson, and Oliver too. Watson, who feared his father and yet tried to emulate his ideals, finally came around. So did Oliver, despite the fact that he was planning to marry sixteen-year-old Martha Brewster. Unhappily for Oliver, the Brewsters disliked the militant Browns and attempted to prevent the marriage; but the young couple defied them and were married on April 7, knowing full well that Oliver might have "to go right away with father." Henry finally "gave *up* going," but two of his brothers—Dauphin and William Thompson—agreed to join Brown later.[14]

Early in April Brown and John Jr. went to Syracuse to confer with Loguen and other Negroes in the area. Then, while John Jr. remained in the States to contact other "interested parties," Brown and Loguen traveled to Canada, where thirty to forty thousand blacks resided, most of them fugitives from the South. At St. Catherines Brown secured the cooperation of Harriet Tubman, a powerful, rotund black woman who was one of the great heroes of the Underground Railroad. Known as "the Moses of her people," she worked in hotels in the summer in order to save money for Underground Railroad expeditions in the winter. Later she told Higginson that she had gone into the South eight times and brought some sixty slaves north to freedom. Apparently she gave Brown what information she had about the Virginia terrain and what allies he might find there. She also agreed to enlist recruits for him among her personal following in the province of Canada. "I am succeeding to all *appearance* beyond my expectation," Brown wrote John Jr. on April 8.

"Hariet Tubman hooked on *his* whole team at once. *He Hariet* is the most of a *man* naturally; that *I ever* met with. There is the most abundant material; & of the *right quality*: in this quarter; beyond all doubt." Then Brown moved on to Chatham, situated on the Thames River in what is now Ontario province, about 45 miles east of Detroit. At Chatham Brown obtained the support of Dr. Martin R. Delany, a prominent Negro who had once said that if he were a slave, he would "boldly strike for LIBERTY—FOR FREEDOM or a Martyr's grave." Brown also made arrangements for a secret convention to meet at Chatham, where he would complete his preparations. On April 14 he wrote Douglass that "I expect to need all the help I can get by first of May."[15]

5

In mid-April Brown returned to Springdale, Iowa, to gather his "flock of sheep." He found them restless and irritable because of their cramped quarters in William Maxson's small farmhouse. Owen explained that they had tried to stay busy while Brown was away: they had debated and talked about war, conducted military maneuvers in a field in back of Maxson's place, studied Forbes's manual, and held sessions of a mock legislature in which they had drawn up laws for a utopian "State of Topeka." Sometimes the sessions had degenerated into boisterous quarreling, much to the irritation of their Quaker neighbors, some of whom regarded the boys suspiciously as "Mormon spies." But for the most part this highly abolitionist Quaker community had sheltered and protected the boys and even allowed them to court Quaker girls. Cook had them chasing after him and had to be censured once for "hugging girls in Springdale Legislature." C. P. Tidd had done more than that with a young girl who lived nearby, laying himself open to a grave accusation by her father. When they were not practicing war or making love, the boys wrote bold letters to their families about the work ahead. William Leeman, a nineteen-year-old who "smoked a good deal and drank sometimes," proudly announced that he was warring against slavery, "the greatest *curse* that ever infested America." And Stevens confided to his sister that "I am ready to give up my life for the oppressed if need be. I hope I shall have your good will and sympathy in this glorious cause."

The company had four additional recruits now: Barclay and Edwin Coppoc, Quaker boys who were living with their mother in Springdale; Stewart Taylor, a young Canadian; and George B. Gill, a twenty-six-year-old Jack-of-all-trades who had worked on a whaling ship in the Pacific before he migrated to Kansas in 1856. Gill had met Brown there, introduced him to Taylor, and sheltered his company in Iowa in 1857.

On April 27 Brown wrote his wife that his sons at North Elba would "probably be called on before the middle of May" and then took all his recruits (except the Coppoc brothers, who would join him later) on to Canada.[16]

6

Chatham, Canada, just before ten o'clock in the morning of May 8, 1858. It was an ordinary Saturday morning for most of the town's 6,000 residents, one third of them fugitive slaves, and the one long shopping thoroughfare named King Street and the wharves on the Thames River all bustled with activity. The streets were crowded with Negroes, who worked as artisans and farmers or as unskilled laborers at $1.25 a day. There was considerable activity at the Negro schoolhouse on Princess Street, too, where 34 Negroes and 12 whites had gathered to organize a Masonic lodge.

It was a blind. The men were delegates to a secret constitutional convention which Brown had called to organize a revolutionary government for the black state he intended to establish in the southern Appalachians. Inside the schoolhouse Brown mingled freely among the black delegates, shaking hands with Dr. Delany and William Charles Munroe, a Negro minister from Detroit, and conversing with James H. Harris, Osborn P. Anderson, and one G. J. Reynolds, who allegedly represented a secret Negro military organization that wanted to cooperate with Brown. The old man was disappointed in the small turnout, for none of the Secret Six were present and neither were Harriet Tubman, Frederick Douglass, Garnet, or Loguen. But Brown was determined to go ahead despite their absence; and when ten o'clock struck he called the meeting to order. First the delegates elected officers for the convention, choosing the Rev. Mr. Munroe as president and Kagi as secretary. Then, on a motion by Dr. Delany, Brown arose to address them on the purpose of the convention. He declared that for twenty or thirty years he had been obsessed with the idea of freeing the slaves. He told them that he had gone to Europe on wool business, had visited the Waterloo battlefield, and claimed to have inspected fortifications and earthworks at other places. Gradually, he said, a "plan" had formed in his mind for mountain warfare in the United States. He had then embarked on a study of Roman warfare, the Spanish uprising against the Romans, the succession of Schamyl (the Circassian chief), and Toussaint L'Ouverture's slave war in Haiti in the 1790's. As he studied such subjects "a plan of action" emerged "spontaneously" in his mind. He was convinced that Southern slaves were ready for revolt, that at the first sign of a leader who wanted to break their chains and lead them to freedom "they would immediately rise all over the Southern states." He "explicitly and emphatically" claimed that he had gone to Kansas "to gain a footing for the furtherance of this matter." From then on he had "devoted his whole being, mental, moral, and physical, all that he had and was to the extinction of slavery." He explained that his company, twelve of whom stood beside him now, would invade Virginia, in the region of the Blue Ridge Mountains, and march into Tennessee and northern Alabama, where the slaves would rally to his standard. They would then wage war upon the plantations on the plains west and east of the mountains, which would serve as the base of operations.

"But what if troops are brought against you?" one of the delegates asked.

Brown waved aside all doubts. A small force trained in guerrilla warfare could easily defend those Thermopylae ravines against Southern militia or the U.S. Army. Yet he hoped that he would not have to shed a great deal of blood. If slaveholders resisted him, he would take them into the mountains as hostages. He believed that "all the free negroes in the Northern states" would also rally to his cause once the invasion began and that "as many of the free negroes in Canada as could accompany him, would do so." He planned to organize the liberated slaves under the Provisional Constitution, which would establish a new state in the territory he had conquered. The blacks would labor on farms and in workshops, build churches and organize schools where "they were to be taught the useful and mechanical arts and to be instructed in all the business of life." Brown was confident that his state could support and govern itself and defy any enemy. Ultimately, he declared, the slave states would be forced to emancipate all their blacks and human slavery would at last be destroyed. Then Brown would reorganize his mountain commonwealth on a permanent basis and new elections would be held.

Brown now presented his Provisional Constitution to the convention. First the delegates took an oath of secrecy, then the preamble and all forty-eight articles of the document were read aloud.

"Whereas slavery, throughout its entire existence in the United States, is none other than a most barbarous, unprovoked, and unjustifiable war of one portion of its citizens upon another portion—the only conditions of which are perpetual imprisonment and hopeless servitude or absolute extermination—in utter disregard and violation of those eternal and self-evident truths set forth in our Declaration of Independence:

"Therefore we, citizens of the United States, and the oppressed people who, by a recent decision of the Supreme Court [the Dred Scott decision], are declared to have no rights which the white man is bound to respect, together with all other people degraded by the laws thereof, do, for the time being, ordain and establish for ourselves the following Provisional Constitution and Ordinances, the better to protect our persons, property, lives, and liberties, and to govern our actions."

The government itself was to consist of a one-house Congress or House of Representatives, a President and Vice-President, and a Supreme Court, to be elected by "all citizens of mature age and of sound mind connected with this organization." A Commander-in-Chief of the Army, to be chosen by the President, Vice-President, and a majority of Congress and the Supreme Court, was to direct military matters and confer with allies. All government officials were to serve without pay; and any of them who committed a crime or shirked their duties would be tried, removed from office, and punished. All treaties must be ratified by the President and Vice-President, the Commander-in-Chief of the Army, and a majority of Congress, the Supreme Court, and the general officers of the army. All property captured from the enemy and all produced by the labor of those associated with the organization would be held "as the property of the whole" and used "for the common benefit, or disposed of for the same object." All money, plates, watches, and jewelry found or captured would be placed in "a liberal safety or intelligence fund." Anybody convicted of a noncapital crime would be sentenced to hard labor on public works or the public roads. Anybody who "forcibly violated" a female prisoner would be put to death. So would anybody who deserted. Those connected with the organization should respect marriages "at all times," keep families together "as far as possible," and reunite broken families. Measures should be taken for moral and religious instruction, for "relief to the suffering, instruction of the young and ignorant, and the encouragement of personal cleanliness." All members of the organization were to treat their prisoners and one another with kindness and respect, "as in the fear of Almighty God, to whose care and keeping we commit our cause." Article 46 stated that the Provisional Constitution should not be construed as an attempt to dissolve the Union or to overthrow "any State Government of the United States," but should be viewed simply as an effort "to Amendment and Repeal." The flag of the Provisional Government would be "the same that our Fathers fought under in the Revolution."

After considerable debate on Article 46, the delegates unanimously approved the constitution and signed it that afternoon. At an evening session, they chose John Brown as Commander-in-Chief and John Henry Kagi, proud and impressive with his large, alert eyes, arched brows, and dark beard, as Secretary of War. The following Monday they appointed Gill as Secretary of the Treasury, Richard Realf as Secretary of State, Owen Brown as Treasurer, and Alfred M. Ellsworth and Osborn P. Anderson as members of Congress. When two black men declined the Presidency, it was decided that a committee of fifteen, headed by Brown, should fill that and other vacant positions at a later time.[17]

The Chatham convention was the climax of all Brown's feverish preparations. Now he was ready to go to war; he had never been more fiercely determined in his life. He refused to worry because none of his influential friends and backers had come to Chatham. Nor was he daunted by the horrors he knew would attend a racial war. Slavery itself, as he stated in his preamble, was "a most barbarous, unprovoked, and unjustifiable War" of one portion of American citizens upon another; and the preamble itself, by invoking "the eternal and self-evident truths" of the Declaration of Independence, provided in Brown's mind a moral and an ideological justification for the violence he was about to unleash upon the South. And anyway he had repeatedly argued that the sins of this nation—and he meant the sin of slavery above all—could never be redeemed without the shedding of blood. He had also memorized the doomsday prophecies of Isaiah and Jeremiah, whose books were among his favorites in the Old Testament. "For these are the days of vengeance," Jeremiah warned a sinning Israel, "and there shall be great distress on this land." "Shall I not visit for these *things*? saith the Lord; and shall not my soul be avenged on such a nation as this?" And Isaiah: "But thus saith the Lord, Even the captives of the mighty shall be taken away, and the prey of the terrible shall be delivered: for I will contend with him that contendeth with thee, and I will save thy children. And I will feed them that oppress thee with their own flesh; and they shall be drunken with their own blood, as with sweet wine."[18]

The Negroes who signed Brown's Constitution wholeheartedly approved of the ideals in its preamble, and they shared the old man's extreme hatred of slavery. Yet many of them were not so sure about joining his force of liberation. The thought of going back to the South must have terrified them. And the plan of invasion itself sounded fantastic—almost mad. Were slaves everywhere on the verge of rebellion? Could the U.S. Army be defeated and a new mountain state maintained? They did not know. They had risked their lives, had suffered much hardship, to get to Canada and freedom. Were they willing to abandon all that now? Were they willing to follow Brown and some boys back to that Gibraltar of slavery and possibly a horrible death in a carnage of racial violence? Furthermore, was Brown really an instrument of God to free the slaves? Or was he merely a poor self-deluded old man?[19]

7

Several frustrating complications delayed Brown's attack. For one thing, Loguen reported from Syracuse that Negroes who would go to

war did not have the money "to get there with" and that he had
decided to "let them all rest for the present." For another, Brown
himself was drastically short of funds. So far the Secret Six had given
him about $600, but the money had melted away in expenses. Brown
wrote Sanborn to send him an additional $300 to $400 at once. But
when no money was forthcoming Brown had to send his men to
Cleveland, where they managed to get enough work to support themselves. Brown remained at Chatham, where he wrote his wife on May
24 that "We are completely nailed down at present for want of funds;
and we may be obliged to remain inactive for months yet."[20]

Meanwhile Hugh Forbes had apparently blown the lid off the
whole conspiracy. Having failed to extract any money out of Brown's
friends with his threatening letters, Forbes had gone to Washington
and started talking to several politicians. He warned William H.
Seward, for example, that John Brown was "a very bad man," "a
reckless man, an unreliable man, a vicious man" who must be
restrained, and partially exposed Brown's plan to Senator Henry
Wilson and others. Alarmed, Wilson wrote Howe on May 9 that the
men who furnished arms for Old Brown to use in Kansas had better
retrieve them and put them in the hands of *reliable men* in the
territory. Above all, the weapons should not be used "for other purposes, as rumor says they may be," because that would harm the supporters of *that very foolish movement.*"[21]

On May 14 Howe received a shocking letter from Forbes himself.
In it the furious drillmaster recounted in detail how he and Brown
had hassled over their rival Virginia plans until Brown had pretended
to agree to their Compromise Project. But Brown was a bigot and a
liar! Forbes declared. He had never intended to honor their agreement, but had betrayed Forbes just as his New England friends had
done, and now his whole "crude" project was a scheme of Amos A.
Lawrence and others involved in New England mills for "grand
speculation in the sudden rise of cotton on the exchanges." Yes, it
was all a cotton hoax! Lawrence and his fellow schemers hoped to
make a pile of money when cotton prices bolted upward during the
panic that followed Brown's attack! Well, Forbes would not tolerate
such a breach of confidence. The mixed plan was partly his and he
denied the right of Brown or Howe ("lying, as you do, out of sight")
or anybody else to abandon the Compromise Project and perpetrate

such an atrocious wrong on him and his "starving family." As for his family, Forbes vowed to defend his "hungry children" to the death from the "foul perfidy" of the New England speculators.[22]

Howe and his colleagues were scandalized. How much did Forbes know about their own involvement in the conspiracy? How much had he told? Already a frantic exchange of letters had begun among the Six and between them and their warrior "nailed down" in Canada. Stearns sent "Hawkins" an official order not to use the weapons collected for Kansas anywhere else. In despair, Howe wrote Higginson that "Wilson as well as Hale and Seward, and God knows how many more, have heard about the plot." Howe, the veteran of the Greek revolution, wanted to go through with the plot anyway, but Parker, Stearns, and Sanborn were so frightened that they were ready to postpone the whole business until next year.[23]

Higginson, too, was emphatically against postponement. He wrote Parker that "if we give it up now at the command or threat of H.F. it will be the same next year." They had to "circumvent the man somehow. . . . When the thing is well started, who cares what he says?" Higginson also wrote Brown about "that fool" and the problems the drillmaster had created. Brown replied: "I have only time to say at this moment that as it is an invariable rule *with me*; to be *governed* by circumstances: or in other words *not to do anything* while I *do not know what to do*: that none of our friends need have any fears in relation to *hasty* or *rash steps* being taken by us." He urged Higginson to stay clear of Forbes personally, asked for $200 to $300 without delay, and promised not to act until they had "perfect *knowledge* of facts in regard to what *F* has *really done*; & *will* do: so that we may ourselves *know how we ought to act*. None of us *here* or with *you* should be *hasty*; or *decide* the course to be taken; while under an excitement. 'In all thy ways acknowledge *Him* & *He* shall direct thy paths.' A *good* course; is *sure* to be *safe* in the hands of an *all good, all wise, & all powerful, Director*: & Father."[24]

This letter reveals more about Brown's attitude toward his own generalship and his projected invasion—both were completely in the hands of God—than practically any letter he ever wrote. Yet his appeal to caution and sober-headedness in the Forbes matter fell largely on deaf ears. Stearns, Parker, Sanborn, and Smith were panic-stricken (would there be investigations? arrests?). Smith demanded that

Brown go no further, insisting that "I never was convinced of the wisdom of his scheme" and that it was madness to continue. On May 24 five members of the secret committee (Higginson refused to attend) held an emergency meeting in the Revere House in Boston. Ironically, Smith had just delivered an address before the American Peace Society, advocating unilateral disarmament in foreign affairs and asserting that America's "irregular but righteous government" deserved the support of "men of good will."[25] In the Revere House meeting Howe joined with the other four in deciding to postpone Brown's attack until things cooled off. They notified "Hawkins" of their decision and urged him to go back to Kansas and create a diversion there that would make whatever Forbes told Wilson and the others seem like meretricious gossip. They promised to raise $2,000 for the old warrior if he would leave for the territory as soon as possible.

When Brown learned of their decision he went to Boston and held several conferences with them and with Higginson. When Brown found that Higginson was infuriated at the postponement and disgusted with the timidity of the other backers, Brown declared that he too was "full of regret" about their decision. He angrily told Higginson that the others *were not men of action*," that Gerrit Smith especially was "a timid man." Brown complained that delay would lower the morale of his followers and discourage the Negroes in Canada as well. Forbes's defection was "injurious" all right, but he agreed with Higginson that "the increased terror" caused by Forbes's confessions might well work to the conspirators' advantage. If Brown had the means he would not delay another hour.

But the others—especially Stearns and Smith—"held the purse," so there was little Brown could do but give in to their demands. However, "the sly old veteran . . . had not said this to them," Higginson noted, "& had appeared to acquiesce far more than he really did; it was essential that they should not think him reckless," since he had to rely on them for money. "But," Higginson added, "he wished me not to tell them what he had said to me."

It was finally agreed among the Secret Six that Brown should "blind F" by some diversionary operation in Kansas and remain there until the spring of 1859, that he would receive $500 now with a promise of an additional $2,000 or $3,000 when he returned to the

East, and that all the arms should be transferred to him "so as to relieve them [the Secret Six] of responsibility." Henceforth Brown was not to "inform them of his plans in detail, nor burden them with knowledge that would be to them both needless and inconvenient." Brown's backers still wanted him to incite insurrection or provoke civil war in the United States, but at a time and in such a way that they would not be held responsible as fellow conspirators in case the experiment failed.

On June 3 the old man left Boston, and Howe, breathing a sigh of relief, notified Higginson that the old warrior "went off in good spirits," with $500 in gold in his pockets and a new alias—"Shubel Morgan."[26]

8

On June 20 and 21 "Shubel Morgan" was in Cleveland, where he gathered his flock around him, gave them what money he could spare, and allowed most of them (Owen, Leeman, Taylor, Parsons, and Moffett) to scatter to various places in Ohio, Illinois, and Iowa, although exhorting them to remain loyal and to come at once when he called.[27] Others he gave special assignments: Realf was to go to New York and keep an eye on Forbes (eventually Realf would return to England in an apparent effort to raise funds for the projected invasion). Stevens and Gill were to solicit money in Springdale and Tabor and then join Brown later in Kansas. And Cook—what was Brown going to do about Cook? Realf had written about Cook's "rage for talking" at Cleveland. He had announced at his boarding-house that he was on a *"secret expedition"* and that the rest of the company was *"under his orders."* He had brandished his guns in public, boasted that he had *"killed 5 men"* in Kansas, talked with alarming candor to "a lady friend," and climaxed his performance by proposing that in the event the attack was postponed, he, Parsons, Gill, and Taylor should raid the South by themselves. Realf believed the worst threat to Brown's plan was not Forbes but Cook's "tongue malady."

That is why Brown was highly dubious when Cook asserted that he wanted to go to Harpers Ferry without delay, to get a job and make investigations as an advance agent. But incredibly enough Brown consented to let him go, with stern orders to keep his garrulous mouth shut and to learn everything he could about the people in the area and the layout of the government arsenal and armory works.[28]

On June 22 Brown left Cleveland with Kagi and Tidd and went to Chicago. There he wrote John Jr. (who had returned to West Andover, Ohio) and instructed him *"with perfect quiet"* to move "the *Tools* (*not the other stuff*) to where they will be safe; & dry: & where *neither my friends or men or any one* but the keeper; & you will know where to find them." The rifles and revolvers had already been shipped to Conneaut, Ashtabula County, Ohio; and John Jr., following his father's orders, soon moved "the tools" to Cherry Valley Village, where they were concealed under a pile of caskets in the King Brothers furniture store.[29]

In the meantime Brown headed west again, and on June 27 he was back in Lawrence.

XVII

MY WORK . . . MY MISSION

ON THE EVENING OF JUNE 27 Brown had dinner with Richard J. Hinton and James Redpath in a hotel in Lawrence. Hinton was amazed at how much Brown had aged since the correspondent had seen him last. Perhaps it was the white, Moses-style beard he had grown, partly to disguise himself from the law, that added so visibly to his age. He was slower in movement, too, and rather grave and reticent as he sat between the young correspondents. Both admired his beard. Redpath said he looked like "a stately old man" in his "patriarchal disguise."

As they talked, Brown inquired about the trend of Kansas politics since he had been away in the East. He was disappointed to learn that, except for isolated outbursts of violence, the territory had remained fairly quiet. Walker, an implacable opponent of the Administration-backed Lecompton Constitution, had resigned as governor, and Buchanan had replaced him with James Wilson Denver, a Virginia lawyer who had lived on the Missouri border before Kansas was opened for settlement. As it turned out, though, Denver was a fair and honest man who tried his best to maintain Walker's policies.

Actually most of the drama in respect to Kansas had taken place in Washington, where the House of Representatives had rejected Buchanan's bill, approved by the Senate, to bring Kansas into the Union with the Lecompton Constitution. In place of the Buchanan measure the House had substituted a compromise known as the English Bill, which called for a popular vote on August 2 and offered the territory a federal land grant should the document be ratified.

The general feeling, however, was that Kansas voters would reject this Congressional bribe and overwhelmingly defeat the proslavery constitution in an election free of fraud and Missouri interference. Then the struggle to make Kansas free would be won at last.

Only in southeastern Kansas around Trading Post and Fort Scott had violence continued. The most spectacular atrocity occurred on May 19, 1858, when a Georgian named Charles A. Hamelton and his proslavery band had taken eleven free-state settlers from their cabins and fields, lined them up in a ravine near the Marais des Cygnes, and shot five of them to death, wounding most of the others. In retaliation, James Montgomery, who had already attacked a company of U.S. cavalry, burned ballot boxes in proslavery elections and threatened proslavery people all over Linn County, now attempted to set Fort Scott afire. Governor Denver, riding into the disturbed area giving speeches and settling feuds, managed to ward off general guerrilla war and to restore some degree of peace to the unsettled border country.

Impressed with what he heard about Montgomery, Brown decided to join forces with the guerrilla captain and make some diversionary move in "the neighborhood of late troubles" that would keep his name associated with Kansas in the public mind. Brown shook hands with Hinton and Redpath and on June 28, said the New York *Tribune* correspondent, "our 'warrior of the Lord and of Gideon' " left Lawrence to "visit Capt. Montgomery."[1]

With Tidd and Kagi at his side, Brown met with Montgomery in his log cabin at Sugar Mound, sometime in early July, and apparently the two agreed to cooperate in protecting the border country from any further proslavery attacks. Initially Brown was fond of Montgomery and thought him "a very intelligent, kind gentlemanly and most excellent man and lover of freedom." But when it became evident that Montgomery had "ideas of his own," Brown came to dislike him and thereafter held his own counsel and went his own way as usual.[2]

Brown also visited his friend Augustus Wattles at his new home in Moneka in Linn County, some twenty-five miles northwest of Fort Scott. Wattles had some unhappy news to report: evidently Charles Robinson and George Washington Brown, editor of the *Herald of Freedom*, had openly criticized the role of Brown and his sons in the troubles of 1856, and Wattles was anxious to publish a history of the Brown family that would set the record straight. Brown agreed, wrote John Jr. to send all letters and documents that would illuminate their family story, and sat down at Wattles' place to compose "A Brief History of John Brown Otherwise (old Brown, & his family: *as connected with Kansas*; by one who knows". He never finished the history. But he complained plenty about "those who do not know and oftener do not care to tell the truth," and wrote Sanborn that "all *honest, sensible* Free State men *in* Kansas consider *George Washington* Brown's '*Herald of Freedom*' one of the most mischievous, traitorous publications in the whole country."

In their discussions about the slave problem Wattles told Brown that "forcible emancipation was worse than slavery." Brown turned on him with disgust. "I have been at your abolition meetings . . . in Massachusetts and Ohio, and your scheme is perfectly futile; you would not release five slaves in a century; peaceful emancipation is impossible; the thing has gone beyond that point." He said he had a plan to place arms in the hands of slaves, "give them their choice, stand behind them so as to protect them in a free choice, and if they chose to go into slavery, let them stay in it; but if they chose to go out, sustain them in it." Wattles said emancipation that way was "a mere matter of opinion" and let it go at that.[3]

Brown and his boys left Moneka and constructed a log and stone fort on the claim of Eli Snyder, "right on a conspicuous place" near the site of the Marais des Cygnes massacre and "in full view for miles around in Missouri." At Fort Snyder he drew up the "Articles of Agreement for Shubel Morgan's Company," signed by fifteen volunteers including himself. Gill and Stevens, who had been soliciting funds in Iowa, joined the old man later in the summer.

While encamped on Snyder's claim Brown wrote Sanborn of the desolation that prevailed along the border. He said that men on both sides of the line lived in "constant fear of new troubles," that companies of armed men were organizing, that "any little affair may open the quarrel afresh," and that rumors had reached him of new proslavery outrages—two murders and several robberies.[4] Actually no such atrocities had taken place—either the old man was misled by rumor or was deliberately exaggerating conditions in Kansas for the benefit of his Eastern backers. He wrote John Jr. that his presence on the border had restored the confidence of free-state settlers, some of whom had returned to their abandoned cabins. He also reported that the election of August 2 "passed off quietly on this part of the line," as Kansas voters, with federal troops standing guard and an anxious nation looking on, defeated the Lecompton Constitution by a margin of 11,300 to 1,788, thereby settling for all time the issue of slavery expansion into Kansas and the rest of the West. Yet, because of powerful Southern opposition in Washington, Kansas would not be admitted as a state until 1861.

All Brown said about the election was that John Jr. had probably heard of its "general result." He went on to say that he had gone to the line "with the utmost quiet" and under an assumed name "to avoid creating any excitement." But word that Old Brown was "improving a Claim" right on the border "leaked out and over into Missouri," producing "a ferment there which you can better imagine than I can describe. Which of the passions most predominated, fear or rage, I do not pretend to say." But he did say that several "spies" from Missouri had visited his camp. The bearded warrior frightened the wits out of one visitor, an avowed proslavery man. Brown pointed out that he had walked into "a perfect *nest* of the most *ultra Abolitionists*" and then recited to him "briefly the story of the Missouri invasions, threatenings, bullyings, boastings, driving off, beating, robbing, burning out and murdering of Kansas people, telling him pro-slavery men of Missouri had begun and carried steadily forward in this manner with most miserably rotten and corrupt pro-slavery Administrations to back them up, shield and assist them while carrying on their Devilish work. I told him Missouri people along the Line might have perfect quiet if they honestly desired it, and further, that if they chose *War* they would soon have all they might *any of them* care for. I gave him the most powerful Abolition lecture of which I am capable, having an unusual gift of utterance for me; gave him some dinner and told him to go back and make a full report and then sent him off. Got no such visits afterwards. I presume he will not soon forget the old Abolitionist 'mit de' white beard on. I gave him also a full description of my views of a Full Blooded Abolitionist and told him who were the *real nigger-stealers* etc."[5]

According to Eli Snyder, Brown, Kagi, Tidd, and Snyder himself made a reconnaissance into Missouri at about this time. On the crest of a hill not far from Pattenville, they saw a cabin in a clump of trees nearby, and Snyder took a look through Brown's field glass. "I declare that is Martin White," Snyder said, "reading a book in a chair in the shade of a tree." Snyder knew that White had killed Frederick and turned to Brown. "Suppose you and I go down and see the old man and have a talk with him." Kagi wanted to go too. But to their surprise, Brown cried, "No, no, I can't do that," and said he had no revenge to gratify.

He had said the same thing to other people—had even tried to head off Watson and Salmon when they had come west to avenge Frederick's death. "People mistake my objects," Brown once told James Hanway. "I would not hurt one hair on [White's] head. I would not go one inch to take his life; I do not harbour the feelings of revenge. *I act from a principle*. My aim and object is to restore human rights."[6]

2

Early in August Brown came down with an acute attack of the ague. Kagi and William Partridge, fearing for the old man's life, carried him to the Rev. Samuel Adair's hospital-cabin at Osawatomie. There Kagi nursed Brown for four weeks before the fever broke and he was strong enough to get out of bed. Hinton called on a visit, and as they talked Brown railed at politicians like Robinson ("a perfect old woman") and angrily predicted that trouble would break out again on the border. Later Kagi took the correspondent aside and told him about the "Great Plan" to liberate the slaves. Hinton protested that they would all be killed. If so, Kagi replied, the result would be worth the sacrifice. He wrote his father and sister a few weeks later: "I believe there are better times dawning, to my sight at least. I am not now laboring and waiting without present reward for myself alone; it is for a future reward for mankind, and for you all. There can be no doubt of the reward in the end, or of the success of a great cause which is to earn it."[7]

When Brown was strong enough to move around he rode down to Pottawatomie Creek to visit James Hanway. As they discussed the civil war of '56, Brown asked what the people on the creek thought about the Pottawatomie massacre. Hanway replied that most settlers in the area now believed it "a justifiable act," because (as Brown himself had often argued) they had come to the conclusion that the victims had been part of a conspiracy to "drive out, burn, and kill" every man, woman, and child on the Pottawatomie who supported the free-state cause. Killing those men had thus saved the lives of free-state people on the creek, and most of them now regarded the slayers as "deliverers."

Brown exclaimed, "Oh, I knew the time would come when people who understood the whole circumstances attending" the massacre "would endorse it." Deep in thought, he paced back and forth for a few moments. Then he turned. "I tell you, Mr. Hanway, that it is infinitely better that this generation should be swept away from the face of the earth, than that slavery shall continue to exist."[8]

During the autumn Brown made frequent trips into Lawrence to demand money, guns, and supplies from the harried agents of the Massachusetts and National Kansas committees, who were never certain what or how much they were authorized to give him. Brown thought he was being betrayed. Where were those revolvers the National Committee had supposedly sent him in 1856? And the rest of the supplies and money it had promised him in New York in 1857? "I hold claims against the National Kansas Committee which are good against them and all persons whatever," Brown indignantly wrote J. T. Cox, and insisted that he was an agent of that committee (which was not the truth) and that he had a right to all supplies and all accounts which Cox or any other agent held in his custody. Meanwhile Brown set about collecting on a batch of promissory notes which Stearns had sent to him in the summer. The notes came from Kansas farmers who had given them to the National Committee in exchange for food and supplies. When Henry B. Hurd found out what Brown was doing, he wrote Whitman that the old man had no authority whatever "to take, receive, collect or transfer" any notes or accounts and that the National Committee would not stand for any such dealings. By now everything was in complete confusion. Whitman, an agent for both committees, did not know whom to believe—Hurd, Brown, or Stearns, who had sent the notes to Brown with instructions to collect on them. In the midst of this "lively dispute in Kansas," the Massachusetts Committee stood firmly behind Brown, and on his own he collected several hundred dollars on the notes at Ottumwa, Emporia, Osawatomie, and Lawrence.

When Brown was in Lawrence he talked frequently with

J. Bowles, an agent of the Kansas Underground Railroad. For over three years Bowles and other abolitionists in Lawrence had been helping fugitives from Missouri, giving them money, food, and shelter and showing them how to get across Iowa and on into Canada. Bowles claimed that "nearly three hundred" runaways had passed through Lawrence since 1855 and that from them he had learned a great deal about Negro slaves. They were usually "very cunning," he said, and believed "about as much as they please of what the master is telling them," although they pretended to accept every word because they knew what would happen if he found out how much they wanted to be free. Brown, of course, was highly encouraged by Bowles's observations and told him "confidentially" that he intended "to make the master pay the way of the slave to the land of freedom." Bowles wrote Sanborn in April, 1859, that Brown's cause was "a good one" and that Brown himself was "a bold cool calculating and far seeing man" who "knows the right and dare maintain it." Bowles also asked Sanborn and Brown's other friends to give some of their money to the Kansas Underground Railroad.[9]

On another trip into Lawrence Brown took a room in the Whitney House near the Kaw River and invited William A. Phillips to come up for a visit. While Kagi stood guard outside the door Brown gave Phillips a lecture on the history of slavery and the South. "And now," he went on, "we have reached a point where nothing but war can settle the question. Had they succeeded in Kansas, they would have a power that would have given them permanently the upper hand, and it would have been the death-knell of republicanism in America. They are checked, but not beaten. They never intend to relinquish the machinery of this government into the hands of the opponents of slavery. It has taken them more than half a century to get it, and they know its significance too well to give it up." If the Republicans won in 1860, there would be war. In fact, at that very moment Buchanan's Cabinet was concentrating the U.S. Army, which for years had been organized "on a Southern basis of power," at strategic points in case "there was danger of having to surrender the government." Brown also believed that the Secretary of the Navy was sending ships away on long voyages so that they could not be available in case of a crisis, and that the treasury would be looted before Northerners could secure control of it.

As Brown talked, Phillips thought: the man is obsessed; he has let one idea carry him away and fog his reason. Phillips argued that surely Brown was mistaken, that he had merely "confounded everyday occurrences with treacherous designs."

"No," Brown insisted, "no, the war is not over. It is a treacherous lull before the storm. We are on the eve of one of the greatest wars in history, and I fear slavery will triumph, and there will be an end of all aspirations for human freedom." For his part, he had drawn his sword in Kansas "when they attacked us" and was not going to sheathe it until "this war is over."

Phillips had the impression that Brown was planning some incursion on the borders of the free and slave states and warned him not to do anything rash. Trust events and peace, he counseled. If the American people deserved a free government, they would maintain it.

"You forget the fearful wrongs that are carried on in the name of government and law," Brown replied.

"I do not forget them," Phillips said, "I regret them."

"I regret and will remedy them with all the power God has given me."

Then the old man brought up Spartacus and analyzed his servile war against the Romans. Phillips reminded him that Spartacus' slaves had been captured from warlike peoples and trained by the Romans to kill in the arena. Negroes, on the other hand, were an "inoffensive race." In all their suffering "they seemed to be incapable of resentment or reprisal."

"You have not studied them right," Brown snapped, "and you have not studied them long enough. Human nature is the same everywhere." They argued for a while longer. Then Brown repeated that "with the help of God, I will do what I believe to be best," said good-by, and escorted Phillips to the door. Phillips never saw him again.[10]

3

As the leaves were falling that October, Brown returned to southeastern Kansas, where Montgomery had continued his guerrilla activities. Again the old man stayed a few days with Augustus Wattles, then returned with his men to his border outpost at Fort Snyder. Except for a brief encounter with an armed posse, which eventually scattered, the company saw little action in those cold windy days. In all the inactivity Brown quarreled constantly with the powerful black-eyed Stevens, who refused to let the old man cow him and raised "merry hell" when Brown became too dictatorial.

On December 14 Montgomery invited Brown to join him in an expedition against Fort Scott, where a free-state man was being held captive. Itching for a fight, Brown advocated burning the town out. But Montgomery now opposed such reckless violence and, to keep Brown in line, assumed over-all command of the raiding party himself. Brown, disappointed in Montgomery's timidity, played only a perfunctory part in the December 16 raid against Fort Scott, in which the free-state captive was liberated and a proslavery man who had fired a shotgun at Kagi was killed and his store plundered.

A day or two later Brown took his men back to Fort Snyder. There were two new recruits with him now. One was Jeremiah Goldsmith Anderson, an Indianan who had served under Montgomery and had twice been arrested by proslavery forces. The other was Albert Hazlett, a blond curly-haired youngster from Pennsylvania who had also ridden with Montgomery. Both of them knew that Brown was planning some operation in Virginia and wanted to go along.

From Fort Snyder Brown sent out daily patrols to scout the line, hoping that God "would provide him a basis of action." One day as Gill was scouting down the line he met a mulatto man who desperately needed help. The man explained that he and his family and another Negro belonged to a slaveowner in Vernon County, Missouri, and that they were about to be sold and his family broken up. Would Gill help them run away? Gill sought out Brown and repeated the slave's story. According to Gill, Brown regarded this as a "Heaven-sent" opportunity to carry his war straight at slaveholders themselves, to execute a bold and dramatic slave-running expedition that would not only link his name sensationally with Kansas in the national press but that might also prove the feasibility of his grand plan to his overcautious Eastern backers.

Accordingly, on the night of December 20–21, Brown and Stevens led separate columns into Missouri, ransacked the homes of two planters, one of whom the hot-blooded Stevens shot dead, and liberated not only their slaves (including the mulatto and his family) but their wagons, horses, mules, harnesses, and other property as well. At daybreak on December 21 the two columns united in Kansas and hid their eleven liberated slaves and two white prisoners in a wooded ravine. That night they set out for Osawatomie, some thirty-five miles to the northwest. The slaves eventually reached there on Christmas Eve and were hidden in an abandoned cabin on the south fork of the Pottawatomie. Brown himself delayed for a time near Fort Scott and Trading Post, to see whether the Missourians would counter-attack. Finally he left the border and arrived in Osawatomie on January 11.[11]

Brown's spectacular expedition—the eighth time free-soil Kansas had raided Missouri—almost started another civil war along the smoldering border. The Missouri General Assembly threatened violent retaliation. Samuel Medary, who had replaced Denver as governor of Kansas, branded the raid as a lawless outrage against innocent people and demanded that the legislature take action. President Buchanan, when he learned of the raid, offered a reward of $250 for Brown's capture.[12]

The proslavery press, of course, shrieked at such a fiendish and bloodthirsty invasion of slavery territory and demanded that the governor of Missouri do "something to protect our people." Free-state newspapers like the *Herald of Freedom* condemned the raid, too, and eventually—as Brown hoped would happen—the news reached the East. Gerrit Smith wrote his wife ecstatically: "Do you hear the news from Kansas? Our dear John Brown is invading Kansas and pursuing the policy which he intended to pursue *elsewhere.*"[13]

Kansans themselves were sharply divided in their opinions about the raid. J. Bowles and S. F. Tappan of Lawrence approved of it. So did William Hutchinson, a correspondent for the New York *Tribune,* who talked with Brown at Wattles' house on December 30 and 31. But if Hutchinson thought the raid "justifiable," he urged Brown not to commit any rash acts and to give peace a chance. Wattles for his part deplored the raid (Brown had promised not to do anything like this) and "censored him for going into Missouri, contrary to our agreement, and getting those slaves." But Brown ignored all criticism and spoke obsessively of "my work," "my great duty," "my mission" to liberate the slaves. On January 1, 1859, he left Moneka and went to the area around Trading Post, to hold himself in readiness in case the Missourians counterattacked.[14]

While he was near Trading Post a settler named George A. Crawford visited him and severely criticized what he had done. They were settlers, Crawford pointed out, and Brown was not. "He could strike a blow and leave. The retaliatory blow would fall on us." Since Crawford was a free-state man, proslavery partisans would hold him personally responsible for Brown's act. Crawford went on to say that Kansas was at peace with Missouri, that the territorial legislature was controlled by free-state men, that even in troubled Bourbon and Linn counties they were in a majority. Brown's attack was a threat to the peace and safety of them all.

Brown replied vaguely that it was no pleasure for him, an old man, to be living in the saddle far away from his home and family and risking his life for the cause of freedom.[15]

Brown called on Montgomery to join him in case the Missourians invaded Kansas. But now even Montgomery was working for peace, giving a speech at a peace meeting at Mapleton and endorsing a set of peace resolutions drawn up by William Hutchinson. In the end sober counsels prevailed on both sides, and except for a few skirmishes the border country remained fairly quiet.

On January 7 Brown was back at Wattles' place in Moneka, defending his raid in a stormy debate with Wattles and Montgomery himself. Kagi was present, too, and while he argued eloquently in behalf of the work, Brown sat down and composed a document entitled "Old Brown's Parallels." In it Brown justified the raid as a retaliation for the Marais des Cygnes massacre, and asserted that he had "forcibly restored" eleven human beings "to their *natural*; & *inalienable rights*" at the expense of only one white man "who fought against the liberation." In doing so Brown had stirred all Hell below and filled "all proslavery conservative Free-State, and dough-faced men & Administration tools" with holy horror. Indeed the widespread alarm his raid had caused was profoundly significant to him. He had heard that planters in western Missouri were terrified and that many had fled into Arkansas. If Brown could incite that much turmoil with a small strike into border Missouri, think what would happen when he invaded a strategic state like Virginia, with its heavy concentration of slaves: the whole peculiar institution was bound to come crashing down. Perhaps that is why Brown turned to Wattles with reckless confidence. "I considered the matter well; you will have no more attacks from Missouri; I shall now leave Kansas; probably you will never see me again; I consider it my duty to draw the scene of the excitement to some other part of the country."[16]

4

On January 20 Brown led his men, the eleven slaves, and all the confiscated horses and wagons out of the territory, eluding posses all along the way. Though he was still weak from the ague, Brown drove his caravan at a killing pace. Gill was awed by Brown's endurance, his fierce determination to get his black people (who called him their Moses) to Canada and freedom.

Yet there were other aspects of Brown's character which Gill did not like at all. While Brown treated Negroes like human beings and felt an almost paralyzing hatred of slavery, he was "essentially vindictive in his nature." He would never "brook a rival" and was intolerant and often unappreciative of others, especially his own sons whom he treated with a special severity. Brown had what Gill called an "imperial egotism." And it was his egotism that, "coupled with love of approbation and his god idea, begot in him [the obsession] that he was the Moses that was to lead the Exodus of the colored people from the taskmasters." The more Brown brooded on this the more he was convinced that he was not merely God's chosen instrument but "the *only one*," and that whatever flaws his plan of operations contained, and whatever mistakes he made, "God would be his guard and shield, rendering the most illogical movements into a grand success." He had written much the same thing to Higginson in the spring of 1858: "In all thy ways acknowledge *Him & He* shall direct thy paths." One way or another, "an *all good, all wise, & all powerful, Director*: & Father" would ensure Brown's ultimate triumph in the South.[17]

5

On February 5 Brown's caravan rolled into Tabor. News of the Missouri raid had preceded them and some of the town's dignitaries, who refused to sanction horse stealing (even from slaveholders), gave Brown a cool reception indeed. When they would not let him speak in the local church, Brown left in a huff and traveled eastward in broad daylight, despite reports that proslavery elements in the state were laying a trap for him. The further east he moved the more he found people sympathetic to what he had done (Southerners had invaded Northern states in search of runaways, now Brown had retaliated with a strike into Missouri). At Des Moines the editor of the *Register* paid Brown's ferriage across the Des Moines River. At Grinnell three Congregational ministers offered Brown sympathy and support in behalf of the townspeople; and Joseph B. Grinnell, founder of the town, provided his company with money and supplies. From February 25 to March 9 they were in Springdale, the Quaker community, vowing to fight to the death should anybody try to take the Negroes. On March 9 a strong guard escorted them to Keith's steam mill at West Liberty, where a boxcar was waiting for them at the railroad station. The Chicago train picked the car up and pulled the party on to Chicago. There the detective Allan Pinkerton not only hid the slaves but raised over $500 for Brown and procured another boxcar to take them to Detroit. All across northern Illinois and Michigan the signs were thrillingly auspicious: not a single peace officer dared to arrest Brown and his liberated blacks because of widespread public resentment toward the fugitive slave law. Thousands of Northwesterners—abolitionists, free-soilers, and Negrophobes alike—more than ever regarded the fugitive slave law as part of the Slave Power conspiracy and not only demanded that the act be nullified but threatened mob action should slavecatchers invade *their* states and *their* neighborhoods under the guise of that enactment. Thousands of others were appalled that free Negroes might be carried off "by accident"—not because they all cared about Negroes as human beings (most Northwesterners, being Negrophobes, did not) but because of the principle involved. If Southerners got away with violating the rights of free blacks, what would prevent them from encroaching on the rights of freē whites? That is why there was such public hostility against the fugitive slave law and anybody who tried to enforce it. And why so many people in Iowa, Illinois, and Michigan applauded Brown's "reprisal raid" and gave aid to him and his refugees (after all, he was not going to leave the blacks in their neighborhoods but was taking them out of the country). Brown, of course, was elated with what he saw and heard in the towns he passed through. If Northwesterners gave him such support for the liberation of eleven slaves, think what they would do when he delivered three million! Confident and full of zeal, he took the Negroes on to Detroit and put them on a ferry which carried them across the river to Canada. Then, while eight of his men went to Ashtabula County in Ohio, where John Jr. had concealed the guns, Brown and Kagi set out for Cleveland to sell the horses and raise additional funds.[18]

Brown and Kagi reached Cleveland on March 15. They found the city in a state of high excitement over the approaching trial of the celebrated "Oberlin rescuers"—thirty-seven businessmen, college professors, students, and free Negroes from Oberlin and Wellington who had been jailed for violating the fugitive slave law. The "Oberlin rescue" had happened in September the previous year, after two slavecatchers had "kidnaped" a young runaway who had been living in Oberlin, a zealous abolitionist community and home of Oberlin College, and taken him to a hotel in Wellington. The news spread like wildfire. Soon a crowd of professors, students, Negroes, and merchants surrounded the hotel, somehow liberated the young Negro, and took him at a gallop back to Oberlin and into hiding. The rescue outraged Southerners and Northern conservatives alike; Clement L. Vallandigham, a Democratic congressman from Ohio, labeled the act "insurrection" and demanded that the lawbreakers be summarily punished. A federal district court soon indicted thirty-seven of the rescuers, who voluntarily entered the Cleveland jail to await their trial. At once the rescuers became a cause célèbre in the Western Reserve, which had become "the hottest piece of abolition territory in the whole United States," and virtually every day delegations from outlying towns came to demonstrate outside the Cleveland jail. In contrast to southern Ohio and other areas in the Northwest, citizens in the Western Reserve, having grown more tolerant of free Negroes since Brown had lived there twenty years before, opposed the fugitive slave law out of genuine concern for the plight of the black man; and they cheered the black rescuers in jail as loudly as the whites. By the time Brown arrived in Cleveland in mid-March the trial had been postponed until April 5 and the demonstrations around the jail had become larger and noisier, leaving the city in a state of intense excitement.

Brown and Kagi visited the rescuers, too, and Kagi himself covered part of their trial (which lasted from April until July) as a reporter for the New York *Tribune* and Cleveland *Leader*. One of the Negro rescuers spoke out eloquently against the law; and his militancy and that of the other Negroes, as Mary Land has suggested, may have confirmed Brown in his belief that blacks everywhere, North as well as South, were ready for revolution.[19]

For ten days Brown walked the streets of Cleveland unmolested, despite the fact that word was out that the President had offered $250 for his arrest. An editor of the Cleveland *Plain Dealer* said that Brown walked defiantly past the marshal's office every day, but the officer was apparently too intimidated by the angry mood in Cleveland to touch the bearded warrior. According to one of Brown's followers, the old man regarded the marshal's failure to arrest him as further proof that the signs were propitious, that the time indeed was here.

Before Brown left Cleveland he auctioned off at the City Hotel stables two "abolitionist" horses and a mule which he had personally "converted." (Later he sent $150 of the proceeds to his family at North Elba.) On March 21 he and Kagi gave a fund-raising lecture, but the attendance was disappointingly "slim." For the benefit of reporters in the audience Brown dwelled at length on his Kansas experiences and his slave-running expedition into Missouri. He pointed out proudly that the President had put a price of $250 on his head—and then in a brilliant publicity stunt he placed a price of $2.50 on the head of Buchanan.[20]

Such remarks, of course, were calculated to keep him dramatically associated with Kansas on the front pages of the newspapers. On March 25 he left Cleveland and set out across Ashtabula County, which Joshua Giddings, Benjamin Wade, and other political abolitionists had made the most fervent antislavery county in the state.

Meanwhile Kagi and Tidd remained in Cleveland, where they joined 10,000 to 12,000 other people—including such antislavery celebrities as Governor Chase and Cassius M. Clay—in a massive protest meeting against the fugitive slave law. Kagi also talked with several of the Oberlin rescuers and recruited two of the Negroes for Brown's force. One was John Anthony Copeland, an Oberlin College student, twenty-three years old, born free at Raleigh, North Carolina, and angry enough to go back there to liberate the slaves. The other recruit was Copeland's uncle, Lewis Sheridan Leary, a mulatto who lived in Oberlin with his wife and six-month-old child. Leary was ready to leave them and sacrifice the comfort and safety of life at Oberlin to fight the slaveholders (although he did not tell his family or his sister so). When all the rescuers were subsequently freed, thanks to an agreement worked out by representatives of both sides, two white rescuers gave Copeland and Leary some money so they could get to "Harpers Ferry, in Virginia."[21]

Meanwhile Brown visited John Jr. in West Andover, instructing him to direct young volunteers from Kansas to Brown's secret rendezvous in Virginia. Then, at the request of Joshua Giddings, Brown traveled to Jefferson to address a crowd of Republicans and Democrats in the Congregational Church. They listened to his stories about Kansas with rapt attention, although had they known what contempt he held for their parties they might not have been so polite. He hated the Democrats because he believed their party was dominated by the South and despised the Republicans because they were too "wishy-washy" on the slavery issue. After he finished talking, Giddings called for contributions and "every Democrat as well as Republican present gave something." Later Brown had tea with Giddings and his wife (he told them nothing about his Virginia plan). Before Brown left the congressman gave him $3 for his "work."[22]

6

In April Brown set out for the East with Jeremiah Anderson, only to fall ill with the old malarial fever and "a terrible gathering" in his head. But illness could not hold him back now. On April 11 he was in

Peterboro for a four-day visit with Gerrit Smith, who was still excited about the Missouri raid and was again prepared to back the Virginia plot all the way (as long as Brown did not reveal his specific plans). Brown lectured to a small gathering of Smith's friends, in a manner so earnest and full of conviction that "Mr. Smith and some others wept." Smith also gave a speech—"the most eloquent speech I ever heard him give," said Edwin Morton. "If I were asked," Smith declared, "to point out—I will say it in his presence—to point out the man in all this world I think most truly a Christian, I would point to John Brown."[23]

All told, Brown collected $435 in Peterboro—$400 of it from Smith himself, with a promise of more to follow.

Brown then returned to North Elba for a much-needed rest. He visited with his daughters, discussed the invasion plans with his sons, examined his farm and sheep, and admired the rock gravemarker of his grandfather, which leaned up against the kitchen side of the house. Early in May he felt strong enough to travel again, went to Concord, and raised a modest $10 in another lecture at the Concord Town House. Sanborn, Emerson, and Thoreau were dutifully present, each remarking how impressive Brown looked with his flowing white beard. Bronson Alcott, the controversial educator and lecturer, was struck by Brown's "courage and religious earnestness." After the lecture Alcott wrote in his journal that, while the captain left them "much in the dark concerning his destination and designs for the coming months," he did not conceal his hatred of slavery or "his readiness to strike a blow for freedom at the proper moment." Alcott thought Brown "equal to anything he dares—the man to do the deed, if it must be done, and with the martyr's temper and purpose." Then, with a final flourish: "I think him about the manliest man I have ever seen—the type and synonym of the Just."[24]

Brown spent most of May 9—his fifty-ninth birthday—with Franklin Sanborn. Sanborn also believed the Kansas diversion had "blinded Forbes" and gave his approval when Brown announced that he would not be trifled with, that he would allow no more postponements. Although Sanborn was a man of small means, he gave his warrior $25 and the next day escorted Brown and Anderson to Boston, where a series of conferences took place with the secret committee. Two members, however, were conspicuously absent.

Parker had become gravely ill with consumption and had left for Europe (by way of Cuba) for health purposes. For Higginson, who was still bitter because of last year's postponement, the plot "had all begun to seem to me rather chimerical," and he remained in Worcester, refusing to attend any of the meetings with Brown in Boston. It was not that Higginson had lost confidence in Brown. On the contrary, as he wrote the old man personally: "I have perfect confidence in you. All you do will be well done. And I long to see you with adequate funds in your hands, set free from timid advisers, & able to act in your own way." "Did I follow only my own inclinations, without thinking of other ties, I should join you in person if I could not in purse. But for the present I am restrained." Yet Higginson did promise to send Brown something once the invasion was truly under way.[25]

Apparently Howe also had second thoughts about the plot, but for different reasons than Higginson. Howe disapproved of Brown's Missouri raid because he did not think confiscating horses or other property—even from slaveholders—was justifiable. Moreover, according to Sanborn, Howe had accompanied Parker to Cuba and then returned through the Carolinas, meeting several congenial planters along the way. "It shocked him," Sanborn claimed, "to think that he might be instrumental in giving up to flames and pillage their noble mansions." However that may be, Howe had decided that he opposed taking property from Southerners—even as a war measure, as outlined in the Provisional Constitution—and told Brown so in two interviews in Boston. Brown, however, argued his case with "great correctness and ingenuity," and the dashing revolutionary finally came back around. But "don't tell me what you are about or where you are going," he warned Brown. Meanwhile, keeping up a good appearance, Howe paraded Brown before his friends as "an honest, keen and veteran backwoodsman," a man "of the Puritan militant order" who had "a martyr's spirit."[26]

For their part, Sanborn and Stearns were steadfast in their support of the experiment. In those last conferences in Boston Stearns agreed that the Missouri raid had successfully screened Forbes (who had mysteriously disappeared) and that it did prove the feasibility of Brown's grand design. With Howe's lackluster support, they gave Brown $2,000 to "raise the mill" somewhere in Virginia, bringing the committee's total contributions to the old man to just over $4,000.[27]

Between these conferences Brown visited the Howes in their home in south Boston. Brown liked Julia Ward Howe, a defiant little woman "all flash and fire." A member of Boston's literati, who was later to become famous for "The Battle Hymn of the Republic," she was a dedicated nonconformist who kept her hair red to spite contemporary fashion. She had written a well-received book, *Passion's Flowers* (1853), could read and speak French, Italian, and German, and fought constantly with her debonair husband, who was twenty years older than she and could never understand why she was unhappy as a mother and housewife. Julia was quite fond of Brown, in whom she saw "a Puritan of the Puritans" who wanted to be the savior of the Negro race.[28]

Brown also met Senator Henry Wilson at the Boston Bird Club and argued with him about the Missouri raid (Wilson thought it injurious to the antislavery cause). Brown was introduced to John A. Andrew, too, a prominent Boston lawyer who was so drawn to this "very magnetic person" that he sent Brown $25. In addition, the old man called on Amos Lawrence, but Lawrence had cooled toward "the Miles Standish of Kansas" because of his "negro stealing" in Missouri. "He has a monomania on that subject," Lawrence recorded in his diary, "and would be hanged if he were taken in a slave State. . . . He and his companion [Jeremiah Anderson] both have the fever and ague, somewhat, probably a righteous visitation for their fanaticism."[29]

Shrugging off Lawrence's coldness, Brown went out to Milton to solicit money from John Murray Forbes, a wealthy industrialist and reformer. Howe, who had arranged the meeting, warned Forbes that Brown was planning something that "might perhaps seem at first to be treason." It consisted of "some plans for delivering our land from the curse of slavery." Sanborn was present, too, and while it rained and thundered outside, Brown and Forbes argued hotly about the slavery question. With a "little touch of insanity" about his "glittering, gray-blue eyes," Brown scornfully rejected Forbes's contention "that firmness at the ballot box might avert the storm." Only bullets and bayonets, Brown said, could settle anything now.[30]

Later, attending a convention of the New England Antislavery

Society, Brown shook his head at all the talk about overthrowing slavery. "Talk! talk! talk!" he cried. "That will never free the slaves." "What is needed is action—action." He was in a strange mood—a different mood—when he called on Judge Russell and his wife. He gave their baby daughter a present of maple sugar, Mrs. Russell recalled, and then held the child so that she stood on his palms. "Now," he said, "when you are a young lady and I am hanged, you can say that you stood on the hand of Old Brown."[31]

On June 3, having collected over $2,000, Brown and Anderson traveled to Collinsville, Connecticut, to see Blair about the long-neglected pikes. Blair had not finished them and could not fathom what Brown wanted them for anyway, since matters in Kansas had been settled. Irritated, Brown replied that if they were finished he would find a way to use them; as they were, they were good for nothing. Reluctantly Blair agreed to finish the pikes for $450. Brown eventually sent him the entire sum.

Soon Brown was on his way across Massachusetts, heading for upper New York. "He means to be on the ground as soon as he can—perhaps so as to begin on the 4th of July," Sanborn wrote Higginson. "Now is the time to help in the movement, if ever, for within the next two months the experiment will be made."[32]

7

On June 11 Brown arrived in North Elba for a last visit with his family. He had already sent them supplies, along with a touching present for Ellen—an inscribed Bible to remember him by. To his dismay Brown found that Salmon—like Henry and Jason, who had given up fighting forever—had "thought the matter over" and decided not to go with his father. Salmon "felt that the trip was a mistake, that it was not the wise thing to do" (later he conceded that he might also have been a little afraid). Brown argued with his son, urged, cajoled, and browbeat him. But Salmon was as stubborn as the old man once he had made up his mind and replied that, no, he wanted to stay at home. Brown regretted Salmon's decision as he "had never regretted the act of any of his children." Around June 16 he gave up arguing, told Mary and the girls good-by, and rode out of the Adirondacks for the last time.

Two days later he was in West Andover, Ohio, where he made final arrangements to have the cache of weapons moved to a secret rendezvous at Chambersburg in Pennsylvania. At his instructions John Jr. was to travel across the East raising recruits and collecting money and guns, despite the fact that John Jr. was suffering from "the most depressing melancholy" and felt unfit for responsible work. Brown may have talked about his plans with the Ashtabula League of Freedom, organized by John Jr. and "Grosh" Giddings, the son of the famous congressman. At Hudson, and later at Akron, Brown threw caution to the winds and announced to certain friends that he planned to invade Virginia.[33]

On June 23, with Oliver, Owen, and Jeremiah Anderson, Brown crossed into Pennsylvania and headed toward Harpers Ferry and the fulfillment of his prophecies.

XVIII

MEN, GET YOUR ARMS

⌒⌒⌒⌒

HARPERS FERRY, THE FIRST TARGET IN Brown's war for slave liberation, was situated on a narrow neck of land at the confluence of the
Shenandoah and Potomac rivers in the Blue Ridge Mountains of
northern Virginia. The Baltimore and Ohio Railroad crossed the
Potomac on a sturdy wooden bridge and ran past the town as it
wound westward toward the Alleghenies and distant Ohio. Baltimore
was some eighty miles due east of Harpers Ferry. And Washington,
D.C., lying on the banks of the Potomac southeast of the mountains,
was less than sixty miles away by turnpike. There were several towns
and villages near Harpers Ferry (Frederick, Hagerstown, Martinsburg, Shepherdstown, Charlestown), but even so the pastoral mountain setting gave Harpers Ferry "an air of remoteness." The
population was a little over 2,500, including 1,251 "free coloreds"
and 88 slaves. A majority of the 1,212 whites were skilled workers
and government employees from the North, whom the native Southerners regarded as "foreigners." Since the climate was too cold and
the terrain too mountainous and wooded for extensive tobacco or
cotton cultivation, there were no large plantations in the region.
What slaveholders there were tilled farms in the country surrounding the town, and their blacks for the most part were "well-kept
house servants." The total population in the entire six-county area
(including four in Virginia and two in Maryland) came to some
115,449 whites, 9,891 free Negroes, and 18,048 slaves. Less than 5,000
of the slaves, however, were men.[1]

From Maryland Heights, just across the Potomac, Harpers Ferry seemed a cramped cluster of homes, saloons, hotels, and shops which extended along the two rivers or climbed up the slopes of Bolivar Heights in helter-skelter fashion. The shops along Potomac Street looked like factories: they were the federal armory where arms were manufactured. The first building in the government complex was the fire-engine house; next came the forging, machine, and stocking shops, and then the arms storehouse, or arsenal. About a half mile above the government shops, on an island in the Shenandoah, stood Hall's Rifle Works, where some sixty expert gunsmiths fashioned firearms for the U.S. Army. All told, the government installation and Hall's Rifle Works employed several hundred persons who could produce 10,000 stands of arms per year.

In the summer of 1858, while Brown made his way back to Kansas, John E. Cook arrived in Harpers Ferry and took a job on a canal across the Potomac. After work he studied the layout of the government armory, ingratiated himself with the townsfolk, and made love to a plump, blonde maid named Mary Kennedy. In April, 1859, he had to marry the girl; she had his son a few months later.

Brown himself arrived at Harpers Ferry on July 3, 1859, with Owen, Oliver, and Jeremiah Anderson, who personally vowed "to make this land of liberty and equality shake to the centre."[2] Brown held a brief consultation with Cook (he was unhappy but probably not surprised to learn about Cook's woman). Leaving his agent in town with orders to keep his mouth shut and his eyes open, Brown set out on Independence Day to locate a secret hideout in the mountains. Eventually he rented from the heirs of Dr. Booth Kennedy a dilapidated two-story farmhouse about seven miles away on the Maryland side of the Potomac, giving his name as "Isaac Smith" and telling neighbors that he was a cattle buyer from New York. While the bearded commander pored over his battle maps and studied population statistics from the U.S. census, a handful of young recruits (all of them except two were under thirty) trickled in. William and Dauphin Thompson and Watson·Brown, who left his wife Belle and a newborn child in North Elba, all arrived on August 6. Tidd, Stevens, Leeman, Hazlett, and Barclay and Edwin Coppoc, the Quaker boys from Springdale, Iowa, all reached the farm within a few weeks of one another. Stewart Taylor, an eccentric young spiritualist and native of Canada, arrived sometime in August; and so did Dangerfield Newby, a forty-eight-year-old free mulatto who was "quiet, sensible, and very unobtrusive." Newby, the oldest of the volunteers, hoped to liberate his wife and seven children from a plantation at Brentville, Virginia. John Henry Kagi, Brown's noble-minded "Secretary of War," was in Chambersburg, Pennsylvania, going by the name of "J. Henrie." Chambersburg was the secret rendezvous for the pikes which Blair was to send from Connecticut and the "Hardware" which John Jr. was to ship from Ohio. The hardware itself—fifteen boxes of Sharps rifles and Maynard revolvers*—reached Chambersburg on August 11 and was later transported to the farm in an old wagon. The revolvers, however, were useless to Brown, for he had mistakenly bought a great quantity of percussion caps for them rather than the Maynard tape primings for which they were fitted.[3]

As the band of men increased, Brown took great pains to conceal them from the neighbors. At his summons seventeen-year-old Martha, Oliver's wife, and fifteen-year-old Annie came down from North Elba to keep house and divert suspicion. The girls cooked meals, washed and hung out clothes, and worked in the garden outside, talking cheerfully with neighbors who dropped by— usually around mealtime—to ask about Mr. Smith's work and to steal glances at the farmhouse (where the men were hiding in the attic scarcely daring to breathe). One barefoot old woman who lived down the road was especially bothersome; she and her flock of children came around "at all hours of the day" to pester the girls and poke around the house while they exchanged worried looks. "One Saturday," Annie recalled, "father and I went to a religious (Dunker) meeting that was held in a grove near the schoolhouse" and the old woman stole into the farmhouse and saw one of the Negro recruits. "She thought these strangers were running off negroes to the North. I used to give her everything she wanted or asked for to keep her on good terms," Annie said, "but we were in constant fear that she was either a spy or would betray us. It was like standing on a powder magazine, after a slow match had been lighted."[4]

While the girls kept a constant vigil at the kitchen window, Brown gathered his handful of recruits upstairs and disclosed the

---

* The revolvers were those which Stearns had purchased for Brown in 1857; the rifles were of the lot given to Brown by the Massachusetts Kansas Committee.

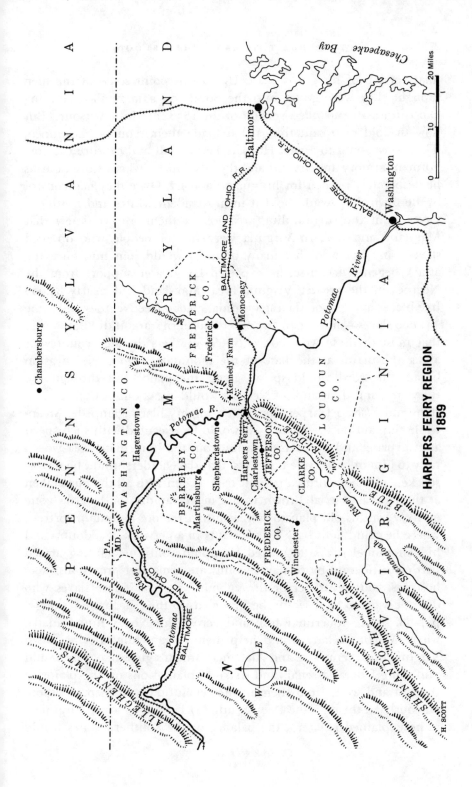

HARPERS FERRY REGION 1859

final version of his grand plan. Up to this point some of the men thought they were going into the South on a large slave-running expedition, an expanded version of the 1858 raid into Missouri. But now the old man said things that made their mouths hang open. They were going to attack Harpers Ferry itself and capture the government armory and arsenal and the rifle works, whose store of arms he desperately needed for his guerrilla army. Once they had control of the town they would hold it until dissident whites and mutinous slaves from the surrounding area joined them. Brown knew that Maryland and western Virginia were full of people who opposed slavery and believed that many of them would join him once the attack began. Of course, he expected far greater support from the Negroes in the greater Virginia area. Maryland had nearly 84,000 free blacks and 87,000 slaves; Virginia, 58,000 free Negroes and some 491,000 slaves—more than any other Southern state. It did not matter that most of these were concentrated in the tidewater country or along the plains at the base of the mountains. Once the invasion began, the word would spread across the plains and through the tidewater, and thousands of Negroes would break out of their plantations and rush to Harpers Ferry in a mighty black stampede. Meanwhile the raid on the town itself would be executed with such speed and surprise, and slaves and whites from the immediate area would rally to him in such large numbers, that slaveholders would be terror-stricken and too confused to fight back. Then with all the guns taken at the federal arsenal Brown would move rapidly southward (gone entirely was his old plan to retreat into a remote mountain fortress, where he could fight back his assailants in a network of redoubts and hidden tunnels). As he moved he would continue sending armed parties to liberate more slaves, confiscate arms and provisions, take hostages, and spread terror throughout Virginia. Those slaves who did not want to fight would be funneled up the Alleghenies (long a popular route for runaways) and across the North into Canada, where Martin Delany would help them. Meanwhile, driving down Virginia into Tennessee and Alabama, Brown's guerrilla army would raid more federal arsenals and strike at plantations on the plains to the east and west; from then on the revolution would spread spontaneously all through the Deep South. "If I could conquer Virginia," as he explained it later, "the balance of the Southern states would nearly conquer themselves, there being such a large number of slaves in them." To show his recruits what he meant, Brown produced maps of seven Southern states, pasted to stout cambric cloth, whose margins contained an impressive array of slave statistics compiled from the 1850 census. He expected tremendous slave support from Tennessee, Alabama, Mississippi, Georgia, and the Carolinas—with a total black population of 1,996,366—and had drawn plain or circled crosses on counties in those states with the heaviest slave concentrations. As his army of liberation stormed into the heart of Alabama, it would ignite a chain reaction of slave uprisings in a diagonal line of marked counties (Augusta, Montgomery, Macon, and Russell) running eastward into Georgia. In Georgia rebellions would break out spontaneously in Monroe, Hancock, Lincoln, Burke, Columbia, Scriven, and other counties with large Negro populations that Brown had marked with crosses. Then the conflagration would roar into South Carolina, across the upcountry around Orangeburg, Sumter, and Darlington, and down the tidewater from Georgetown to Charleston and on into Jasper County (which Brown had branded with a cross circled twice). At the same time, back in Alabama, the revolution would sweep inexorably westward through a cluster of counties (Wilcox, Washington, Sumter, and Dallas near the town of Selma) and on into Mississippi and Louisiana. Insurrections would continue to break out in the farthest reaches of the South, until the demoralized planters liberated all the slaves or, in case of widespread resistance, until the whole South was ablaze from the Potomac to the Gulf of Mexico. If the U.S. Army intervened, Brown would easily defeat it with his Spartacus-style guerrilla force, for he regarded all regular soldiers in terms of those he had seen in Kansas and on the Michigan front in the War of 1812 —they were all "an inefficient lot." Throwing back all assailants and growing increasingly powerful as thousands of mutinous slaves swarmed to him from all directions, he believed he could maintain impregnable positions in the hills and mountains, just as runaway blacks in Jamaica and Guiana—the celebrated Maroons—had done for generations.[5]

A mad scheme? Some of Brown's recruits who listened to him in the upstairs of their farmhouse certainly worried about the first part of it—the raid on Harpers Ferry. First Tidd and then Brown's own sons strenuously objected, arguing that it was suicidal for a mere handful of men to attempt to capture and then hold a whole town against militia and possibly federal troops, no matter how inefficient Brown thought they were. Evidently Brown's sons—Oliver especially —pointed out that because of the terrain (the converging rivers, the mountains in back of town) they might easily be trapped in Harpers Ferry and cut to pieces. The discussions became "warm" and "earnest" on this point. Cook and Kagi hurried back to the farm to take part in the deliberations. Cook, who had studied the layout of the government buildings and the habits of the watchmen, "favored the capture quite forcibly." Stevens, Leeman, and Jeremiah Anderson voiced their support of the raid. So did John Henry Kagi, who argued that if they took the Ferry by surprise and then moved rapidly into the mountains they might avoid a fight and possible capture. Then, maintaining their advantage of celerity and surprise, they might be able to carry off the revolution and set up the mountain state.

But Tidd and the other dissidents continued to object; they were as immovable as their fierce-eyed commander. Tempers flared; twice there was a threat of mutiny. Tidd himself became so irate that he left the farm and went down to Cook's house in Harpers Ferry "to cool off." In a show of anger Brown then resigned as Commander-in-Chief—a calculated move that warded off mutiny and brought all his men back to his side. "We have all agreed to sustain your decisions," Owen declared in behalf of the others, "until you have *proved incompetent*, & many of us will adhere to your decisions as long as you will." Although Stewart Taylor was among those who returned to Brown's side, he was obsessed with the idea that he would be the first to die.[6]

In the seemingly endless late summer and early autumn days, the men tried to keep occupied: they read yellowed copies of the Baltimore *Sun* and Thomas Paine's *Age of Reason*; they studied warfare with Stevens, polished their rifles, played checkers, and wrote letters to their families, wives, or girl friends. "I think of you all day," Watson wrote his wife Belle on September 8, "and dream of you at night. I would gladly come home and stay with you always but for the cause which brought me here,—a desire to do something for others, and not live wholly for my own happiness."

Would she kiss the baby for him? "I am thinking of you and him all the time." When Stevens was not leading discussions on warfare he was writing love letters to Jennie Dunbar back in West Andover, Ohio ("if you can love as poor a mortal as I am, it will be more than I expect . . . I hope your heart will be with me in this cause"). Some of the boys' letters were amazingly explicit. "Our mining company will consist of between twenty-five and thirty men well equipped with tools," Jeremiah Anderson wrote his brother late in September. "We go to win, at all hazards. So if you should hear of failure, it will be after a desperate struggle, and loss of capital on both sides. . . . I expect (when I start again travelling) to start at this place and go through the State of Virginia and on south, just as circumstances require; mining and prospecting, and carrying the ore with us." "I am now in a Southern slave state," William Leeman wrote his mother on September 9, "and before I leave it, it will be a free state, and so will every other one in the South." Then, to make certain she got the message: "We are now all privately gathered in a slave state, where we are determined to strike for freedom, incite the slaves to rebellion, and establish a free government." He asked her not to divulge a word of this outside the family—and not to worry, because "mother it will bring me a *Name* & *Fortune* If we succeed we will not *want* any more."[7]

As the days passed and Brown himself wrote a procession of letters to his Northern allies, the recruits became edgy and irritable in the cramped farmhouse. During a thunderstorm, when they were certain the neighbors could not hear them, they jumped around, ran up and down the stairs and shouted to let off steam. But in time the crowded quarters and constant worry that they might be discovered got to them all. When Hazlett and Leeman derided Barclay Coppoc and Dauphin Thompson (the youngest of a family of eighteen children, a frail curly-haired blond with blue eyes) "as too nearly like girls to make good soldiers," there must have been a near fight. They were all like caged animals. Hazlett and Leeman took to stealing out of the house at night and roaming through the woods and even going down to Harpers Ferry to see Cook.[8]

Brown, of course, gave them a tongue-lashing for this. But he knew what the trouble was. If they did not attack soon they might all break from the tension. Yet he could not attack now—not with all the problems and uncertainties he faced. For it was an invariable rule with him to be governed by circumstances, to take no hasty or rash steps while under pressure, "in other words *not to do anything while I do not know what to do*" and to trust his course to Providence. The most crucial problem was money. He had spent all the $2,000 from the secret committee—along with another $200 Smith had sent him on June 4—for freight costs, supplies, and expenses for John Jr., who was traveling across New York, Massachusetts, and Canada in an attempt to raise more recruits and solicit more weapons and funds. Howe had sent him an additional $50 and Sanborn another $155 ($50 of it from Mrs. Russell of Boston and $35 or so from Smith), but that was hardly enough to sustain him in an all-out war.[9] And where were all the weapons and money his other friends were to have sent? Where were the pikes? And all the volunteers Brown had expected from Pennsylvania, New York, New England, Ohio, and Kansas? Where were Parsons, Moffett, Hinton, and Gill, Secretary of the Treasury of the Provisional Government who had written Brown: "At the right hour, by all you deem sacred, remember me"? "I shall rejoice over '*one* that repenteth,' " Brown wrote John Jr., and dispatched urgent calls to his friends—"all miners will come at once!"—as well as to his Negro allies in New York, Massachusetts, and Canada. Where were the Negroes? They had more of a stake in this than any of the whites. Where were the friends of Loguen, Tubman, and Garnet? Where were Osborn Anderson and Richard Richardson? Frederick Douglass and Shields Green?[10]

At Brown's request, Douglass and Green met him for a consultation at an old stone quarry in Chambersburg (August 19–21). Kagi also was present. After giving Brown $10 from Mrs. Gloucester, who sent "her best wishes," Douglass studied his old friend, who was disguised as a fisherman in an "old and storm-beaten" hat. Brown's face "wore an anxious expression" as he told Douglass, apparently for the first time, about his plan to raid the Harpers Ferry arsenal. Douglass was shocked. He pointed out that if Brown attacked federal property, it would "array the whole country" against him and the invasion would be stamped out at once. But Brown argued that the attack was both feasible and necessary, because it would "serve notice to the slaves that their friends had come, and as a trumpet to rally them to [my] standard." Douglass continued to object, insisting that the old man was "going into a perfect steel-trap, and that once in he would never get out alive." How, Douglass exclaimed, could his friend "rest upon a reed so weak and broken"? Douglass was certain that Virginia would "blow him and his hostages sky-high, rather than that he should hold Harper's Ferry an hour." Brown categorically disagreed with that. "Come with me, Douglass," he pleaded; "I will defend you with my life. I want you for a special purpose. When I strike, the bees will begin to swarm, and I shall want you to help hive them." But Douglass shook his head. No, he told his friend, he would not go with him this time. Then Douglass turned to Shields Green and asked what he was going to do. Green, a runaway himself, could not have had much confidence in Brown's plan; yet he felt a tremendous loyalty to Brown personally; and after thinking the matter through, he replied that he would go with the old man.[11]

Douglass had refused to follow him; Richardson, Gill, Hinton, Parsons, and the others still had not arrived. A Negro member of the Chatham convention had written a note from Cleveland that he was not coming and that he was disgusted with himself "and the whole negro set, G— D—'em." Moreover, John Jr.'s journey across the East and Canada was an unmitigated failure, partly because Brown himself was vague in his instructions and partly because John Jr., in deep personal anguish, appears to have given contradictory and incoherent directions to Brown's allies. As the failures and disappointments multiplied, Brown began to doubt that the invasion would ever take place. Why had his friends betrayed him? Was it an ill omen? Had he misjudged his own destiny? He prayed to God for guidance. He made his recruits attend morning Bible services. He wrote John Jr. (and told himself) that the time was exactly right for the destruction of slavery and prayed that their "own impudence & folly" would not defeat them. Yet he still did not move. He wrote more letters, begging "for further support." He looked for signs. He worked furiously, hunched over the kitchen table, preparing "General Orders No. 1" which provided for the organization of the Provisional Army. He wrote notes about the "Duty of all persons in regard to this *matter*" and the "Criminality of neglect in this *matter*" and composed a ringing "VINDICATION OF THE INVASION" in the past tense, as though the raid had already failed and he was facing a jury and a divided nation beyond. First: "It was in accordance with my settled policy." Second: "It was intended as a discriminating blow at *Slavery*." Third: "It was calculated to lessen the value of Slaves." And finally: "It was (over and above all others) *Right*."[12]

2

It has been estimated that at least eighty people knew about Brown's projected invasion and that many others—Senators Seward and Wilson, for example—had reason to expect that Brown was planning some incendiary move against the South, although they did not know what for certain. And anybody who read James Redpath's *The Roving Editor; or, Talks with Slaves in the Southern States*, published in New York early in 1859, would have to be monumentally naïve not to have suspected that something large was underfoot. Redpath wrote the book after he and a young abolitionist named Francis Jackson Meriam had visited Haiti and made a trip across the South in 1858. The volume was dedicated "TO JOHN BROWN, Senior, of Kansas." "You have proven that the slaver has a soul as cowardly as his own 'domestic institution,'" Redpath wrote in the Dedication. "I do not hesitate to urge the friends of the slave to incite insurrections, and encourage, in the North, a spirit which shall ultimate in servile and civil wars." "You, Old Hero! believe that the slave should be aided and urged to insurrection, and hence do I lay this tribute at your feet." In the text itself Redpath announced that there were a number of young men, trained in guerrilla warfare in the ravines of Kansas, who were eager to avenge their murdered comrades in Georgia and the Carolinas.[13]

One of the most incredible things about Brown's plot was how the authorities managed to remain completely ignorant of what was going on. In fact, it was not until August, 1859, while Brown was hiding out on the Maryland border, that one of his many confidants decided to expose the conspiracy. In Springdale, Iowa, a Quaker named David J. Gue talked over Brown's scheme with his brother and another Quaker, and all three decided that Brown and his followers would be killed. To "protect Brown from the consequences of his own rashness," Gue sent an anonymous letter (dated August 20)

to Secretary of War John B. Floyd, who was vacationing at Red
Sweet Springs in Virginia. The letter warned darkly that " 'old John
Brown,' late of Kansas," was organizing "a secret association" to
incite a slave uprising in the South. He had a secret agent "in an
armory" in Maryland and a large number of arms at his secret rendezvous. He planned to move in a few weeks, passing down Maryland
and entering Virginia at Harpers Ferry. Gue told Floyd that he was
afraid to reveal his identity, but trusted that the Secretary of War
would not disregard this warning "on that account." Gue hoped that
Floyd would send soldiers to Harpers Ferry at once, and that Brown,
observing the troop build-up, would abandon his plans and return
safely to the North.

When Floyd read this remarkable letter, he was a bit confused
(he did not associate the "old John Brown" in the letter with the
Brown for whom the President had offered a $250 reward). Floyd
knew there was no armory or arsenal in Maryland. Besides, "a scheme
of such wickedness and outrage could not be entertained by any
citizens of the United States." Deciding that the author was a crank,
Floyd filed the letter away and forgot about it.[14]

At almost the same time, on August 27, Gerrit Smith wrote a
letter to the "Jerry Rescue" Anniversary Committee in New York.
"No wonder," Smith declared, "that in this state of facts which I have
sketched, intelligent black men in the States and Canada should see
no hope for their race in the practice and policy of white men. No
wonder they are brought to the conclusion that no resource is left to
them but in God and insurrections. For insurrections then we may
look any year, any month, any day. A terrible remedy for a terrible
wrong! But come it must unless anticipated by repentance and the
putting away of the terrible wrong."[15]

                                3

As the September days passed, Brown's recruits grew more restless
and more fearful than ever that the neighbors were on to them, that
any moment now a "nigger-hating" mob would converge on the
farmhouse, burn it, and lynch them all.

Yet Brown continued to wait, hoping that support from the North might still come through. Perhaps to Watson he seemed to be "dally-ing," just as Salmon predicted would happen before Watson had left home ("you know father," Salmon had said, and his "peculiarity for insisting on *order*"—he "would insist on getting everything arranged just to suit him before he would consent to make a move" and the long delay would probably get him trapped) . In desperation, Brown and Kagi made a secret trip to Philadelphia "on some final important business"—doubtless to plead with his white and Negro friends there to join him. But the trip was fruitless, and Brown returned to the farm with "a saddened heart" and a growing realization that God, who was master of all their fates, wanted them to attack with what they had.[16]

Late in September there were propitious signs. For one thing, 950 pikes from Charles Blair came in from Chambersburg, which the boys stored in boxes along with the 200 revolvers and 198 Sharps repeating rifles from the Kansas committees. For another, Osborn P. Anderson, a brave young Negro who had attended the Chatham convention, arrived from Canada and said he was ready for war. On September 30 Brown sent the two girls back to North Elba and the next day wrote a moving letter to his wife and daughters, advising them about their worldly concerns and imploring them to remain good and sincere Christians. Then, knowing that he might never see them again, he asked that Annie "*Save this letter* to remember your Father by."

He also scratched off a note to John Jr.: "If you were here, I could fully *explain* all but cannot do so now. From Harrisburg by Rail Road remember."[17] Then he sent Cook down the Charleston pike to collect statistics on the slave population and the planters in the area. Apparently Cook reported back that the old man could indeed expect the slaves to "swarm like bees" when the attack began. Kagi thought "the moon was just right," too, because (as he wrote John Jr.) the slaves were more discontented after the crops had been harvested than at any other season. Also, "a great religious revival is going on, and has its advantages. Under its influence, people who are commonly barely *unfavorable* to Slavery under religious excitement in meetings speak boldly against it. In addition to this and as a stimu-lant to the religious feeling, a fine slave man near our headquarters, hung himself a few days ago because his master sold his wife away from him. This also arouses the slaves. There are more reasons which I could give, but I have not time."[18]

Beyond Kagi's observations (a "right moon," a hanging black man) and Cook's single ride down the Charlestown pike, Brown made no further effort to gather information about the slaves or to learn anything else about the region. He even refused to send agents out to alert the blacks, arguing that they would hear of the attack as the news spread through the countryside and would rush to a school-house, on the Maryland side of the Potomac, which Brown had chosen as their rendezvous. From either carelessness or ineptitude, or because he trusted everything to the Almighty ("in all thy ways acknowledge Him & He shall direct thy paths"), Brown made no reconnaissance of the area in order to familiarize himself with the roads, the hidden trails and places of refuge, which he might utilize once he left Harpers Ferry. Nor did he bother to work out an escape plan should militia and federal troops come to the town's defense, believing as he did that God would "guard and shield" him and alone would determine the outcome.

Yes, the signs were encouraging, the time was undoubtedly near. Brown stored all his vital documents—his maps, his Constitution, his "VINDICATION OF THE INVASION," and a number of letters (explicit letters, incriminating letters) from Sanborn, Howe, Smith, Douglass, Delany, Gill, John Jr., Blair, and others—in a carpetbag, which he left in a trunk in the downstairs of the farmhouse. Then he ordered Kagi and Cook to the farm and sent Cook's wife (who was ignorant of everything) to Chambersburg. The last obstacles to the attack—and any lingering doubts Brown had about his destiny—were removed when three late recruits reached the farm on October 15: John Copeland and Lewis Leary, the Negro rescuers from Oberlin, and Francis Jackson Meriam, who had visited Haiti with Redpath and wanted to help in "stealing slaves down South." A nephew of a prominent abolitionist, frail, one-eyed, and either emotionally unbalanced or mentally retarded, Meriam had learned of Brown's plot from a Negro in Boston and eagerly approached Sanborn and Higginson about "the shepherd" and his "business operation." Both of them knew enough about Brown's whereabouts to direct Meriam to the Kennedy farm.

Meriam not only volunteered his services but contributed $600 in

gold. For Brown, that gold was an unmistakable sign that God
wanted him to move. With awakened resolution, he told his men that
tomorrow night, Sunday, October 16, the revolution would begin.[19]

4

As the first rays of light spread through the farmhouse that Sunday
morning, Brown assembled his twenty-one recruits—sixteen whites
and five Negroes—in the living room for a final worship service. He
read a passage from the Bible that was applicable to the slaves, then
"offered up a fervent prayer to God," recalled Osborn P. Anderson,
"to assist in the liberation of the bondmen in that slaveholding
land."

Later that morning Brown explained his battle plans to the new
recruits, pointing out that they would barricade the two bridges
leading to Harpers Ferry, seize the federal armory complex and the
rifle works, and use hostages to negotiate with any militia that
attacked them. Since no federal troops were stationed at Harpers
Ferry, he thought he would have plenty of time to gather the arms,
terrorize the town, wait for slave reinforcements from Virginia to
join him there, and then take to the hills. Nobody questioned
the soundness of the plan of operation; nobody raised any objections
at all, as Stevens read the Constitution in his rich baritone voice and
Brown administered the oath of secrecy to the new recruits. At a war
council that afternoon Brown gave out battle assignments: Owen,
Barclay Coppoc, and the one-eyed Meriam were to remain at the
farm as a rear guard. At a prescribed time Owen would move the
guns and pikes to the schoolhouse near the Potomac and arm the
slaves from Maryland and the dissident whites from southern Pennsylvania and western Virginia who came to join the revolution. The
other eighteen volunteers, with Kagi, Stevens, Tidd, and Cook serving as captains in the Provisional Army, would follow Brown to the
Ferry.

As darkness closed over the farmhouse Brown warned his men
not to spill blood needlessly but not to hesitate in defending themselves either. As Brown spoke and the tension mounted in those final
minutes before the attack began, they all knew they might be killed

in the glorious struggle ahead, but they were willing to die—to follow Brown straight to their graves—in order to strike a blow for freedom and justice in this "slave-cursed land." For it was as Brown had told them earlier: "We have here only one life to live, and once to die; and if we lose our lives it will perhaps do more for the cause than our lives would be worth in any other way."

While Brown spoke to them on that last Sunday night, he too realized that the raid stood a strong chance of failure and that they might all be killed. But even if the raid did fail (as he had repeatedly told the Secret Six), the attempt would provoke such a violent sectional crisis that hopefully a war would break out in which slavery would be destroyed and the sins of this whole nation would be washed away with blood. "God has honored but comparatively *a very small* part of mankind with any possible chance for such mighty & soul satisfying rewards," Brown had written Sanborn the year before. "I expect to effect a mighty conquest even though it be like the last victory of Sampson." Of course, Brown would not question the will of God, and it was possible that the Almighty would carry out the invasion just as Brown had planned it. But whatever happened, God would use the attack this night to suit His own purposes.

It was eight o'clock. John Brown, an old man with glaring eyes and a white beard, who called himself an avenging angel of the Lord, faced his meager army. "Men, get on your arms; we will proceed to the Ferry." Leaving the rear guard at the farmhouse, Brown climbed into a wagon loaded with pikes and tools and led his men "as solemnly as a funeral procession" down the county road toward the Potomac. It was a chill, overcast night with a slight drizzle of rain. There was no moon.[20]

XIX

INSURRECTION!

❧

NOBODY SAID ANYTHING AS THE PROVISIONAL ARMY marched solemnly behind the creaking wagon, the bent figure of their commander barely visible in the darkness. With rifles on their shoulders, they made their way down the steep, winding road, passing farmhouses here and there on the wooded hillsides, until at last they could see the lights of Harpers Ferry through the moving trees, a twinkling fairy-tale city on a mountainside, unaware of the violence about to descend upon it this Sabbath night.

In a moment they reached the canal that ran along the Potomac, and headed for the covered railroad and wagon bridge that led across the river into town. There was not a sound in the darkness except the sloshing of the river and the dull, mechanical hoofbeats of the wagon team. Ahead, outlined against the cloudy sky, were the shadows of Maryland Heights.

Soon Cook and Tidd fell out of line and headed into the woods to cut telegraph lines east and west of town. The others marched stiffly on behind the old man, their stomachs tightening as they reached the bridge. *Now.* Brown turned in the wagon and motioned: crouching low, Kagi and Stevens darted across the bridge and captured the night watchman, who thought it was all a joke until the raiders made it clear they were in deadly earnest. The others came up fast and deployed noiselessly across the Shenandoah bridge. Except for a few figures crossing the streets, the town showed hardly a sign of life. While Newby, Will Thompson, Oliver, and another recruit guarded the bridges, the other raiders stole past the well-lit

Wager House (a combination railroad station and hotel) and a saloon called the Galt House on the bank of the Shenandoah. Straight ahead, on Potomac Street, they could make out the shadows of the arsenal and armory buildings. Quickly now they ran across the intersecting streets and took the watchman at the government shops by surprise, pinning him against the gate and securing both the armory and arsenal. "I came here from Kansas," Brown told the frightened watchman, "and this is a slave State; I want to free all the negroes in this State; I have possession now of the United States armory, and if the citizens interfere with me I must only burn the town and have blood."[1]

While Brown brought the wagon into the armory yard at a clatter, his men captured a few people in the streets and herded all the prisoners into the engine house near the gate. Then the old man himself led a party up Shenandoah Street, seized Hall's Rifle Works, and took another prisoner. Kagi and John Copeland, the Oberlin College student, garrisoned the rifle works and Lewis Leary later reinforced them.

Brown hurried back to the armory, convinced that so far everything was going like clockwork. He had possession of all his prime military targets, including several million dollars' worth of federal munitions and arms. He next sent out a special detachment of raiders to seize hostages in the surrounding countryside—among them Colonel Lewis W. Washington, a small but prosperous planter and a great-grandnephew of the first President. By now Owen should have moved to the schoolhouse where shouting slaves from Maryland would soon be congregating. The word was spreading through Virginia, too, and in the next twenty-four hours slaves from all over that state should be pouring into Harpers Ferry, reporting to Oliver at the Shenandoah bridge and to Kagi at the rifle works.

Not long after midnight the special detachment rode into the armory yard in a four-horse wagon loaded with ten liberated slaves and three hostages—Colonel Washington and a farmer named John Allstadt and his son. The raiders had also confiscated several household weapons, including a magnificent sword of Washington's which Frederick the Great had allegedly given his illustrious relative. In the glare of a large stove in the engine house Brown told Washington, "I wanted you particularly for the moral effect it would give our cause having one of your name, as a prisoner," and then armed the bewildered slaves with pikes and ordered them to guard the hostages. Brown was admiring Washington's sword—a fine symbol for the revolution that had begun this night—when one of his men reported that all the telegraphs had been cut. Now, as soon as the slaves arrived, he could garrison the town, take more hostages, and move on.[2]

A gunshot punctuated the darkness. Below the government shops Brown's sentinels had just fired at a relief watchman, driving him back to the Wager House with his head bleeding from a flesh wound. They had barely constructed a barricade across the railroad bridge when an express train from Wheeling came chugging into Harpers Ferry, only to grind to a stop when the wounded night watchman warned the conductor that he had been attacked by men with guns. In a moment the engineer and another employee came walking down the track to investigate, but the raiders opened fire and drove them back on the run. Then the train itself backed up out of rifle range and stopped again, while the engineer shouted the alarm and anxious faces pressed against the windows of the passenger coaches. At that moment a free Negro named Hayward Shepherd, who worked at the station as baggage master, came down the trestlework looking for the night watchman. "Halt!" one of the raiders cried. Just as Shepherd started to retrace his steps there was a crack of gunfire, and the Negro staggered back along the trestlework and fell mortally wounded. The night watchman dragged him back into the station where he later died in great agony. The first real blood in Brown's war against slavery had been spilled.[3]

By now the gunfire and the unusual commotion around the armory had aroused the townspeople; they gathered in the streets with knives, axes, squirrel rifles, with any weapon they could pick up. What was it? What was happening? A slave insurrection, somebody cried: hundreds of niggers with some bloodthirsty abolitionists murdering and looting around the armory. They had killed the colored baggage master—one of their own—and somebody else reported that Thomas Boerley, the Irishman, had also been shot and was lying dead in the street. Panic-stricken, the townsmen fled with their families to the top of Bolivar Heights in back of Harpers Ferry. But in all the confusion and hysteria they seemed not to notice a few of the very Negroes they dreaded cowering in their midst, as terrified as any of the whites.[4]

Down in town the bell on the Lutheran church was tolling the alarm, calling to farmers all over the countryside: *insurrection, insurrection*: tolling on into the mist-swept morning. By that time the alarm was spreading to nearby towns, as two villagers galloped madly along separate roads yelling at the top of their lungs: insurrection at Harpers Ferry! Slaves raping and butchering in the streets! The thing all Southerners had dreaded since Nat Turner's terrible uprising in 1831 was now upon them like a black plague. Soon church bells were tolling in Charlestown, in Shepherdstown and Martinsburg. At the same time Brown had allowed the express train to push on; and it was now carrying the news to Monacacy and Frederick. From Monocacy the alarm would click over the telegraphs to Baltimore and from there to Richmond and Washington, D.C., and the news would soon be blazing in headlines throughout the South and East, "Negro Insurrection at Harper's Ferry!" Fire and Rapine on the Virginia Border!"[5] In the meantime all over the Blue Ridge Mountains of northern Virginia, in every town and village within a 30-mile radius of the stricken hamlet, men were running about like angry ants, forming militia companies and setting out to repress the rebellion with terrible shouts.

By eleven o'clock on Monday morning a general battle was raging at Harpers Ferry, as armed farmers and militiamen poured into the town and laid down a blistering fire on both the rifle works and the fire-engine house of the armory where Brown and a dozen of his men were gathered. The speed with which the countryside had mobilized had taken Brown completely by surprise; flustered, he did not know what to do. He had had abundant opportunities to gather his hostages and the government weapons and make a run for it; Kagi, in fact, had sent him frantic messages all morning that they must leave the town at once. But the old man had mysteriously delayed, his own men milling about the armory compound in confusion. Brown had even taken the time to order breakfast from the Wager House for all his prisoners (including a number of employees captured as they came to work that morning). With his small force already badly scattered, he had loaded Cook, Tidd, Leeman, and several of the liberated slaves into Washington's four-horse wagon and sent them across the Potomac to help Owen move the "tools" and to marshal black and white reinforcements at the schoolhouse (Leeman later returned to the armory with another prisoner, a Maryland slave-owner). Even as armed farmers arrived and opened fire on the raiders, Brown continued to disregard Kagi's pleas and refused to budge. Was he waiting for a sign? Holding his ground because he did not know what else to do? Still hoping that God would send the bees swarming to his side? To Osborn P. Anderson the old man seemed "puzzled" as he watched the bustle of armed men in the streets and the gray sky beyond.[6]

As Brown waited at the armory, the Jefferson Guards from Charlestown arrived on the Maryland side of the Potomac and charged across the bridge with rifles blazing. They routed Oliver and the other sentinels, secured control of both bridges, and barricaded themselves in the Wager House, thus cutting off Brown's only means of escape back to his rear guard in Maryland. As Brown and some of his men exchanged volleys with the militia, Oliver and one of the other sentinels made it back to the armory, but Dangerfield Newby fell from a sniper's bullet, fired from one of the homes between the hill and the armory. Newby was the first of the raiders to die and the last hope of his slave wife whose letter he carried in his pocket: "Oh dear Dangerfield, com this fall without fail monny or no Monney I want to see you so much that is the one bright hope I have before me." Newby lay in the street, "his throat cut literally from ear to ear" by the iron slug shot into him, until somebody—an inflamed villager, a half-drunk militiaman—dragged him into the gutter and sliced his ears off as souvenirs. Other "infuriated people" beat the body with sticks. Then as final humiliation a pack of hogs came to root on the body.[7]

As the townsmen, encouraged by the arrival of the Jefferson Guards, came down from Bolivar Heights and joined in the fighting around the armory, Brown had to admit that he might be trapped, that he could not wait for white or slave reinforcements. The only thing he could do, cut off as he was from Kagi at the rifle works and from the rear guard in Maryland, was to negotiate for a cease fire, offering to release his thirty-odd prisoners if the militia would let him and his men go free. He sent Will Thompson and one of the prisoners out under a flag of truce, but the excited crowd seized

Thompson and took him off to the Galt House at gun point. Would they shoot him like a dog? Would they lynch him? Brown grew desperate. With Hazlett and Osborn P. Anderson holding the arsenal, Brown gathered his other men, the armed slaves, and eleven of his most important prisoners into the fire-engine house, a brick building with three heavy oak doors in front and arched windows above them. The other prisoners remained unguarded in the watch-room of the engine house, too frightened by all the shooting to escape. Brown then sent his son Watson, Aaron Stevens, and the acting superintendent of the armory out under another white flag, but the mob gunned down both of the raiders. Watson crawled back to the engine house and doubled up in agony at the feet of his father. Stevens, however, lay bleeding in the gutter and might have died there had not one of the prisoners, a man named Joseph Brua, volunteered to leave the watch-room and go to Stevens' aid. Thanks to this brave and humane man, Stevens was carried to the railroad station and given medical attention. Then, incredibly enough, Brua returned to the watch-room of the engine house and took his place there among the other prisoners.

But if there were acts of mercy on this dark, fog-ridden day, there were shocking indignities and uninhibited hatred: the outrages committed on Newby, the shooting of Watson and Stevens under a flag of truce. The mob in the streets wanted blood; it wanted revenge— revenge for the insurrection these fanatics had tried to incite—and that meant a fight to the death. Many of the militiamen were already crazy with liquor (the Galt House was doing a booming business) and their bloodthirsty shouts, "*Kill them, Kill them,*" rang through the armory yard. It was no wonder that twenty-year-old William Leeman, the youngest raider, lost his nerve, ran across the armory yard, leaped over the gate, and fled for his life toward the Potomac. Some militiamen saw him and gave chase, firing at him on the run. Two of them finally overtook Leeman on a small islet and shot him to death at point-blank range. His body lay there for hours, a target for a dozen marksmen that afternoon, until somehow, riddled with bullets, it slid into the water and floated in slow silent eddies toward the bridge.[8]

Newby, Watson Brown, Stevens, and Leeman. The killing—and the vengeance—continued. About two o'clock the raiders shot a slaveowner named George Turner, whose death added to the frenzy and the anger of the crowd that day. Above the armory a party of whites stormed Hall's Rifle Works, driving Kagi and the two Negroes back toward the Shenandoah, where they were caught in a cross fire. Knowing better than to surrender, they turned and ran into the river, but the militia blazed away at the fleeing figures. Kagi "fell and died in the water," his body punctured with bullets. Leary was mortally wounded (he died the next morning in a cooper's shop on the island) and Copeland was taken prisoner. A black man with a gun. The whites went berserk. "Lynch him! Lynch the nigger!" They were tying their handkerchiefs together in a makeshift noose when a local physician rode up, saw what was about to happen, and shielded the trembling Negro with his horse until some other militia arrived and took Copeland away to a safe place.[9]

By late afternoon the town was in chaos as half-drunken and uncontrolled crowds thronged Potomac and Shenandoah streets. Hearing their shouts from behind the trestlework below the armory, kindly old Fontaine Beckham, the mayor of Harpers Ferry and an agent of the Baltimore and Ohio Railroad, was extremely upset over what was happening to his town. In his agitation he kept venturing out on the railroad, between some freight cars and the water station, trying to see what was going on around the beleaguered armory. Inside the engine house, Edwin Coppoc, the Quaker boy from Springdale, Iowa, thought the mayor was trying to shoot at them and drew a bead on him from the doorway: Coppoc fired, missed, fired a second time, "and the dark wings again brushed the little town" as Mayor Beckham—the best friend the Negroes had in the county— slumped to the timbers. For in his Will Book the mayor had provided for the liberation upon his death of a Negro named Isaac Gilbert, his wife, and three children. The Quaker's shot had freed them all.[10]

At that moment it began to rain, compelling the townspeople and militiamen to take cover. During the downpour word spread that the mayor had been killed, touching off one explosion of rage after another. The drunks in the saloon banged on the bars, fired their revolvers out the windows, and clamored for revenge. When the rain stopped and men spilled angrily into the streets, a mob led by the saloonkeeper and Harry Hunter, a militiaman from Charlestown and a relative of the mayor, marched over to the Wager House where Will Thompson had been taken; Hunter and the saloonkeeper went inside and started to shoot Thompson then and there, but a girl threw herself before him and begged the two men, both of them mad with hate, to leave Thompson to the laws. They grabbed him and dragged him outside by the throat. "You may take my life," he cried, but "80,000 will arise up to avenge me, and carry out my purpose of giving liberty to the slaves." The mob carried him kicking and screaming down to the Potomac, where they shot him in the head with revolvers and flung his body into the shallow water between the roadway and the bridge. For the rest of the afternoon "sharp-shooters" filled his body with bullets. According to one writer, Thompson "could be seen for a day or two after, lying at the bottom of the river, with his ghastly face still exhibiting his fearful death agony."[11]

While sporadic fighting continued around the armory that afternoon, more reinforcements were on their way, as the alarm spread through Virginia and Maryland. At Baltimore five militia companies boarded a special train and started for Harpers Ferry while thousands of citizens cheered wildly around Camden Station. All along the Baltimore and Ohio Railroad crowds gathered to hear the latest news. Three companies from Frederick and another from Martinsburg, composed mainly of railroad employees, were marching on the town at a killing pace. Meanwhile the nation's capital was in a state of panic (was it a series of coordinated insurrections? how many cities and towns had been attacked?). The mayor of Washington had mobilized the entire police force and garrisoned all routes into the capital. And President Buchanan, hearing that "700 whites and Negroes" were involved in the Harpers Ferry invasion, ordered three artillery companies to the town and then instructed some ninety U.S. Marines under Lieutenant Israel Green, stationed at Washington Barracks, to move as well. Buchanan also sent Brevet Colonel Robert E. Lee of the 2nd Cavalry and Lieutenant J. E. B. Stuart of the 1st Cavalry up to Harpers Ferry where Lee was to take command.

While federal troops were on the march, the company from Martinsburg reached Harpers Ferry not long after the mayor had been killed; the company rushed through the armory yard from the rear, thus cutting off Brown's last means of retreat, and broke out the windows in the watch-room of the engine house so that the prisoners there could escape. Had the railway employees been able to rally the drunken men in the streets they might have stormed the engine house

and ended the fighting entirely. As it was, Brown's raiders fired back
testily; and at last the company withdrew, dragging away eight
wounded men. The company formed picket lines around the armory
and the arsenal, only to find it deserted (for Hazlett and Osborn
Anderson had escaped in all the confusion, paddled across the
Potomac in a stolen boat, and were now running through the Maryland woods toward the farmhouse). From a mountain on the Maryland side of the Potomac John E. Cook saw that Brown was trapped
in the engine house and under heavy siege. Hoping to draw off some
of the fire, Cook scaled a tree and started shooting at a party of men
on High Street; instantly they returned his fire—one shot cut away a
limb Cook was clinging to and he fell fifteen feet to the ground.
Bruised and cut, Cook made his way down to the canal and hurried
to the schoolhouse, where Owen, Barclay Coppoc, Meriam, and Tidd
were waiting anxiously for news.[12]

Meanwhile, back at Harpers Ferry, two militia companies from
Shepherdstown and three from Frederick had arrived, joining in the
noisy melee around the armory. Again Brown had tried to negotiate,
sending out a note, signed "John Brown," in which he offered to
release his hostages if he and his men could escape across the Potomac
into Maryland. This signed note was perhaps the first evidence the
militia had as to the identity of the bearded chief of the insurrectionists, whom somebody had already recognized as the mysterious
Maryland farmer, "Isaac Smith." (The next day dispatches out of
Harpers Ferry revealed that the notorious John Brown of Kansas was
the leader of the raiders and newspapers soon carried his name to the
outside world.) [13] If Brown hoped his assailants would agree to
terms he was incredibly misguided. They knew that federal troops
were on the way, and in any case they were not about to let him go
when they had him trapped. More reinforcements arrived that evening; and rifle fire and drunken shouting continued to punctuate the
drizzly darkness all that night.

2

It was painfully cold and pitch dark inside the engine house, as
Brown, four uninjured raiders, and eleven prisoners watched the
night drag by. Stewart Taylor lay near the doorway, where he had

been shot dead that afternoon. Watson and Oliver Brown, who had
been wounded shortly after the killing of Mayor Beckham, lay side
by side on the floor, both of them choking and crying in intense pain.
The old man, distraught and exhausted, still wearing Washington's
sword, paced back and forth in the darkness, muttering to himself
and occasionally calling out, "Men, are you awake?" He made sure
that his prisoners were comfortable (throughout the fighting that
day he had been extremely kind to them). He paused, listening to
the yelling and clank of arms outside, then started pacing again.
Oliver, one of the prisoners remembered later, begged his father
"again and again to be shot, in the agony of his wound." But Brown
turned on him. "If you must die, die like a man." Then he turned
to the prisoners in despair. "Gentlemen, if you knew of my past
history you would not blame me for being here. I went to Kansas
a peaceable man, and the proslavery people hunted me down like
a wolf. I lost one of my sons there." He stood there trembling for
a moment, then called to Oliver. There was no answer. "I guess he
is dead," the old man said, and started pacing again.[14]

3

When the first cold gray light of morning spread through the high
windows of the engine house, Brown and the remaining raiders—
Edwin Coppoc, Jeremiah Anderson, Dauphin Thompson, and
Shields Green—took their places at the gun holes which one of
Allstadt's slaves had dug out of the walls. The men winced at what
they saw in the yard outside: the company of United States Marines
had arrived during the night and was now deployed in front of the
engine house with bayonets and sledge hammers, while two thousand
spectators looked on from sidewalks and buildings as far as the raiders could see. Brown had the doors barricaded and loopholed, but
he knew they would not hold against sledge hammers, he knew that
his attempted insurrection had failed and that this was the end for
him and the young men who stood by his side. Yet his face wore an
expression of proud resolution, as though this was what he wanted
and expected to happen all along. Brown "was the coolest and firmest
man I ever saw," Colonel Washington observed. "With one son
dead by his side, and another shot through, he felt the pulse of his

dying son with one hand and held his rifle with the other, and commanded his men with the utmost composure, encouraging them to sell their lives as dearly as they could."

But the Marines did not attack. With Lee looking on from a slight elevation about forty feet away, J. E. B. Stuart, a flamboyant young trooper and a son of Virginia, approached the engine house under a flag of truce. Brown cracked the door, and with his rifle aimed at Stuart's head he took a note from the trooper's hand. As the old man read it, Stuart recognized him as Osawatomie Brown, "who had given us so much trouble in Kansas," where Stuart had served in 1856. Lee's note summoned Brown to surrender unconditionally, with assurances that he would be protected from harm and turned over to the proper authorities. Brown handed the note back with his fierce eyes on Stuart's. He would surrender, he declared, only on terms that would allow him and his men to escape. At that some of the prisoners begged Stuart to ask Colonel Lee himself to come and reason with Brown. Stuart replied that Lee would agree only to the terms offered in the note. Then suddenly the trooper jumped away from the door and waved his cap; and storming parties, with the spectators cheering wildly, rushed the engine house and started battering at the thick oak doors. The raiders fired back, powder smoke wreathing out of the gun holes and cracks in the building, but nothing could stop the marines: they tore down one of the doors with a heavy ladder and stormed inside; two of them fell, but the others swarmed on, pinning Jeremiah Anderson to the wall with a bayonet and running Dauphin Thompson through as he crawled under a fire engine. Both raiders died from the bayonet wounds. Colonel Washington then pointed to Brown, who was kneeling with his rifle cocked, and said, "This is Ossawatomie." Lieutenant Israel Green, leader of the storming party, struck Brown with his light dress sword before the old man could fire, and then tried to run him through with such a savage thrust it almost lifted him off the floor, but the blade struck either a bone or Brown's belt buckle and bent double. Had Green been armed with his heavy battle sword, which he had left in the Washington Barracks in all the excitement, he would probably have killed Brown with that thrust. As Brown fell, Green beat him on the head with the hilt of his dress sword until the old man was unconscious. When Green at last got control of himself he had Brown and the other dead and wounded raiders carried

outside and laid on the grass. Colonel Lee inspected Brown himself
and when he regained consciousness the colonel had a doctor tend
his wounds.[15]

After Brown's capture word came that more insurrectionists had
been seen at the schoolhouse on the Maryland side of the Potomac. A
column of Baltimore militia hurried across the river, only to find the
schoolhouse deserted. On the floor inside, though, they saw something
that made their blood freeze: boxes of Maynard revolvers and Sharps
carbines that were obviously intended for slave allies and abolitionist
reinforcements. Later that morning a special detachment under
Lieutenant Stuart marched up to the Kennedy farm, but nobody was
there. The patrol confiscated all the pikes from Charles Blair and an
incredible collection of incriminating documents found strewn about
the farmhouse: the marked maps, Forbes's *Manual*, the "Provisional
Constitution," "General Orders No. 1," the "VINDICATION OF THE
INVASION," and the carpetbag filled with letters that implicated
Brown's secret backers and a number of innocent friends. These
documents eventually found their way into the hands of the Virginia
authorities, who began extradition proceedings to get all of Brown's
Northern collaborators.[16]

4

Thus Brown's war for slave liberation, thirty-six hours after it began,
had ended in dismal failure. No uprisings had taken place anywhere
in Virginia and Maryland, because the slaves there, lacking organization and leadership, having little if any knowledge of what was going
on and being dreadfully afraid of Southern reprisals, had been both
unable and unwilling to join him. Not a single slave had come to
Harpers Ferry of his own volition; and the handful Brown had forcibly liberated had refused to fight back once the shooting began
around the armory. Those with the rear guard in Maryland had
deserted during the night, returning to their masters with stories
about how they had been held against their will (for they knew what
terrible fate awaited slaves who were accused of insurrection). One
slave was captured with Brown at Harpers Ferry and later taken to
jail at Charlestown, where he died from a combination of pneumonia
and fear of what the White Man would do to him. And another slave

was found drowned in one of the rivers at Harpers Ferry, where some townsmen had probably chased him as he tried to escape.[17] This was the extent of the black revolution Brown had hoped to ignite in northern Virginia.

The raid cost a total of seventeen lives (including the two slaves who had died). Three townsmen, a slaveholder, and one Marine had been killed, and nine men had been wounded. Ten of Brown's own recruits, including two of his sons, had been killed or fatally injured. Five raiders had been captured and the rest had escaped into the Maryland mountains. Hazlett and Cook were caught in Pennsylvania several days later and returned to Virginia under heavy guard. But Owen, Meriam, Tidd, Barclay Coppoc, and Osborn P. Anderson all escaped for good.[18]

Brown himself, "cut thrust and bleeding and in bonds," was lodged along with Aaron Stevens—who was also gravely wounded— in the paymaster's office of the armory, where Brown displayed a "cool, collected, and indomitable" spirit even as a lynch mob formed in the street outside and cried for his head. Green, Edwin Coppoc, and Watson Brown, still clinging to his life, were locked in the watch-room of the engine house under a strong guard. A South Carolinian who championed slavery and nullification visited the watch-room that Tuesday morning and was profoundly impressed by the raiders' courage, remarking that he could not help "but feel respect for men who offer up their lives in support of their convictions." The man gave Watson a cup of water, lifted him to a bench, and fashioned a pillow for him out of a pair of overalls. Watson searched his eyes with a look the South Carolinian would never forget. "What brought you here?" the man asked. "Duty, sir," Watson replied. "Is it then your idea of duty to shoot men down upon their own hearth-stones for defending their rights?" Watson answered with great difficulty, his face contorted with pain. "I am dying; I cannot discuss the question; I did my duty as I saw it." Early the next morning he was dead.[19]

5

Early on Tuesday afternoon, Governor Henry A. Wise of Virginia and a retinue of officers, newspaper reporters, and United States congressmen (including Senator James M. Mason of Virginia and

Representative Clement L. Vallandigham of Ohio) arrived at Harpers Ferry, which was still in a state of wild excitement. The governor conferred with Lee, who showed him Brown's Constitution and some of the other captured documents, and then entered the paymaster's office to interrogate "the commander of the abolitionist filibuster army," who lay on a pile of old bedding with bandages on his head. Lee made the introductions, surveyed the crowded room, and said he would remove all visitors if Brown and Stevens were annoyed. Brown said let them stay; he wanted "to make himself and his motives clearly understood." With Lee, Stuart, Colonel Washington, Andrew Hunter, Governor Wise, a Virginia congressman, and several reporters and bystanders looking on, Mason started firing questions at Brown, and the interview was under way, to last a full three hours. Knowing that his words would be read by people all over the United States, Brown struck such a heroic pose, with his eyes "flashing" at everybody, that even Governor Wise had to admit that "He is the gamest man I ever saw." A reporter for the Baltimore *American and Commercial Advertiser* was impressed, too. "In the midst of enemies, whose home he had invaded; wounded, and a prisoner; surrounded by a small army of officials, and a more desperate army of angry men; with the gallows staring him full in the face, he lay on the floor, and, in reply to every question, gave answers that betokened the spirit that animated him."[20]

"Can you tell us, at least, who furnished the money for your expedition?" Senator Mason began.

Brown replied: "I furnished most of it myself. I cannot implicate others. It is by my own folly that I have been taken. I could easily have saved myself from it had I exercised my own better judgment, rather than yielded to my feelings."

"You mean if you had escaped immediately?" Mason asked.

"No," Brown answered. "I had the means to make myself secure without any escape; but I allowed myself to be surrounded by a force by being too tardy. I should have gone away; but I had thirty odd prisoners, whose wives and daughters were in tears for their safety, and I felt for them. Besides, I wanted to allay the fears of those who believed we came here to burn and kill. For this reason I allowed the train to cross the bridge, and gave them full liberty to pass on. I did it only to spare the feelings of those passengers and their families, and to allay the apprehensions that you had got here in your vicinity a band of men who had no regard for life and property, nor any feelings of humanity."

Congressman Vallandigham, a conservative Democrat who suspected that Joshua Giddings and other "radicals" in the Western Reserve were behind Brown's invasion, asked him who had sent him here.

"No man sent me here; it was my own prompting and that of my Maker, or that of the Devil—whichever you please to ascribe it to. I acknowledge no master in human form."

"Did you get up this document that is called a Constitution?" Vallandigham asked.

"I did," Brown replied. "They are a constitution and ordinances of my own contriving and getting up."

Mason asked: "What was your object in coming?"

"We came to free the slaves, and only that."

A volunteer interrupted. "How many men, in all, had you?"

"I came to Virginia with eighteen men only, besides myself."

The volunteer was astonished. "What in the world did you suppose you could do here in Virginia with that amount of men?"

"Young man, I do not wish to discuss that question here."

"You could not do anything," the volunteer said.

"Well," Brown said testily, "perhaps your ideas and mine on military subjects would differ materially."

Mason asked: "How do you justify your acts?"

"I think, my friend, you are guilty of a great wrong against God and humanity—I say it without wishing to be offensive—and it would be perfectly right for any one to interfere with you so far as to free those you wilfully and wickedly hold in bondage. . . ."

There were further questions about Brown's beliefs. Then Mason asked: "Did you consider this a military organization in this Constitution? I have not yet read it."

"I did, in some sense." Brown beckoned at the Constitution. "I wish you would give that paper close attention."

Vallandigham wanted to know more about Brown's connections with abolitionists in Ohio. When was he there last? Had he visited Joshua Giddings?

"I did. I would not tell you, of course, anything that would implicate Mr. Giddings; but I certainly met with him and had conversations with him."

"About that rescue case?"

"Yes; I heard him express his opinions upon it very freely and frankly."

"Justifying it?"

"Yes, sir; I do not compromise him, certainly, in saying that."

"Will you answer this: Did you talk with Giddings about your expedition here?"

"No, I won't answer that; because a denial of it I would not make, and to make any affirmation of it I should be a great dunce." Now there was no doubt in Vallandigham's mind that Giddings and other "insurrectionary" abolitionists in Ohio were behind Brown's plot, and the congressman later said so publicly. Vallandigham went on: "Have you had correspondence with parties at the North on the subject of this movement?"

Brown replied that he had.

A bystander interrupted. "Do you consider this a religious movement?"

"It is, in my opinion, the greatest service man can render to God."

"Do you consider yourself an instrument in the hands of Providence?"

"I do."

"Upon what principle do you justify your acts?"

"Upon the Golden Rule. I pity the poor in bondage that have none to help them: that is why I am here; not to gratify any personal animosity, revenge, or vindictive spirit. It is my sympathy with the oppressed and the wronged, that are as good as you and as precious in the sight of God."

Vallandigham turned to Aaron Stevens, lying nearby, and pressed him about his connections with Ohio. "Be cautious, Stevens," Brown warned. "I would not answer that." Stevens turned away, groaning in pain, and said nothing.

Vallandigham snapped back to Brown. "Who are your advisers in this movement?"

"I cannot answer that. I have numerous sympathizers throughout the entire North."

A bystander wanted to know whether Brown had read Gerrit

Smith's letter to the "Jerry Rescue" Anniversary Committee, warning that a slave insurrection was at hand. Brown said he had not. But
"I agree with Mr. Smith that moral suasion is hopeless. I don't think
the people of the slave States will ever consider the subject of slavery
in its true light till some other argument is resorted to than moral
suasion."

"Did you expect a general rising of the slaves in case of your
success?" Vallandigham asked.

Brown deliberately lied. "No, sir; nor did I wish it. I expected
to gather them up from time to time, and set them free."

A bystander later asserted that setting the slaves free "would
sacrifice the life of every man in this community."

"I do not think so," Brown said.

"I know it," the bystander said. "I think you are fanatical."

"And I think you are fanatical. 'Whom the gods would destroy
they first made mad,' and you are mad."

"Robber!" somebody shouted in the crowd.

"You are the robbers," Brown retorted. "If you have your opinions about me, I have my opinions about you."

There were other questions about where Brown had obtained his
guns. Then a reporter told Brown: "I do not wish to annoy you; but
if you have anything further you would like to say, I will report it."

Brown addressed the entire gathering, with one eye on the
martyrdom that was nearly his now. "I have nothing to say, only that
I claim to be here in carrying out a measure I believe perfectly
justifiable, and not to act the part of an incendiary or ruffian, but to
aid those suffering great wrong. I wish to say, further more, that you
had better—all you people of the South—prepare yourselves for a
settlement of this question, that must come up for settlement sooner
than you are prepared for it. The sooner you are prepared the better.
You may dispose of me very easily—I am nearly disposed of now; but
this question is still to be settled—this negro question I mean; the
end of that is not yet...."[21]

XX

LET THEM HANG ME

ᘓᗭᗊ

ON THE TUESDAY EVENING AFTER BROWN'S capture, Harpers Ferry was still in a state of panic: rumors flew through the stricken town that slaves had been "seen in the mountains" and that thousands of abolitionists were "coming down through Pleasant Valley, killing all the citizens." While women and children gathered "crying and screaming" in the Lutheran church, armed men patrolled the streets and bridges, maintaining a sleepless vigilance through the night. The same was true in other towns in northern Virginia and Maryland. "The intelligence from Harper's Ferry," reported a shocked Baltimore *American and Commercial Advertiser,* "has created an excitement in our community and throughout the whole length and breadth of the country that has scarcely been equalled by any preceding occurrence of the present century." When Wednesday dawned and no abolitionists appeared, however, fear again turned to rage, and "lynch law" took "a vice-like grip on the area."[1]

Fearing that Brown and the other captured raiders would be murdered, the authorities hurried them by train to Charlestown, eight miles southwest of Harpers Ferry, and lodged them in the county jail under a heavy guard. Governor Wise then made a decision that was to bear significantly on the outcome of Brown's raid: although Brown had attacked and seized federal property at Harpers Ferry, the governor decided to prosecute him in a Virginia court rather than turn him over to federal authorities. Wise argued that federal prosecution would take too long anyway, that if the law did not act swiftly, Brown would be lynched. But that by no means covered his motivations. He also wanted to enhance the prestige of Virginia at the expense of Washington, thus adding luster to his own political career among his fellow Southerners. Luckily for the governor, the court calendar offered him an opportunity for a rapid trial: a grand jury was already in session in Charlestown, and Judge Richard Parker had just opened the semiannual term of the county circuit court. Thus the governor ordered Brown to stand trial in Parker's court only one week after his capture, thereby allaying Southern demands that this crime be quickly avenged and at the same time invoking the power of the state of Virginia.

On October 25, while a fierce debate over Brown's raid was taking shape between the South and antislavery Northerners, Brown and the other raiders underwent a preliminary examination before the magistrates' court. Andrew Hunter, the governor's special prosecutor, told the court that it must of course observe "the judicial decencies" in this case, but "in double quick time." Otherwise Stevens would die of his wounds before he could be hanged. Or worse yet: a mob might break into the jail and lynch the prisoners without due process. The court must move at once.

While various Northern reporters sharply criticized the haste of these proceedings, Brown himself was indifferent. When asked whether he had counsel, Brown snorted: "Virginians, I did not ask for any quarter at the time I was taken. I did not ask to have my life spared. The Governor of the State of Virginia tendered me his assurance that I should have a fair trial. I have had no counsel; I have not been able to advise with any one. . . . But if we are to be forced with a mere form—a trial for execution—you might spare yourselves that trouble. I am ready for my fate. I do not ask a trial. I beg for no mockery of a trial, no insult—nothing but that which conscience gives, or cowardice, would drive you to practice. . . . I have now little further to ask, other than that I may not be foolishly insulted only as cowardly barbarians insult those who fall into their power."

Reporters scribbled down Brown's speech and newspapers recounted it to thousands of readers during the next few days. Had the magistrates been more perceptive they might have realized that their wounded prisoner, with his "piercing eyes" and "resolute countenance," was determined to use the Charlestown court as a forum to rally Northern sentiment to his cause. But the magistrates allowed themselves to remain cheerfully ignorant of the drama Brown intended to stage and went on to assign Lawson Botts and Charles J. Faulkner, both of Virginia, as Brown's defense lawyers. But Faulkner withdrew, so the magistrates replaced him with Thomas C. Green, mayor of Charlestown, and then asked if Brown would accept these gentlemen as his counsel. "I do not care anything about counsel," Brown snapped. "It is unnecessary to trouble any gentlemen with that duty." At that one of the state's attorneys assured the old man that "You are to have a fair trial." When the other raiders accepted the assigned counsel, the magistrates ordered them taken to the county circuit court to stand trial.

At two o'clock on the afternoon of October 25 law men whisked Brown into the red-brick courthouse, where the circuit court, with Judge Parker sitting on the bench, was anxiously waiting. Although militiamen guarded all approaches to the courthouse, an angry mob was moiling in the streets outside. Judge Parker, hearing the tumult, was convinced that, unless Brown was prosecuted in a hurry, the mob would break into his court and drag the prisoner away to the nearest tree. Wasting no time, the court charged the grand jury, and the next day the jury reported a true bill against Brown for murdering four whites and one Negro, for conspiring with slaves to rebel, and for committing treason against Virginia, even though he was not a citizen of that state and owed it no allegiance. The jury presented similar indictments against Copeland, Coppoc, Shields Green, and Aaron Stevens, who was held on his feet by two bailiffs. Brown's lawyers entered pleas of "not guilty" and requested separate trials for the raiders; the court consented, electing to try Brown first. Because of his wounds the old man then asked the court for continuance, and so did Botts. But the court refused. A doctor who had examined Brown reported that his wounds were not serious enough to impair his reason or his memory. And the incendiary atmosphere in and around Charlestown, the court believed, had become too dangerous to permit further delay. The court selected a jury of twelve (Brown's counsel did not challenge any of them) and on October 27 the trial began, with Brown, composed and heroic, lying on a cot in full view of the crowded courtroom—and the nation beyond.[2]

2

Brown had hoped that, even if his invasion failed (as he probably knew it would), it would still provoke a crisis over the slavery issue, and that was exactly what was happening. As John Jay Chapman put it, millions of Americans who read about Brown's raid in their newspapers "shuddered not only with horror, but with awe. The raid took place. It took place, not in Kansas, a long way off, but within a few miles of Washington. Innocent men were killed. No one could tell whether a slave insurrection would follow. A wave of panic swept across the South, and of something not unlike panic across the North. The keynote was struck. There was no doubt about that, anywhere."[3]

Predictably, Northern and Southern Democrats branded the invasion as a Republican plot and demanded a Congressional investigation to root out "Black Republican" conspirators. Stephen A. Douglas argued that the invasion was the "natural, logical, inevitable result of the doctrines and teachings of the Republican party." Clement Vallandigham singled out Joshua Giddings as one of the Republican ringleaders. And Sumner, Seward, and Thaddeus Stevens were also accused of complicity. Backpedaling for all they were worth, Republican leaders disparaged the raid as the work of a solitary fanatic, pointing out that they neither advocated nor sanctioned attacks upon the South. Party bosses fretted over what the raid might do to Republican candidates in the forthcoming fall elections. "We are damnably exercised here about the effect of Brown's wretched fiasco in Virginia upon the moral health of the Republican party," the editor of a Chicago paper wrote Lincoln. "The old idiot—the quicker they hang him and get him out of the way the better." John Brown was no Republican," declared Lincoln himself, "and you have failed to implicate a single Republican in his Harper's Ferry enterprise."[4]

Initially the Republican press agreed with the party leaders, calling Brown "a madman" for believing that he could start a slave war where Negroes were "not abundant" and where "no Abolitionists were ever known to peep."[5] But as Brown's trial progressed, and the old man uttered some of the most stirring words ever to come from an American courtroom, much of the Republican press—and thousands of Republican readers—came to admire Brown's courage, his faith, and his noble ideals. What he had done was admittedly a crime, but there were extenuating circumstances because of his worthy motives: he wanted to rid America of slavery, the central paradox of her history. Dozens of Republican newspapers—and scores of Northern readers—agreed with the New York *Tribune* that Brown and his followers "dared and died for what they felt to be right, though in a manner which seems to us fatally wrong."[6]

Even Lincoln had to concede that Brown's ideals were noble ("he agreed with us in thinking slavery wrong"), yet that could not "excuse violence, bloodshed and treason. It could avail him nothing that he might think himself right." Another Republican presidential hopeful, speaking for scores of antislavery Northerners, was more sympathetic. "Poor old man!" said Salmon P. Chase. "How sadly misled by his own imaginations! How rash—how mad—how criminal then to stir up insurrection which if successful would deluge the land with blood and make void the fairest hopes of mankind!" Yet Chase could not forget "the unselfish desire to set free the oppressed —the bravery—the humanity towards his prisoners which defeated his purposes! It is a tragedy which will supply themes for novelists & Poets for centuries—Men will condemn his act & pity his fate forever." On the other hand, "how stern will be the reprobation which must fall on the grafting of public slavery upon Kansas which began it all and then slavery itself which underlies it all."[7]

There were, of course, a number of Northern newspapers—the New York *Herald* and the New York *Observer*, for example—and thousands of Northern conservatives who viewed Brown as a criminal, his raid as an inexcusable and unpardonable outrage, and demanded that he and his men "be dealt with as their guilt deserves." But the proslavery New York *Journal of Commerce*, while violently denouncing Brown, warned Virginia that "To hang a fanatic is to make a martyr of him and fledge another brood of the same sort. Better send these creatures to the penitentiary, and so make of them miserable felons" than to lynch them as many Virginians demanded. For "Monsters are hydra-headed, and decapitation only quickens vitality, and power of reproduction." The Portage (Ohio) *Weekly Sentinel*, speaking for conservative Northwesterners, blamed the invasion not on Brown but on the Republicans who had inspired his grisly work. "Already the Black Republican press has commenced to apologize for him," the *Sentinel* pointed out. "They say he reasoned thus, 'that the slave drivers tried to put down Freedom in Kansas by force of arms and he would try to put down Slavery in Virginia by the same means.' " This was the irrepressible conflict of Seward, Smith, and Giddings, carried into practical effect "by a bold, bad, desperate man." And who was responsible? "Not Brown, for he is mad; but they, who by their countenance and pecuniary aid have induced him thus to resort to arms to carry out their political schemes, must answer to the country and the world for this fearfully significant outbreak."[8]

Well, had any abolitionists or Republicans given Brown money for the raid? Northern readers wanted to know. They had their answer when both the New York *Herald* and the *New York Times* described how the authorities had confiscated Brown's secret documents, including shockingly incriminating letters from Franklin Sanborn, Gerrit Smith, Samuel Gridley Howe, "John Smith, Jr.," Martin Delany, Augustus Wattles, Frederick Douglass, and many other black and white abolitionists who had aided or supported Brown. The newspapers announced that these documents were now in the possession of Governor Wise and that he was negotiating for the arrest of Smith, Sanborn, Howe, and Douglass particularly. The New York *Herald* printed Gerrit Smith's letter of June 4, in which he called Brown "My Dear Friend" and sent him a draft for $200, and editorially accused both Smith and Douglass of being "accessories before the fact." The *Times* published a number of Brown's papers, including his ringing "VINDICATION OF THE INVASION" and a description of Brown's marked Southern maps, the publicity of which caused another round of convulsions in the South. Then the New York *Herald* scooped everybody when Hugh Forbes gave the editors an explicit account of his dealings with Brown and the Secret Six, and several letters he had written to Howe, including that which described the formulation of the "Well-Matured Plan."[9]

By now nobody knew how many well-to-do Northerners were involved in the conspiracy. Rumors had it that Southern agents, working in cooperation with Northern governors and federal authorities, were on the track of everybody who had ever given Brown money or help of any kind. Men like Amos Lawrence and Charles Blair were understandably shocked; they had known nothing about Brown's Virginia plan, nothing at all. Lawrence wrote Governor Wise that while he and several others had given Brown money, it was for his family at North Elba and for nothing else. Then Lawrence struck a note that was to be sounded in other letters to Wise and in Brown's trial itself: "the hardships & excitements of the past three years, together with fever & ague from which he now suffers," had disordered his mind and made him "a monomaniac."[10]

Meanwhile four of the actual conspirators were panic-stricken when they read the sensational news. They had been willing to give money and guns for Brown's cause, but they did not want to hang for it. How could he have been so careless as to leave behind all his letters and secret papers? Gerrit Smith, reading his own letters in both the *Times* and the *Herald*, became hysterical. "I am going to be indicted, sir, indicted! . . . If any man in the Union is taken, it will be me." In "hasty, nervous agitation" he burned all his letters that bore on Brown's plot, then sent his brother-in-law to destroy other incriminating evidence in Boston and Ohio. Unable to sleep, plagued with fears that he would be captured and put to death, Smith went "temporarily insane." On November 7 friends had him confined in the State Asylum for the Insane at Utica. When it became evident that he would not be arrested, however, he "recovered his reason" and late in December was able to return to Peterboro, where he steadfastly insisted that he had "neither been implicated in nor acquainted with Brown's plans."[11]

Howe, the dashing veteran of the Greek revolution, was hysterical too. Possessed "with a dread that threatened to overwhelm his reason," he fled to Stearns's home in Medford, where he walked up and down, wildly insisting that he would go insane if he and Stearns did not flee at once. Stearns was worried, too, and on October 25 they set out for Canada. From there Howe sent a statement to the New York *Tribune*: "The outbreak at Harper's Ferry was unforseen and unexpected by me; nor does all my previous knowledge of John Brown enable me to reconcile it with his characteristic prudence, and his reluctance to shed blood, or excite servile insurrection. It is still to me a mystery and a marvel. As to the heroic man who planned and led that forlorn hope, my relations with him in former times were such as no man ought to be afraid or ashamed to avow." Afterward Howe claimed lamely that he wrote this letter to help Brown, by showing that he had acted alone at Harpers Ferry, without agents or allies. "It is true," Howe confessed to Higginson, "that I ought to have expected an explosion and onslaught *somewhere*; but the point is, that I did not expect anything like what happened, or anything more than a stampede."[12]

Meanwhile Franklin Sanborn spent two consecutive nights obliterating letters and manuscripts that would implicate him in the raid; then he, too, fled to Canada. On October 22 he wrote Parker: "Our old friend struck his blow in such a way,—either by his own folly or the direction of Providence,—that it has recoiled, and ruined him, and perhaps those who were his friends." Sanborn knew that he was in trouble, "but this is little compared to the loss of Brown, and the premature explosion of the mine." Four days later, however, Sanborn was back in Concord, believing that if he were arrested he would be tried in Massachusetts, not in Virginia. In November he worked secretly with Higginson, John W. Le Barnes, and others in plotting a bold scheme to liberate Brown from the jail in Charlestown. Several weeks later a Senate investigating committee, headed by James M. Mason of Virginia, summoned the Concord schoolteacher for interrogation; Sanborn defiantly refused (there were a thousand better ways of fighting slavery than lying in a Washington prison, he told Higginson) ; he fled to Canada again when the Senate voted his arrest.[13]

Edwin Morton sought refuge in England lest he, too, be arrested and turned over to Virginia. Frederick Douglass fled to Canada and then sailed for England as well (he had planned to go there anyway) . Douglass had become extremely alarmed when friends warned him that the New York governor would surrender him to the Virginia authorities, who would not hesitate to hang a Negro abolitionist. Douglass "barely evaded his pursuers," for Virginia officials had already charged him with "murder, robbery and inciting to servile insurrection in the State of Virginia," and Wise had requested that President Buchanan and the U.S. Postmaster General allow two Virginia agents to seize Douglass and bring him to trial. So quite understandably Douglass sought refuge abroad, even though he had refused to participate in the Harpers Ferry attack. He tried to explain that fact—and to deny a charge by John E. Cook that *he* had caused the raid to fail—in a letter to the Rochester *Democrat and American*. Douglass confessed that, "tried by the Harper's Ferry insurrection test," he was "most miserably deficient in courage— even more than Cook, when he deserted his old brave captain, and fled to the mountains." Douglass had opposed the raid, he explained, because he had deemed it a wild and rash enterprise. Yet he would willingly support a movement against slavery when there was "a reasonable hope of success" and believed that *any* effort to over- throw that institution was moral. Still, Douglass hoped that Brown's attack was not without significance. Two weeks after the raid he wrote wishfully: "Posterity will owe everlasting thanks to John Brown," for he "has attacked slavery with the weapons precisely adapted to bring it to the death. . . . Like Sampson, he has laid his hands upon the pillars of this great national temple of cruelty and blood, and when he falls, that temple, will speedily crumble to its final doom, burying its denizens in its ruins."[14]

Of all Brown's backers and confederates only the fiery Higginson stood his ground, remained in the country, refused to destroy his letters (much to the dismay of the other conspirators), and defied anybody to arrest him. When he first heard the news of the attack, he was overcome with joy, praising the raid as "the most formidable insurrection that has ever occurred." Then came the shattering reports that the raid was not a success but an unmitigated disaster, that Brown had been easily overcome, and that no insurrection had taken place at all. Higginson was bitterly disappointed: he had hoped that a slave rebellion would destroy once and for all the prevailing Northern opinion that all slaves were feeble and submis- sive Sambos. As for Brown, "I don't feel sure that his acquittal or rescue would do half as much good as being executed; so strong is the personal sympathy with him." But Higginson soon changed his mind about that and helped plot a dramatic rescue scheme to save Brown's life. Bristling with defiance, he chided his fellow conspira- tors for their timidity and cowardice. "Sanborn, is there no such thing as *honor* among confederates?" he cried, and plagued the harried young schoolteacher by refusing to burn their correspond- ence. Meanwhile he lavished praise on heroic "Old Osawatomie Brown" and asserted that if he were a lawyer he would go to Virginia and stand by Brown's side. Since Higginson was not a lawyer, the least he could do was help John A. Andrew, Wendell Phillips, and Le Barnes in providing Brown with counsel.[15]

Le Barnes himself had already hired lawyer George H. Hoyt, "a beardless boy" from Athol, Massachusetts, and sent him to Charlestown ostensibly to assist in Brown's defense. Actually Hoyt was to act as a spy. His orders: seize that satchelful of incriminating letters and arrange the jail break which Le Barnes, Higginson, Sanborn, and others were plotting.

As Brown's backers planned his escape or fled to Canada, relatives of the killed and captured raiders gradually learned the fateful news. Mrs. Leeman went into shock and for eighteen months lay in bed, unable to speak. In Nebraska the Kagi family went into mourning, in memory of a young man who had given his life in a cause he believed would benefit the human race. Aaron Stevens' father and sisters, reading about the proceedings at Charlestown, took immense pride in Stevens, who lay wounded, defiant and unrepentant, in that Virginia jail. In Springdale, Iowa, a grieving Mrs. Coppoc, who had begged her sons not to go with Brown, awaited news of Barclay (who had escaped and would eventually rejoin her). Leary's widow wept in Oberlin, while "her Virginia sister," Harriet Newby, was sold to a Louisiana slave dealer. In Chambersburg, Pennsylvania, Cook's wife "cowed in bewildered dread" when she learned that Cook had been captured in Pennsylvania and had given Virginia authorities a "confession" admitting that he was one of the raiders. Back in Ohio, Jason anxiously waited for news of Owen, whose whereabouts were filled with "tedious uncertainty" (to Jason's immense relief Owen finally turned up in Ohio, with an incredible tale to tell about his role at Harpers Ferry and how he had escaped). In the meantime John Jr. had gone into hiding in the office of the Ashtabula *Sentinel*, whose editor was sympathetic to Brown's raid. Members of the Ashtabula League of Freedom, who may have known about the raid all along, pinned black stripes or bands to their lapels, took an oath never to reveal information about the invasion, and watched the roads that led to Jefferson, in case any federal officers came to arrest suspects.[16]

At North Elba Brown's family read about his capture and the deaths of Watson and Oliver in the New York *Tribune*, which a neighbor brought over. Annie recalled that "There was very little 'weeping or wailing' on the part of our brave household; we were most of us struck dumb, horror stricken with a grief too deep and hard to find expression in words or even tears." First Mary, then Annie and Salmon's wife became ill. But stoic Martha, a widow at seventeen, dutifully took care of the farmhouse, consoled Watson's wife Belle, and nursed the others back to health—only to fall ill herself and die in March, 1860, after her baby too had died.[17]

Out in Kansas Brown's relatives and friends were dismayed at what had happened at Harpers Ferry, but most of them were completely on the old man's side. Adair and other Osawatomie abolitionists approved not only of his lofty ideals but also of his methods. "How in the name of common sense do Christians propose to do away with this enormous sin if not with John Brown's method," Sarah Everett wrote; "you know very well and every body knows that southern slaveholders will not allow any kind of Christian teaching in all their borders only the christianity of devils and how is the great southern heart to be reached but by God's ministers of vengeance." Mary Partridge (whose brother George had fallen in the battle of Osawatomie), Hinton, Redpath, and others planned various jail-break schemes, all of which failed for lack of funds. Redpath himself set about energetically promoting the image of Brown as a Great Warrior-Saint on his way to martyrdom. He wrote articles for the Boston *Atlas & Daily Bee* entitled "Notes on the Insurrection" and "Reminiscences of the Insurrection." Redpath welcomed Brown's execution. "Living he acted bravely, dying, he will teach us courage. A Samson in his life; he will be a Samson in his death. Let cowards ridicule and denounce him; let snake-like journalists hiss at his holy failure—for one, I do not hesitate to say that I love him, admire him, and defend him. GOD BLESS HIM!" Then Redpath started writing a legend-building biography to be entitled *The Public Life of Capt. John Brown*, but decided not to publish it "until Old B. is in heaven."[18]

A number of free-state Kansans, of course, condemned Harpers Ferry as the same kind of violent lawlessness which proslavery forces had visited on Kansas. But a belligerent little infantry captain at Fort Riley, an ultra-abolitionist who was later to play a crucial role in the Missouri secession crisis, emphatically demurred. Brown's raid, said Nathaniel Lyon, had administered "a handsome rebuke" to "proslavery arrogance." Brown himself was a "simpleton" who "deserved his fate, though sympathy is natural, for so earnest, sincere and brave a character." And the Southerners whom Brown had attacked? "The people of the South make fools of themselves about the matter, as they always do on the subject of slavery. This affair will probably assume other shapes in course of time."[19]

Northeastern abolitionists thought it would, too, and they set about zealously to make Brown a martyr for their cause. Garrison himself, while reminding everybody that he was still nonviolent, nevertheless declared that "let no one who glories in the revolutionary struggle of 1776 deny the right of the slaves to imitate the example of our fathers." "It will be a terribly losing day for all Slavedom," Garrison wrote later, "when John Brown and his associates are brought to the gallows." Other abolitionists—black and white alike—asserted that the South had asked for an invasion like Brown's; they trumpeted Harpers Ferry as "the best news that America ever had"—maybe now she would face the slavery curse forthrightly—and proclaimed Brown himself "the bravest and humanest man in all the country." Harpers Ferry, declared Wendell Phillips, "is the Lexington of to-day." And Virginia? "Virginia . . . is a pirate ship, and John Brown sails the sea a Lord High Admiral of the Almighty, with his commission to sink every pirate he meets on God's ocean." And the Lord High Admiral of the Almighty, Phillips exclaimed, "has twice as much right to hang Governor Wise, as Governor Wise has to hang him."[20]

Emerson, who at first was pained at what he thought a mad and violent act, finally spoke out in Brown's defense. In lectures at Boston and Concord, Emerson called him "that new saint, than whom none purer or more brave was ever led by love of men into conflict and death,—the new saint awaiting his martyrdom, and who, if he shall suffer, will make the gallows glorious like the cross." But Emerson's heart was not entirely in the crusade to make Brown an abolitionist saint. After a speech at Salem he told Bronson Alcott, in reference to Brown, that "we have had enough of this dreary business."[21]

Henry Ward Beecher, for his part, wanted Brown to hang and become the martyred leader of a new crusade against the South. "Let no man pray that Brown be spared!" Beecher declared in a sermon on October 30. "Let Virginia make him a martyr! Now, he has only blundered. His soul was noble; his work miserable. But a cord and a gibbet would redeem all that, and round up Brown's failure with a heroic success." (Brown wholeheartedly agreed with Beecher; shown a newspaper report of Beecher's sermon while he was in jail, Brown scratched "Good" above the passage about making him a martyr.) [22]

Thoreau also wanted Brown to hang. "I almost fear to hear of his deliverance," Thoreau asserted, "doubting if a prolonged life, if any life, can do as much good as his death." Thoreau then launched a one-man campaign to ensure Brown's martyrdom. On October 30 he delivered a "Plea for Captain John Brown" at Concord, a lecture that mixed eloquence and pugnacity in behalf of the old warrior, "a transcendentalist above all, a man of ideas and principles," who dared to sacrifice his life for the liberation of the slaves. Thoreau repeated his eloquent "Plea" at Worcester and Boston and gave another address at Concord on December 2 called "After the Death of John Brown." Thoreau confronted everybody—Republicans and Democrats, Garrisonians, newspapermen, and Christians—until at last it seemed that the entire North—"I mean the *living* North"— was beginning to recognize "the eternal justice and glory" of Brown's vision.[23]

Theodore Parker, writing from Rome, Italy, where he had gone to die, declared that Brown's raid had created a storm across the United States: "the Northern sky is full of lightning long treasured up: Brown was one bright, clear flash into the Southern ground." And that flash, Parker predicted, would detonate a civil war in which "The Fire of Vengeance" would run "from man to man, from town to town" across a South drenched with the "white man's blood!"

"How much longer," said Lydia Maria Child, "the volcano will smoke, before the lava pours down, God alone know[s]. One thing is certain slavery or freedom must die in this struggle." Henry Wadsworth Longfellow agreed. Brown's raid and his death "will be a great day in our history; the date of a new Revolution,—quite as needed as the old one. Even now as I write, they are leading old John Brown to execution in Virginia for attempting to rescue slaves! This is sowing the wind to reap the whirlwind, which will come soon."[24]

3

For the South the whirlwind was already here. Southern leaders were virtually united in damning the raid as "an act of war" perpetrated by "murderers, *traitors*, robbers, insurrectionists," and "wanton, malicious, unprovoked felons." While some reflective Southerners warned Governor Wise that to execute the raiders would only make them martyrs in the North, a majority of Southern newspapers screamed for the blood of Brown and his men. Hang that "notorious old thief and murderer" who committed such "foolhardy treason," demanded the Albany (Georgia) *Patriot*. "An undivided South says let him hang." John Forsyth's Mobile *Register* agreed, and went on to say: "The ark of covenant has been desecrated. For the first time the soil of the South has been invaded and its blood has been shed upon its own soil by armed abolitionists" who "invoked our slaves to rebellion." The raid was indisputably an abolitionist-Republican plot; and if the South did not secure guarantees against further abolitionist outrages it should withdraw from the Union. "The day of compromise is passed," intoned the Charlestown *Mercury*. Brown's ignominious raid proved even to "the most bigoted Unionist that there is no peace for the South in the Union. The South must control her own destinies or perish."[25]

Other Southerners, in an ecstasy of rage and insecurity, believed that not just the Black Republicans and abolitionists but the entire North was behind the raid: the work of "fanatics"—all Northerners were fanatics—who thrilled at the prospects of Negroes murdering their masters and raping Southern girls. After all, were Northerners not singing Brown's praises? Were Republican newspapers not ranting and raving about his "noble ideals" while they rationalized or explained away the crime of the invasion itself? Were not the abolitionists applauding Brown as an abolitionist saint—another Jesus Christ? For thousands of Southerners this was dramatic, conclusive proof that slave insurrection was what the abolitionists had wanted all along. To Southerners who were in no mood for "subtle" distinctions between sympathy and support for Brown, the North seemed to be teeming with "mad John Browns"—with abolitionists and Black Republicans who were mobilizing in a cacophony of hate to invade the South and incite a servile war.[26]

Then came the widespread publicity of Brown's maps—small, elaborate maps of seven Southern states—with crosses drawn on those counties where slaves overwhelmingly outnumbered white people. Even greater hysteria swept over the South. Conspirators were everywhere. Reports flooded Governor Wise's office that Brown's agents had been arrested and that incipient slave plots had been uncovered in other parts of the South, especially in Alabama.[27] The tension was heightened when the Southern press published another document found among Brown's papers: it was a letter written by an alleged agent named "Lawrence Thatcher," who had made a tour of the South and reported that slaves in Arkansas and Tennessee were ripe for rebellion. Tennessee reeled from shock; the governor announced that a terrible plot was underfoot; and Memphis girded itself for a "Harpers Ferry outbreak." Everywhere in the South people gathered and talked in frightened tones about the latest rumors, spawned by reports of "great slave agitation in Kentucky" and "a stampede of Negroes in Missouri."[28]

Fearing slave revolts from within and invasion from without, Southern towns from Jackson to Richmond alerted militia units and local defense companies, declared martial law, and embarked upon a reign of terror, repression, and censorship. A minister in Texas who criticized the treatment of slaves was publicly whipped. A man in Baltimore who "gave vent to sympathetic utterances concerning Brown's invasion" was thrown in the county jail. And the new president of an Alabama college fled for his life because he was a Northerner. Alabama itself, trying to protect impressionable pupils "from abolitionist teachers," passed a law that only citizens who had resided there for ten years could teach in Alabama's schools. And in Texas, Mississippi, and South Carolina, vigilante citizens confiscated all books considered "anti-Southern" and destroyed them in ceremonial book burnings. All over the South local leaders employed whippings, proscription, and arraignment to make slavery defense, in the words of Louis Filler, "the *sine qua non* of southern patriotism." At the same time plantation owners tightened the discipline in their slave quarters, threatening to whip or hang any Negro who even *looked* rebellious. As Allan Nevins put it, "The raid of twenty-two men on one Virginia town had sent a spasm of uneasiness, resentment, and precautionary zeal from the Potomac to the Gulf."[29]

Nowhere was the tension worse than in Virginia, whose slave

frontier lay exposed to invasion from both Pennsylvania and Ohio. Newspapers kept the populace continuously aroused with reports that armies of abolitionists had crossed into the state to incite the Negroes "to rapine and murder." A joint committee of the Virginia legislature investigated the Harpers Ferry attack and reported that a widespread Northern conspiracy existed all right, "not merely against Virginia, but against the peace and security of all the Southern States." The committee cited as proof "the sympathy with the culprits which has been manifested by large numbers of persons in the Northern States" and the fact that "all countenance and encouragement which was extended to [Brown] were by citizens of the Northern States" who wished "to make war upon and overthrow an institution intimately interwoven with all the interests of the Southern States." While the Richmond *Enquirer* predicted that secession of the Southern states was bound to follow, Governor Wise added to the statewide jitters by repeatedly mobilizing militia units and countermarching them in noisy confusion. Rumors also flew about that the governor "has spies throughout Ohio and the other Northern states who report large bodies of men are arming and leaving for Virginia with the intention to rescue Brown." Reports like these kept the Charlestown-Harpers Ferry vicinity in a state of "perpetual excitement." Fire bells shattered the night as "unknown incendiaries" set fire to wheat and haystacks, barns and outhouses, illuminating the darkness with an eerie glow that citizens took as "signals for the slaves to rebel." At Charlestown pranksters set fire to the barns and "other property" of Brown's jurors, throwing the town into another panic. Hysterical women, afraid that they would be raped and killed, barricaded themselves in their homes at Charlestown; militia units marched noisily through the streets and a heavy guard, with two cannons, stood around the jail where Brown and the other raiders were lodged. As the terror increased in Charlestown, Governor Wise himself hurried there with some 400 Virginia militia, who quartered themselves in homes, schools, and churches. Another 150 troops marched to Harpers Ferry, whose citizens expected another invasion at any moment. By December 2 an estimated 4,000 men were under arms in Virginia and thousands more in the other Southern states.[30]

Thus, as other writers have pointed out, Brown's raid had created

a "Great Fear" in the South comparable to that which prevailed in
rural France in the summer of 1789, when the peasants lived in
mortal terror that the king's brigands were coming to slaughter them
all. In that state of anxiety compromise between South and North—
as the Charlestown *Mercury* asserted—was henceforth impossible.
For Brown's raid had terrified not only the planters in the South but
the masses of nonslaveholding whites as well. Since 1850 most of
these people had opposed secession and the notion of a planters' war
for Southern independence, but Brown's lone-hand blow at Harpers
Ferry changed all that. Now most of the yeoman farmers and poor
whites closed ranks behind the slaveowners and vowed that they,
too, would fight to their deaths to protect their homes from a Negro
insurrection or another Black Republican invasion. Nobody was
more exultant about the effects of Harpers Ferry than fire-eating
Southern secessionists like George Fitzhugh and J. D. B. De Bow,
editor of *De Bow's Review*, and they used Harpers Ferry to whip up
Southerners into a frenzy of anti-Northern, anti-Republican hatred.
The North "has sanctioned and applauded theft, murder, treason,"
cried *De Bow's Review*, "and at the hands of our Northern Brethren,
has shed Southern Blood on Southern soil! There is—there can be
no peace!" Harpers Ferry, the journal asserted, was "the first act in
the grand tragedy of emancipation, and the subjugation of the South
in bloody treason. . . . The vanguard of the great army intended for
our subjugation has crossed our borders on Southern soil and shed
Southern blood." And the only solution for the South—the only way
to save "our wives and daughters"—was secession and an independent
Southern confederacy.[31]

Thus "The Harper's Ferry invasion," announced the Richmond
Enquirer, "has advanced the cause of Disunion more than any other
event that has happened since the formation of the Government."
"The North and South," asserted O. G. Memminger, "are standing
in battle array." "All Virginia," exhorted General James L. Kemper
of the Virginia General Assembly, "should stand forth as one man
and say to fanaticism, in her own language, whenever you advance
a hostile foot upon our soil, we will welcome you with bloody hands
and hospitable graves."

"I have said of Mr. Seward and his followers," cried a state senator of Mississippi, "that they are our enemies and we are *theirs*. He

has declared that there is an 'irrepressible conflict' between us. So there is! He and his followers have declared war upon us, and I am for fighting it out to the bitter end."[32]

4

While the Southern states girded themselves for war, the violent, visionary old Calvinist "who was the stone God threw into the black pool of slavery" listened stolidly on his makeshift cot, as Judge Parker pounded his gavel and Brown's trial opened in a crowded Charlestown courtroom. No sooner had the trial commenced, however, than Lawson Botts made a crucial defense move that caught everybody (including Brown) by surprise. Botts introduced a telegram from A. H. Lewis of Akron, who stated that Brown and several of his family had lived in and around Akron for many years. "Insanity is hereditary in that family," Lewis declared. "His mother's sister died with it, and a daughter of that sister has been two years in a lunatic asylum. A son and daughter of his mother's brother have also been confined in the lunatic asylum, and another son of that brother is now insane and under close restraint. These facts can be conclusively proven by witnesses residing here, who will doubtless attend the trial if desired."

While the court buzzed with whispers Botts explained that he had discussed the telegram with Brown in jail and that he had admitted instances of insanity on his mother's side but had denied that anybody in his father's family had been afflicted. Brown confessed that his first wife had exhibited symptoms and so had two of their sons (Frederick and John Jr.).[33]

Obviously this was a move to save Brown's life, by having him declared insane and placed in an asylum. But Brown would have none of it. Rising up on his cot he said: "I will add, if the court will allow me, that I look upon [the plea of insanity] as a miserable artifice and pretext of those who ought to take a different course in regard to me, if they took any at all, and I view it with contempt more than otherwise. As I remarked to Mr. Green, insane persons, so far as my experience goes, have but little ability to judge their own sanity; and, if I am insane, of course, I should think I know more than all the rest of the world. But I do not think so. I am perfectly unconscious of insanity, and I reject, so far as I am capable, any attempt to interfere in my behalf on that score."

Botts then asked the court for delay, on the grounds that new counsel for Brown was coming from Cleveland. Thus, as Richard Morris has observed, Botts had raised two critical issues which no impartial court could quickly dismiss: the legal question of Brown's sanity and the defendant's right to select his own counsel. Yet Judge Parker was so impatient that he rejected Botts's plea, and the trial went on. The insanity question did not come up in court again.

As Brown lay on his cot, sometimes with his eyes closed, the prosecution paraded witnesses before the court. Colonel Washington told how Brown had denounced the shooting of his son Watson under a white flag but otherwise had uttered no violent threats to his prisoners or to his enemies outside the engine house. Two witnesses claimed that Brown had declared his purpose was not to kill whites but to free Negroes and destroy slavery. But Archibald M. Kitzmiller, the watchman captured at the armory gate, overheard Brown say that if necessary he would fight slaveholders to set the Negroes free.

Only when Harry Hunter—a relative of the special prosecutor—took the witness stand and told how he and a saloonkeeper shot William Thompson and flung his body into the river ("I felt it my duty, and I have no regrets") did Brown lose his composure. Rising to his feet he argued that this was not a fair trial, repudiated his counsel (which now included young Hoyt), and demanded that he be given until tomorrow morning to have "something done" about getting proper counsel. Hoyt asked the court to grant Brown's request, but Judge Parker refused. By now Botts and Green, who had labored honestly and fairly to defend Brown, had had enough and withdrew from the case. The next day the court assigned two other lawyers to the defense—Samuel Chilton of Washington and Hiram Griswold of Cleveland. The judge banged his gavel. "The trial must go on," he announced, and the court proceeded without giving the new lawyers opportunity to prepare their defense.

The trial moved to a rapid conclusion. On October 31 Griswold gave an able summation for the defense, pointing out that Brown could not be guilty of treason against Virginia because he owed that state no loyalty and that Brown's relatively insignificant raid, in failing to incite a slave revolt, had not constituted any real threat to the state of Virginia. Now that the South was "alarmed and armed in every direction," Griswold was positive that there was not the remotest possibility of another raid like Brown's. Griswold hoped the jurors would consider such facts and treat Brown's case fairly.

Now it was Andrew Hunter's turn for the prosecution. He "whip-lashed" Brown for wanting "the citizens of Virginia calmly to fold their arms and let him usurp the government, manumit our slaves, confiscate the property of slaveholders, and without drawing a trig-ger or shedding blood, permit him to take possession of the Common-wealth and make it another Haiti." Brown knew what he was doing, Hunter insisted, and that proved malice. He turned to the jury. "Administer [justice] according to your law—acquit the prisoner if you can—but if justice requires you by your verdict to take his life, stand by that column uprightly, but strongly, and let retributive justice, if he is guilty, send him before that Maker who will settle the question forever and ever."

The jury took only forty-five minutes to find Brown guilty as charged, but left his sentencing for a later session. During the inter-im Edwin Coppoc's trial commenced, to last for less than two days. On November 2, while the jury was out deciding Coppoc's fate, Brown was carried back into the packed courtroom and asked if there was any reason why he should not be sentenced. He stood. "I have, may it please the Court, a few words to say." He promptly denied everything the prosecution had said about his motives con-nected with the raid and insisted that he had only intended to liber-ate slaves and carry them to Canada. "I never did intend murder or treason," he argued, "or the destruction of property, or to excite or incite the slaves to rebellion, or to make insurrection." (It is hard to tell whether Brown was coolly and deliberately lying for the benefit of his Northern sympathizers or whether he was confused or simply so excited, so carried away with his own drama, that he actually believed what he was telling the court. But the court in any case was fairly sure that what he was saying was false, as were other state-ments he made elsewhere in his oration.) Now Brown drew himself up for a final burst of eloquence and delivered a five-minute discourse that was to awe an entire generation. "I see a book kissed," he sang out, "which I suppose to be the Bible, or at least the New Testament, which teaches me that all things whatsoever I would that men should do to me, I should do to them. It teaches me further to remember them that are in bonds, as bound with them. I endeavored to act up to that instruction. I say I am yet too young to understand that God is any respecter of persons. I believe that to have interfered as I have done in behalf of His despised poor, is no wrong, but right. Now, if it is deemed necessary that I should forfeit my life for the furtherance of the ends of justice, and mingle my blood with the blood of millions in this slave country whose rights are disregarded by wicked, cruel, and unjust enactments, I say let it be done."

Scores of Northerners who read Brown's speech in their newspapers, unaware of its falsehoods and factual inaccuracies, were deeply moved by the majesty—the moral grandeur—of the five-minute peroration. That discourse probably converted to his side countless people who until now had been highly dubious about his invasion. The old man said he did not intend to incite insurrection; he was sacrificing his life for liberty and justice. How could one help but sympathize with a man who said and did such a noble thing as that? Ralph Waldo Emerson was later to compare Brown's oration to Lincoln's Gettysburg Address.[34]

Judge Parker was unmoved, however, and sentenced Brown to hang on the gallows on December 2.

5

There was not much doubt about the outcome of the other trials. Just after Brown was sentenced, on November 2, the jury found Edwin Coppoc guilty on all counts in his indictment. The two Negroes—first Shields Green and then John Copeland—were tried in two days. George Sennott, a young Boston lawyer and a Democrat who had come down to help the defense, did what he could to save the Negroes' lives. He argued that a Negro, deprived of U.S. citizenship by the Dred Scott decision, could not be guilty of treason against Virginia. The prosecution concurred, but pressed for conviction on the other charges. Sennott even went so far as to suggest that Green and Copeland were justified in resisting the enslavement of their race—something no Southerner in that court wanted to hear. The jury emphatically rejected Sennott's argument and found both Negroes guilty of murder and conspiring with slaves to rebel.

Next came Cook, who had been captured in Pennsylvania on October 26, identified as one of the insurgents, and brought to Charlestown two days later. At the request of Cook's influential relatives, Governor A. P. Willard of Indiana—Cook's own brother-in-law—and two Indiana lawyers, one the venerable Daniel W. Voorhees, came to Charlestown to defend him. Although Cook had given the authorities a "confession" about his involvement in the Harpers Ferry conspiracy, his lawyers waged a courtroom battle with the prosecution that was "hotly contested" and occasionally "very severe." But inevitably Hunter won the battle; and on the night of November 9 the jury convicted John E. Cook of murder and inciting slaves to insurrection.

The next day all the convicted raiders came before Judge Parker for sentencing. When asked if there was any reason why sentence should not be pronounced, the two Negroes refused to say anything. But Coppoc and Cook—the latter speaking in a "somewhat vehement" manner—insisted that they had not known about Brown's plans to seize the arsenal at Harpers Ferry until the Sunday of the raid. Both expected to be punished for what they had done but did not think they should hang for it. Judge Parker disagreed. After denouncing the prisoners for their crimes, he sentenced them all to die on the gallows on December 16, 1859.

That left only Aaron Stevens and Albert Hazlett. Hazlett had been arrested in Pennsylvania and illegally extradited to Virginia on November 5 (nobody at the extradition proceedings gave evidence that he had been at Harpers Ferry). But the two raiders were to have a long wait. Just before Stevens was to stand trial Governor Wise intervened and ordered that Stevens be turned over to the federal government, in hopes that his trial in a national court might elicit evidence from federal authorities that would incriminate "leading abolitionists of the North." Stevens, however, remained in jail at Charlestown throughout the winter. As for Hazlett, going by the name of "William H. Harrison," the district court decided not to try him until the next term, to begin in February, 1860.* At that, on November 10, 1859, the court at Charlestown adjourned.[35]

6

Meanwhile Brown's own lawyers made a last desperate attempt to save his life. In November Hoyt visited Washington and talked with Montgomery Blair, a Maryland Republican who was convinced that Southern fire-eaters would use Harpers Ferry to break up the Union. Anxious to block their efforts Blair suggested that "a demonstration of Brown's insanity might please Wise," that the governor might be willing to commit Brown to an asylum. Blair thought that if Brown could be presented to the divided nation as a "lunatic" who had perpetrated an "insane act," it might quell the sectional storm which Harpers Ferry had provoked.[36]

Inspired by Blair's suggestion, Hoyt traveled to Ohio and collected affidavits regarding Brown's "insanity" from nineteen of his relatives and friends, who were anxious indeed to save him from the gallows.[37] Among the affiants were Jeremiah Brown, a half brother; Sylvester Thompson and Gideon Mills, relatives on his mother's side; Milton Lusk, Dianthe's brother (who had never liked Brown but did not want him to hang either) ; and old friends like Orson M. Oviatt, George Leach, and Edwin Wetmore. To begin with, many of the affiants claimed that "insanity" ran in the maternal side of Brown's family and that Brown himself was "laboring under hereditary insanity." Thompson and others asserted that Brown's grandmother (Ruth Humphrey Mills) was "said to be insane" during the last six years of her life. Contrary to what several writers have claimed, there were no references made to any mental trouble on the part of Brown's mother, Ruth Mills Brown.[38] But one or two of her brothers and three of her sisters—Thompson's mother, Susan Richardson, and Sarah Woodruff—were alleged to have been

---

* Stevens and Hazlett both came to trial at Charlestown in February, 1860. Although George Sennott challenged the legality of Stevens' imprisonment and trial (since Governor Wise had supposedly given him over to the federal government) and stressed the lack of convincing proof that Hazlett, still going by the alias "William H. Harrison," was one of the Harpers Ferry raiders, they, too, were convicted and sentenced to hang on the scaffold on March 16, 1860.

"insane." Three of Gideon Mills's children and two children of
Oliver Mills were "intermittently insane." Brown's "only sister"
and his brother Salmon were "thought to be at times insane." Other
cousins and relatives of Brown's on his mother's side had shown
symptoms. The affiants also pointed out that Brown's wife Dianthe
had been "afflicted" and so had two of her sons—John Jr. and
Frederick.

As for Brown himself, the affidavits varied as to the degree and
nature of his "mental derangement." Many of the affiants stated that,
while Brown was "an honest," "deeply religious," "very conscientious" man, he had always had an "excitable mind" when it came to
religious matters and slavery. Milton Lusk and Sylvester Thompson
both claimed that Brown's behavior had been "erratic" and "peculiar" after he moved from Pennsylvania back to Ohio in 1835. Lusk
(who mentioned nothing about his sister's troubles) argued that
Brown had been "more or less insane" since shortly after Dianthe's
death. His penchant "for wild & desperate projects" was proof that
he had "an unsound mind." George Leach, who had known Brown
from boyhood, contended that Brown had been "a monomaniac"
in some of his business affairs in Ohio. S. Goodale agreed. "I have
known John Brown for 15 years," Goodale testified, "and never saw
any business transaction conducted by him which indicated a Sane
mind—excepting while engaged in Summit County in growing sheep
& wool." Brown's wool crusade in Springfield, Goodale argued,
showed that Brown was "clearly insane." Jonathan Metcalf, a
seventy-two-year-old physician of Hudson, had always thought Brown
subject to "fits of insecurity" and at times "completely insane."
Metcalf had talked with Brown in 1855, when he was on his way to
Kansas, and thought him "fanatically insane" on the subject of
slavery. (It would be instructive to know the physician's opinions
about slavery, just to keep the record straight.) Metcalf's wife had
known Brown's grandmother, and the doctor had "heard her say"
that the grandmother was "insane"—although Metcalf admitted that
he had no "personal knowledge of this fact." Several of the other
affiants believed that it was the horror Brown had experienced in
Kansas that had caused his mind to become "deranged." Jeremiah
Brown had seen the old man in 1857 and recalled how he spoke
obsessively about his mission to free the slaves. William Otis, who

had known Brown at Ravenna and Akron, said that Brown had long suffered from "religious fixations" and that after Kansas he had become a "monomaniac" on the subject of slavery. Otis concluded this from two conversations he'd had with Brown "after his return from Kansas." David L. King of Akron said he had talked with Brown in April, 1859, and had also decided that "on the subject of slavery he was crazy—he was armed to the teeth & remarked among other things that he was an 'instrument in the hands of God to free the slaves.' " Other affiants thought that the fighting in Kansas combined with the loss of Frederick and a lifetime of sickness and hardship had "deranged his mind." Gideon Mills, who thought Brown had been of unsound mind for twenty years, was frankly shocked at Brown's invasion of Virginia. Mills had thought Brown's "insanity" was "harmless." He never dreamed it would lead Brown to Harpers Ferry.

Since many writers have accepted these affidavits at face value and have used them as proof that Brown was a "madman" out of touch with "reality," the documents—and the whole insanity question—merit careful examination. To begin with, the word "insanity" is a vague, emotion-charged, and clinically meaningless term. Modern psychology has long since abandoned it in describing mental and emotional disorders. And historians should abandon it as well. As C. Vann Woodward has reminded us, the term even in historical context is misleading, ambiguous, and relative—it has meant different things to different peoples in the past, and what seems "insane" in one period of time may seem perfectly "sane" at other times. Even in nineteenth-century parlance, "insanity" was a catchall term used to describe a wide range of odd or unacceptable behavior, including epilepsy and multiple sclerosis. Consequently, when Brown's relatives and friends talk about instances of "insanity" in the family, we do not know what sort of disorders they were describing. Maybe some of the cases were epileptics or mentally retarded.

The whole argument about Brown's alleged "hereditary insanity" is open to dispute. Modern psychologists themselves do not agree on how much of the human personality is inherited (if any of it is) and how much is the result of the environment. Any biographer or historian who argues that "insanity" is hereditary intrudes upon his craft the controversies and disagreements of what is still an imprecise science. And even if one persists in arguing that Brown labored from "hereditary insanity," one must rest one's case on the assumption that his disorders came from his grandmother. And there is no evidence at all as to what her trouble was. Maybe she was just senile.

Historians have described "the instances of insanity" in Brown's family as "a fearful record."[39] But in truth the record is more fearful for the Mills and Thompson sides of the family than for the Browns. Probably it did not occur to Gideon Mills or Sylvester Thompson, as they testified to the "insanity" of their mothers, their aunts and uncles, and Mills's own children, that they might be raising far more serious questions about their own mental health than about John Brown's—*if* one accepts the moot argument that emotional and mental disorders can be inherited at all.

In the case of Brown's immediate family, the affidavits contained a great deal of information based not on direct knowledge of the condition of Brown's sister and his brother Salmon but on hearsay (as Sylvester Thompson admitted). In fact, there is no evidence that Salmon, who was editor of the New Orleans *Bee* and a prominent lawyer of that city, was "insane." As for Brown's sons (Frederick and John Jr.), if one accepts the assumption that "mental aberrations" are hereditary, then one must face the argument that both sons inherited their "troubles" from Dianthe, not from Brown. Actually a much more plausible explanation is that John Jr.'s depression and melancholia resulted from his experiences in Kansas: the constant haggling with his father as to what they should do during the Lawrence crisis, the tension and lack of sleep, the humiliation he had suffered when his friends turned against him after the Pottawatomie massacre, and the cruel treatment he received at the hands of U.S. troops following his capture. And what of Frederick? If we may believe Samuel Adair, Frederick was suffering from what doctors at that time diagnosed as "an accumulation of blood on the brain" that caused "blinding headaches" and occasionally left him "flighty" and incoherent. He could have had a brain tumor. Or perhaps his trouble was epilepsy.

Finally—and this is a crucial point—the affidavits Hoyt collected in Ohio were intended first and foremost to save Brown's life, by convincing Governor Wise and the state of Virginia that Brown was "insane," that he was not responsible for his acts, and that he should be placed in an asylum. The documents were not objective clinical evidence gathered by doctors who wanted to establish as clearly as possible what Brown's "mental disorders" were. When the affiants asserted that Brown was "insane," they were giving their opinions for a partisan objective. And, although many of them doubtless believed their opinions were true, they were still opinions. Except for Dr. Metcalf, none of the affiants were educated in medical matters and none of them were psychologists.

All this is not to argue that Brown was a "normal," "well-adjusted," "sane" individual. These terms are meaningless too. That he was a revolutionary who believed himself called by God to a special destiny (a notion that stemmed from his Calvinist beliefs), that he had an excitable temperament and could get carried away with one idea, that he was inept, egotistical, hard on his sons, afflicted with chronic attacks of the ague, worn down from a lifetime of hardship, and enraged enough at his "slave-cursed" country to contemplate destroying it, that he could have five men he regarded as his enemies assassinated in cold blood (after proslavery forces had murdered six free-state men in cold blood), and that he wanted to become either an American Spartacus at the head of a slave army or a martyred soldier who was the first to die in a sectional war over slavery—all this is true. Yet to dismiss Brown as an "insane" man is to ignore the tremendous sympathy he felt for the suffering of the black man in the United States; it is to disregard the fact that at a time when most Northerners and almost all Southerners were racists who wanted to keep the Negro at the bottom of society, John Brown was able to treat America's "poor despised Africans" as fellow human beings. And to label him a "maniac" out of touch with "reality" is to ignore the piercing insight he had into what his raid—whether it succeeded or whether it failed—would do to sectional tensions that already existed between North and South. Nor can John Brown be removed from the violent, irrational, and paradoxical times in which he lived. A man of "powerful religious convictions" who believed to his bones that slavery was "a sin against God," he was profoundly disturbed that a nation which claimed to be both Christian and free should condone, protect, and perpetuate that "sum of villanies." It was not only Brown's angry, messianic mind, but the racist, slave society in which he lived—one that professed "under God" to provide liberty and justice for all—that helped bring John Brown to Harpers Ferry.

"John Brown may be a lunatic," the Boston *Post* declared, but if so "then one-fourth of the people of Massachusetts are madmen" and three-fourths of the ministers of the gospel. At a time when thousands of Northerners remained indifferent to the contradiction of slavery in a self-proclaimed "free and just" Republic, at a time when Christians, scientists, and politicians (in North and South alike) heralded Negro slavery as "enlightened" and "inevitable," at a time when thousands of Southerners were plagued with fears of a Black Republican invasion and haunted by nightmares of Negro rebels raping "our wives and daughters," it was indeed (as Wendell Phillips said) "Hard to tell who's mad."[40]

                              7

Once Hoyt had gathered the affidavits (certified by a federal judge in Ohio), he sent them forthwith to Samuel Chilton in Washington. Chilton forwarded the documents to Governor Wise, along with a plea that the governor stay Brown's execution and have him tried again on the grounds that he was criminally insane.

Already Wise had been besieged with similar testimonies (one from a "near relative" of Brown's who lived in Wisconsin), urging the governor to spare the life of "that *poor, unfortunate* fanatic"— that "monomaniac," that "sick," "crazy," "deluded" old man—and put him away in an asylum where he belonged.[41] Other letters from fellow Southerners fell on the governor's desk, warning that if he allowed Brown to hang it would make him a martyr in the North and inspire other "fanatics" to emulate his deeds. Prevailed upon from all sides, the learned but inept governor did not know what to do. Had he not stated publicly that Brown was a truthful, courageous, clear-headed man—even if he was a felon and a fanatic? Still the pressure to consider the insanity plea was considerable, and the governor decided briefly to look into the matter. On November 10 he asked the superintendent of the state lunatic asylum at Staunton to examine Brown and find out whether he was "sane, in the legal responsibility of crime." On second thought Wise canceled the directive. The Court of Appeals had confirmed Brown's sentence and anyway Wise himself entertained no doubts whatever of the "perfect sanity" of that "cool, collected, and indomitable" old man. The governor rejected the affidavits and comparable testimony and refused to stay Brown's execution. In doing so the governor unwittingly gave Brown the opportunity—as a Cincinnati minister put it—to "die a pure, and noble martyr to liberty—to sympathy for poor, crushed, degraded, and wronged humanity—aye, for the very principles which brought his prototype to our Shores, and for which our noble Sires periled their lives, their fortunes, and their honors."[42]

Let them hang me, Brown rejoiced. "I am worth inconceivably more to *hang* than for any other purpose."[43] Believing that the great object of his life would now be accomplished on the scaffold, the old man rejected the jail-break scheme which Higginson, Sanborn, Le Barnes, and Hoyt were plotting. He told Hoyt emphatically that he did not want to escape—he wanted to hang. In despair the young lawyer reported to his Eastern colleagues what the old man said, adding that escape was probably impossible anyway, as "the country all around is guarded by armed patrols & a large body of troops are constantly under arms."[44]

Although the jail-break scheme was finally canceled, Virginia authorities were convinced right up to the end that some mad attempt would be made to liberate Brown. They had heard "a thousand rumors" about armed men from Ohio crossing into Virginia; about a wholesale invasion of screaming abolitionists; about secret plots to take place in and around Charlestown (one of them involved a balloon which was to float over the execution site and blow up the gallows with makeshift bombs). The authorities believed as many of these rumors as they discounted and the result was that the Charlestown vicinity remained in a constant state of alarm. Edmund Ruffin, an implacable Virginia secessionist, visited the town after Brown's trial and noted that the streets were filled with troops, that telegrams arrived warning of "trouble ahead," and that night patrols saw rockets shooting up from the mountains nearby. Ruffin recorded in his diary that "with the great population at the North, & the violent fanatical hatred of the South & of negro slavery there prevailing, it is not impossible that a large body of desperadoes may be sent out to attempt a rescue." Military officers in Charlestown agreed and kept troops on alert in case of any emergency. "We are ready for them," declared Colonel J. L. Davis, "if an attack be made the Prisoners will be shot by the inside guards."[45]

Higginson meanwhile was undaunted when he learned that Brown did not want to be rescued. He traveled to North Elba, where he persuaded Mary to go to Charlestown herself and convince Brown to let his friends liberate him. Higginson took this "simple, kindly, slow, sensible creature" back to Boston and there placed her on a train to Philadelphia and Virginia. When Brown learned that she was coming, he telegraphed Higginson to stop her at once. If she saw him now, Brown explained in a following letter, it would only distract her mind *"ten fold"* and add to his own worries. And besides she "cannot possibly do me *any good*." Mary, in the meantime, had reached Philadelphia, where the abolitionist J. Miller McKim joined her, and both of them had taken the train to Baltimore. Brown's message reached her on November 8, just as she and McKim were preparing to take the train to Virginia. That same day Brown wrote her and the children, explaining that her trip into the South would only subject her to threats and "gazing-stock" and that the pain of a final separation would be too much for them both. "I am besides, quite cheerful," he declared, "having (as I trust) 'the peace of God, which passeth all understanding,' to 'rule in my heart,' and the testimony (in some degree) of a good conscience that I have not lived altogether in vain. I can trust God with both the time and the manner of my death, believing, as I now do, that for me at this time to seal my testimony for God and humanity with my blood will do vastly more toward advancing the cause I have earnestly endeavored to promote, than all I have done in my life before. I beg of you all meekly and quietly to submit to this, not feeling yourselves in the least *degraded* on that account. Remember, dear wife and children all, that Jesus of Nazareth suffered a most excruciating death on the cross as a felon, under most aggravating circumstances. Think also of the prophets and apostles and Christians of former days, who went through greater tribulations than you or I, and try to be reconciled. May God Almighty comfort all your hearts, and soon wipe away all tears from your eyes! To him be endless praise!"[46]

XXI

I, JOHN BROWN

DURING THE LAST MONTH BEFORE HE WAS HANGED, Brown struck such a heroic pose that nearly everybody who saw him was impressed. Even Southerners who hated him had to concede that he was a spirited old man who was not afraid to die. John Avis, the jailer, a native of Charlestown, admired his courage so much that he treated Brown with reverential kindness throughout his imprisonment. (Avis, Brown wrote his family, was like the jailer who took charge of Paul and Silas.) Newsmen also praised Brown for his courage and wrote such graphic descriptions of his prison setting that Northern readers could almost hear the tumult of militia outside, smell the musty odor of Brown's cell, hear the clank of his chain, and see him lying on his cot, giving interviews or writing letters, with the self-assurance of a man who is certain that he is right.

Nothing seemed to ruffle him. He remained composed and proudly unrepentant as a number of visitors—militiamen, a Methodist preacher, local newsmen, Governor Wise and a retinue of soldiers, and others who were curious—came to see the self-styled savior of the Negro and his young followers (including Cook and Hazlett now). Edwin Coppoc claimed that during two days in November more than 800 people visited the jail, some to express sympathy for the prisoners, others to curse them bitterly.

Brown's men drew strength from his steadfastness. "Whatever may be our fate," Coppoc wrote some Quaker friends in Iowa, "rest assured we shall not shame our dead companions by a shrinking fear. They lived and died like brave men. We, I trust, shall

do the same." "I am not terrified by the gallows," John Copeland, the Negro college student, wrote his parents in Oberlin. "Could
I die in a more noble cause? Could I die in a manner and for a cause
which would induce true and honest men more to honor me, and the
angels more ready to receive me to their happy home of everlasting
joy above?" Shields Green retained a quiet dignity as he waited for
the gallows like the others; even some Virginians had to concede that
the two Negroes were "perservering" and "manly" (although Governor Wise refused to give up the bodies of Green and Copeland,
after they were executed, unless "white men came after them").
Cook spent his last days writing poetry. And Aaron Stevens, who
shared Brown's cell, echoed the old man when asked why he had
come to Virginia. "It was to help my fellow men out of bondage.
You know nothing of slavery—*I* know a great deal. It is the crime of
crimes. I hate it more and more the longer I live. Even since I have
been lying in this cell, I have heard the cryings of slave-children
torn from their parents."

The Virginia authorities, in a display of leniency, permitted
Brown to answer letters of sympathy from Northerners and to write
freely to his friends and family. As a result, the authorities only
contributed to Brown's canonization as an abolitionist martyr
because the old man, taking advantage of this God-sent opportunity,
sent out from that Charlestown jail some of the most eloquent statements ever to come from the pen of a condemned man. Even the
sheriff, who examined Brown's letters as a matter of duty, frequently
had to wipe tears from his eyes.[1] "I have been *whiped* as the
saying *is*," Brown wrote his wife; "but am sure I can recover all
the lost capital occasioned by that disaster; by only hanging a few
moments by the neck; & I feel quite determined to make the utmost
possible out of defeat. I am dayly & hourly striving to gather up what
little I may from the wreck." But he did not think he was striving
alone. He said over and over that he felt the presence of God in his
cell, guiding his pen across the paper, filling his mind with noble
words, ringing words, prophetic words—words that would hopefully
win an entire generation to his side.[2]

2

Letters of sympathy poured into Brown's cell from all over the North. A Quaker woman wrote him from Iowa: "You can never know how very many dear Friends love thee with all their hearts for thy brave efforts in behalf of the poor oppressed; and though we, who are non-resistants, and religiously believe it better to reform by moral and not by carnal weapons, could not approve bloodshed, yet we know thee was animated by the most generous and philanthropic motives." She said that "thousands" prayed for him every day and that posterity would do him justice. "If Moses led out the thousands of Jewish slaves from their bondage . . . then surely, by the same reasoning, we may judge thee a deliverer who wished to release millions from a more cruel oppression. If the American people honor Washington for resisting with bloodshed for seven years an unjust tax, how much more ought thou to be honored for seeking to free the poor slaves."

Brown replied that he loved his Quaker friends too. He went on to say: "You know that Christ once armed Peter. So also in my case I think he put a sword into my hand, and there continued it so long as he saw best, and then kindly took it from me. . . . I wish you could know with what cheerfulness I am now wielding the 'sword of the Spirit' on the right and on the left. I bless God that it proves 'mighty to the pulling down of strongholds.' " He felt no guilt about taking up arms in behalf of the slaves. "God will surely attend to his own cause in the best possible way and time, and he will not forget the work of his own hands."[3]

Three days later, on November 4, Brown wrote Lydia Maria Child, who had offered to come and tend his wounds. He thanked her and said he would "be greatly pleased to become personally acquainted with one so gifted; & so kind." But he was under the care of "a most humane gentleman" already and was recovering sufficiently from his wounds ("these light afflictions," he called them). He proposed that she give her sympathies not to him but to his wife and children and the widows of his dead sons and followers. Perhaps she could contribute 50 cents now and "a like sum yearly for the relief of these very poor; & deeply afflicted persons." She could do him *"immence good"* in that way. He was cheerful and believed that "the peace of God which passeth all understanding" ruled in his heart.[4]

On November 10 he wrote Mary that Hoyt had just informed him that she was with "dear kind friends in Philadelphia" (the McKims and Lucretia Mott) and that she would still like to see him again "in this world of 'sin & sorrow.' " He repeated what he had already told her, that coming south would subject her to "gazing-stock" and would be painful for them both. "I will here say that the sacrifizes you; & I, have been called to make in behalf of the *cause we love* the *cause of God; & of humanity*: do not seem to me as at all too great." After his execution, if she could bear the expense and trouble of gathering his bones and those of their sons and if the people here would allow her to do so, he was entirely willing to have her come to Charlestown. He did not have the strength to write all his friends and relatives. Could she answer a letter he had received from his brother Jeremiah?[5]

On second thought he wrote Jeremiah himself, asking him to tell his children in Ohio—especially Jason and Ellen—never to grieve on his account. Perhaps Jeremiah could ask the same of Brown's "sorrowing friends" there, for whom he felt "a thousand times more" anguish than he did for himself. As for his own fate, it was "all joy." " 'I have fought the good fight,' and have, as I trust, 'finished my course.' " He sent his love and asked that God be merciful to them all.[6]

In a letter to George Adams of West Newton, Massachusetts, Brown remarked that God "in His Infinite grace" had most wonderfully strengthened him. "May I use that strength in 'showing *his strength* unto this generation, & his power to every one that is to come.' " On that same day (November 15) Brown answered a letter from the Rev. H. L. Vaill, Brown's old teacher at Morris Academy in Litchfield. Brown asked Vaill not to grieve for him, because God was with him in Charlestown. "I tell you that I am 'joyfull in all my tribulations': that I do not feel condemned of Him whose judgment is just; nor of my own conscience. Nor do I feel degraded by my imprisonment, my chains or prospects of the Gallows." On the contrary, he believed that "I have not only been (*though utterly unworthy*) permitted to suffer affliction with God's people,' but have also had *a great many* rare opportunities for 'preaching righteousness in the great congregation.' " He truly felt the presence of Jesus now. "Christ the great captain of *liberty*; as well as of salvation; & who began his mission, as foretold of him; by proclaiming it, *saw fit* to take from me a sword of steel after I had carried it for a time but he has put another in my hand ('The sword of the Spirit,') & I pray to God to make me a faithful soldier wherever he may send me." He went on to say that "I have often passed under the rod of him whom I *call* my Father; & certainly no son ever needed it oftener; & yet I have enjoyed much of life. . . . It has been in making theprosperity, & the happiness of others *my own*." He said he was "looking forward to a time when 'peace on Earth & good will to *men* shall every where prevail.' " Brown thanked Vaill for the profession of sympathy from friends in his native state and assured him that Harpers Ferry would further the cause of God and humanity. Before "I began my work at Harpers Ferry; I felt assured that in the *worst event*; it would certainly PAY. . . ." He was disappointed only in "not keeping up *to my own plans*." But now he was even reconciled to that, "for Gods plan, was Infinitely better."[7]

The next day he wrote Mary again, expressing his gratitude for those persons who had generously helped relieve the wants and sufferings of his family. He especially praised *"dear gentle"* Sarah Wattles, whom Mary had contacted, for Sarah and her family "like angels of mercy" had frequently helped him and his sons. Then Brown turned to the proposal of certain friends (among them Franklin Sanborn) to educate his daughters. He gratefully left the details of this task to his friends but did hope that the girls would pursue a "plain but practical" education that would "enable them to transact the common business of life, comfortably and respectably, together with that thorough training to good business habits which prepares both men and women to be *useful though poor*, and to meet the *stearn* Realities of life." Mary had asked whether she might visit him, not to talk about escape but merely to be with him one last time. He replied: "If you feel sure that you can endure the trials and the shock, which will be *unavoidable* (if you come) , I should be most glad to see you *once more*." But he asked her to wait until after November 27 or 28.[8]

"I do not feel myself in the least degraded by my imprisonment, my chain, or the *near prospect* of the Gallows," Brown wrote the son of a business friend in Massachusetts. "Men cannot *imprison*, or *chain*; or *hang* the *soul*. I go joyfully in behalf of Millions that 'have no rights' that this 'great, & glorious'; 'this Christian Republic,' 'is bound to respect.' "

"I also feel," he wrote his cousin, the Rev. Luther Humphrey of Windham, Ohio, "that I have *long been endeavoring* to hold exactly 'such a fast as God has chosen.' See the passage in Isaiah which you have quoted. . . . 'Let us hold fast that we already have.' 'Thanks be *ever* unto God; who giveth us the victory through Jesus Christ our Lord.' And now my old warmhearted friend, 'Good bye.' "9

"My Dear Wife," he wrote on November 21, "I am very glad to learn from yourself that you feel so much resigned to your circumstances, so much confidence in a wise and good Providence, and such composure of mind in the midst of all your deep afflictions. This is just as it should be; and let me still say, 'Be of good cheer,' for we shall soon 'come out of all our great tribulations;' and very soon, if we trust in him, 'God shall wipe away all tears from our eyes.' " He said that he was uneasy because of the fires that blazed around Charlestown by night and by day. He did not know who had caused them (were they Negroes? pranksters?) . He did not think his friends had started the fires, but did believe they would be blamed for them. He said that Governor Wise had been deluged with ominous and threatening letters. Because of the state of public feeling in the South, he was understandably worried about Mary's coming to Charlestown; but she could decide that matter on her own. Meanwhile, would she write him about their crops—which ones had matured? He would never again "intermeddle" with her worldly concerns, but he was still interested in them.

The next day he wrote his "Dear Children" at North Elba. Annie's letter had just arrived, and he was happy that they were cheerful in Mary's absence. May God grant them the same comfort he enjoyed. "I feel just as content to die for God's eternal truth and for suffering humanity on the scaffold as in any other way; and I do not say this from any disposition to 'brave it out.' No; I would readily own my wrong were I in the least convinced of it." He said that he had been in jail a month (only ten days remained before his execution) and, reflecting on that, he implored them to remain in good cheer. "This life is intended as a season of training, chastisement, temptation, affliction, and trial; and the 'righteous shall come of' it all. Oh, my dear children, let me again entreat you all to . . . 'Trust in the Lord and do good, so shalt thou dwell in the land.' "

On the same day (November 22) he wrote Jason and Ellen, thanking them for their letters and praising God that they were holding up well. As for himself, "A calm peace, perhaps like that which your own dear mother [Dianthe] felt in view of her last change, seems to fill my mind by day and night." He urged them not to grieve for him. God would make his death "a thousand times more valuable to his cause" than all the "miserable service" Brown had rendered in his life. He beseeched them to trust in God and Jesus Christ and again thanked them for writing.[10]

Then he scratched off a few lines of gratitude to Higginson, "for your journey to visit & comfort my family." Since his imprisonment, Brown said, Higginson had proved himself again and again "a friend in need." Brown appreciated the help of Mary Stearns, Hoyt, and other friends as well. He had not written them yet—he was still weak from his wounds—but he had not forgotten their "love, & kindness." He sent his own love to all his "dear friends" and signed the letter: "Yours for God & the right, John Brown."[11]

3

One day that November Brown received an unexpected visit. John Avis opened the cell door, and there stood Judge and Mrs. Russell, who had come down from Boston on the train. Brown rose from his cot and greeted them with his lips trembling a little. "My dear," he told Mrs. Russell, "this is no place for you." Then he excused himself and lay down again.

As they talked, Mrs. Russell was amazed at his composure. He did not feel sorry for himself but "was calm and at peace, and earnestly desired to maintain that mind, with unshaken self-control, to the end." Brown said little about the raid, suggesting only that "something had gone very wrong—that something had been done that he had expressly forbidden"—and adding a few sharp words about Frederick Douglass. Of his sons who had died at Harpers Ferry he merely said that they had not been gently killed.

Mrs. Russell did not wish to hear any more about the raid anyway, for she had never sympathized with Brown on "such subjects" and had tried to avoid them in their conversations. She wanted to remember Brown not for the violence in him or his bloody pilgrimage into Virginia but for "his integrity, high purpose, courage and singleness of heart." When it was time to go she kissed him and left the jail in tears. For the rest of her life she would think of him—as many others would think of him—as one of the most noble idealists the country had ever known. "He could form beautiful dreams of things, as they should occur, and forthwith go into action on the basis of those dreams, making no sufficient allowance for some things occurring as they should not. John Brown's dreams were not always practical. But we loved and trusted *John Brown*."[12]

4

But millions of other Americans—Southerners and Northern Negrophobes especially—hated Brown with a passion. "The rage for vengeance which is felt by the citizens of this place," cried the Charleston *Mercury*, "can only be fully and satisfactorily satisfied by the blood of John Brown." A score of hate letters from all over the Union piled up on Governor Wise's desk, calling Brown a murderer, calling him a maniac. . . . A New York physician angrily protested when Governor Wise agreed to let Mary have Brown's body for burial at their farm in the Adirondacks. "A bloody outrage," the man wrote. Brown's body ought to be given to a medical school for dissection; otherwise it would be marched "in a triumphal procession through all the Eastern states, and they will make a hero martyr of him," and other fanatics would try to follow his example.[13]

Then there was the letter Mahala Doyle sent him from Tennessee: "Altho' vengeance is not mine, I confess that I do feel gratified to hear that you were stopped in your fiendish career at Harper's Ferry, with the loss of your two sons, you can now appreciate my distress in Kansas, when you then and there entered my house at midnight and arrested my husband and two boys, and took them out of the yard and in cold blood shot them dead in my hearing. You can't say you done it to free slaves. We had none and never expected to own one." Then in a bitter postscript: "My son John Doyle whose life I beged of you is now grown up and is very desirous to be at Charlestown on the day of your execution."[14]

Brown did not answer that letter or make any attempt to justify the Pottawatomie murders as he did the Harpers Ferry attack. When questioned about the slayings he merely remarked that "I did not kill any of those men, but I approved of their killing." Which *was* the truth—if not the whole truth. He left the ambiguities and contradictions for his inquisitors to figure out, for he was no longer personally concerned with the Pottawatomie massacre, as he told Judge Russell.[15]

In the eyes of the authorities his objectives in the Harpers Ferry attack remained ambiguous, too, because Brown persisted in giving confused and contradictory statements about his intentions. In his interview after his capture he had denied that he wanted to incite a slave insurrection; yet he had told one of his prisoners during the raid itself that if he could conquer Virginia the rest of the Southern states would practically conquer themselves because they had so many slaves in them. He remarked to Governor Wise that he had expected plenty of slave support, especially from Virginia, Tennessee, and the Carolinas. Yet, in his now famous court oration of November 2 he had told the jury—and his Northern sympathizers beyond—that he had not intended to spill a drop of Southern blood but had merely planned to run slaves off to the North. In his exalted state of mind he probably believed every word of this. And in any case it was easy for him to rationalize his erroneous and contradictory statements, for whatever he said to further the cause of liberty was not only right, it was the will of God.

When Governor Wise visited him in jail, however, and pointed out his contradictory assertions, Brown wrote Andrew Hunter forthwith, saying that he wanted to correct some of the things he had told the court on November 2. When the clerk had asked about his sentencing, Brown had been taken by surprise: he had not expected to be sentenced before the other raiders. In "the hurry of the moment," he forgot much of what he had intended to say and had not fully considered what he did say. "I intended to convey this idea," Brown told Hunter, "that it was my object to place the slaves in a condition to defend their liberties, if they would, *without any bloodshed*, but *not that I intended to run them out of the slave*

States. I was not *aware* of any such apparent confliction until my attention *was called* to it, and I do not suppose that a man in *my then circumstances* should be superhuman in respect to the *exact purport* of every word he might utter."[16]

5

The end was only nine days away. Brown wrote the Rev. James W. McFarland of Wooster, Ohio, who had sent him a friendly letter. Brown said he would love to have McFarland "or any of my liberty-loving ministerial friends, to talk and pray with me." In his youth Brown had aspired to be a minister, but God had had other work for him. Now that his time was near he would take much pleasure in having a preacher to lead him in meditation and prayer.[17]

Yet when some Southern Methodists, followed by Governor Wise's son and a Virginia colonel, offered the old man a minister, to give him "the consolations of religion," Brown answered with a resounding no. He did not, he said, recognize slaveholders or defenders of slavery (lay or clerical) as Christians. He would rather be escorted to the scaffold by "blacklegs" than by proslavery preachers. "I have asked to be *spared* from having any *mock; or hypocritical prayers made over me,* when I am publicly *murdered,*" he wrote George Stearns, "& that my only *religious attendants* be poor *little, dirty, ragged, bare headed, & barefooted Slave Boys; & Girls;* led by some old *grey headed Slave* Mother. I should feel much prouder of such an escort, and I wish I could have it."[18]

Another cousin, the Rev. Heman Humphrey, sent a letter containing "a doleful lamentation" about Brown's "infatuation" and "madness." In reply to this "very sorrowful, kind, and faithful letter," Brown said that he sympathized with Humphrey but that he had entertained no murderous intentions at Harpers Ferry. Furthermore, "I must say that I am neither conscious of being 'infatuated' nor 'mad.' You will doubtless agree with me in this,—that neither imprisonment, irons, nor the gallows falling to one's lot are of themselves evidence of either guilt, 'infatuation, or madness.' " If Humphrey could spend some time with Brown in prison he would find much to reconcile his mind about Brown's execution. "He shall begin to deliver Israel out of the land of the Philistines," Brown quoted. "This was said of a poor erring servant many years ago; and for many years I have felt a strong impression that God had given me powers and faculties, unworthy as I was, that he intended to use for a similar purpose." This "unmerited honor" God had seen fit to bestow on him; and whether his death would have as much value as that "same poor frail man" he had alluded to, he still felt that in spite of his sins he too would die "in faith."[19]

Then another letter to Mary, again expressing his gratitude that so many people (Lucretia Mott and John Jay, among others) were helping her and the family in such countless ways. He was feeling better—good enough to sit up, in fact. He read his Bible and wrote letters "pretty much all day: as well as part of the night." Yes, the day was rapidly approaching; yet he trusted that God would give him courage when he was out there on that scaffold. "My only anxiety is to be properly assured of my *fitness* for the company of those who are washed from all *filthiness*: '& *for the presence* of Him who is infinitely pure.' "[20]

"My dearly beloved Sisters Mary A., & Martha," he wrote on November 27. "There are 'things dear Sisters that God hides *even* from the wise & prudent' I feel astonished that one *so exceedingly vile, & unworthy* as *I am* would even be suffered to have a place *any how or any where* amongst the *very least of All* who when they came to die (as all must:) *were permitted* to pay the debt of nature' in defense of the *right*: & of Gods eternnal *& immutable truth*. Oh my dear friends can you believe *it possible* that the scaffold *has no terrors* for your *own* poor, old, unworthy brother? *I thank God* through Jesus Christ *my Lord: it is even so* I am now sheding tears: but they *are no longer* tears of *grief or sorrow* I trust I have nearly DONE with those. I am weeping for *joy* & *gratitude* that I can *in no other way* express."[21]

On November 30 he composed "what is probably the last letter I shall ever write" to Mary and the children. He mentioned that he had received and sent to them drafts for $150 from well-wishers John Jay and Edward Harris. But what he wanted to discuss in his last message was God and the conduct of their lives after he was dead. He beseeched his children to love and fear God, to give their whole hearts to Him as Brown had tried to do. He implored them to make the Bible their *"dayly & Nightly study;* with a *childlike honest, candid, teachable spirit,"* out of love and respect for their husband and father. And he prayed that the God of his fathers would open their eyes so that they might discover the truth and be consoled in their time of need by the Christian religion. "I only *ask* you," he said, "to make a candid, & sober *use of your reason:* My dear younger children will you listen to this last poor admonition of one who can only love you?" He implored them not to be vain and thoughtless, but sober-minded, and entreated them "to love *the* whole *remnant* of our once great family" and try to rebuild their broken walls. He also urged them to abhor slavery "with *undiing hatred"* and reminded them that "he that is *slow* to *anger* is *better* than the mighty: and he that ruleth his *spirit*; than he that taketh a city," and that "they that be *wise* shall *shine*; and they that *turn* many to *righteousness*: as the stars forever; & ever."

As for himself, he was awaiting the hour of his execution with "great composure of mind," knowing that "a *wise,* & *merciful,* as *well* as *Just, & holy* God: rules not only the affairs of *this world*; but of all worlds. . . . I have now no doubt that our seeming *disaster*: will ultimately result in the most *glorious success* So my dear *shattered*; & *broken* family; . . . Do not feel ashamed on my account; nor for one moment despair of the cause; or grow *weary* of *well doing.* I bless God; I never felt stronger confidence in the certain & near approach of a *bright Morning*; & a *glorious day."*[22]

6

Just before 3:30 in the afternoon of December 1, the last afternoon of Brown's life, the jailer opened the cell door and Mary entered. For a moment they both shed tears. Then, regaining their composure, they sat down together for the last time.

Mary herself had already given way to uncontrollable anguish in Philadelphia, where she had received word from Governor Wise, in answer to her pleas, that there was no hope for her husband. She took some consolation, however, in the governor's permission to take Brown home for burial.

Brown was pleased when he learned this. He asked John Avis to help Mary move his body—and also to assist her in gathering the remains of his sons and the Thompson brothers, for burial with him. In addition, Brown asked that the bodies of the other dead raiders be burned and their ashes taken with him to the Adirondacks.

The Browns had supper with Avis in his room (it was perhaps the first time Brown had been out of his cell since November 2). Then they discussed his will, her future, and the education of their daughters. When it was time for her to leave, Brown lost control of himself for the first time. He could not understand why she had to go—why she could not stay with him during his last night. But General William B. Taliaferro, who was in command of the town, had explicit orders from the governor that Mary must return to Harpers Ferry that night. For a moment Brown lost his temper completely, inveighing against such a thoughtless and arbitrary decision. Then he checked himself. He was perfectly calm and composed when he took Mary into Avis' room and there told her good-by . . . good-by to this woman who had endured such hardship and such tragedy with him since their marriage in Pennsylvania twenty-six years before. Mary wept as he embraced her and prayed for God to take care of her and give her strength. Then she was gone, out into the night, on her way back to Harpers Ferry to wait for his coffin.[23]

Brown returned to his cell and lay awake on his cot for a long while. Then, to get his mind off Mary, he wrote a short letter to his brother Jeremiah in which he insisted that he was "quite cheerful & composed."[24] Then he lay down again. Sometime late that night he slept.

7

He arose at dawn, quite certain that this *was* the beginning of a bright morning and most glorious day. He read his Bible, marking those passages in Genesis, Exodus, Leviticus, Deuteronomy, Job, Proverbs, Ecclesiastes, Isaiah, Jeremiah, Matthew, and Revelation, which had had a strong influence on his life. Then he wrote a last note to his wife and enclosed his will which he had forgotten to give her the night before. He also sent the following instructions:

To be inscribed on the old family Monument at North Elba.
"Oliver Brown born   1839 was killed at Harpers ferry Va
Nov 17th 1859.
"Watson Brown, born   1835 was wounded at Harpers ferry
Nov 17th and died Nov 19th 1859
(My Wife can) supply *blank* dates to above
"John Brown born May 9th 1800 was executed at Charlestown,
Va, December 2d 1859."

An hour before his execution Brown dashed off a reply to Lora
Case of Hudson, Ohio, who had written him on November 28.
Brown thanked him for his "outburst of warm hearted sympathy"
and declared that such sentiments made Case shine "in the midst of
this wicked; & perverse generation as light in the world."[25]

Avis and the guard unlocked the cell door. It was time now. Both
men stood aside as Brown walked out without hesitation. Because
they had been kind to him he gave his Bible to the guard, his silver
watch to Avis. Then Brown started down the corridor to say good-by
to the other captive raiders. He stopped first at the cell of Copeland
and Green. "Stand up like men," he exhorted the Negroes, "and
do not betray your friends." Then on to the cell of Cook and Coppoc.
"You have made false statements," Brown accused Cook, referring to
the confession Cook had given the authorities, "that I sent you to
Harper's Ferry; you knew I protested against your going." Cook
retorted that Brown most certainly did order him to the Ferry, that
he had a good memory and recalled the orders clearly. They quarreled for a moment. Then Brown cut the argument off, pointing out
that it would not do them any good to bicker because they were
all going to die for a good cause. And not one of them, he added,
should deny that cause now. Brown turned to Coppoc. "You also
made false statements, but I am glad to hear you have contradicted
them. Stand up like a man!" He shook hands with them both and
then walked back to Stevens. "Good by, Captain," Stevens said. "I
know you are going to a better land."

"I know I am," Brown replied; "bear up, as you have done, and
never betray your friends."

Brown said nothing to Albert Hazlett. All the raiders pretended
not to know him, in hopes the authorities would decide they had the
wrong man and let him go.

"God bless you, my men," Brown called out. "May we all meet in

Heaven." Then the guard escorted him down the corridor and out into the street.[26]

Brown paused in front of the jail, looking over the wagon that was to carry him to the gallows (his coffin rested in the wagon bed— he would have to ride on his coffin). The streets around the jail were full of armed guards and soldiers, for rumors still circulated that some desperate attempt would be made to save Brown from the gallows. "I had no idea that Gov. Wise considered my execution so important," Brown said bitterly. Then he turned and handed one of his attendants a last prophetic message he had written to his countrymen:

> Charlestown, Va, 2d, December, 1859.
> I John Brown am now quite *certain* that the crimes of this *guilty, land: will* never be purged *away;* but with Blood. I had *as I now think: vainly* flattered myself that without *very much* bloodshed; it might be done.[27]

8

The gallows had been set up in an open field on the outskirts of Charlestown. On the way out Brown sat on his coffin in the wagon bed, his arms "closely pinioned at the elbows." He wore slippers, a low broad-brimmed hat, and his ragged Harpers Ferry clothes. It was nearly eleven o'clock by the time the wagon and armed escort reached the execution site, where 1,500 cavalry and militia and scores of spectators had gathered to witness Brown's hanging. A balmy wind was blowing out of the south and "a warm & dreamy haze" lay over the landscape: the broad, fertile fields dotted with corn shocks, the white farmhouses just visible through the leafless trees—all set against the pastoral Blue Ridge Mountains.

"This *is* a beautiful country," Brown remarked. "I never had the pleasure of seeing it before." But when the wagon moved past the scaffold Brown fixed his eyes on it and stared at it intently. One reporter thought that Brown wore "a grim & greisly smirk" as he stepped down from the wagon and approached the steps of the scaffold. But Professor Thomas J. Jackson of the Virginia Military Institute saw only "unflinching firmness" in Brown's whole manner; and Edmund Ruffin, who stood behind the professor in the ranks of the V.M.I. cadets, said that Brown ascended the scaffold with "seeming alacrity" as though he were "a willing assistant, instead of the victim."

On the platform now, in full view of the soldiers and spectators, Brown stared straight ahead as the jailer removed his hat, adjusted the halter around his neck, then pulled a white linen hood over his head. But the hood flapped in the wind so annoyingly that the sheriff finally had to pin it. "Move ahead," the sheriff ordered. "You will have to guide me," Brown replied. The sheriff led him over the trap door, hooked the halter to the beam overhead, and tied Brown's ankles together. "Do you want a handkerchief dropped as a signal to cut the rope?" the sheriff asked. "No," Brown said, "I don't care; I don't want you to keep me waiting unnecessarily."

But for a full ten minutes confusion reigned around the scaffold as soldiers scurried about trying to locate their assigned positions. In all the commotion Ruffin could not take his eyes from the condemned man; the Virginia secessionist grudgingly admired the "one virtue" Brown possessed: his "physical or animal courage," his "complete fearlessness of & insensibility to danger and death." But in the ranks of the 1st Virginia Regiment out of Richmond, John Wilkes Booth viewed the old man with contempt, thinking how abolitionists like him were "the *only* traitors in the land."

At last the troops were in their places. "We are ready," an officer shouted out. A great hush fell over the troops and spectators as the civilian officials stepped off the scaffold. Now Brown stood there alone, "as motionless as a statue," as he waited to be taken from this world.

Below, the sheriff raised the hatchet and severed the rope with a single blow; there was a crash as the platform fell and Brown plummeted through space . . . the rope caught, his arms below the elbow flew up and his body struggled convulsively . . . then at last John Brown "was hanging between heaven and earth," while the crowd looked on in silence. In a moment the voice of Colonel J. T. L. Preston of the Virginia Military Institute rang out on the wind: "So perish all such enemies of Virginia! All such enemies of the Union! All such foes of the human race!"[28]

XXII

BEYOND THE GALLOWS

∾

As THE VIRGINIA AUTHORITIES took Brown down from the gallows and sent him northward in a black walnut coffin, most Southerners took grim satisfaction that justice had been done. Said the Savannah *Daily Morning News*, speaking for the Deep South: Thus, "the notorious horsethief, murderer, insurrectionist and traitor, expiated his guilt. Would that his might be the fate of the craven-hearted instigators and plotters of the treason which he so recklessly endeavored to execute— There are thousands of white-cravated necks in New England and the Northern States to-day, that are as deserving of John Brown's hempen tie as well as his own."[1]

Perhaps the *News* did not know it, but a great mass of conservative Northerners shared these sentiments. In Union meetings at Boston and later at New York, Yankees who sympathized with the South not only repudiated Brown's raid but approved of his hanging, acclaimed the Union, and asserted Virginia's right to enslave Negroes. Stephen A. Douglas of Illinois, a Democratic presidential hopeful who needed Southern support, condemned Brown for invading Missouri and stealing horses, pronounced him a "notorious man who has recently suffered death for his crimes," and again blamed those crimes on the Republican party. But Republican leaders, including Seward and Lincoln, continued to disparage Brown's raid as a criminal act—even if Brown's motives were admirable—and conceded that hanging him was just.

But the abolitionists, and moderate and liberal Northerners who had never liked slavery anyway, had been so moved by Brown's

353

courage, by his inspired speeches and eloquent prison letters and interviews, that they were profoundly disturbed when the old man was executed. And on that day they gathered by the hundreds— Northerners of various political and religious persuasions—to pay tribute to what Brown symbolized and to condemn the South for hanging him.

At the very hour Brown was hanging, in fact, town officials in Albany, New York, were firing a 100-gun salute to honor his martyr- dom; and church bells were tolling in commemoration from New England to Kansas. At Lawrence a crowd of antislavery settlers adopted eleven resolutions, three of which praised Brown's inten- tions at Harpers Ferry and asserted that he had given his life for the liberty of man.[2] In Hudson and virtually all the other towns in Ohio's Western Reserve, hundreds of people who hated slavery crowded into their churches to hear commemorative services and bear witness to Brown's "sublime purpose." There were comparable services in Akron, where banks, business establishments, and public offices closed for the entire day of December 2 as a tribute to Brown's memory. At Cleveland banners stretched over the streets proclaim- ing: "I cannot better serve the cause I love than to die for it." And 1,400 citizens held a memorial meeting there, during which the Rev. J. C. White repeated what Brown himself had often said: "The great and sinful system of American slavery will never be overthrown by pacific means. 'Without the shedding of blood, there can be no remission of such a sin.' " Then the crowd adopted an uncompromis- ing resolution: "The irrepressible conflict is upon us, and it will never end until Freedom or slavery go to the wall. In such a contest and under such dire necessity we say 'without fear and without reproach' let freedom stand and the Union be dissolved."[3]

At that same moment church bells were tolling in Iowa, in Chicago and northern Illinois, and all along the Mohawk Valley; and a group of antislavery Pennsylvanians were holding a public prayer meeting in Philadelphia—a meeting that was broken up by a mob of Southern medical students. Public prayer meetings were also taking place at New York City, Syracuse, and Rochester; at Fitchburg, Plymouth, New Bedford, and Manchester. In the Town House at Concord Thoreau delivered an address in honor of the "crucified hero," while at the Tremont Temple in Boston a great crowd gathered to hear speeches and to parade placards, one of them quoting Lafayette: "I never would have drawn my sword in the cause of America if I could have conceived that thereby I was helping to found a nation of slaves." The highlight of the meeting came when William Lloyd Garrison, heretofore an uncompromising apostle of nonviolent abolitionism, rose to speak. Garrison's friends knew that he had been haunted by the question of Brown's guilt since the Harpers Ferry debacle. Garrison never doubted that Brown had believed himself divinely inspired. Yet, as one of Garrison's biographers phrased it, "he could not help thinking [Brown] misguided and rash, 'powerfully wrought upon by the trials through which he has passed.'" By the standards of Lexington or Bunker Hill, Brown had died a patriot. But what of the standards of peace? "Was there a place in history for the Gideons, the Joshuas and Davids?" Standing before the huge crowd in Tremont Temple, Garrison had his answer to that question. He pointed out that he was a nonresistant who had labored for over twenty-eight years to bring about the peaceful abolition of slavery. "Yet, as a peace man— I am prepared to say: 'Success to every slave insurrection at the South, and in every slave country.' And I do not see how I compromise or stain my peace profession in making that declaration. . . . I thank God when men who believe in the right and duty of wielding carnal weapons are so far advanced that they will take those weapons out of the scale of despotism, and throw them into the scale of freedom. It is an indication of progress and positive moral growth; it is one way to get up the sublime platform on non-resistance; and it is God's method of dealing retribution upon the head of the tyrant. Rather than see men wearing their chains in a cowardly and servile spirit, I would, as an advocate of peace, much rather see them breaking the head of the tyrant with their chains. Give me, as a nonresistant, Bunker Hill and Lexington, and Concord, rather than the cowardice and servility of a Southern slave-plantation."

The message was emphatically clear to all present: John Brown had converted Garrison; now he, too, "had capitulated to the need for violence" to destroy slavery in the United States.[4]

In the weeks that followed Brown's execution Northern writers, poets, and intellectuals enshrined him in an almost endless procession of poems, songs, letters, essays, and public addresses. William

Dean Howells, Edmund Clarence Stedman of Kansas, Herman Melville, and Walt Whitman all composed poems immortalizing Brown. "I would sing," wrote Whitman in the *Year of Meteors*, "how an old man, tall, with white hair, mounted the scaffold in Virginia (I was at hand, silent I stood with teeth shut close, I watch'd, I stood very near you old man when cool and indifferent, but trembling with age and your unheal'd wounds you mounted the scaffold)." Victor Hugo, writing from France, praised Brown as "the champion of Christ" and damned "the whole American Republic" for crucifying him. Ministers, lecturers, composers, and essayists by the score agreed with Lydia Maria Child when she wrote of Brown: "Leaning on the Almighty arm, he passed triumphantly through the Valley of the Shadow of Death, and I think a vision of heaven will open to him as glorious as it did to St. Stephen." "His soul is marching on."

"It is safe to say," said the Lawrence *Republican*, in surveying the reaction to Brown's execution, "that the death of no man in America has ever produced so profound a sensation. A feeling of deep and sorrowful indignation seems to possess the masses. The religious element is most profoundly stirred."[5]

2

On the afternoon of December 2, with church bells tolling in the North, a military escort took Brown's coffin from Charlestown up to Harpers Ferry. To the credit of the citizens of the area, who still feared a Northern invasion, no incidents occurred along the way. At Harpers Ferry, Mary and her escort—Hector Tyndale and J. Miller McKim—received the coffin and had it placed on a train for Philadelphia. Mary had hoped to take Watson and Oliver home, too, but Watson's body had been given to the Winchester Medical College and Oliver's had been piled in "store boxes," along with the other raiders killed at Harpers Ferry, and buried in the woods on the other side of the Shenandoah. Mary did not have the strength to identify Oliver's body, so she left her sons in Virginia and took only the old man out of the South.

The funeral train reached Philadelphia at one o'clock on the afternoon of December 3. A large and boisterous crowd had gathered around the station. There were some Negroes present, wanting to catch a glimpse of the coffin. Groups of white racists were there, too, milling about the station and eyeing the Negroes. Fearing that trouble might break out, the authorities sent an empty hearse to the undertaker's parlor, which drew the crowd away, and then smuggled Brown's coffin into a furniture car which carried it secretly down to the Walnut Street wharf. From there a boat took the coffin up the coast to New York. Mary followed by train the next day.

In New York a friend of the family removed Brown from his coffin (the old man was not going to be buried in a Southern coffin) and placed him in another. From New York, Wendell Phillips and J. Miller McKim escorted Mary and the coffin north toward the Adirondacks. At every town they passed through—Troy, Rutland, Vergennes, Westport—bells tolled and people gathered in the streets to watch the procession. In the courthouse at Elizabethtown an honor guard stood watch over the coffin until dawn. Then the party started up the steep roads that led to North Elba, moving through the mountains Brown had loved, and arrived at the Brown farm toward evening on Wednesday, December 7. Mary met her daughters with "a burst of love and anguish," while the coffin was placed in the main room of the farmhouse. There the old man lay in state for those of his neighbors who wanted to look at him for the last time.

The next day—December 8—final services for Brown were held in the farmhouse. Present were Brown's younger daughters (Annie, Sarah, and Ellen), Mary and Salmon Brown, Ruth and Henry Thompson, and the widows of Watson, Oliver, and William Thompson—and several black and white neighbors. Lyman Epps, a close friend of the family who had Indian as well as Negro ancestry, was there with his wife and children. McKim bore testimony to Brown's memory. Then Wendell Phillips gave the eulogy to that "marvellous old man" who "has loosened the roots of the slave system; it only breathes—it does not live—hereafter."

Early that afternoon the pallbearers led the funeral party out to a freshly dug grave by a large boulder near the farmhouse (where Grandfather Brown's gravemarker, yet to be inscribed, still leaned against the kitchen). It was a chill winter day in the mountains; and the mourners stood shivering around the graveside as the Rev. Joshua Young of Burlington, Vermont, read from the Bible and offered a final prayer. Then, as the coffin was lowered into the earth, Lyman Epps's family, who loved that old man because he had tried to help black people and had treated them as human beings, sang "Blow ye the trumpet, blow," the hymn Brown used to sing to his children as he held them on his knees.[6]

> Blow ye the trumpet, blow
> Sweet is Thy work, my God, my King.
> I'll praise my Maker with my breath.
> O, happy is the man who hears.
> Why should we start, and fear to die.
> With songs and honors sounding loud.
> Ah, lovely appearance of death.

But the story of John Brown does not end with a silent grave in the stillness of the mountains. His raid and public execution had set in motion a spiral of accusation and counteraccusation between Northerners and Southerners that spun the nation inexorably toward civil war. Nowhere was the mutual hostility more visible than in Congress when it assembled on Monday, December 5, only three days after Brown was hanged. The specter of his corpse haunted the legislative halls; the atmosphere was tense with pent-up violence. "The members on both sides are mostly armed with deadly weapons," one senator wrote his wife, "and it is said that the friends of each are armed in the galleries."

Once again Southern Democrats blamed the Republican party for Harpers Ferry and the sectional crisis it had provoked. One Southern representative, pointing an angry finger at his Republican colleagues, cried that he would "shatter this Republic from turret to foundation stone" before he would surrender a single Southern right (a cry repeated countless times in the South itself). There followed a sharp exchange of insults between the Southern representative and Thaddeus Stevens of Pennsylvania. A Mississippian became so outraged that he rushed at Stevens with a drawn Bowie knife. A bloody fight was averted only when Stevens' friends rushed to his defense and the House clerk shouted for order. Finally the Southerners, glowering at their Republican enemies, returned to their side of the House chamber, which, like the nation itself, was divided into mutually resentful and suspicious halves.[7]

In the Senate Southern Democrats were able to get a special investigating committee set up on December 14, with James M. Mason of Virginia as chairman and Jefferson Davis of Mississippi as chief inquisitor, to find out whether any "subversive organizations" —in other words, any Republicans—were involved in Brown's crime. The committee questioned such Republican notables as William H. Seward, Henry Wilson, John A. Andrew, and Joshua Giddings, but found no evidence that they were guilty of complicity in the raid and had to let them go. The committee also interrogated two of Brown's secret backers—Howe and Stearns—as well as Charles Blair, Martin Conway, Richard Realf, Charles Robinson, and Augustus Wattles. With the capital in a violent mood, the committee was impelled to confront its witnesses with extreme caution, lest by overzealousness it plunge the Congress into a battleground between antislavery Republicans and angry Southerners. Later Howe and Stearns, breathing sighs of relief, both remarked that their questions were asked in such a way that they could make honest replies and still not implicate themselves. Finally, on June 15, 1860, with Congress degenerating into a circus of threatened duels and brandished weapons, the Mason Committee reported that it had found no evidence that any organizations or any individuals beyond those who had accompanied Brown were accessory to the crime.[8]

But the South itself was never convinced that the Republican party had nothing to do with Brown's invasion. Unable to believe that the mass of conservative Northern opinion (which had condemned the raid) was typical of the region, Southerners continued to regard the North as a land of Brown-loving abolitionist, "Black Republican" fanatics. And so the Great Fear persisted and deepened in that fateful year of 1860, as rumors of Black Republican invasions multiplied over the South and "delusions of persecution and impending disaster flourished."[9] *From Texas came shocking reports that incendiary fires were blazing against the night, that abolitionists were plotting with slaves to incite a full-scale race war, such as Brown had tried to ignite at Harpers Ferry. As summer wore on and the crucial election of 1860 approached, prosecessionist orators harangued crowds with terrifying prophecies: if Abraham Lincoln and the "Black Republicans" won control of the federal government, they would invade the South and incite the slaves to insurrection, rape, and murder. Secessionist newspapers damned Lincoln under lurid, black headlines as a "black-hearted abolitionist fanatic," "a human viper," who, like John Brown, had committed himself to the violent destruction of the South's "ancestral institution" and the whole Southern Way of Life. Southerners who viewed the ownership of slaves not only as a status symbol but as the cornerstone of their whole society listened intently to what the fire-eaters said. Had Lincoln not proclaimed that this nation could not endure half slave and half free? Was he not of the same party as William H. Seward, who had asserted that the North and South were locked in an irrepressible conflict? Did Southerners have any choice but to protect their homes and families—their whole society—through an independent Confederacy? Thus when Lincoln won the election of*

*1860 without receiving a single popular vote in ten Southern states,
the seven states of the Deep South seceded from the Union. They
did so because (as the Texas secession ordinance phrased it) "the
destruction of the existing relations between the two races, as advocated by our sectional enemies, would bring inevitable calamities
upon both and desolation upon the fifteen slaveholding States."
Southern Unionists pleaded frantically for moderation. "Wait for an
overt Republican act," they cried, and begged Lincoln to clarify his
position, even though he had made repeated assertions that he had
no intention of harming the South's native institutions (he did not
believe he had the authority to do so and in any case the Democrats,
though divided themselves, had still won control of Congress). There
followed a series of tragic political blunders, failures at compromise,
misunderstandings and dramatic confrontations between the two
sides that culminated in the firing on Fort Sumter and the beginning
of civil war—the very thing Brown had hoped and prayed would be
the ultimate consequence of his Harpers Ferry attack. Soon Northerners were marching into Virginia, into the very region where
Brown had hoped to free the slaves by insurrection, and they were
marching to the song of "John Brown's Body."*[10]
    *At the outset, of course, the destruction of slavery was not a
Northern objective in the war; Lincoln painstakingly argued (to the
dismay of the abolitionists and antislavery members of his own party)
that his only purpose was to save the Union, not to free the slaves.
But a combination of problems and pressures (and perhaps his own
conscience) caused him to change his mind; and in September, 1862,
he issued the Preliminary Emancipation Proclamation, a symbolic
move that made the eradication of slavery one of the North's principal war objectives. Emancipation for all slaves, though, was not
assured until the Confederacy fell and the 13th Amendment was
adopted in December, 1865. The liberation of the black man in the
muck and rubble of civil war signaled the triumph of Brown's own
prophecy, that the "crime of slavery" would never be purged from
this "guilty land" except with blood. And "John Brown's Body"
became a Northern legend, a symbol of noble idealism and self-
sacrifice, in the aura of which the man himself was all but forgotten.*

NOTES

PROLOGUE

1. Nearly all the early biographies were either defenses or eulogies of Brown as a great abolitionist hero "incapable of anything selfish or base." They include James Redpath, *Public Life of Capt. John Brown* (Boston, 1860); Richard D. Webb, *Life and Letters of Captain John Brown* (London, 1861); Franklin B. Sanborn, *Life and Letters of John Brown* (Boston, 1885), still a helpful volume if used with care, because of the many letters and recollections it contains; Hermann von Holst, *John Brown* (Boston, 1889); Richard J. Hinton, *John Brown and His Men* (New York, 1894); Joseph Edgar Chamberlin, *John Brown* (Boston, 1899); William E. Connelly, *John Brown* (Topeka, 1900); John Newton, *Captain John Brown of Harper's Ferry* (London, 1902); and W. E B. Du Bois, *John Brown* (Philadelphia, 1909). Oswald Garrison Villard's *John Brown, 1800-1859: A Biography Fifty Years After*, published in Boston in 1910 and reissued (without textual revision) in New York in 1943, is a compendium of information about Brown based on prodigious research in manuscript materials and on interviews with surviving members of Brown's family. Villard presents a well-tempered version of the traditional view of Brown himself, defending his memory "as at once a sacred, a solemn and an inspiring American heritage." Hill Peebles Wilson, *John Brown, Soldier of Fortune: A Critique* (Lawrence, Kans., 1913), written deliberately to "correct" the sympathetic portrait in Villard, is high-decibel, anti-Brown polemicism. Robert Penn Warren's *John Brown, the Making of a Martyr* (New York, 1929), drawing most of its facts from Sanborn and Villard, offers a pro-Southern indictment of Brown as a common thief whose only virtue was his courage. David Karsner's *John Brown, Terrible Saint* (New York, 1934) is a eulogistic sketch which borrows most of its information from Villard.

I. FIRST AWAKENING

1. Unless otherwise cited, my account of Owen and Ruth Mills Brown was drawn from Owen Brown's "Autobiography," in Franklin B. Sanborn, *Life and Letters of John Brown* (Boston, 1885), 4-11. For a sketch of Torrington in 1799 see John H. Thompson, *A History of Torrington* (3rd ed., Torrington, Conn., 1940), 13-19.

2. Genealogists are still arguing about the correct lineage of the Brown family. According to family tradition, the Browns were descendants of Peter Brown of the *Mayflower*. Captain John Brown—Owen's father—was allegedly of the fourth generation from Peter Brown, "one of the Pilgrim Fathers who landed at Plymouth Mass Dec 22 1620." Thus Owen's son John, who was to attain such notoriety in 1859, was supposed to have had the blood of one of America's cherished pilgrims flowing in his veins. The National Society of Mayflower Descendants, however, will not recognize any male descent from Peter Brown of the *Mayflower*, and many authorities believe that the Brown family tradition is false. See Donald Lines Jacobus, "Peter Brown of Windsor, Connecticut," *American Genealogist*, XXXIII (October, 1957), 214-222. Rev. Clarence S. Gee of Lockport, N.Y., who has done extensive research on Brown genealogy, wrote me on Feb. 27, 1968, that neither the evidence for nor that against the family tradition "is clearly and *finally* established." He remarked that an expert genealogist of Washington, D.C., was compiling a genealogy of the Brown clan, which presumably will attempt to settle the dispute.

3. Gideon Mills—Ruth's father—descended from Dutch immigrants who settled in Windsor, Conn., and anglicized their name from van der Meulen to Mills. Ruth's mother—Ruth Humphrey Mills—was alleged to have been an emotionally troubled woman who "died insane." See Oswald Garrison Villard, *John Brown, 1800-1859: A Biography Fifty Years After* (2nd ed., New York, 1943), 15, 508-509, and chap. XX of the present work.

4. Samuel Orcutt, *History of Torrington, Connecticut* (Albany, N.Y., 1878), 43, 317-319; Clarence S. Gee, "Brown Genealogy" and "Hannah Owen Brown Genealogy," typescript, Gee Collection.

II. A CALVINIST UPBRINGING

1. Unless otherwise cited, my account of Brown's early life in Connecticut and Ohio is based on John Brown to Henry L. Stearns, July 15, 1857, photostatic copy, Boyd B. Stutler Collection, and on Owen Brown's "Autobiography" in Sanborn, *Life and Letters of John Brown*, 8-9. The letter Brown wrote to Henry Stearns gave a fairly detailed account of the first twenty years of his life. While it was intended to convince young Henry's father—George Luther Stearns, a prominent Massachusetts businessman and reformer—that Brown was an honest soldier of the Lord whom Stearns should assist in his private war against slavery, portions of the letter never-

theless are remarkably revealing—more so than Brown probably realized. Where possible I have sought to corroborate Brown's recollections with reminiscences of those who knew or worked with him in Ohio. Still there is a dearth of such sources, and to provide a portrait of Brown's crucial formative years at all I had to rely heavily on his letter to Stearns. As far as I am concerned, in view of the kind of man Brown was to become, the things he tells about his boyhood in this letter all sound accurate enough. The document is printed in full in Louis Ruchames, *A John Brown Reader* (London and New York, 1959), 35-51, and in Sanborn and Villard.

2. See Christian Cackler, *Recollections of an Old Settler* (Ravenna, Ohio, 1874), 20-21, 29.

3. There is no evidence that Ruth died insane, as Allen Johnson, Allan Nevins, C. Vann Woodward, and others have asserted. For a detailed analysis of this point, see chap. XX of the present biography.

4. Milton Lusk's statement in Sanborn, *Life and Letters of John Brown*, 33.

5. Owen's eight children by Sally Root were born between 1811 and 1832. She died in 1840. In April, 1841, Owen took a widow named Lucy Hinsdale as his third wife. They had no children. Clarence S. Gee, "Brown Genealogy," typescript, Gee Collection.

6. According to the Rev. Mr. Gee, who made a thorough examination of the records of the Hudson, Ohio, Congregational Church, Brown "was examined and approved for membership on March 6, 1816; and received into the church on March 31, 1816."

7. Sanborn, *Life and Letters of John Brown*, 31-32.

8. Villard, *John Brown*, 17; Richard J. Hinton, *John Brown and His Men* (New York, 1894), 13.

9. See letter of the Rev. H. L. Vaill, who was Brown's teacher at the Morris Academy, in James Redpath, *Echoes of Harpers Ferry* (Boston, 1860), 388-398.

10. Lusk's statement in Sanborn, *Life and Letters of John Brown*, 34; James Foreman to James Redpath, Dec. 28, 1859, Richard J. Hinton Papers, Kansas State Historical Society.

11. Lusk's statement in Sanborn, *Life and Letters of John Brown*, 33.

12. Foreman to Redpath, Dec. 28, 1859, Hinton Papers, Kansas State Historical Society; George B. Delamater, address about John Brown given at Meadville sometime after Brown's death, MS, copy in Stutler Collection.

13. Foreman to Redpath, Dec. 28, 1859, Hinton Papers, Kansas State Historical Society. See also Samuel A. Lane, *Fifty Years and Over of Akron* (Akron, 1892), 828-829; and Mary Land, "John Brown's Ohio Environment," *Ohio Archaeological and Historical Quarterly*, LVII (January, 1948), 28.

14. Villard, *John Brown*, 17-18.

15. Lusk's statement in Sanborn, *Life and Letters of John Brown*, 33-34. Later Brown and Lusk enjoyed something of a reconciliation. When Brown was living in Pennsylvania, Milton got into a controversy with the church in Hudson over "the issue of colonization for the colored people." Brown

came back to see Lusk, prayed with him, and told him he was "nearer right" in opposing the church than Brown had thought.

16. Foreman to Redpath, Dec. 28, 1859, Hinton Papers, Kansas State Historical Society.

17. See Boyd B. Stutler, "John Brown and the Masonic Order," *Ohio History,* LXXI (January, 1962), 24-32.

18. Statements of relatives, friends, and members of Brown's own family in Villard, *John Brown,* 19, 592. When the subject of Dianthe's emotional troubles came up during Brown's trial in 1859, he admitted that she had had problems. See chap. XX of this biography.

19. Deed of sale, Nov. 12, 1825, Stutler Collection.

20. Brown's correspondence with Seth Thompson, 1826-1849, is in the Atlanta University Library.

III. SMARTING UNDER THE ROD OF PROVIDENCE

1. Edward Arf, "An Abolitionist," Pittsburgh (Pa.) *Post,* May 28, 1899; Foreman to Redpath, Dec. 28, 1859, Hinton Papers, Kansas State Historical Society; Delamater's address about John Brown, Stutler Collection; "His Soul Goes Marching On," Cleveland *Press,* May 3, 1895; William B. Lingo, *The Pennsylvania Career of John Brown* (Corry, Pa., 1926), 30; Ernest C. Miller, *John Brown, Pennsylvania Citizen* (Warren, Pa., 1952), 3-5.

2. Henry L. Kellogg's interview with Owen Brown, "How John Brown Left the Lodge," *Christian Cynosure,* XIX (March 31, 1887), 2; Brown to his father, June 12, 1830, John Brown Collection, Ohio Historical Society; Ernest C. Miller, "John Brown's Ten Years in Northwestern Pennsylvania," *Pennsylvania History,* XV (January, 1948), 25-26.

3. Boyd B. Stutler, "Abraham Lincoln and John Brown—A Parallel," *Civil War History,* VIII (September, 1962), 297; Mary Ann Brown's statement in James Redpath, *Public Life of Capt. John Brown* (Boston, 1860), 70.

4. Foreman to Redpath, Dec. 28, 1859, Hinton Papers, Kansas State Historical Society; Delamater's address, Stutler Collection; Miller, John Brown, *Pennsylvania Citizen,* 6-7.

5. Notes for a sermon in John Brown's handwriting, undated, Stutler Collection.

6. Brown to his father, June 12, 1830, John Brown Collection, Ohio Historical Society; Sanborn, *Life and Letters of John Brown,* 37-39; Delamater's address, Stutler Collection; Foreman to Redpath, Dec. 28, 1859, Hinton Papers, Kansas State Historical Society.

7. Delamater's address, Stutler Collection; Jason Brown's statement in Villard, *John Brown,* 19; Ruth's statement in Sanborn, *Life and Letters of John Brown,* 93-95. See also Arthur W. Calhoun, *A Social History of the American Family* (reprint ed., 3 vols., New York, 1960), II, 92-93.

8. John Jr.'s statement in Sanborn, *Life and Letters of John Brown,* 91-93;

Ruth's statement in *ibid.*, 39; Foreman to Redpath, Dec. 28, 1859, Hinton Papers, Kansas State Historical Society; Villard, *John Brown*, 20.

9. Brown to Thompson, April 13, 1832, Brown Letters, Atlanta University. See also letters of Sept. 6, 1830; March 4, July 23, Oct. 1, 1831; Aug. 17, Nov. 3, Dec. 24, 1832; Jan. 11, March 2, 1833; and March 1, 1834.

10. See for example Brown to Thompson, Aug. 13 and 20, 1831; Nov. 3 and Dec. 24, 1832, *ibid.*

11. Brown to his father, Aug. 11, 1832, in Ruchames, *A John Brown Reader*, 41; Brown to Thompson, Aug. 13, 1831 [1832], Brown Letters, Atlanta University.

12. Robert Penn Warren, *John Brown, the Making of a Martyr* (New York, 1929), 29; Foreman to Redpath, Dec. 28, 1859, Hinton Papers, Kansas State Historical Society; John S. Duncan, "John Brown in Pennsylvania," *Western Pennsylvania Historical Magazine*, XI (January, 1928), 50; Villard, *John Brown*, 24-25.

13. Brown to Thompson, Jan. 11, 1833, and March 1 and Nov. 20, 1834, Brown Letters, Atlanta University.

14. *The Liberator*, Jan. 1, 1831, and Jan. 1, 1833; John L. Thomas, *The Liberator: William Lloyd Garrison* (Boston, 1963), 71-280 and *passim*.

15. The best and most recent general studies of the abolitionist crusade are Louis Filler's *The Crusade Against Slavery, 1830-1860* (New York, 1960) and Dwight Lowell Dumond's *Antislavery: the Crusade for Freedom in America* (Ann Arbor, Mich., 1961). But see also Martin Duberman (ed.), *The Antislavery Vanguard: New Essays on the Abolitionists* (Princeton, N.J., 1965).

16. Hudson *Observer and Telegraph*, issues of July 12, 1832, through Jan. 31, 1833; Edward C. Reilley, "Early Slavery Controversy on the Western Reserve" (unpublished Ph.D. dissertation, Western Reserve University, 1940), 3-52; Mary Land, "John Brown's Ohio Environment," *Ohio Archaeological and Historical Quarterly*, LVII (January, 1948), 30-32; Frederick Clayton Waite, *Western Reserve University: the Hudson Era* (Cleveland, 1943), 44-45.

17. Villard, *John Brown*, 49; Brown's remarks about Garrison in chap. III of "Sambos Mistakes" (1848), MS, Maryland Historical Society. The document is printed in Ruchames, *A John Brown Reader*, 61-64.

18. *Ibid.*; Foreman to Redpath, Dec. 28, 1859, Hinton Papers, Kansas State Historical Society; Thomas Wentworth Higginson's statement in Redpath, *Public Life of Capt. John Brown*, 69.

19. Sanborn, *Life and Letters of John Brown*, 40-41.

20. See Brown's letter to Kent in April, 1835, in "John Brown of Harper's Ferry," Kent (Ohio) *Courier*, Sept. 14, 1906; Villard, *John Brown*, 26.

IV. OHIO AGAIN

1. R. Carlyle Buley, *The Old Northwest: Pioneer Period, 1815-1840* (2 vols., Bloomington, Ind., 1951), I, 563.

2. Agreement of Seth Thompson and John Brown, Jan. 13, 1836, and Brown to Thompson, Feb. 8 and 25, 1836, Apr. 4, June 25, and July 23, 1836, Brown Letters, Atlanta University; bond for a deed to a lot in Hudson, written and signed by John Brown, June 1, 1836, Stutler Collection. Also see Villard, *John Brown*, 27.

3. Buley, *The Old Northwest*, II, 260.

4. Brown to Thompson, Dec. 30, 1836, Brown Letters, Atlanta University.

5. Brown to Thompson, Feb. 24, March 25, and Aug. 2, 1837, *ibid*. According to Villard, Brown had twenty-one lawsuits brought against him in Ohio between 1829 and 1845—many of them involving his land speculations in 1836-1837. Brown lost ten of these suits, settled two out of court, and saw three others thrown out as invalid cases for action. He actually won four cases—one of them involving a suit which an alleged horse thief brought against Brown for false arrest and assault and battery, after Brown had assisted a constable in apprehending the man. Of the other two suits one was a judgment against Brown entered by his own consent; the other "was an amicable suit in debt." Villard, *John Brown*, 36-37.

6. Kent's statement in Villard, *John Brown*, 28; Cincinnati *Daily Gazette*, Feb. 12, 1840; John Jr.'s statement in Sanborn, *Life and Letters of John Brown*, 88.

7. Villard, *John Brown*, 37-41. Hill Peebles Wilson, in his diatribe against Brown, *John Brown, Soldier of Fortune: A Critique* (Lawrence, Kans., 1913), 29, charged that the methods Brown employed in the Westlands controversy "were of the most fradulent and criminal nature." There is no evidence that Brown deliberately perpetrated a fraud on Oviatt or that Oviatt or anybody else accused him of doing so.

8. Buley, *The Old Northwest*, II, 620; Reilley, "Early Slavery Controversy on the Western Reserve," 53-61, 124, 191-204, 378-379; C. Bruce Staiger, "Abolitionism and the Presbyterian Schism of 1837-1838," *Mississippi Valley Historical Review*, XXXVI (December, 1949), 391-414; Harold Davis, "Religion in the Western Reserve," *Ohio Archaeological and Historical Quarterly*, XXXVII (July, 1929), 491-493; Fairchild, "The Story of Congregationalism on the Western Frontier," *Papers of the Ohio Church Society*, V (Oberlin, Ohio, 1894), 22-23.

9. Cleveland *Herald*, Aug. 11, 1835; Hudson *Observer and Telegraph*, Sept. 7, 1835; Reilley, "Early Slavery Controversy on the Western Reserve," 146-148, 235-238; Buley, *The Old Northwest*, II, 620-621.

10. Cincinnati *Philanthropist*, Jan. 20, 1837; Reilley, "Early Slavery Controversy on the Western Reserve," 240.

11. Reminiscence of the Rev. Edward Brown (a cousin of John Brown who was a student at Western Reserve College at the time of the public meeting where Brown made his vow against slavery), *Nation*, XCVIII (Feb. 12, 1914), 157. The reminiscence is reprinted in edited form in Ruchames, *A John Brown Reader*, 179-181, and is discussed at length in J. Newton Brown, "Lovejoy's Influence on John Brown," *Magazine of History*, XXIII

(Sept.-Oct., 1916), 97-103. Lora Case, another Hudson citizen who was present at the prayer meeting, gave a slightly different version from that of the Rev. Mr. Brown. Said Case: "John arose and in his calm, emphatic way says: 'I pledge myself with God's help that I will devote my life to increasing hostility towards slavery.'" Copy of Lora Case's Reminiscences (from the scrapbook of George A. Miller of Hudson, Ohio), Stutler Collection.

12. Members of Brown's family and all the legend-building biographies—most notably those by Brown's friends and associates, James Redpath, Franklin B. Sanborn, and Richard J. Hinton—claimed after Harpers Ferry that the "greatest or principal object" of Brown's adult life was the destruction of slavery. Villard, on the basis of family recollections, also maintained this traditional view. Actually, as the present biography attempts to show, the facts of Brown's life belie the traditional picture of Brown as a fighting abolitionist single-mindedly committed to eradicating slavery from the 1830's and 1840's on. This is *not* to say that Brown was no abolitionist or that he did not hate slavery and oppose all those who defended it or who practiced racial discrimination in the North as well, because he did— passionately. Yet it was not until 1855-1856, as this volume shows, that fighting slavery became the major concern of Brown's life.

13. Sanborn, *Life and Letters of John Brown*, 53; Waite, *Western Reserve University: the Hudson Era*, 167; Land, "John Brown's Ohio Environment," *Ohio State Archaeological and Historical Quarterly*, LVII, 30-32; C. B. Galbreath, "John Brown" and "Anti-slavery Movement in Columbiana County," *ibid.*, XXX (July, 1921), 184-289, 355-396.

14. I am heavily indebted to the Rev. Clarence S. Gee of Lockport, N.Y., for information regarding Brown's membership in both the Congregational Church in Hudson and that in Franklin Mills. Dr. Gee served as pastor of the Hudson church from 1921 to 1926 and during that time made a careful study of the records of that institution as well as those of the church in Franklin Mills (now Kent). He was kind enough to share the fruits of his labors with me.

15. Foreman to Redpath, Dec. 28, 1859, Hinton Papers, Kansas State Historical Society.

16. Higginson's statement in Redpath, *Public Life of Capt. John Brown*, 69.

17. Statements of John Jr. and Ruth Brown Thompson in Sanborn, *Life and Letters of John Brown*, 37, 52-53. According to Jason, Brown called him, Owen, and John Jr. into the kitchen of their home in Franklin Mills one night in 1839 and there had them join with him in a solemn pledge "to do all in their power to abolish slavery." If this incident happened, Brown doubtless meant that they should help convert Northern opinion to abolitionism, try to educate free blacks, and assist runaways on the Underground Railroad, as other abolitionists dedicated to overthrowing slavery were doing. John Jr. told Sanborn that Brown, on the night of the family pledge, "informed us of his determination to make war on slavery . . . by

force of arms." No contemporary evidence exists that Brown at this time planned to oppose slavery with force.

18. Statement of Simon Perkins in Sanborn, *Recollections of Seventy Years* (2 vols., Boston, 1909), I, 109. In 1853 Brown seriously considered uniting with a little community church in North Elba, N.Y., where he lived intermittently after 1849. I could find no evidence, however, that he ever joined that or any other church during these years. See Brown to Ruth Brown Thompson, June 30, 1853, Sanborn, *Life and Letters of John Brown*, 109-110.

19. Brown, "Sambos Mistakes," MS, Maryland Historical Society; Perkins' statement in Sanborn, *Recollections*, I, 109; Stutler, "Abraham Lincoln and John Brown—A Parallel," *Civil War History*, VIII, 290-299.

20. Brown to his wife and children, June 12, 1838, and Jan. 23, 1839, Franklin B. Sanborn Folder, Houghton Library of Harvard University.

21. Brown to Thompson, Dec. 13, 1838, and May 28, 1839, Brown Letters, Atlanta University; Brown to his wife and children, Feb. 6 and June 12, 1839, Sanborn Folder, Houghton Library of Harvard University; Brown to his wife and children, May 28, 1839, John Brown Jr. Papers, Ohio Historical Society; Brown to George Kellogg, Aug. 27, 1839, photostatic copy in John Brown Papers, Library of Congress.

22. Villard, *John Brown*, 31.

23. Boyd B. Stutler, "John Brown and the Oberlin Lands," *West Virginia History*, XII (Apr., 1951), 189, 192-193, 195-198. As Stutler implies, Brown was not contemplating any sort of attack against slavery when he went to survey the Oberlin lands in western Virginia, nor did he return to Ohio with any such plan. See also his letter to his wife, Apr. 27, 1840, John Brown Papers, Henry E. Huntington Library.

24. Jan. 18, 1841, John Brown Jr. Papers, Ohio Historical Society.

25. Clipping of John Brown Jr.'s autobiographical statement in Cleveland *Leader* (ca. 1879), Sanborn, Scrapbooks, IV, Stutler Collection.

26. Arrangement between Brown and Oviatt, Jan. 3, 1842, Stutler Collection. Oviatt said of Brown in 1859: "Through life he has been distinguished for his integrity, and esteemed a very conscientious man by those who have known him." Sanborn, *Life and Letters of John Brown*, 67.

27. Brown to Kellogg, Nov. 15, 1841, Stutler Collection; Salmon Brown, "My Father, John Brown," *Outlook*, CIII (Jan. 25, 1913), 212-213; Brown to Thompson, September, 1842, Brown Letters, Atlanta University; Brown's agreement with Kellogg in Sanborn, *Life and Letters of John Brown*, 55-56; Brown's agreement with Oviatt, Oct. 29, 1842, Brown Letters, Western Reserve Historical Society. A list of the property Brown retained after the bankruptcy settlement is in the Stutler Collection.

28. Ruth's statement in Sanborn, *Life and Letters of John Brown*, 33-40, 93-95; Salmon Brown, "My Father, John Brown," *Outlook*, CIII, 212-214; quotation about Brown's father from Brown to his wife and children, May 28, 1839,

John Brown Jr. Papers, Ohio Historical Society; Villard, *John Brown*, 19-20.

29. Brown to Franklin B. Sanborn, Feb. 24, 1858, John Brown Jr. Papers, Ohio Historical Society.

30. Sept. 25, 1843, Brown Letters, Illinois State Historical Library; Mary Ann Brown's statement in Sanborn, *Life and Letters of John Brown*, 497.

V. SPRINGFIELD CRUSADER

1. Jan. 11, 1844, John Brown Jr. Papers, Ohio Historical Society; agreement between Brown and Perkins, Jan. 9, 1844, Sanborn Folder, Houghton Library of Harvard University.

2. Brown to John Jr., June 22, 1844, Sanborn, *Life and Letters of John Brown*, 61; Brown to John Jr. and Ruth, May 8, 1846, Stutler Collection; Perkins' statement in Sanborn, *Recollections*, I, 109; John Brown, Memorandum Book, 1843-1846, John Brown Papers, Henry E. Huntington Library.

3. Brown to Giddings, June 22, 1848, Oswald Garrison Villard Collection, Columbia University; Brown to Giddings, Feb. 20, 1856, Villard, *John Brown*, 131; Louis Filler (ed.), "An Interview with Charles S. S. Griffing," *Ohio Archaeological and Historical Society Quarterly*, LVIII (April, 1949), 215-216; James Harris Fairchild, *Underground Railroad* (Cleveland, 1895), 103-106; Delamater's address, Stutler Collection.

4. Filler (ed.), "An Interview with Charles S. S. Griffing," *Ohio Archaeological and Historical Society Quarterly*, LVIII, 216.

5. Perkins' statement in Sanborn, *Life and Letters of John Brown*, 57; Brown to John Jr., March 24, 1846, *ibid.*, 62; Brown to John Jr., Jan. 27, 1846, John Brown Jr. Papers, Ohio Historical Society; John Brown, Memorandum Book, 1843-1846, MS, entry of March 17, 1846, John Brown Papers, Huntington Library; Aaron Erickson to Henry A. Wise, Nov. 8, 1859, John Brown Papers, Library of Congress. Brown had actually been suspicious of wool buyers for several years. See Brown's letter of Sept. 25, 1842, written at Pittsburgh, Pa., copy in Sanborn Folder, Houghton Library of Harvard University.

6. Brown to his wife, March 17, 1844 [1847], Stutler Collection, and Nov. 8, 1846, Villard, *John Brown*, 35-36.

7. John Brown, Letterbooks of Perkins & Brown, 1846-1847, 1849-1850, MSS, Stutler Collection; Brown to his wife, Nov. 29, 1846, *ibid.*; Brown to his father, Oct. 29, 1846, Sanborn, *Life and Letters of John Brown*, 21; Brown to Perkins, July 23, 1846, John Brown Letters, Yale University; Brown to Perkins, Dec. 16, 1846, Stutler Collection; Villard, *John Brown*, 59-60.

8. Brown to John Jr., April 12, June 25, July 6, 1847, John Brown Jr. Papers, Ohio Historical Society; Jason to John Jr., July 14, 1848, *ibid.*; Brown to John Jr., July 9, 1847, Stutler Collection.

9. Villard, *John Brown*, 60-61; statements of E. C. Leonard and Reuben Chap-

man in Sanborn, *Life and Letters of John Brown*, 64-65, 87; Brown, Letter-books of Perkins & Brown, Stutler Collection.

10. Erickson to Henry A. Wise, Nov. 8, 1859, John Brown Papers, Library of Congress. There seems no reason to question the reliability of Erickson as a witness. He was neither a close friend nor a relative of Brown's and was not trying to save him from the gallows by persuading Wise to declare him insane after the Harpers Ferry raid. Of course there is the possibility that Erickson never liked Brown and was giving a strongly biased picture of him. But in my judgment Erickson's letter reads as though he was a man of integrity who wanted to add his experience with Brown to the public record.

11. Sanborn, *Life and Letters of John Brown*, 65; Brown to his father, Jan. 16, 1848, *ibid.*, 24-25; Brown to his father, Dec. 2, 1847, John Brown Papers, Huntington Library; Erickson to Wise, Nov. 8, 1859, John Brown Papers, Library of Congress; Brown to Simon Perkins, Jan. 3, 1848, John Brown Collection, Brown Farm.

12. Mason A. Green, *Springfield, 1636-1886* (Springfield, Mass., 1888), 442, 470-471; Wilbur H. Siebert, *The Underground Railroad from Slavery to Freedom* (New York, 1898), 73; U.S. Bureau of the Census, *The Seventh Census of the United States: 1850* (Washington, D.C., 1853), 51.

13. Brown to John Jr., Apr. 24, 1848, John Brown Jr. Papers, Ohio Historical Society; Brown to Giddings, June 22, 1848, Villard Collection, Columbia University.

14. The original of "Sambos Mistakes" is in the Maryland Historical Society. See also Villard, *John Brown*, 49-50, 68, 659-661. Annie Brown Adams later claimed that Abby Kelly and Lucretia Mott both had influenced Brown and that he had been an advocate of woman suffrage and women's rights. I could find no corroboratory evidence of this.

15. Henry Highland Garnet, *A Memorial Discourse* (Philadelphia, 1865), 44-52.

16. Frederick Douglass, *Life and Times* (Hartford, Conn., 1882), 277-282; Philip S. Foner, *Life and Writings of Frederick Douglass* (4 vols., New York, 1950-1955), II, 49-50; *North Star*, Feb. 11, 1848, and also issues of Nov. 17, 24, and Dec. 8, 1848. See also Thomas Thomas' statement in Sanborn, *Life and Letters of John Brown*, 133. While Brown was in Springfield he had a photograph taken of himself; it shows him with right hand upraised as though he were taking an oath and his left hand holding a banneret. Richard J. Hinton, *John Brown and His Men* (New York, 1894), 27, 32, claimed that another daguerreotype was taken at about the same time; this one showed Brown's Negro helper, Thomas Thomas, standing beside Brown and holding a banneret which contained the letters SPW—Subterranean Pass Way.

17. *North Star*, Feb. 11, 1848.

18. Boyd B. Stutler, who has spent more than fifty years doing research on Brown and his family and owns one of the most valuable Brown collections in the United States, agrees with me that Brown had it in his mind to

interfere directly with slavery in the South in 1846 and 1847. Later Brown himself and some of his Negro friends made repeated references to his old "Subterranean Pass Way" scheme. I am not arguing, of course, that Brown intended to attack Harpers Ferry and incite a general insurrection in 1847, as members of his family insisted in later years. But the Harpers Ferry scheme obviously grew out of Brown's Subterranean Pass Way plan.

19. Villard, *John Brown*, 16; Ruth's statement in Sanborn, *Life and Letters of John Brown*, 38-39; New York *Illustrated News*, Dec. 10, 1859; and see sec. 2, chap. VI, of this biography.

20. Brown to his father, Dec. 2, 1847, and Jan. 16, 1848, Sanborn, *Life and Letters of John Brown*, 23-25; Brown to his father, Dec. 2, 1847, John Brown Papers, Huntington Library. For Frederick's illness, see Brown to Ruth, Sept. 1, 1847, John Brown Collection, Brown Farm, and S. L. Adair, "Life of Frederick Brown," MS, Kansas Collection, University of Kansas.

21. Sanborn, *Life and Letters of John Brown*, 96-97; Ralph V. Harlow, *Gerrit Smith: Philanthropist and Reformer* (New York, 1939), 246.

22. Brown's statement in Jason to John Jr., Feb. 15, 1853, John Brown Jr. Papers, Ohio Historical Society.

23. Brown to his father, Jan. 10, 1849, John Brown Papers, Kansas State Historical Society; Sanborn, *Life and Letters of John Brown*, 96-101; Villard, *John Brown*, 73.

24. Brown to Perkins, March 12 and March 30, May 24, 1849, John Brown Papers, Library of Congress; Brown to Perkins, May 1, 1849, Higginson Papers, Boston Public Library.

25. Erickson to Wise, Nov. 8, 1859, John Brown Papers, Library of Congress.

26. Ruth's statement in Sanborn, *Life and Letters of John Brown*, 44.

27. *Ibid.*, 100-101; Brown to Gerrit Smith, June 20, 1849, Stutler Collection; Villard, *John Brown*, 72-73. The deed to Brown's 244-acre farm, dated Nov. 8, 1849, is in the John Brown Collection, Brown Farm.

28. Richard Henry Dana Jr., Journal, June 23 and 29, 1849, MS, Massachusetts Historical Society; Dana, "How We Met John Brown," *Atlantic Monthly*, XXVIII (July, 1871), 6-7; Samuel Shapiro, *Richard Henry Dana, Jr.: 1815-1882* (East Lansing, Mich., 1961), 34.

29. Brown to Perkins, July 27 and Aug. 15, 1849 (typescript), John Brown Papers, Library of Congress; Brown to John Jr., Aug. 31, Sept. 21, and Oct. 5, 1849, John Brown Jr. Papers, Ohio Historical Society.

30. October, 1849, Brown Letters, Yale University.

VI. FEELING OUR DEPENDENCE

1. Sanborn, *Life and Letters of John Brown*, 64-65, 67-68, 87; Erickson to Wise, Nov. 8, 1859, John Brown Papers, Library of Congress; Thomas Musgrave's statement in *Hampshire Gazette* (Northampton, Mass.), Dec. 6, 1859.

2. Apr. 12, 1850, John Brown Jr. Papers, Ohio Historical Society. Other documents relating to the last disastrous months of Perkins & Brown are in the

John Brown Papers, Huntington Library, the Stutler Collection, and the Brown Letters, Illinois State Historical Library.

3. Brown to John Jr., Nov. 4, Dec. 6, 1850, and Brown to his children, Dec. 14, 1850, John Brown Jr. Papers, Ohio Historical Society; Brown to his wife, Aug. 22, 1850, John Brown Papers, Huntington Library; Brown to his wife, Sept. 4, 1850, copy in Sanborn Folder, Houghton Library of Harvard University.

4. John Jr. to his father, Nov. 29, 1850, and Brown to his wife, Nov. 28, 1850, Sanborn Folder, Houghton Library of Harvard University; Brown to his children, Dec. 4, 1850, John Brown Jr. Papers, Ohio Historical Society.

5. Nov. 28, 1850, Sanborn Folder, Houghton Library of Harvard University.

6. Ruchames, *A John Brown Reader*, 76-78; Brown to his wife, Jan. 17, 1851, Sanborn, *Life and Letters of John Brown*, 132.

7. Ruth's statement in Sanborn, *Life and Letters of John Brown*, 132.

8. Brown to John Jr., March 24, 1851, John Brown Jr. Papers, Ohio Historical Society; Villard, *John Brown*, 75

9. For documents pertaining to Brown's litigation, see Brown to Thomas Middleton, Apr. 2, 1851, John Brown Papers, Huntington Library; Brown to his wife, Oct. 15, 1851, Brown to Perkins, Dec. 3, 1852, Brown letters, Yale University; Brown to Perkins, Oct. 20, 1851, Stutler Collection; Brown to his family, Apr. 16, 1858, Villard, *John Brown*, 65; and Sanborn, *Life and Letters of John Brown*, 79-84.

10. Brown to John Jr., Dec. 1, 1851, and May 14, 1852, John Brown Jr. Papers, Ohio Historical Society; Brown to Ruth and Henry Thompson, Aug. 10, 1852, John Brown Papers, Huntington Library; Brown to Ruth and Henry Thompson, Jan. 23, 1852, John Brown Papers, Chicago Historical Society; Brown to John Jr., Aug. 23 and 26, 1853, Stutler Collection.

11. Brown to Ruth and Henry Thompson, May 10, 1853, Stutler Collection.

12. Brown to Ruth and Henry Thompson, Jan. 23, 1852, Brown Papers, Chicago Historical Society; Brown to John Jr., Aug. 6, 1852, Villard, *John Brown*, 70; Brown to Ruth and Henry Thompson, Aug. 10, 1852, John Brown Papers, Huntington Library.

13. Aug. 26, 1853, John Brown Papers, Stutler Collection. See also Brown to Ruth and Henry Thompson, Sept. 23, 1853, *ibid.*, and Brown to Ruth and Henry Thompson, Sept. 24, 1853, Sanborn, *Life and Letters of John Brown*, 154-155.

14. Jason to John Jr., Feb. 15, 1853, and Brown to John Jr., Feb. 21, 1853, John Brown Jr. Papers, Ohio Historical Society; Brown to Henry and Ruth Thompson, May 10, 1853, Stutler Collection.

15. Sanborn, *Life and Letters of John Brown*, 57, 156-157; Sanborn, *Recollections*, I, 109; John Jr. to his father, Dec. 1, 1850, Feb. 1, 1851, and Brown to John Jr., Apr. 3, 1854, John Brown Jr. Papers, Ohio Historical Society.

16. Brown to Ruth and Henry Thompson, June 30, 1853, and Jan. 25, 1854, Sanborn, *Life and Letters of John Brown*, 109-111, 155; Brown to Ruth and Henry Thompson, Sept. 23, 1853, Stutler Collection.

17. *Frederick Douglass' Paper* (Rochester, N.Y.), Jan. 27, 1854, Spingarn Collection, Howard University; photostatic copy in Stutler Collection.
18. Allan Nevins, *Ordeal of the Union* (2 vols., New York and London, 1947), II, 153-154.
19. Brown to Perkins, June 7, 1854, Stutler Collection; Brown to his wife, June 7 and June 22, 1854, Sanborn Folder, Houghton Library of Harvard University; Brown to John Jr., June 26, 1854, John Brown Jr. Papers, Ohio Historical Society; Brown to John Jr., Aug. 3, 1854, John Brown Papers, Huntington Library; Brown to Ruth and Henry Thompson, Aug. 24, 1854, Byron Reed Collection, Omaha Public Library.

VII. WEST TO THE PROMISED LAND

1. Eli Thayer, *A History of the Kansas Crusade* (New York, 1889), 25ff; Bruce Catton, *This Hallowed Ground* (New York, 1956), 4. See also Samuel A. Johnson, *The Battle Cry of Freedom: the New England Emigrant Aid Company in the Kansas Crusade* (Lawrence, Kans., 1954).
2. James C. Malin, "The Proslavery Background of the Kansas Struggle," *Mississippi Valley Historical Review*, X (December, 1923), 287-297; Nevins, *Ordeal of the Union*, II, 306-311; Lester B. Baltimore, "Benjamin F. Stringfellow: the Fight for Slavery on the Missouri Border," *Missouri Historical Review*, LXII (October, 1967), 14-29.
3. Brown to John Jr., Aug. 21, 1854, Sanborn, *Life and Letters of John Brown*, 191.
4. Aug. 21 and Nov. 2, 1854, *ibid.*, 110-111, 191; Brown to Ruth and Henry Thompson, Sept. 30, 1854, Brown Letters, Western Reserve Historical Society.
5. James Malin, *John Brown and the Legend of Fifty-Six* (Philadelphia, 1942), 492-497, and Appendix; John Jr. to Brown, June 22, 1855, John Brown Papers, Kansas State Historical Society.
6. Brown to Ruth and Henry Thompson, Feb. 13, 1855, Sanborn, *Life and Letters of John Brown*, 192; Brown to John W. Cook, Feb. 13, 1855, John Brown Letters, Torrington Public Library. The Missourians had illegally voted in an election for a territorial congressman back on Nov. 29, 1854, but there is no evidence that the episode had any influence on Brown's decision early in 1855 to go to Kansas.
7. John Jr. to his father, May 6, 1855, copy in Sanborn Folder, Houghton Library of Harvard University; John Jr.'s statement in Sanborn, *Life and Letters of John Brown*, 189; Salmon Brown's statement (typescript) commemorating Jason's death in 1912, Stutler Collection. For descriptions of the terrain around Osawatomie, see Edward P. Bridgman to "Cousin Sidney," May 25, 1856, M. M. Quaife (ed.), "Bleeding Kansas and the Pottawatomie Murders," *Mississippi Valley Historical Review*, VI (March, 1920), 557; and John Everett to his wife, Oct. 28, 1854, "Letters of John and Sarah Everett, 1854-1864," *Kansas Historical Quarterly*, VIII (February, 1939), 5.

8. Salmon to his mother and family, Aug. 10, 1855, Stutler Collection.

9. Sanborn, *Life and Letters of John Brown*, 193.

10. Salmon's letter is in the Sanborn Folder, Houghton Library of Harvard University. Members of Brown's family later claimed that Brown had already developed his "Virginia Plan" to strike a blow at Harpers Ferry and incite a slave insurrection before he went to Kansas; Annie in fact insisted that he regarded Kansas as a training ground for his larger project. There is no contemporary evidence to support this contention. Thus the "plan" Salmon referred to in his letter could only have been Brown's old Subterranean Pass Way scheme.

11. John Jr.'s letter in the Dreer Papers, Historical Society of Pennsylvania; [John Brown], "A Brief History of John Brown Otherwise (old Brown, & his family: *as* connected with Kansas; by one who knows," MS, *ibid.*

12. Brown to his wife, June 28, 1855, Richard D. Webb, *Life and Letters of Captain John Brown* (London, 1861), 416; Lawrence *Herald of Freedom*, Oct. 29, 1859; Harlow, *Gerrit Smith*, 339-341; Hinton, *John Brown and His Men*, 18-19.

13. John Brown Papers, Kansas Historical Society.

14. Copy in Sanborn Folder, Houghton Library of Harvard University.

15. Villard, *John Brown*, 76-78, 84-85, 93, made the inaccurate generalization that Brown went to Kansas to fight slavery from the outset and never gave a thought to settling there. Malin, on the other hand, contends that John Jr.'s reports of impending violence in Kansas did not alter Brown's original intentions for going out, that Brown's decision to collect money and guns in New York, Massachusetts, and Ohio was "unquestionably an afterthought," and that he headed for Kansas, with a wagonload of guns and artillery broadswords, to find "a business deal." (Malin, *John Brown and the Legend of Fifty-Six*, 10-16.) This contention not only disregards John Jr.'s remarks about the lack of business opportunities in his letters of June 22 and 29 but is inconsistent with vital aspects of Brown's character (which Malin disregarded throughout his study)—Brown's belligerent abolitionism, his intense Calvinism and religious zeal, his obvious sense of mission, and his hatred and fear of the "Slave Power" as evidenced in numerous letters, documents, and public utterances quoted throughout the preceding chapters of the present work. Thus (Malin to the contrary) it would seem that Brown himself most accurately described his ultimate reason for going to the territory. "Four of my sons had gone there to settle, and they induced me to go," he told a retinue of interrogators after Harpers Ferry. "I did not go there to settle, but because of the difficulties." See Sanborn, *Life and Letters of John Brown*, 563. Brown implied the same thing in a letter to Jason, Aug. 11, 1856, Kansas Collection, University of Kansas.

16. Brown to his family, Aug. 15, 1855, Villard, *John Brown*, 85-86; Brown to his family, Aug. 23, 1855, Sanborn, *Life and Letters of John Brown*, 199; Sept. 4, 1855, John Brown Papers, Kansas State Historical Society; Sept. 15, 1855, Stutler Collection; Brown to Jason, Aug. 11, 1856, Kansas Collection,

University of Kansas. See also Henry Thompson's statement in Sanborn, *Recollections*, I, 127-128; and [Brown], "A Brief History of John Brown," MS, Dreer Papers, Historical Society of Pennsylvania; and Brown's letter to the editor of the Akron *Summit Beacon*, Dec. 20, 1855, in Ruchames, *A John Brown Reader*, 89.

VIII. THE WICKED SHALL CEASE FROM TROUBLING

1. Brown to his father, Oct. 19, 1855, Clarence S. Gee Collection; Brown to his wife and children, Oct. 13 and Nov. 2, 1855, John Brown Papers, Kansas State Historical Society; Brown to the editor of the Akron *Summit Beacon*, Dec. 20, 1855, in Ruchames, *A John Brown Reader*, 89.

2. August Bondi's statement in Sanborn, *Life and Letters of John Brown*, 272; James Townsley's statement in *ibid.*, 270; S. J. Shively's statement (typescript), Dec. 1, 1903, John Brown Papers, Kansas State Historical Society; Montgomery Shore's interview with William E. Connelley, June 4, 1892, *ibid.*; James Hanway, "Reminiscences [1869]," in Malin, *John Brown and the Legend of Fifty-Six*, 327; testimony of George W. and H. C. Grant, Lawrence *Daily Journal*, Dec. 5, 1879.

3. Affidavit of Louisa Jane Wilkinson, June 13, 1856, "Howard Report," *U.S. House Committee Reports* (3 vols., 34th Cong., 1st Sess., 1855-1856), vol. II, no. 200, pp. 1179-1181; testimony of William Chestnut (an election judge for the Pottawatomie precinct), May 9, 1856, *ibid.*, 231; Hanway, "Reminiscences [1869]," in Malin, *John Brown and the Legend of Fifty-Six*, 327; Hanway, Memorandum Book, entry about June 1, 1856, James Hanway Papers, Kansas State Historical Society; Shively's statement, Dec. 1, 1903, John Brown Papers, *ibid.*; Mrs. Rising's statement in Sanborn, *Life and Letters of John Brown*, 271n.

4. Salmon's statement in Villard, *John Brown*, 158; John Everett to his father, Jan. 25 and Feb. 1, 1856, "Everett Letters," *Kansas Historical Quarterly*, VIII, 25-27; Eugene H. Berwanger, *Frontier Against Slavery: Anti-Negro Prejudice and the Slavery Extension Controversy* (Urbana, Ill., 1967), 97-115.

5. Five conventions met in Lawrence on or before August 15 to resist the proslavery territorial government. John Brown Jr. was vice-president of one that convened on June 25. Villard, *John Brown*, 91.

6. *Ibid.*, 103-104; Malin, "Proslavery Background of the Kansas Struggle," *Mississippi Valley Historical Review*, X, 299.

7. Wealthy and John Brown Jr. to Mary Ann Brown, Sept. 16, 1855, copy in Sanborn Folder, Houghton Library of Harvard University.

8. John Brown Papers, Kansas State Historical Society; see also Brown to his father, Oct. 19, 1855, Gee Collection. Actually, as Malin pointed out, neither John Jr., Jason, Owen, Frederick, nor Salmon had completed title to their claims. Whether they would have done so eventually is impossible to say. In any case, after the Pottawatomie Massacre, Missourians burned

their cabins and shanties and stole their livestock; and the ensuing civil war ended any plans on their part for permanent settlement in Kansas.

9. Brown to the editor of the Akron *Summit Beacon*, Dec. 20, 1855, in Ruchames, *A John Brown Reader*, 89; Brown to his wife and children, Nov. 2, 1855, John Brown Papers, Kansas State Historical Society; Ellen's letter quoted in Villard, *John Brown*, 112; Brown to his wife and children, Nov. 20, 1855, Stutler Collection, and Nov. 23, 1855, Webb, *Life and Letters of Captain John Brown*, 416.

10. Adair told this to John and Sarah Everett, who repeated the statement in a letter to a relative, Dec. 31, 1859, John Everett Papers, Kansas State Historical Society. Adair and the Everetts were honest people, and I see no reason to question Adair's assertion that Brown (a Calvinist who believed in predestination) thought God had raised him to "break the jaws of the wicked." A Quaker named Richard Mendenhall, in Sanborn, *Life and Letters of John Brown*, 327, said he heard Adair make a comparable remark about Brown.

11. Unless otherwise cited, my account of Brown's activities in the Wakarusa War was drawn from Brown's letter to the Akron *Summit Beacon*, Dec. 20, 1855, Ruchames, *A John Brown Reader*, 89-93; Brown to his wife and children, Dec. 16, 1855, John Brown Papers, Kansas State Historical Society; Brown to *Frederick Douglass' Paper*, letter dated Dec. 17, 1855, published on Jan. 11, 1856; Brown to Orson Day, Dec. 14, 1855, John Brown Jr. Papers, Ohio Historical Society; and John Jr.'s letter of Dec. 22, 1855, in Western Reserve *Chronicle* (Warren, Ohio), Jan. 16, 1856, copy in Stutler Collection.

12. Lawrence *Herald of Freedom*, Dec. 15, 1855, and Oct. 29, 1859; G. W. Brown's statement in Sanborn, *Recollections*, I, 102. The muster roll of Brown's company (in the Ferdinand Julius Dreer Papers, Historical Society of Pennsylvania) gives the dates of its services from Nov. 27 to Dec. 12, 1855, although the company was not organized until Dec. 7.

13. Lawrence *Herald of Freedom*, Oct. 29, 1859; James F. Legate's statement in Leavenworth *Weekly Press*, Oct. 23, 1879, clipping in John Brown, Scrapbooks (16 vols.), I, Kansas State Historical Society; Villard, *John Brown*, 123-124; Henry Thompson's statement in Sanborn, *Recollections*, I, 129. A correspondent wrote the New York *Evening Post* that the defenders of Lawrence were ready to fight. "The great difficulty is to restrain our men from making a sally upon the camp on Wakarusa." Nevins, *Ordeal of the Union*, II, 410.

14. William Phillips, *The Conquest of Kansas, by Missouri and Her Allies* (Boston, 1856), 220-222; Brown to his wife and children, Dec. 16, 1855, John Brown Papers, Kansas State Historical Society.

15. Legate's statement in Leavenworth *Weekly Press*, Oct. 23, 1879. At this distance Legate's story seems sound enough. It is inconceivable that Brown would not ask him what slaves in the South were like.

16. Nevins, *Ordeal of the Union,* II, 411; Leverett W. Spring, *Kansas, the Prelude to the War for the Union* (Boston, 1885), 97-101.

17. James Malin, *John Brown and the Legend of Fifty-Six,* 3, claimed that Brown was a dishonest criminal-type before he came to Kansas and was thus unreliable as a witness (see note 9, chap. XII for a brief critique of the Malin thesis of Brown). True, Brown had a talent for overstatement, especially when he was excited. And true, after he had embarked on his grand scheme to invade the South he could distort facts or leave them out, and even lie about his true intentions, because he believed that his mission to free the slaves was divinely inspired and so anything he did in pursuit of that end was justifiable. Still at other times Brown could be as honest as Moses. And the letters he composed about the Wakarusa War are a case in point. They are all consistent in their presentation of the facts (no "compulsive liar" would tell a consistent story over and over), and they are also commendably accurate eyewitness accounts. For biblographical particulars of these letters, see note 11 in this chapter.

18. Redpath, *Public Life of Capt. John Brown,* 103-104. Returns for the Pottawatomie precinct in the December 15 elections are in "Howard Report," *U.S. House Committee Reports,* 1855-1856, II, 733-734.

19. Dec. 20, 1855, in Ruchames, *A John Brown Reader,* 93.

IX. SIGNS AND PORTENTS

1. Brown to his wife and children, Dec. 16, 1855, and Feb. 1, 1856, John Brown Papers, Kansas State Historical Society; Jan. 1, 1856, Stutler Collection; Feb. 6, 1856, Sanborn, *Life and Letters of John Brown,* 222-223. See also Owen Brown's letters to John Brown, Nov. 26, 1855, and March 27, 1856, John Brown Papers, Kansas State Historical Society; Adair, "Life of Frederick Brown," MS, Kansas Collection, University of Kansas.

2. Jan. 1, 1856, Stutler Collection; Brown to Orson Day, Feb. 21, 1856, Kansas Collection, University of Kansas; Brown to his wife and children, Feb. 1, 1856, John Brown Papers, Kansas State Historical Society; Salmon's statement commemorating Jason's death, *ibid.* On January 15 Brown purchased a $20 share in the capital stock of the New England Emigrant Aid Society. It is not clear whether he did so before or after he sold his horse and wagon.

3. Brown to his wife and children, Feb. 1, 1856, John Brown Papers, Kansas State Historical Society; Villard, *John Brown,* 93, 127.

4. "Howard Report," *U.S. House Committee Reports,* 1855-1856, II, 779; Hanway, "Reminiscences [1869]," in Malin, *John Brown and the Legend of Fifty-Six,* 325.

5. Villard, *John Brown,* 129; "Howard Report," *U.S. House Committee Reports,* 1855-1856, II, 981ff.

6. John Brown Papers, Kansas State Historical Society.

7. Sanborn, *Life and Letters of John Brown,* 223; Brown to Giddings, Feb. 20,

1856, Villard, *John Brown*, 131; Giddings to Brown, March 17, 1856, John Brown Papers, Kansas State Historical Society.

8. Appeal of the Lafayette Kansas Emigration Society, March 25, 1856, *National Intelligencer*, Apr. 12, 1856; Nevins, *Ordeal of the Union*, II, 430.
9. See James B. Abbott of Lawrence to his mother, Feb. 17, 1856, Abbott Papers, Kansas State Historical Society; Brown to his wife and children, Feb. 20, 1856, Sanborn, *Life and Letters of John Brown*, 223; and John Jr.'s letter of Apr. 4, 1856, in *Frederick Douglass' Paper*, May 2, 1856, copy in Stutler Collection.
10. "The Topeka Movement," *Publications of the Kansas State Historical Society* (17 vols., Topeka, 1875-1928), XIII, 188-192; Malin, *John Brown and the Legend of Fifty-Six*, 509-536; Wealthy Brown to "Friend Louisa," March 23, 1856, Stutler Collection; Villard, *John Brown*, 133.
11. John Jr.'s letter of Apr. 4, 1856, in *Frederick Douglass' Paper*, May 2, 1856, copy in Stutler Collection. John Jr. said that Lane initiated him into the Kansas Regulators in a room of Garvey's Hotel in Topeka (Sanborn, *Life and Letters of John Brown*, 344-346). There is no contemporary evidence that John Brown himself ever joined the secret society.
12. John Jr. to "Friend Louisa," March 29, 1856, Stutler Collection.
13. Brown to his wife and children, Apr. 7, 1856, John Brown Papers, Kansas State Historical Society. Brown's biblical quote, "Their foot shall slide in due time" (Deut. 32:35), also formed the basis for the text in the older Jonathan Edwards' famous sermon, "Sinners in the Hands of an Angry God," which Brown had read.
14. John Jr.'s letter of Apr. 29, 1856, in Lawrence *Herald of Freedom*, May 10, 1856; Malin, *John Brown and the Legend of Fifty-Six*, 531. Hill Peebles Wilson, *John Brown, Soldier of Fortune*, 99, conjectures that Brown and Henry Thompson were about to engage in "the theft of a large number of horses on Pottawatomie Creek," and that is why they planned to leave the neighborhood. There is not only no evidence but no excuse for Wilson's assertion. In fact, his entire volume is so biased against Brown (it was written to correct the favorable portrait of Brown in Villard) and is so rife with unsupported conjectures to prove that Brown was an unscrupulous soldier of fortune (an American "Captain Kidd") that nobody should take the book seriously as history. As it turned out, Mrs. Sara T. Robinson, whose late husband had challenged the legend of Brown as presented in the hero-worshiping biographies by James Redpath, Franklin Sanborn, and Richard J. Hinton, had promised Wilson $5,000 to do this book. She died without paying up, however, and Wilson had to sue her heirs to get his money. James Malin (who wrote to destroy the Brown legend) later claimed that Wilson had arrived at his views before Mrs. Robinson commissioned him to write his book. If so, that still does not alter what the book is: an anti-Brown tract that will always be enjoyed, as C. B. Galbreath put it, "by the critically inclined who place a low estimate upon humanitarian

endeavor and reluctantly accord unselfish motives to others." Galbreath, "John Brown," *Ohio Archaeological and Historical Quarterly*, XXX, 194.

15. Hanway, "Reminiscences [1869]," in Malin, *John Brown and the Legend of Fifty-Six*, 325. The exact date the Rifles were organized is not known; it was probably around mid-April. The outfit may have been formed as part of a general program of home defense advised by the Topeka legislature. See *ibid.*, 536.

16. My account of the settlers' meeting at Osawatomie was drawn from Martin White's speech before the territorial legislature, Feb. 13, 1857, in the Leavenworth *Herald*, March 21, 1857; White's letter to the Bates County (Mo.) *Standard*, Jan. 14, 1860; Samuel L. Adair to J. H. Holmes, July 9, 1894, in Villard, *John Brown*, 134; Mendenhall's statement in Sanborn, *Life and Letters of John Brown*, 326; O. C. Brown, "The Settlers' Meeting and Protest of April 16, 1856, in Osawatomie," MS, and "Pioneer Life in Kansas, 1854 to 1861," MS, O. C. Brown Papers, Kansas State Historical Society; and Joseph B. Higgins' testimony in Malin, "The Hoogland Examination," *Kansas Historical Quarterly*, VII (May, 1938), 146. The official report of the meeting, prepared by Mendenhall and Dayton and published in the Lawrence *Free State*, May 5, 1856, stated that the gathering was "large and enthusiastic" and that the resolutions were "unanimously" adopted. The report mentioned nothing about Brown and White's speeches or the conservative bolt. Obviously these were left out of the report on purpose, so that the territorial officers might think Osawatomie and Pottawatomie stood united in opposition to the proslavery laws.

17. Brown to his wife and children, Apr. 17, 1856, Webb, *Life and Letters of Captain John Brown*, 420.

18. Journal of U.S. Court of Second Judicial District, Kansas Territory, in session at Dutch Henry's Crossing, entries for Apr. 21 and 22, 1856, Federal Records Center, Kansas City, Mo. See also Malin, *John Brown and the Legend of Fifty-Six*, 540-547.

19. Affidavits of Mahala and John Doyle, June 7, 1856, "Howard Report," *U.S. House Committee Reports*, 1855-1856, II, 1175, 1176; Maggie Moore and Mahala Doyle to A. A. Lawrence, May 26, 1885, in Villard, *John Brown*, 156.

20. Hanway, "Reminiscences [1869]," in Malin, *John Brown and the Legend of Fifty-Six*, 325-326; John Jr.'s letter of Apr. 29, 1856, in Lawrence *Herald of Freedom*, May 10, 1856; Brown to Adair, Apr. 22, 1856, copy in Sanborn Folder, Houghton Library of Harvard University; Salmon's statement in Villard, *John Brown*, 135-136; Henry Thompson's statement in Sanborn, *Recollections*, I, 129. Salmon and Henry both claimed that the court "got out warrants for all the Browns," but there is no evidence of that in the court's records and neither Brown himself nor John Jr. mentioned any such warrants in the letters cited above.

21. Hanway, "Reminiscences [1869]," in Malin, *John Brown and the Legend of Fifty-Six*, 326; and Hanway, "The Settlement of Lane and Vicinity," MS, Hanway Papers, Kansas State Historical Society. The reader will note my frequent citations to Hanway's letters and published writings about Brown's Kansas career in 1856. Hanway, as Malin pointed out, "was the first friend of John Brown to make a determined effort to establish the facts with regard to him in Kansas, especially those touching the controversial Pottawatomie massacre question. He believed that the facts did not discredit Brown but, on the contrary, justified the act." Even though Hanway was a friend of Brown's, his writings constitute some of the most accurate and honest eyewitness accounts of the Kansas troubles of 1856. Even James Malin, who distrusted free-state witnesses (especially those friendly to Brown), had to admit that Hanway strove to tell the truth. See *John Brown and the Legend of Fifty-Six*, 310-343.

22. Journal of the U.S. Court of Second Judicial District, Kansas Territory, entries for Apr. 21-22 and Apr. 28-May 1, 1856, Federal Records Center, Kansas City, Mo.; Malin, *John Brown and the Legend of Fifty-Six*, 559.

23. John Jr.'s letter of Apr. 4, 1856, in *Frederick Douglass' Paper*, May 2, 1856, copy in Stutler Collection, and letter of Apr. 29, 1856, in Lawrence *Herald of Freedom*, May 10, 1856; Hanway, "Reminiscences [1869]," in Malin, *John Brown and the Legend of Fifty-Six*, 325; O. C. Brown to [?], June 24, 1856, O. C. Brown Papers, Kansas State Historical Society; Florilla Adair to "Martha," May 16, 1856, Villard Collection, Columbia University.

24. The evidence that open hostility existed between the proslavery and free-state factions on the Pottawatomie and that the Wilkinson-Sherman-Doyle faction flung threats and insults at their free-state rivals seems quite convincing. See James Hanway's Memorandum Book, MS, entry about June 1, 1856, Hanway Papers, Kansas State Historical Society; Hanway to James Redpath, March 12, 1860, *ibid.*; Samuel Adair to "Dear Bro. & Sis. Hand & Other Friends," written shortly after the Pottawatomie Massacre, Villard Collection, Columbia University; Edward P. Bridgman to "Cousin Sidney," May 27, 1856, in Quaife (ed.), "Bleeding Kansas and the Pottawatomie Murders," *Mississippi Valley Historical Review*, VI, 559; James H. Carruth to the Watertown (N.Y.) *Reformer*, letter dated May 31, 1856, reprinted in the Overbrook (Kans.) *Citizen*, June 25, 1908; and O. C. Brown to [?], June 24, 1856, O. C. Brown Papers, Kansas State Historical Society. For corroborative accounts, see James Hanway's Scrapbook as quoted in Hanway to Judge Adams, Feb. 1, 1878, John Brown Papers, *ibid.*; Sanborn, *Life and Letters of John Brown*, 253-256; James Townsley's statement in *ibid.*, 269-270; and William G. and H. C. Grant's testimony in Lawrence *Daily Journal*, Dec. 5, 1879.

25. Had free-state men continued to regard the local proslavery threat as more serious than the long-expected Missouri invasion, thirty-four of them

would not have marched away to defend Lawrence on May 21, leaving their families and the older free-state settlers virtually defenseless.

26. James Hanway concluded by 1860 that the Shermans, Doyles, and Wilkinson had actually worked out a plan to burn out the free-state men of Pottawatomie (see note 6 of chap. XI). However, there is no convincing contemporary evidence that this was so.

27. Villard, *John Brown*, 139-142; Walter L. Fleming, "The Buford Expedition to Kansas," *American Historical Review*, VI (October, 1900), 39-43.

28. There are so many versions of the "surveyor story" that it is impossible to say exactly when it happened or what Brown actually learned in the Georgians' camp. Brown mentioned the incident in "An Idea of Things in Kansas," MS, John Brown Papers, Kansas State Historical Society, which was drawn from several speeches he delivered in the East in the spring of 1857, but he did not state specifically what he overheard. Salmon and Hanway's versions (probably based on what Brown himself said in conversation) asserted that the incident happened around April 21 or April 22 (over a week before the Southerners actually arrived in Kansas); John Jr. said it occurred a few days before the sacking of Lawrence. See Salmon Brown, "John Brown and Sons in Kansas Territory," *Indiana Magazine of History*, XXXI (June, 1935), 142-150, and Salmon Brown to William E. Connelley, May 28, 1913, Stutler Collection; Hanway, "Reminiscences [1868]," in Malin, *John Brown and the Legend of Fifty-Six*, 333; and John Jr.'s statement in Sanborn, *Life and Letters of John Brown*, 260n.

29. Nevins, *Ordeal of the Union*, II, 435; Malin, "Proslavery Background of the Kansas Struggle," *Mississippi Valley Historical Review*, X, 285-305; James Ford Rhodes, *History of the United States from the Compromise of 1850* (7 vols., New York, 1894-1913), II, 158.

30. John Jr.'s statement in Cleveland *Leader*, Nov. 29, 1883; H. H. Williams' letter in the New York *Tribune*, Aug. 20, 1856; Brown to his wife and children, June 24, 1856, Brown Letters, Illinois State Historical Library.

X. BLOODY POTTAWATOMIE

1. John Brown Jr.'s letter in the Cleveland *Leader*, Nov. 29, 1883; H. H. Williams' letter in the New York *Tribune*, Aug. 20, 1856; Hanway, "Reminiscences [1869]," in Malin, *John Brown and the Legend of Fifty-Six*, 329; statements of Jason, Salmon, and Wealthy Brown and of Mrs. B. F. Jackson in Villard, *John Brown*, 173.

2. Brown to his wife and children, June 24, 1856, Brown Letters, Illinois State Historical Library; Hanway, "Reminiscences [1868 and 1869]," in Malin, *John Brown and the Legend of Fifty-Six*, 328-329; Williams' letter in New York *Tribune*, Aug. 20, 1856; Hanway to James Redpath, March 12, 1860, Hanway Papers, Kansas State Historical Society; testimony of Joseph B. Higgins, Daniel W. Collis, and Harvey Jackson at the Hoogland

examination at Tecumseh, Kans., on June 20, 1856, in the *New York Times,* July 8, 1856; see also Malin, "Hoogland Examination," *Kansas Historical Quarterly,* VII, 149-152.

3. Salmon Brown, "John Brown and Sons in Kansas Territory," *Indiana Magazine of History,* XXXI (June, 1935), 142-150; statements of Salmon, Jason, and John Jr. in Villard, *John Brown,* 151-152. There are so many conflicting accounts and interpretations as to what actually motivated Brown to instigate the Pottawatomie massacre that the exact reasons may never be known. I have accepted the "retaliatory blow" thesis (but only after lengthy deliberation) because it seems to fit the logic of events and the behavior of Brown in all the frustration and hysteria that surrounded the sacking of Lawrence. Yet one cannot be certain, and I make no claim that I have proved beyond doubt that the retaliatory blow argument is the final answer to the controversy. Here are some of the other reasons given for the Pottawatomie murders (along with a brief explanation why I question them).

(1) In 1875 Samuel Walker claimed that Brown told him in the summer of 1856 that Lane and Robinson had actually instigated the massacre and that Brown merely executed it. For lack of any convincing corroborative evidence, I have rejected this contention (as did Villard).

(2) Salmon and John Jr. both claimed later that the entire Pottawatomie company knew the complete details of the massacre beforehand, approved of it, and cheered Brown when he left on his mission, and that some of them (Salmon mentioned H. H. Williams specifically) even helped compile the list of proscribed men. This argument is not in accord with the facts given in more contemporary accounts by Williams, Hanway (who seems the most reliable of the free-state witnesses), Townsley, Higgins, Collis, Jackson, and the Grants. Furthermore, if the company knew and approved of the massacre, why did many if not most of the men bitterly condemn the killings on Sunday and Monday?

(3) Numerous witnesses later claimed that a mysterious messenger (they could not agree on who he was) brought news to Ottawa Creek that trouble was expected back on the Pottawatomie. The Doyles (and possibly the Shermans "and others") had vowed to kill "old Squire" Morse, who owned a store near Dutch Henry's Crossing and had sold lead to free-state volunteers, if he did not leave the creek "in five days." This news was supposedly the final blow which moved Brown to strike back at the enemy on the Pottawatomie in a burst of unleashed Calvinist fury. The threat to Morse seems actually to have happened. But whether a messenger brought news of it to Brown before he set out on his "secret mission" is highly questionable. Salmon vigorously denied the messenger story, and the events of Thursday and Friday and the behavior of the old man himself seem to support Salmon's contention. In none of the accounts, for example, did Brown mention the threat to Morse as the reason why he was going

back to "regulate matters" on the creek (nor did he ever mention the Morse incident after the massacre as having had anything directly to do with it). Moreover, if the entire company was apprised of the threat to Morse (and possibly other settlers), why did not John Jr. send a detachment back to protect the threatened men? Would the Rifles still have regarded the Doyles as more bluff than fight? Space does not permit a more detailed analysis of the questions and riddles raised by the controversial messenger story. Suffice it to say that I have not included it in my own narrative as a cause of the massacre because it sounds implausible to me and because there is not enough convincing evidence to support it. But because of the persistence of the story in free-state accounts, one cannot dismiss it completely.

(4) Finally, there is the argument Brown advanced himself, after the massacre. He claimed on several different occasions between the summer of 1856 and December of 1859 that he had found that proslavery men on the creek were on the verge of killing all free-state settlers there and that he had conceived the massacre to save their lives. There is (as I've noted above) scarcely any contemporary evidence to suggest that any such conspiracy was onfoot or that Brown had heard of any such plot before he set out on his secret expedition. Of course, in his rage over the Missouri invasion and the sacking of Lawrence he may well have *thought* such a conspiracy was being plotted, or simply convinced himself that eventually the men he killed would have carried out their recriminations to "exterminate" their free-state neighbors.

(5) James C. Malin gave still another interpretation of why Brown committed the massacre, which I've examined in note 7 of chap. XI.

4. Hanway, "Reminiscences [1868]," in Malin, *John Brown and the Legend of Fifty-Six*, 329 (see also 562-563); Hanway to Richard J. Hinton, Dec. 5, 1859, Hinton Papers, Kansas State Historical Society; Salmon Brown, "John Brown and Sons in Kansas Territory," *Indiana Magazine of History*, XXXI, 142-150; Salmon's statement in Villard, *John Brown*, 154; John Jr.'s letter in Cleveland *Leader*, Nov. 29, 1883; August Bondi, "With John Brown in Kansas," *Publications of the Kansas State Historical Society*, VIII, 279; Bondi, "Narrative," MS, Bondi Papers, Kansas State Historical Society; Grants' testimony in Lawrence *Daily Journal*, Dec. 5, 1879; and Lawrence *Herald of Freedom*, Nov. 5, 1879.

5. Townsley's "Confession" in Lawrence *Daily Journal*, Dec. 10, 1879; Hanway to Hinton, Dec. 5, 1859, Hinton Papers, Kansas State Historical Society; Hanway, "Reminiscences [1868]," in Malin, *John Brown and the Legend of Fifty-Six*, 329-330.

6. Amos Hall's testimony, June 20, 1856, W. I. R. Blackman Papers, Kansas State Historical Society; Williams' letter in the New York *Tribune*, Aug. 20, 1856; Hanway's letter in the Lawrence *Daily Journal*, Nov. 27, 1879; John Jr.'s letter in the Cleveland *Leader*, Nov. 29, 1883; Jason to F. G.

Adams, Apr. 2, 1884, John Brown Papers, Kansas State Historical Society; Church's report, May 26, 1856, *Publications of the Kansas State Historical Society*, IV, 441.

7. Blood's statement in the Lawrence *Daily Journal*, Dec. 3, 1879.

8. Townsley's "Confession" in *ibid.*, Dec. 10, 1879; Townsley's remarks in Sanborn, *Life and Letters of John Brown*, 268; statement of an unnamed member of the party in *ibid.*, 269-270; Salmon's statement in Villard, *John Brown*, 157; and Salmon's statement, MS, Stutler Collection.

9. Salmon's statement, Stutler Collection; Salmon Brown, "John Brown and Sons in Kansas Territory," *Indiana Magazine of History*, XXXI, 142-150; Townsley's "Confession" in the Lawrence *Daily Journal*, Dec. 10, 1879; affidavits of Mahala and John Doyle, June 7, 1856, "Howard Report," *U.S. House Committee Reports*, 1855-1856, II, 1175; statements of Salmon Brown and Henry Thompson in Villard, *John Brown*, 158-160.

10. Affidavit of Louisa Jane Wilkinson, June 13, 1856, "Howard Report," *U.S. House Committee Reports*, 1855-1856, II, 1179-1181. Salmon claimed that the company divided at Wilkinson's place and went on "separate errands"—Thompson and Weiner in one party; Townsley, Owen, Frederick, Salmon, and Oliver in the other. The old man, said Salmon, ran "back and forth between the two parties." Townsley, on the other hand, implied that the company stayed together and so did the descriptions of Brown's party in the affidavits by the Doyles, Mrs. Wilkinson, and James Harris.

11. Affidavit of James Harris, June 6, 1856, *ibid.*, 1178-1179.

12. Townsley's "Confession" in the Lawrence *Daily Journal*, Dec. 10, 1879.

XI. WAR HAS COMMENCED

1. Jason's statement in Sanborn, *Life and Letters of John Brown*, 273; Jason to F. G. Adams, Apr. 2, 1884, John Brown Papers, Kansas State Historical Society; Hanway to Redpath, March 12, 1860, Hanway Papers, *ibid.*; Bridgman to "Cousin Sidney," May 27, 1856, in Quaife (ed.), "Bleeding Kansas and the Pottawatomie Murders," *Mississippi Valley Historical Review*, VI, 559; testimony of Hall and Higgins, June 20, 1856, in Malin, "Hoogland Examination," *Kansas Historical Quarterly*, VII, 147-148; and the Grants' testimony in the Lawrence *Daily Journal*, Dec. 5, 1879.

2. Hanway to Redpath, March 12, 1860, Hanway Papers, Kansas State Historical Society; Hanway, "Reminiscences [1868]," in Malin, *John Brown and the Legend of Fifty-Six*, 331-332; Grants' testimony in the Lawrence *Daily Journal*, Dec. 5, 1879; Sanborn, *Life and Letters of John Brown*, 271. There is some question as to when and why John Jr. resigned his command. In retrospect he said he did so because of the slave liberation episode on Sunday, May 25. Jason, Hanway, and George Grant, however, said that John Jr. resigned on Monday morning, after Brown and his company returned to camp with the confiscated horses. Jason said that

the other men were bitter toward the Browns because of the murders and that John Jr. may have resigned because of their bitterness.

3. Jason's statements in the Lawrence *Daily Journal*, Feb. 8, 1880, and in Sanborn, *Life and Letters of John Brown*, 273; Jason to F. G. Adams, Apr. 2, 1884, John Brown Papers, Kansas State Historical Society; Lawrence *Herald of Freedom*, Nov. 5, 1859; statements of Jason and Salmon in Villard, *John Brown*, 166-167; Collis' testimony, June 20, 1856, in Malin, "Hoogland Examination," *Kansas Historical Quarterly*, VII, 141.

4. Hanway, Memorandum Book, MS, entry about June 1, 1856, Hanway Papers, Kansas State Historical Society; Hanway, "Reminiscences [1869]," in Malin, *John Brown and the Legend of Fifty-Six*, 333-334; Hanway's letter in Cincinnati *Commercial*, July 23, 1856; Hanway to Redpath, March 12, 1860, Hanway Papers, Kansas State Historical Society; Leavenworth *Weekly Herald*, June 14, 1856; Grants' testimony in the Lawrence *Daily Journal*, Dec. 5, 1879.

5. Collis' testimony, June 20, 1856, in Malin, "Hoogland Examination," *Kansas Historical Quarterly*, VII, 141; Hall's testimony, June 20, 1856, Blackman Papers, Kansas State Historical Society; J. G. Grant's statement as cited in Villard, *John Brown*, 167.

6. Hanway, Memorandum Book, entry about June 1, 1856, Hanway Papers, Kansas State Historical Society; Adair to "Dear Bro. & Sis. Hand & Other Friends," written a few days after the massacre, Villard Collection, Columbia University; Carruth to the Watertown (N.Y.) *Reformer*, letter dated May 31, 1856, reprinted in Overbrook (Kans.) *Citizen*, June 25, 1908; O. C. Brown to [?], June 24, 1856, O. C. Brown Papers, Kansas State Historical Society. Hanway and many other free-state settlers later accepted Brown's own after-the-fact justification for the massacre. "I am fully satisfied," Hanway wrote James Redpath on March 12, 1860, "as everybody else is who lived on the Creek in 56; that a base conspiracy was on foot to drive out, burn, and kill;—in a word the Pottawatomie Creek from its mouth to its founded head was to be cleared of every man, woman, or child who was for Kansas being a free state." In murdering those five men (who were allegedly involved in this conspiracy) Brown had saved the lives of his free-state neighbors. This thesis will probably always be argued by some writers; but it seemed to me, in evaluating the mass of contradictory and confusing evidence on the massacre, that Brown never had any proof that such a conspiracy was under way.

7. James Malin, who wrote to demolish the legend of Brown as a free-state hero, accepted and elaborated upon the thesis advanced by the Westport *Border Times* in its issue of May 27, 1856. Malin argued that the Pottawatomie massacre was largely "political assassination," that Brown selected his victims, on the one hand, because they had been associated with Cato's court when it sat in session at Pottawatomie and, on the other hand, because (according to the *Border Times*) they were going to testify against Brown at the Lykins County session of the court, to open on May 26, on

a charge of treasonably resisting the territorial government. However interesting this thesis might be, it hardly provides an adequate explanation for the massacre, and it raises several questions which Malin did not answer. He did confess that one problem existed in his interpretation: Brown spared the life of James Harris, who had been a juror on Cato's court. "If the assassination was directed at those who participated in the court, why was he permitted to go free?"

Malin did not answer his own question. Nor did he address himself to other problems which his thesis contained. For one thing, neither Brown nor any of his sons had been indicted at the Pottawatomie session of the court, so why should Brown be preoccupied with the personnel of the court beyond any other considerations? Why indeed did Brown allow Harris, as well as other members of the court who resided on the creek, to live? Wasn't it because they had not actively aided the Missourians or threatened to kill their free-state neighbors? Furthermore, Malin gave no evidence that Brown knew he was going to be indicted for treason by the court when it opened in Lykins County (I could find no such evidence either). And even if he had known, would he have cared? The Cato court had indicted several free-state men for crimes and misdemeanors, but no attempt had been made to arrest them. And if it was feared that arrests might be made this time, why did not John Jr. and some of the others who had resisted the laws (and who were subsequently indicted by the court on a treason charge) accompany Brown on the massacre? See Malin, *John Brown and the Legend of Fifty-Six*, 537-592, 754-755. Perhaps troubled by his own interpretation, Malin argued elsewhere in his book that Brown may also have had some devious psychological purpose for the murders. Since John Jr. had defeated Brown "on all points relative to the expedition" to defend Lawrence, the massacre may have been in part "the explosive self-assertion of a frustrated old man . . . a means by which he might enjoy untrammelled authority and restore his confidence in himself."

8. Quoted in *ibid.*, 57, 753.
9. Shannon's letter of May 31, 1856, *Publications of the Kansas State Historical Society*, IV, 416; Cato to Shannon, May 27, 1856, *ibid.*, 419-420; Journal of the U.S. Court of Second Judicial District, Kansas Territory, in session at Paola, Lykins County, entries for May 27-31, 1856, U.S. Federal Records Center, Kansas City, Mo. A copy of the warrant for the arrest of Brown, John Jr., and eight other men indicted for treason, filed on May 30, 1856, is in the John Brown Papers, Kansas State Historical Society.
10. Jason's statements in Sanborn, *Life and Letters of John Brown*, 277-278, and in Villard, *John Brown*, 194-195. It was not until the publication of Mahala Doyle's testimony that the proslavery press connected John Brown with the mysterious "Captain Brown" and the Pottawatomie murders. See Malin, *John Brown and the Legend of Fifty-Six*, 61-62.
11. Since the murders had occurred after the Howard Committee had arrived in Kansas, the other two members (Howard himself and John Sherman)

did not believe they were authorized to investigate the affair and refused to take testimony regarding it. Oliver, representing proslavery Missouri, criticized the two congressmen (who were free-soil) for their position in his "Minority Report," *U.S. House Committee Reports*, 1855-1856, II, 105-106.

12. Malin, *John Brown and the Legend of Fifty-Six*, 111; Nevins, *Ordeal of the Union*, II, 479.

13. Quaife (ed.), "Bleeding Kansas and the Pottawatomie Murders," *Mississippi Valley Historical Review*, VI, 559; Adair to "Dear Bro. & Sis. Hand," Villard Collection, Columbia University; John Everett to his family, June 27, 1856, "Everett Letters," *Kansas Historical Quarterly*, VII, 31-33.

14. New York *Tribune*, July 2 and 7, 1856; William Hutchinson ("Randolph") to the *New York Times*, letter dated June 23, 1856, clipping in Hutchinson Scrapbook, Kansas State Historical Society; H. H. Williams' letter to the New York *Tribune*, Aug. 20, 1856; Jason's statement in Villard, *John Brown*, 195.

15. *New York Times*, July 8, 1856; Malin, "Hoogland Examination," *Kansas Historical Quarterly*, VII, 133-153.

16. Adair to "Dear Bro. & Sis. Hand," Villard Collection, Columbia University.

XII. GOD WILL KEEP AND DELIVER US

1. See, for example, Hanway to Redpath, March 12, 1860, Hanway Papers, Kansas State Historical Society; Samuel Walker to Hanway, Feb. 18, 1875, *ibid.*; E. A. Coleman's statement, reported by T. J. Tilley, at an old settlers' meeting, Bismarck, Kans., in 1879, John Brown Papers, *ibid.*; Hanway, "Reminiscences [1868]," in Malin, *John Brown and the Legend of Fifty-Six*, 333; Sanborn, *Life and Letters of John Brown*, 622-623; Walker's statement in *ibid.*, 337-338.

2. August Bondi, "With John Brown in Kansas," *Publications of the Kansas State Historical Society*, VIII, 281-282; Bondi's statement in Sanborn, *Life and Letters of John Brown*, 271-272; Collis' testimony in Malin, "Hoogland Examination," *Kansas Historical Quarterly*, VII, 141, 150-151.

3. Brown to his wife and children, June 24 and 26, 1856, Brown Letters, Illinois State Historical Library.

4. Bondi, "With John Brown in Kansas," *Publications of the Kansas State Historical Society*, VIII, 284-285; Sanborn, *Life and Letters of John Brown*, 296-297; Villard, *John Brown*, 200.

5. Redpath, *Public Life of Capt. John Brown*, 112-114; Bondi, "With John Brown in Kansas," *Publications of the Kansas State Historical Society*, VIII, 282-286; G. W. E. Griffith, "The Battle of Black Jack," *ibid.*, XVI, 527.

6. Villard, *John Brown*, 200.

7. My account of Black Jack was drawn from Pate's version, published first in the St. Louis *Republican* and reprinted in the New York *Tribune*, June 17, 1856 (and also included in Pate's diatribe against Brown, "John Brown,"

MS, Kansas Collection, University of Kansas); Brown's report, with lists of wounded, June 2, 1856, John Brown Papers, Kansas State Historical Society; Brown's retort to Pate's account in the New York *Tribune*, July 11, 1856; Brown to his wife and children, June 24 and 26, 1856, Brown Letters, Illinois State Historical Library; Henry Thompson's statement in Sanborn, *Recollections*, I, 130-132; Griffith, "Battle of Black Jack," *Publications of the Kansas State Historical Society*, XVI, 524-528; prisoner exchange agreement, June 2, 1856, John Brown Papers, Kansas State Historical Society.

8. Parsons had come to Kansas from Illinois in May, 1856, and bought a claim four miles west of Lawrence. Parsons to J. H. Beach, Apr. 21, 1913, John Brown Papers, Kansas State Historical Society.

9. See especially Wilson, *John Brown, Soldier of Fortune*. James Malin, who set out to demolish the legend of Brown as an abolitionist hero and any other favorable interpretation of the man and his career, argued that Brown was not a great villain as Wilson portrayed him, but an insignificant frontier crook and petty horse thief, a compulsive liar, and a fraud. As has become apparent already, I strongly disagree with the now famous Malin conception of Brown. While I have learned a great deal from Malin about the Kansas civil war and the growth of the Brown legend, I am dismayed by the biased and distorted picture which Malin presented of Brown himself—all the more so because Malin claimed his interpretation was a "scientific" one, imbued with dispassionate objectivity and based on "the critical technique of modern historiography." Yet Malin based *John Brown and the Legend of Fifty-Six* almost exclusively on materials in the Kansas State Historical Society, either ignoring or using in a limited manner valuable Brown collections in more than a dozen other libraries and private and public repositories in the United States. His view is that before Kansas Brown was a dishonest ne'er-do-well, that "two or more" of his business ventures had ended in "crime" (an inaccurate statement), that he was already unreliable as a character witness (see note 17, chap. VIII), and that he had no extraordinary interest in "the negro question." Always restless, Brown migrated to Kansas (with a wagonload of guns and swords, mind you) only to find "a business deal" (see note 15, chap. VII). Ignoring Brown's intense Calvinist faith and militant abolitionism, Malin insisted that Brown had no genuine interest in the free-state cause or in resisting the advance of slavery into the West. Malin went on to argue that all the threats of murder and invasion issued by proslavery forces had no impact on Brown (a considerable body of evidence to the contrary), that he instigated the Pottawatomie massacre largely for political reasons (see note 7, chap. XI), that he used the guerrilla war that ensued as a pretext for stealing horses and other property, and that when the war ended the dishonest and thieving Brown turned to his Harpers Ferry scheme, less to free the slaves than to loot and plunder on a grand scale in the South itself. Malin also suggested that Brown was crazy, using as evidence a letter written in 1859 by a Christian minister named C. G.

Allen, who remarked that he had "heard" several persons say that they thought Old Brown was "insane" after the battle of Osawatomie. Malin regarded this as "a damaging piece of evidence," despite the fact that in his analysis of the Pottawatomie massacre and the growth of the Brown legend he repeatedly castigated pro-Brown writers for using "hearsay" evidence.

10. For details of the raid on Bernard's store, see the testimony of Bernard himself and six other witnesses in "Report of Commissioners of Kansas Territory," *U.S. House Committee Reports* (3 vols., 36th Cong., 2nd Sess., 1861), III, pt. I, 842-846; Bondi's "Narrative," MS, Bondi Papers, Kansas State Historical Society; Bondi, "With John Brown in Kansas," *Publications of the Kansas State Historical Society*, VIII, 284.

11. Brown to his wife and children, June 24 and 26, 1856, Brown Letters, Illinois State Historical Library; Sumner's report, June 23, 1856, *Publications of the Kansas State Historical Society*, IV, 445; Major General John Sedgwick, *Correspondence* (2 vols., New York, 1902), II, 7-8. The story goes that William Preston, allegedly a U.S. marshal, rode with Sumner's force and had warrants for Brown's arrest. But, seeing Brown, Preston turned coward and did not arrest Brown because he was afraid of him. Malin exposed the story as myth, pure and simple, pointing out that there is no evidence that Preston was a U.S. marshal or that he carried any warrants. See Malin, *John Brown and the Legend of Fifty-Six*, 87-88, 591-592.

12. June 24 and 26, 1856, Brown Letters, Illinois State Historical Library.

13. Nevins, *Ordeal of the Union*, II, 478-482; Spring, *Kansas*, 163-170; Malin, *John Brown and the Legend of Fifty-Six*, 593-602.

14. June 24 and 26, 1856, Brown Letters, Illinois State Historical Library.

15. Phillips, *Conquest of Kansas*, 332-342; and Phillips, "Three Interviews with Old John Brown," *Atlantic Monthly*, XLIV (Dec., 1879), 738-741.

16. John Jr. to his father, July 26, 1856, Sanborn Folder, Houghton Library of Harvard University.

17. Nevins, *Ordeal of the Union*, II, 482; Samuel J. Reader to J. H. Beach, Apr. 7, 1913, John Brown Papers, Kansas State Historical Society; Reader's statement in Sanborn, *Recollections*, I, 93-95.

18. Aug. 11, 1856, Kansas Collection, University of Kansas.

19. Aug. 16, 1856, John Brown Papers, Kansas State Historical Society; Malin, *John Brown and the Legend of Fifty-Six*, 124-125, 606-609.

XIII. JOHN BROWN OF OSAWATOMIE

1. Allen to James Redpath and Richard J. Hinton [December, 1859?], Hinton Papers, Kansas State Historical Society.

2. Leonard Ehrlich, *God's Angry Man* (New York, 1932), 5.

3. John Brown's Notebook, II, MS, Boston Public Library.

4. Allen to Redpath and Hinton [December, 1859?], Hinton Papers, Kansas

State Historical Society; James H. Holmes, "Kansas Experiences," Dec. 8, 1856, MS, Thaddeus Hyatt Papers, Kansas State Historical Society.

5. My account of the campaign on South Middle Creek and Sugar Creek is based on Malin, *John Brown and the Legend of Fifty-Six*, 613-619; the accounts of Allen, Thomas Bedoe, N. W. Spicer, Samuel Anderson, and the joint statement of "McArthur-Hall-Hazen," in the Hyatt Papers, Kansas State Historical Society; Cline's report, New York *Tribune*, Sept. 17, 1856; and the testimonies of settlers looted by the free-state companies in "Report of Commissioners of Kansas Territory," *U.S. House Committee Reports*, 1861, vol. III, pt. II, *passim*.

6. Sanborn, *Life and Letters of John Brown*, 326-327.

7. Webb, *Life and Letters of Captain John Brown*, 423-426.

8. George Cutter, "Kansas Experiences," Jan. 1, 1857, MS, Hyatt Papers, Kansas State Historical Society; Adair, "Life of Frederick Brown," MS, Kansas Collection, University of Kansas; Martin White's speech before the proslavery Kansas legislature, Feb. 13, 1857, Leavenworth *Journal*, March 12, 1857; Hanway, "Reminiscences [1871], in Malin, *John Brown and the Legend of Fifty-Six*, 338.

9. Unless otherwise cited, my account of the battle of Osawatomie was drawn from Brown's report, Sept. 7, 1856, in Sanborn, *Life and Letters of John Brown*, 318-320; Luke F. Parsons' statement in *ibid.*, 285; Brown to his wife and children, Sept. 7, 1856, John Brown Papers, Kansas State Historical Society; Bedoe's statement and Holmes' "Kansas Experiences," MS, in Hyatt Papers, *ibid.*; Cline's account in the New York *Tribune*, Sept. 17, 1856; Spencer K. Brown's Diary, MS, 6-8, O. C. Brown Papers, Kansas State Historical Society; John Everett to [?], written a day or so after the battle, "Everett Letters," *Kansas Historical Quarterly*, VIII, 147-149; reports in the St. Louis *Missouri Republican*, Sept. 6, 1856, and St. Louis *Daily Democrat*, Sept. 8, 1856; Malin, *John Brown and the Legend of Fifty-Six*, 619-628; and Villard, *John Brown*, 241-247.

10. Villard, *John Brown*, 245-246, 248.

11. *Ibid.*, 253-254; Malin, *John Brown and the Legend of Fifty-Six*, 625-628.

12. Villard, *John Brown*, 253-254.

13. Allen to Redpath and Hinton [December, 1859?], Hinton Papers, Kansas State Historical Society.

14. John Brown Papers, *ibid.*; Sanborn, *Life and Letters of John Brown*, 318-320.

15. Coleman's statement, as reported by T. J. Tilley, at the old settlers' meeting in Bismarck, Kans., 1879, in John Brown Papers, Kansas State Historical Society (in this statement Coleman said his discussion with Brown took place on Sept. 13, 1856, which seems to fit actual events, but in Charles S. Gleed [ed.], *The Kansas Memorial* [Kansas City, Mo., 1880], Coleman gave the date as "one evening, not long before the fight at Osawatomie"). On many occasions after he left the territory Brown declared that he was an

instrument in the hands of God (his letters and recorded public utterances are filled with such statements, many of them quoted in the text of this biography); of course such a belief was an outgrowth of his Calvinist faith. Several persons who knew Brown in Kansas believed that the battle of Osawatomie and the shock of Frederick's death affected Brown's mind and gave vent to all his pent-up hatred of the South. From then on he was obsessed with the destruction of slavery there, laboring under "a religious hallucination" that he had "a mission" just as Christ did, that he was "the appointed instrument for putting an end to human slavery" (after Harpers Ferry Brown told his Southern interrogators much the same thing). See George P. Gill, "Reminiscences," MS, Hinton Papers, Kansas State Historical Society; and statements by Mrs. J. E. Partridge to Andrew Reeder, Nov. 11, 1905, John Brown Papers, *ibid.*; by Charles Robinson, in Sanborn, *Life and Letters of John Brown*, 269n; by the correspondent to the Chicago *Tribune* in 1860 in Nevins, *Emergence of Lincoln*, II, 9.

16. Hinton's Journal and Robinson's letter to his wife, Sept. 20, 1856, in Malin, *John Brown and the Legend of Fifty-Six*, 630, 634; Robinson to Brown, Sept. 13, 1856, John Brown Papers, Kansas State Historical Society.

17. Nathaniel Parker's statement, Dec. 5, 1856, Hyatt Papers, Kansas State Historical Society; T. W. Higginson ("Worcester") to New York *Tribune*, Oct. 17, 1856; Walker's statement in Sanborn, *Life and Letters of John Brown*, 336; Malin, *John Brown and the Legend of Fifty-Six*, 632-633; Hinton, *John Brown and His Men*, 48-52.

18. Both documents are in Sanborn, *Life and Letters of John Brown*, 330-331.

19. Augustus Wattles' testimony, "Mason Report," *U.S. Senate Committee Reports* (2 vols., 36th Cong., 1st Sess., 1859-1860), vol. II, no. 278, p. 214; Brown to his wife and children, Oct. 11, 1856; Stutler Collection. Sanborn, *Life and Letters of John Brown*, 339-340, stated that Geary ordered Walker himself to arrest Brown. But in his reports Geary mentioned nothing about such an order, even though he had been told that Brown was second only to Lane among free-state guerrilla captains resisting the territorial laws. Geary was probably apprised, too, that Cato had twice issued warrants for Brown's arrest (the second time on July 7, 1856). The only one of the Pottawatomie slayers arrested was James Townsley. As Malin pointed out, Cato's court met on Nov. 17, 1856, at Tecumseh, charging Townsley for the Pottawatomie massacre and William Partridge for larceny and theft in connection with the Sugar Creek raid. Partridge was found guilty and sentenced to ten years in prison. The court's case against Townsley, however, was too weak to bring about a conviction: Glanville (the traveler at James Harris' house that tragic night) had been mysteriously assassinated, and Mrs. Doyle, Mrs. Wilkinson, and John Wightman had all left the territory. Many other settlers refused to testify. Finally, the case against Townsley was dropped. Malin, *John Brown and the Legend of Fifty-Six*, 682-683.

20. Brown to his wife and children, Oct. 11, 1856, Stutler Collection; Brown, Notebook, II, MS, Boston Public Library; Villard, *John Brown*, 267-270.

XIV. FOR THE CAUSE OF LIBERTY

1. Quotations from Anna Mary Wells, *Dear Perceptor: the Life and Times of Thomas Wentworth Higginson* (Boston, 1963), 104-105.
2. Sanborn, *Recollections*, I, 11-50, 75-76, 91-92; Thomas Wentworth Higginson, *Letters and Journals, 1846-1906* (ed. by Mary Thacher Higginson, Boston and New York, 1921), 86.
3. A copy of Brown's plan to defend Kansas is in the Sanborn Folder, Houghton Library of Harvard University.
4. Sanborn, *Life and Letters of John Brown*, 341, 620, 626-636; Sanborn, *Recollections*, I, 75, 83, 88; Octavius Brooks Frothingham, *Theodore Parker: A Biography* (Boston, 1874), 453-454.
5. Higginson Papers, Boston Public Library.
6. Sanborn, *Life and Letters of John Brown*, 511; Henry Steele Commager (ed.), *Theodore Parker: An Anthology* (Boston, 1960), 257-266; Harold Schwartz, *Samuel Gridley Howe: Social Reformer, 1801-1876* (Cambridge, Mass., 1956), 117; Higginson, *Letters and Journals*, 94; Commager, *Theodore Parker* (2nd ed., Boston, 1947), *passim*.
7. Wendell Phillips Garrison and Francis Jackson Garrison, *William Lloyd Garrison* (4 vols., Boston and New York, 1894), III, 487-488; Thomas, *Garrison*, 396-397; and Commager (ed.), *Theodore Parker: An Anthology*, 257.
8. William Lawrence, *Life of Amos A. Lawrence* (Boston, 1888), 124-125.
9. Sanborn, *Life and Letters of John Brown*, 332-333.
10. Schwartz, *Howe*, 1-217; Howe, *Letters and Journals* (ed. by Laura E. Richards, 2 vols., Boston, 1909), II, 418-437.
11. Franklin Preston Stearns, *Life and Public Services of George Luther Stearns* (Philadelphia, 1907), 129; votes of Massachusetts Kansas Committee giving money and guns to Brown, and correspondence, freight bill, and receipted statements for 200 pistols from Massachusetts Arms Co., paid for by Stearns, in Stutler Collection; Stearns's testimony in "Mason Report," *U.S. Senate Committee Reports*, 1859-1860, II, 227-228.
12. Higginson, *Letters and Journals*, 1-77; Higginson, *Cheerful Yesterdays* (Boston and New York, 1898), 1-216; Mary Thacher Higginson, *Thomas Wentworth Higginson: the Story of His Life* (Boston, 1914), 22-189; Tilden G. Edelstein, *Strange Enthusiasm: A Life of Thomas Wentworth Higginson* (New Haven, 1968), 7-196.
13. Higginson, *Letters and Journals*, 77; Edelstein, *Higginson*, 196, 203-204.
14. Statement of Henry Stearns, Oct. 26, 1902, Villard Collection, Columbia University; Stearns, *George Luther Stearns*, 133-134.
15. David Donald, *Charles Sumner and the Coming of the Civil War* (New York, 1961), 350.

16. H. B. Hurd to George L. Stearns, March 19, 1860, Stearns Papers, Kansas State Historical Society; "Memorandum of articles wanted for Fifty volunteers," John Brown Papers, *ibid.*; documents pertaining to the meeting of the National Kansas Committee in the Astor House and correspondence between Brown and Hurd in *ibid.*; Sanborn, *Life and Letters of John Brown*, 348-349, 360; Villard, *John Brown*, 275-276.

17. Ralph V. Harlow, "Gerrit Smith and the John Brown Raid," *American Historical Review*, XXXVIII (October, 1932), 32-34; Brown to John Jr., Feb. 14, 1857, John Brown Jr. Papers, Ohio Historical Society.

18. Annie's statements in Villard, *John Brown*, 277, and Sanborn, *Life and Letters of John Brown*, 387. For how Mary, Watson, and the girls managed during the winter of 1855-56, see Brown to Mary, Nov. 23, 1855, Webb, *Life and Letters of Captain John Brown*, 416-417; Watson to Brown, Dec. 4, 1855, copy in Sanborn Folder, Houghton Library of Harvard University; and Owen Brown to Mary, Dec. 25, 1855, John Brown Jr. Papers, Ohio Historical Society.

19. Brown's speech before the Massachusetts legislative committee, Feb. 18, 1857, Stutler Collection; Sanborn, *Life and Letters of John Brown*, 372-373; and Sanborn to Brown, Jan. 28 and Feb. 11, 1857, Sanborn Letters, Atlanta University.

20. The exact date of Brown's Concord lecture is not known. Several writers said the lecture took place variously in January or February. Actually Brown may not have delivered the address until after March 9, 1857, for Sanborn lamented to him in a letter of that date that "I think we [the citizens of Concord] must give up the expectation of seeing you here at all, now that we have tried twice to appoint a time for you and have not succeeded in it. . . ." See Sanborn to Brown, Feb. 11, March 1 and 9, 1857, Sanborn Letters, Atlanta University.

21. Notes for speeches Brown made at Concord and elsewhere in New England and New York, John Brown Papers, Kansas State Historical Society (printed in Sanborn, *Life and Letters of John Brown*, 243-245); Thoreau, *Writings* (20 vols., Boston, 1906), IV, 413-416; XVIII, 437; Emerson, *Works* (12 vols., 1903), XI, 208; Sanborn, *Recollections*, I, 112; Gilman M. Ostrander, "Emerson, Thoreau, and John Brown," *Mississippi Valley Historical Review*, XXXIX (March, 1953), 713-726. Brown also told Sanborn and Stearns that it was better that a whole generation should pass away in violent death than that "one jot or one tittle" of the Golden Rule or the Declaration of Independence be not fulfilled. On Emancipation Day, Jan. 1, 1863, Stearns distributed cards with Brown's statement (and a woodcut portrait of the old man) printed on them. Copies of the cards are in the Stutler Collection.

22. Lawrence to Brown, Feb. 19, 1857, John Brown Papers, Kansas State Historical Society.

23. Sanborn Letters, Atlanta University.

24. Brown to his wife and children, March 12, 1857, John Brown Papers,

Kansas State Historical Society; Brown to John Jr., Apr. 15, 1857, Stutler Collection; Blair's testimony in "Mason Report," *U.S. Senate Committee Reports,* 1859-1860, II, 121-129. Brown and Blair signed a contract on March 30 and Brown paid him $50. On April 25 Brown sent Blair an additional $200. Their correspondence during 1857 and 1858 is in the John Brown Papers, Kansas State Historical Society.

25. Forbes's statement in the New York *Herald,* Oct. 27, 1859, including Forbes's letter to Howe, May 14, 1858; *New York Times,* Oct. 28, 1859; Brown to Forbes, June 22, 1857, Ferdinand Julius Dreer Papers, Historical Society of Pennsylvania; Villard, *John Brown,* 285-286; Hinton, *John Brown and His Men,* 146-147; Edelstein, *Higginson,* 203.

26. Sanborn to Brown, March 25, 1857, Sanborn Letters, Atlanta University; Sanborn, *Recollections,* I, 115-118; Sanborn to Higginson, Sept. 11, 1857, Higginson Papers, Kansas State Historical Society; Sanborn to Henry Richards, May 15, 1908, Higginson Papers, Houghton Library of Harvard University.

27. March 31, 1857, Stutler Collection.

28. Hurd to Brown, Apr. 1, 1857, John Brown Papers, Kansas State Historical Society.

29. Brown to William Barnes, Apr. 3, 1857, Villard, *John Brown,* 283; Brown to Lawrence, March 19, 1857, Massachusetts Historical Society; Lawrence to Brown, March 20, 1857, *ibid.;* Brown to Wattles and Holmes, Apr. 8, 1857, in "Mason Report," *U.S. Senate Committee Reports,* 1859-1860, II, 220.

30. Interview with Mrs. Thomas Russell, by Katherine Mayo, New York *Evening Post,* Oct. 23, 1909.

31. Brown, "Farewell," John Brown Papers, Kansas State Historical Society (other original copies are in the Stutler Collection and the Chicago Historical Society); Brown to Hurd, John Brown Papers, Chicago Historical Society; Villard, *John Brown,* 291-292.

32. Brown to John Jr., Apr. 15, 1857, Stutler Collection; statement of Mary Stearns in Sanborn, *Life and Letters of John Brown,* 509-511; Stearns's testimony in "Mason Report," *U.S. Senate Committee Reports,* 1859-1860, II, 227-228; Stearns, *George Luther Stearns,* 159.

33. Apr. 15, 1857, Stutler Collection; Brown to Stearns, May 23, 1857, *ibid.;* Brown to Eli Thayer, Apr. 16, 1857, John Brown Papers, Huntington Library.

XV. RAILROAD BUSINESS ON AN EXTENDED SCALE

1. John Jr. to Brown, Apr. 23, 1857, in Villard, *John Brown,* 290-291.

2. John Brown, Notebook, II, MS, Boston Public Library, entries of June 9, 11, 16, 21, 22, 1857; Chase to Brown, June 6, 1857, John Brown Papers, Kansas State Historical Society; Bryant to Brown, June 1 and 25, 1857, *ibid.;* Brown to his family, May 27, 1857, Sanborn, *Life and Letters of John*

Brown, 410-411; Brown to Augustus Wattles, June 3, 1857, "Mason Report," *U.S. Senate Committee Reports*, 1859-1860, II, 221; Brown to William A. Phillips, June 9, 1857, as cited in Villard, *John Brown*, 292-293.

3. Brown to his wife and children, June 22, 1857, and Brown to George L. Stearns, Aug. 8, 1857, Stutler Collection; Brown to his wife and children, June 25, 1857, Brown Letters, Illinois State Historical Library; Smith to Hyatt, July 25, 1857, Hyatt Papers, Kansas State Historical Society; Harlow, *Gerrit Smith*, 394.

4. Brown, Notebook, II, MS, 1856-1859, Boston Public Library; Brown to his wife and children, July 17, 1857, John Brown Papers, Kansas State Historical Society.

5. A photostatic copy of Brown's letter to Henry Stearns in Stutler Collection; [John Brown], "A Brief History of John Brown," MS, Dreer Papers, Historical Society of Pennsylvania.

6. Brown to Stearns, Aug. 8, 1857, Stutler Collection; Sanborn to Stearns, Lawrence, and other subscribers [1857], *ibid.*; Sanborn to Brown, Aug. 14 and 28, 1857, Sanborn Letters, Atlanta University; Brown to Sanborn, Aug. 27, 1857, Stutler Collection.

7. Brown to Sanborn, Oct. 1, 1857, Stutler Collection; Smith to Hyatt, July 25, 1857, Hyatt Papers, Kansas State Historical Society; Sanborn, *Life and Letters of John Brown*, 399, 412-414; Villard, *John Brown*, 289.

8. Forbes to Samuel Gridley Howe, May 14, 1858, in New York *Herald*, Oct. 27, 1859, and in *New York Times*, Oct. 28, 1859.

9. Brown to his wife and children, Aug. 17, 1857, John Brown Papers, Kansas State Historical Society; Brown to Sanborn, Oct. 1, 1857, Stutler Collection; Villard, *John Brown*, 297-298.

10. Brown, Notebook, II, MS, Boston Public Library. The entries pertaining to guerrilla warfare and the list of Southern towns are undated but obviously were made in the summer of 1857, as the notes that precede and follow them were recorded at that time. Villard, *John Brown*, 53, erroneously asserts that Brown made the notations "early in 1855" and so Villard's contention that Brown had evolved his final Virginia Plan before he went to Kansas also is in error.

11. Villard, *John Brown*, 293, 297; Sanborn, *Life and Letters of John Brown*, 397-398.

12. The correspondence between Brown and Lane, during September and October, 1857, is in the John Brown Papers, Kansas State Historical Society.

13. Sanborn to Brown, Sept. 14 and 19, Oct. 19, 1857, Sanborn Letters, Atlanta University.

14. Sept. 11, 1857, Higginson Papers, Kansas State Historical Society.

15. Brown to Sanborn, Oct. 1, 1857, Stutler Collection; Middlesex County, Mass., Kansas Aid Society to "Nelson Hawkins," Sept. 14, 1857, John Brown Papers, Kansas State Historical Society; Brown to Whitman, Oct. 5, 1857; W. B. Edmonds [E. B. Whitman] to Brown, Oct. 5, 1857, *ibid*.

16. Stearns to Whitman, Nov. 14, 1857, Stearns Papers, Kansas State Historical

Society; Howe to Brown, Nov. 7, 1857; and Stearns to Brown, Feb. 4, 1858, Stutler Collection. A copy of Howe's letter to Brown is in the Howe Papers, Massachusetts Historical Society.

17. See Forbes to Howe, May 14, 1858, in New York *Herald*, Oct. 27, 1859, and *New York Times*, Oct. 28, 1859; Sanborn to Brown, Jan. 12, 1857, Sanborn Letters, Atlanta University; Sanborn, *Life and Letters of John Brown*, 427-430; Stearns to Brown, Feb. 4, 1858, in Stutler Collection; Villard, *John Brown*, 299.

18. Lane to Brown, Oct. 30, 1857, and Whitman to Brown, Oct. 24, 1857, John Brown Papers, Kansas State Historical Society; Brown to Adair, Nov. 17, 1857, in Villard, *John Brown*, 306.

19. Whitman to Stearns, Feb. 28, 1858, Stearns Papers, Kansas State Historical Society; John E. Cook, "Confession," in Hinton, *John Brown and His Men*, 700-701; Brown to Stearns, Nov. 16, 1857, in Villard, *John Brown*, 305; Brown to John Jr., Nov. 16, 1857, John Brown Jr. Papers, Ohio Historical Society.

20. There are biographical sketches of Cook, Stevens, and Kagi in Hinton, *John Brown and His Men*, 453-504; Villard, *John Brown*, 679-691; and Thomas Featherstonhaugh, "John Brown's Men: the Lives of Those Killed at Harper's Ferry," *Publications of the Southern History Association*, III (Washington, D.C., 1899), 281-306.

21. Brown, Notebook, II, MS, Boston Public Library; Cook, "Confessions," in Hinton, *John Brown and His Men*, 701; Allan Nevins, *Emergence of Lincoln* (2 vols., New York and London, 1960), II, 17-18.

22. Extracts from the diary Owen kept between Aug. 25 and Dec. 8, 1857, in *New York Times*, Oct. 24, 1859 (the *Times* erroneously asserted that Jason was the author); Realf's testimony in "Mason Report," *U.S. Senate Committee Reports*, 1859-1860, II, 91; Cook, "Confession," in Hinton, *John Brown and His Men*, 702; Luke Parsons' statement in Villard, *John Brown*, 310; Brown to his wife and children, Dec. 30, 1857, Stutler Collection.

23. Brown, Notebook, II, MS, Boston Public Library; Villard, *John Brown*, 312-313; Sanborn, *Life and Letters of John Brown*, 425-426; and Irving B. Richman, *John Brown Among the Quakers* (Des Moines, Iowa, 1894), 12ff.

24. Douglass, *Life and Times*, 318-321; U.S. Bureau of the Census, *Negro Population, 1790-1915* (Washington, D.C., 1918), 44. For an analysis of Brown's relationships with Douglass and other Negro leaders, see David Potter, *The South and the Sectional Conflict* (Baton Rouge, La., 1968), 201-218.

25. Sanborn, *Life and Letters of John Brown*, 440-441.

26. Brown to Higginson, Feb. 2, 1858, Higginson Papers, Boston Public Library. For comparable letters to Brown's other friends, see Frothingham, *Theodore Parker*, 457-458, and Sanborn, *Recollections*, I, 142-143.

27. Sanborn to Brown, Jan. 12, 1858, Sanborn Letters, Atlanta University; Sanborn, *Life and Letters of John Brown*, 427-428; Stearns to Brown,

Feb. 4, 1858, Stutler Collection; Stearns, *George Luther Stearns*, 162.

28. Brown to John Jr., Feb. 9, 1857, in Sanborn, *Life and Letters of John Brown*, 432-433; Brown, Notebook, II, MS, Boston Public Library.
29. Stearns to Brown, Feb. 4, 1858, Stutler Collection; Stearns, *George Luther Stearns*, 162; Higginson to Brown, Feb. 7, 1858, and Brown to Higginson, Feb. 12, 1858, Higginson Papers, Boston Public Library.
30. Sanborn to Higginson, Feb. 11 and 19, 1858, and Brown to Sanborn, Feb. 17, 1858, Higginson Papers, Boston Public Library; Sanborn, *Recollections*, I, 143; Sanborn, *Life and Letters of John Brown*, 436-438.
31. Feb. 20, 1858, John Brown Jr. Papers, Ohio Historical Society.

XVI. THE CONSPIRACY BEGINS

1. Salmon claimed that he heard his father and John Jr. discuss "by the hour" the possibilities of provoking a civil war over the slavery issue and that "the Harper's Ferry raid had that idea behind it far more than any other." Villard, *John Brown*, 56. The scenes sketched in the text are from Sanborn, *Recollections*, I, 145-148. Gerrit Smith himself gave the most complete expression of Brown's own arguments about the consequences of a slave insurrection, in a letter written on Aug. 27, 1859, to the "Jerry Rescue" Anniversary Committee. Harlow, *Gerrit Smith*, 405-406, also believes that this document is a key to some of the "unreported conversations" that took place between Brown and Smith at Peterboro.
2. Harlow, *Gerrit Smith*, 345-350, and "Gerrit Smith and the John Brown Raid," *American Historical Review*, XXXVIII, 32-37; Brown to his wife and children, Feb. 24, 1858, in Villard, *John Brown*, 320.
3. Sanborn, *Recollections*, I, 147, and *Life and Letters of John Brown*, 438-440; Frothingham, *Theodore Parker*, 458-459.
4. Feb. 24, 1858, John Brown Jr. Papers, Ohio Historical Society.
5. Gloucester to Brown, Feb. 19 and March 19, 1858, John Brown Papers, Kansas State Historical Society.
6. Villard, *John Brown*, 323; Brown to his wife, March 2, 1858, John Brown Papers, Kansas State Historical Society.
7. Stearns, *George Luther Stearns*, 164; Villard, *John Brown*, 324; Higginson to Smith, Nov. 22, 1856, Smith Papers, Syracuse University; J. C. Furnas, *Road to Harpers Ferry* (New York, 1959), 344.
8. Stampp, *The Peculiar Institution: Slavery in the Ante-Bellum South* (New York, 1956), 141-191; William W. Freehling, *Prelude to Civil War: the Nullification Controversy in South Carolina, 1816-1836* (New York, 1965), 49-86, 301-360; Charles G. Sellers, Jr., "The Travail of Slavery," in Sellers (ed.), *The Southerner as American* (Chapel Hill, N.C., 1960), 40-71; John Hope Franklin, *The Militant South, 1800-1860* (Cambridge, Mass., 1956), especially 72-90; and W. J. Cash, *The Mind of the South* (New York, 1941), 30-102.

9. Higginson, *Cheerful Yesterdays*, 219; Stearns, *George Luther Stearns*, 164; Sanborn, *Life and Letters of John Brown*, 446; Schwartz, *Howe*, 227; Nevins, *Emergence of Lincoln*, II, 21, 22, 31.

10. Giddings Papers, Ohio Historical Society.

11. See, for example, Leon F. Litwack, *North of Slavery: the Negro in the Free States, 1790-1860* (Chicago, 1961), 64ff.; Berwanger, *Frontier Against Slavery*, 30-59; Forrest G. Wood, *Black Scare: the Racist Response to Emancipation and Reconstruction* (Berkeley, Calif., 1968), 1-16; and V. Jacque Voegeli, *Free But Not Equal: the Midwest and the Negro During the Civil War* (Chicago, 1967), 1-9.

12. Sanborn, Personal Reminiscences of John Brown (Apr. 7, 1897), typescript, Sanborn Folder, Houghton Library of Harvard University.

13. Brown, Notebook, II, MS, Boston Public Library; Sanborn, *Life and Letters of John Brown*, 451; Hinton, *John Brown and His Men*, 169.

14. Ruth to Brown, Feb. 20, 1858, in Webb, *Life and Letters of Captain John Brown*, 426; Oliver to Brown, Apr. 14, 1858, Stutler Collection; Annie's statement in Sanborn, *Recollections*, I, 171.

15. Brown to John Jr., Apr. 8, 1858, Stutler Collection; Brown, Notebook, II, MS, Boston Public Library; Higginson, *Letters and Journals*, 81.

16. Villard, *John Brown*, 315-316, 328-329; Brown to his wife and children, Apr. 27, 1858, Stutler Collection; Sanborn, *Life and Letters of John Brown*, 454.

17. My account of the Chatham convention is based on Richard Realf's testimony in "Mason Report," *U.S. Senate Committee Reports*, 1859-1860, II, 96-99; John Henry Kagi's "Journal of the Chatham Convention," *ibid.*, 45-47; Brown's Provisional Constitution in *ibid.*, 48ff. (also printed in Hinton, *John Brown and His Men*, 619-633); Cook, "Confession," in *ibid.*, 703-704; Gill, "Reminiscences," Hinton Papers, Kansas State Historical Society; Osborn P. Anderson, *A Voice From Harper's Ferry* (Boston, 1861), 9.

18. Before he was hanged at Charlestown, Va., in 1859, Brown made a list of those passages in the Bible that had most influenced his life. Among them were Isaiah 49:24-26, and Jeremiah 5:25-29, which I quoted in the text. See New York *Illustrated News*, Dec. 10, 1859.

19. Of the thirty-four Negroes who attended the Chatham convention, only Osborn P. Anderson joined Brown in the Harpers Ferry attack. According to Martin R. Delany, "the plan and purpose of the Canada Convention" was to establish a massive slave-running enterprise called "the Subterranean Pass Way," an extended version of Brown's old scheme. Brown, Delany said, was elected president of "the permanent organization." Delany claimed that nobody at the convention except perhaps Kagi knew that Brown planned to attack the government armory and rifle works at Harpers Ferry. Frank A. Rollins, *Life and Public Services of Martin R. Delany* (Boston, 1868), 90.

20. Loguen to Brown, May 6, 1858, John Brown Papers, Kansas State Historical Society; Sanborn, *Life and Letters of John Brown*, 456.

21. Villard, *John Brown*, 339; Henry Wilson's testimony in "Mason Report," *U.S. Senate Committee Reports*, 1859-1860, II, 141-143; Howe to Forbes, May 10, 1858, *ibid.*, 177-179.

22. New York *Herald*, Oct. 27 and 29, 1859, and *New York Times*, Oct. 28, 1859.

23. Sanborn, *Life and Letters of John Brown*, 456-460, and *Recollections*, I, 155-158; Howe to Brown, May 14 and 15, 1858, in "Mason Report," *U.S. Senate Committee Reports*, 1859-1860, II, 231.

24. Higginson to Parker, May 9, 1858, and Brown to Higginson, May 14, 1858, Higginson Papers, Boston Public Library.

25. Smith to Sanborn, May 7, 1858, *ibid.*; Harlow, *Gerrit Smith*, 400-401.

26. Memorandum of Higginson, June 1, 1858, outlining the Revere House decision, Higginson Papers, Boston Public Library; Sanborn, *Recollections*, I, 157-158, and *Life and Letters of John Brown*, 462-466.

27. Richard Richardson was already in Canada and was never to go to Harpers Ferry. Owen, Leeman, and Taylor went to stay with Jason in Akron, while Parsons and Moffett started west, too, and eventually returned to their respective homes in Illinois and Iowa.

28. Realf to "Dear Uncle" [Brown], May 21, 1858, John Brown Papers, Kansas State Historical Society; Gill, "Reminiscences," Hinton Papers, *ibid.*; Hinton, *John Brown and His Men*, 473; Villard, *John Brown*, 344, 629.

29. June 22, 1858, John Brown Jr. Papers, Ohio Historical Society. John Jr. moved his family to West Andover by May 10, 1858, and remained there, chopping wood, plowing, and planting potatoes, through December. See entries from May 10 to Dec. 27, 1858, John Brown Jr.'s Diary, MS, *ibid.*

XVII. MY WORK . . . MY MISSION

1. Hinton, *John Brown and His Men*, 205; Redpath, *Public Life of Capt. John Brown*, 199-200; New York *Tribune*, July 8, 1858; Brown to Sanborn, June 28, 1858, Higginson Papers, Boston Public Library.

2. Brown to his wife and children, July 9, 1858 (photostatic copy), and Brown to John Jr., July 9, 1858, Stutler Collection; Gill to Hinton, July 7, 1893, and Gill, "Reminiscences," Hinton Papers, Kansas State Historical Society.

3. Brown to Sanborn (from July 20 to Aug. 6, 1858), Higginson Papers, Boston Public Library; Brown to John Jr., July 9, 1858, Stutler Collection; Brown's "History," MS, in Dreer Papers, Historical Society of Pennsylvania; Wattles' testimony in "Mason Report," *U.S. Senate Committee Reports*, 1859-1860, II, 215.

4. Higginson Papers, Boston Public Library.

5. Brown to John Jr., Aug. 9, 1858, in Villard, *John Brown*, 354-355.

6. Snyder to James H. Holmes, in 1894, as quoted in *ibid.*, 357; Hanway to Hinton, Dec. 5, 1859, Hinton Papers, Kansas State Historical Society.

7. Sept. 23, 1858, in Hinton, *John Brown and His Men*, 464. See also Hinton's statement in Redpath, *Public Life of Capt. John Brown*, 202-205; Brown to his wife and children, Sept. 13 and Dec. 2, 1858, Stutler Collection; and Brown to his wife and children, Oct. 11, 1858, John Brown Jr. Papers, Ohio Historical Society.

8. Hanway to Redpath, March 12, 1860, Hanway Papers, Kansas State Historical Society; Hanway's "Reminiscences" [1868] in Malin, *John Brown and the Legend of Fifty-Six*, 333.

9. Villard, *John Brown*, 359-360; Bowles' letter of Apr. 9, 1859, in Siebert, *Underground Railroad*, 347-350.

10. Phillips, "Three Interviews with Old John Brown," *Atlantic Monthly*, XLIV, 743-744.

11. Gill, "Reminiscences," Hinton Papers, Kansas State Historical Society; Gill to F. G. Adams, Aug. 15, 1883, John Brown Papers, *ibid.*; John Brown, "Old Brown's Parallels," January, 1859, *ibid.*; James Townsend's statement [no date], MS, *ibid.*; Luke F. Parsons to J. H. Beach, Apr. 21, 1913, *ibid.*; [Floyd C. Shoemaker], "John Brown's Missouri Raid: A Tale of the Kansas-Missouri Border Wars Retold with Some New Facts," *Missouri Historical Review*, XXVI (October, 1931), 78-83.

12. [Shoemaker], "John Brown's Missouri Raid," *Missouri Historical Review*, XXVI, 80-83. The governor of Missouri did not offer a $3,000 reward for Brown's capture as mistakenly claimed in the biographies of Brown by Redpath, William E. Connelley, and Villard.

13. Jan. 10, 1859, in Harlow, *Gerrit Smith*, 403.

14. Hutchinson to his wife, January, 1859, in *Publications of the Kansas State Historical Society*, VII (Topeka, 1901-1902), 398-399; Hutchinson's statement in Villard, *John Brown*, 373; Wattles' testimony in "Mason Report," *U.S. Senate Committee Reports*, 1859-1860, II, 223.

15. Crawford to Eli Thayer, Aug. 4, 1879, George W. Brown Papers, Kansas State Historical Society.

16. Brown, "Old Brown's Parallels," John Brown Papers, *ibid.*; Jeremiah Anderson to his brother, late in September, 1859, in Sanborn, *Life and Letters of John Brown*, 545; Wattles' testimony in "Mason Report," *U.S. Senate Committee Reports*, 1859-1860, II, 223.

17. Gill to Hinton, July 7, 1893, and Gill, "Reminiscences," Hinton Papers, Kansas State Historical Society; Brown to Higginson, May 14, 1858, Higginson Papers, Boston Public Library.

18. Villard, *John Brown*, 380-390.

19. Land, "John Brown's Ohio Environment," *Ohio State Archaeological and Historical Quarterly*, LVII, 28, 38-41; Cincinnati (Ohio) *Enquirer*, Oct. 22, 1859; Fairchild, *Underground Railroad*, 112-120; William C. Cochran, *The Western Reserve and the Fugitive Slave Law* (Cleveland, 1920), 187.

20. Cleveland *Plain Dealer*, March 22 and 30, 1859; J. W. Schuckers, "Old John

Brown," Cleveland *Leader*, Apr. 29, 1894; Cook, "Confession," in Hinton, *John Brown and His Men*, 705; "John Brown's Speech," in Redpath, *Public Life of Capt. John Brown*, 239-240.

21. Ralph Plumb's testimony in "Mason Report," *U.S. Senate Committee Reports*, 1859-1860, II, 179, 181-184; Cleveland *Leader*, Nov. 1, 1859; Villard, *John Brown*, 684-686.

22. New York *Tribune*, Oct. 31, 1859; Giddings' testimony in "Mason Report," *U.S. Senate Committee Reports*, 1859-1860, II, 147-148; Stutler, "Abraham Lincoln and John Brown—A Parallel," *Civil War History*, VIII, 290-299; Villard, *John Brown*, 394.

23. Brown to his wife and children, Apr. 7, 1859, Byron Reed Collection, Omaha Public Library; Morton to Sanborn, Apr. 13, 1859, in Sanborn, *Recollections*, I, 161-162; Harlow, *Gerrit Smith*, 403.

24. Sanborn, *Recollections*, I, 163-164.

25. Higginson, *Cheerful Yesterdays*, 222-223; Edelstein, *Higginson*, 217-218; Higginson to Brown, May 1, 1859, Higginson Papers, Boston Public Library.

26. Howe to Higginson, Feb. 16, 1860, Higginson Papers, Boston Public Library; Sanborn, *Life and Letters of John Brown*, 491n-492n; Howe to Parker, Jan. 22, 1860, Howe, *Journals and Letters*, II, 442; Howe's letter of introduction to John Murray Forbes, Feb. 5, 1859, in Forbes, *Letters and Recollections* (ed. by Sarah Forbes Hughes, 2 vols., Boston and New York, 1899), I, 178; Henry Richards to Sanborn, May 14, 1908, and Sanborn to Richards, May 15, 1908, Higginson Papers, Houghton Library of Harvard University. Schwartz, *Howe*, 239-240, suggests that "it is possible that [Howe] did not realize fully what Brown had in mind" in his Virginia plan. But all the evidence points to the fact that Howe knew the plan perfectly well but not the exact place where Brown intended to strike. None of the backers—except perhaps Sanborn—knew the spot where Brown hoped to launch the experiment.

27. Sanborn to Higginson, May 30 and June 4, 1859, Higginson Papers, Boston Public Library; Villard, *John Brown*, 396-397; Sanborn, *Life and Letters of John Brown*, 523; Brown to his wife and children, May 12, 1859, Byron Reed Collection, Omaha Public Library.

28. Howe, *Journals and Letters*, II, 434-435; Schwartz, *Howe*, 328-329; Louise Hall Tharp, *Three Saints and a Sinner* (Boston, 1956), 4.

29. Andrew's testimony in "Mason Report," *U.S. Senate Committee Reports*, 1859-1860, II, 192; Lawrence, *Life of Amos Lawrence*, 130.

30. Forbes, *Letters and Recollections*, I, 178-182; Howe to Forbes, May 25, 1859, Howe Papers, Massachusetts Historical Society.

31. Sanborn, *Life and Letters of John Brown*, 131; Thomas, *Garrison*, 397; interview with Mrs. Judge Thomas Russell, by Katherine Mayo, in the New York *Evening Post*, Oct. 23, 1909.

32. Charles Blair's testimony in "Mason Report," *U.S. Senate Committee Reports*, 1859-1860, II, 124-125, 127; Sanborn to Higginson, June 4, 1859, Higginson Papers, Boston Public Library.

33. Salmon Brown, "My Father, John Brown," *Outlook*, CIII, 212-217; E. C. Lampson, "The Black String Bands," Cleveland *Plain Dealer*, Oct. 8, 1899; Villard, *John Brown*, 402, 637; John Brown Jr.'s statement in Cleveland *Press*, May 3, 1895.

XVIII. MEN, GET YOUR ARMS

1. My statistics are from *Population of the United States in 1860; Compiled from . . . the Eighth Census* (Washington 1864), I, 214, 516-517, 519. In 1850 there were 20,335 slaves in the six-county area (Washington and Frederick counties in Maryland; Berkeley, Jefferson, Loudoun, and Frederick counties in Virginia). See *New York Times*, Oct. 20, 1859.
2. Cook, "Confession," in Hinton, *John Brown and His Men*, 705-708; Villard, *John Brown*, 408, 682.
3. John Smith Jr. to Henrie, July 23 and Sept. 2, 1859; J. Henrie to I. Smith and sons, Aug. 11, 1859, in "Mason Report," *U.S. Senate Committee Reports*, 1859-1860, II, 62-65.
4. Annie's statements in Hinton, *John Brown and His Men*, 265; in Villard, *John Brown*, 416-420; and in Sanborn, *Recollections*, I, 171-178.
5. Brown's maps are described in detail in the *New York Times*, Oct. 22, 1859. See also Brown's remarks quoted in "Mason Report," *U.S. Senate Committee Reports*, 1859-1860, II, 1-12; Jeremiah Anderson to his brother, late in September, 1859, in Sanborn, *Life and Letters of John Brown*, 545.
6. Owen to Brown, Aug. 18, 1859, Dreer Papers, Historical Society of Pennsylvania; Owen's statements in Sanborn, *Life and Letters of John Brown*, 541, and *Recollections*, I, 182-183; and Hinton, *John Brown and His Men*, 258-259.
7. Anderson's letter is in Sanborn, *Life and Letters of John Brown*, 545; Leeman's is in the Hinton Papers, Kansas State Historical Society.
8. Annie's statements in Villard, *John Brown*, 418-420, and in Sanborn, *Recollections*, I, 171-178; and Osborn P. Anderson, *A Voice From Harper's Ferry* (Boston, 1861), 23-25.
9. Brown to Higginson, May 14, 1858, Higginson Papers, Boston Public Library; Brown to John Jr., August, 1859, New York *Herald*, Oct. 25, 1859; Sanborn, *Recollections*, I, 165-166, and *Life and Letters of John Brown*, 534-536, 548; Smith to Henrie, July 10, 1859, Dreer Papers, Historical Society of Pennsylvania; [Sanborn] to "Dear Friend" [Brown], Aug. 27, 1859, in "Mason Report," *U.S. Senate Committee Reports*, 1859-1860, II, 67-68.
10. *New York Times*, Oct. 22, 1859; Brown to John Jr., Aug. 6, 1859, Dreer Papers, Historical Society of Pennsylvania. Richard Richardson refused to leave Canada and Harriet Tubman was said to be too ill to move (see Sanborn, *Life and Letters of John Brown*, 535). Hinton and Gill both started for Harpers Ferry, only to receive news of the fateful results en route. Parsons had elected not to accompany Brown on his Virginia

invasion and was at Council Bluffs on his way to the Pikes Peak gold-rush site when Brown's call reached him. Parsons heeded his mother's advice, "They are bad men. You have got away from them, now keep away from them." And he went on to Colorado. Villard, *John Brown*, 344.

11. Douglass, *Life and Times*, 322-325.
12. Villard, *John Brown*, 413; Brown to John Jr., Aug. 6, 1859, Dreer Papers, Historical Society of Pennsylvania; Brown, "VINDICATION OF THE INVASION," in *New York Times*, Oct. 22, 1859. Martin Delany apparently was left in the dark about Brown's specific plans. He wrote Kagi on Aug. 16, 1859, that "I have been anxiously looking and expecting to see something of uncle's movements, but as yet have seen nothing." Would Kagi send him information about their activities? "All are in good spirits here, hoping and waiting for the good time coming." *Ibid.*
13. Redpath, *Roving Editor*, iii-iv, 306.
14. Floyd's testimony in "Mason Report," *U.S. Senate Committee Reports*, 1859-1860, II, 250-252; Villard, *John Brown*, 410-411.
15. Harlow, *Gerrit Smith*, 405-406.
16. Villard, *John Brown*, 420, 424; Anderson, *A Voice From Harper's Ferry*, 26-27.
17. Brown to his wife and daughters, Oct. 1, 1859, John Brown Papers, Huntington Library; Brown to John Jr., Oct. 1, 1859, Higginson Papers, Boston Public Library.
18. Villard, *John Brown*, 422-423; Cook, "Confession," in Hinton, *John Brown and His Men*, 707; Anderson, *A Voice From Harper's Ferry*, 31.
19. Sanborn, *Life and Letters of John Brown*, 548n; Edelstein, *Higginson*, 219-220.
20. Anderson, *A Voice From Harper's Ferry*, 27-32; Owen's statement in Sanborn, *Recollections*, I, 183; Cook, "Confession," in Hinton, *John Brown and His Men*, 708.

XIX. INSURRECTION!

1. Daniel Whelan's testimony in "Mason Report," *U.S. Senate Committee Reports*, 1859-1860, II, 22; Anderson, *A Voice From Harper's Ferry*, 32.
2. Washington's testimony in "Mason Report," *U.S. Senate Committee Reports*, 1859-1860, II, 29-36; John H. Allstadt's testimony in *ibid.*, 40-42; Cook, "Confession," in Hinton, *John Brown and His Men*, 708-709; Anderson, *A Voice From Harper's Ferry*, 33-35.
3. B. Phelp's testimony in *Life, Trial and Conviction of Captain John Brown* (New York, 1859), 69; statements of C. W. Armstrong (a passenger on the express train) and W. W. Throckmorton in the New York *Herald*, Oct. 19 and 24, 1859; Dr. John D. Starry's testimony in "Mason Report," *U.S. Senate Committee Reports*, 1859-1860, II, 13-24; Patrick Higgins' statement quoted from Baltimore *American* in the Savannah (Ga.) *Daily Morning News*, Oct. 26, 1859.

4. Starry's testimony in "Mason Report," *U.S. Senate Committee Reports,* 1859-1860, II, 24-26; Jennie Chambers, "What a School-Girl Saw of John Brown's Raid," *Harper's Monthly Magazine,* CIV (Jan., 1902), 311-318; Baltimore *American and Commercial Advertiser,* Oct. 17, 1859.

5. Telegram from the mayor of Frederick to Henry A. Wise, Oct. 17, 1859, John Brown Papers, Library of Congress; Baltimore *American and Commercial Advertiser,* Oct. 17, 1859; Savannah (Ga.) *Daily Morning News,* Oct. 18, 1859.

6. Anderson, *A Voice From Harper's Ferry,* 36; Cook, "Confession," in Hinton, *John Brown and His Men,* 709.

7. Harriet Newby to Dangerfield Newby, Apr. 11, 1859, in Virginia Governor (Henry A. Wise), *Governor's Message and Reports of the Public Officers of the State* (Richmond, 1859), Doc. I, 116-117; Alexander R. Boteler, "Recollections of the John Brown Raid," *Century,* XXVI (July, 1883), 399-411; Hinton, *John Brown and His Men,* 311; Frederick (Md.) *Herald,* as cited in the *Liberator* (Boston), Nov. 11, 1859; Patrick Higgins' statement in Villard, *John Brown,* 439, 640.

8. See Villard, *John Brown,* 440, for conflicting accounts of the manner of Leeman's death.

9. Copeland's statement (dictated in jail in Charlestown, Va., in 1859), MS, Stutler Collection; Boteler, "Recollections," *Century,* XXVI, 399-411; Starry's testimony in "Mason Report," *U.S. Senate Committee Reports,* 1859-1860, II, 27; Villard, *John Brown,* 445.

10. John T. Allstadt's statement in Villard, *John Brown,* 441; George W. Chambers' testimony in "Mason Report," *U.S. Senate Committee Reports,* 1859-1860, II, 29; Mayor Beckham's Will Book, Jefferson County Court Records, Charlestown, W. Va.

11. Villard, *John Brown,* 443. See also Harry Hunter's testimony, given during John Brown's trial, in the New York *Tribune,* Oct. 29, 1859, and in the New York *Herald,* Oct. 31, 1859.

12. Cook, "Confession," in Hinton, *John Brown and His Men,* 710-711; Anderson, *A Voice From Harper's Ferry,* 47-55. Anderson claimed that he and Hazlett escaped on Tuesday morning, after the storming of the engine house, which was impossible. Probably they left the arsenal late in the afternoon or early in the evening of Monday, October 17, during all the skirmishing that followed the arrival of the Martinsburg company.

13. "Capt. John Brown answers," in Villard, *John Brown,* 447. For newspaper accounts identifying Brown as the commander of the insurgents, see *New York Times,* Oct. 19, 1859, and New York *Herald* and New York *Tribune* of the same date; and the Savannah (Ga.) *Daily Morning News,* Oct. 19 and 20, 1859.

14. Allstadt's statement in Villard, *John Brown,* 448.

15. Washington's statement in *ibid.,* 453; J. E. B. Stuart to his mother, Jan. 31, 1860, H. B. McClellan, *Life and Campaigns of J. E. B. Stuart* (Boston, 1885), 28-30; "Mason Report," *U.S. Senate Committee Reports,* 1859-1860,

II, 40-43; Washington's testimony in *ibid.*, 38; New York *Herald*, Oct. 21, 1859; Villard, *John Brown*, 451-455.

16. *New York Times*, Oct. 22, 1859; Stuart to his mother, Jan. 31, 1860, McClellan, *Life and Campaigns of J. E. B. Stuart*, 28-30; Villard, *John Brown*, 467.

17. Villard, *John Brown*, 468.

18. The following raiders died at Harpers Ferry: Oliver and Watson Brown, William and Dauphin Thompson, John Henry Kagi, William H. Leeman, Jeremiah Anderson, Stewart Taylor, Dangerfield Newby, and Lewis Leary. The captured raiders, in addition to Brown himself, included Shields Green, John A. Copeland, Aaron D. Stevens, and Edwin Coppoc. Hazlett and Cook were captured later and returned to Charlestown for trial.

19. C. W. Tayleure to John Brown Jr., June 15, 1879, in Villard, *John Brown*, 455.

20. Baltimore *American and Commercial Advertiser*, Oct. 21, 1859; New York *Tribune*, Oct. 22, 1859.

21. The original text of the interview was published in the New York *Herald*, Oct. 21, 1859, and reprinted with minor variations in Sanborn, Villard, and Ruchames. My quotes are from Sanborn, *Life and Letters of John Brown*, 562-569.

XX. LET THEM HANG ME

1. Baltimore *American and Commercial Advertiser*, Oct. 19, 20, and 21, 1859; Chambers, "What a School-Girl Saw of John Brown's Raid," *Harper's Monthly Magazine*, CIV, 318; Richard B. Morris, *Fair Trial* (New York, 1967 ed.), 268.

2. Villard, *John Brown*, 476-489; Morris, *Fair Trial*, 268-270; New York *Herald*, Oct. 26 and 27, 1859; New York *Tribune*, Oct. 28, 1859; *Life, Trial and Execution of Captain John Brown* (New York, 1859), 59-61.

3. Chapman, *Learning and Other Essays* (New York, 1910), 130-134.

4. Stutler, "Abraham Lincoln and John Brown—A Parallel," *Civil War History*, VIII, 296; Lincoln's Cooper Union Address, Feb. 27, 1860, in Roy P. Basler (ed.), *Collected Works of Abraham Lincoln*, III, 538.

5. New York *Tribune*, Oct. 18 and 19, 1859. See also the Topeka (Kans.) *Tribune*, Oct. 21, 1859, and the Hartford *Evening Press*, Oct. 20, 1859. For more extensive quotations from the Northern press, see Villard, *John Brown*, 472-474.

6. Nevins, *Emergence of Lincoln*, II, 86; Villard, *John Brown*, 480-481, 568-569.

7. Lincoln's speech at Troy, Kans., Dec. 2, 1859, in Topeka *Capital*, Oct. 25, 1908; Villard, *John Brown*, 564; Chase to H. H. Barrett, Oct. 29, 1859, Stutler Collection.

8. "Justice" of Massachusetts to Wise, Nov. 21, 1859, John Brown Papers,

Library of Congress; the *Liberator*, Nov. 4, 1859; Portage (Ohio), *Weekly Sentinel*, Oct. 26, 1859.

9. New York *Herald*, Oct. 18, 20, 21, 27, and 29, 1859; *New York Times*, Oct. 21, 22, 24, and 28, 1859; Baltimore *American and Commercial Advertiser*, Oct. 20, 21, and 24, 1859.

10. Oct. 25, 1859, John Brown Papers, Library of Congress.

11. Harlow, *Gerrit Smith*, 407-422; Sanborn, *Recollections*, I, 168-169; New York *Herald*, Nov. 2, 1859.

12. Statement of Mary Stearns (n.d.), Hinton Papers, Kansas State Historical Society; New York *Tribune*, Nov. 6, 1859; Howe, *Letters and Journals*, 437-439; Howe to Higginson, Feb. 16, 1860, Higginson Papers, Boston Public Library; Schwartz, *Howe*, 237-238.

13. Sanborn Folder, Houghton Library of Harvard University; Sanborn, *Recollections*, I, 187-207.

14. Foner, *Life and Writings of Frederick Douglass*, II, 91-93, 460-463; Douglass, *Life and Times*, 310-317, 325-330.

15. Higginson, *Cheerful Yesterdays*, 223, and *Letters and Journals*, 86-87; Edelstein, *Higginson*, 221-232.

16. Mrs. Sarah H. Braun [?] to John Brown Jr., Sept. 6, 1887, John Brown Papers, Kansas State Historical Society; Hinton, *John Brown and His Men*, 332-334, 553-567; "Owen Brown's Story of His Escape from Harper's Ferry," typescript, John Brown Jr. Papers, Ohio Historical Society; E. C. Lampson, "The Black String Bands," Cleveland *Plain Dealer*, Oct. 8, 1899.

17. Annie's statement in Hinton, *John Brown and His Men*, 445-446.

18. Sarah Everett to "Dear Jennie," Dec. 31, 1859, John and Sarah Everett Papers, Kansas State Historical Society; Villard, *John Brown*, 512-517; Boston *Atlas & Daily Bee*, Oct. 24, 1859; Redpath to Higginson, Nov. 13, 1859, Higginson Papers, Boston Public Library; Edelstein, *Higginson*, 230.

19. Ashbel Woodward, *Life of General Nathaniel Lyon* (Hartford, Conn., 1862), 229.

20. *Liberator*, Oct. 21 and 28, 1859; Phillips, *Speeches, Lectures, and Letters* (Boston, 1863), 272; C. Vann Woodward, "John Brown's Private War," in Woodward, *The Burden of Southern History* (Baton Rouge, La., 1960), 53-54; and Benjamin Quarles, *Black Abolitionists* (New York, 1969), 240-244.

21. Franklin B. Sanborn, *The Personality of Emerson* (Boston, 1903), 87-88; J. E. Cabot, *Memoir of Ralph Waldo Emerson* (2 vols., Boston, 1887), II, 597; Ostrander, "Emerson, Thoreau, and John Brown," *Mississippi Valley Historical Review*, XXXIX, 713-726.

22. Hinton, *John Brown and His Men*, 433-437.

23. Thoreau, *Journal*, XII, 429, and *Writings*, IV, 443, VI, 358-369; Ostrander, "Emerson, Thoreau, and John Brown," *Mississippi Valley Historical Review*, XXXIX, 724-726.

24. Parker to Francis Jackson, Nov. 24, 1859, in Commager (ed.), *Parker: An Anthology*, 267; Lydia Maria Child to "Dear Mary," Nov. 3, 1859,

Stutler Collection; Samuel Longfellow, *Life of Henry Wadsworth Long-fellow* (3 vols., Boston, 1891), II, 347.

25. Villard, *John Brown*, 465; Albany (Ga.) *Patriot*, Oct. 27 and Dec. 1, 1859; Mobile *Register*, Oct. 25, 1859; Charleston *Mercury*, Nov. 3, 1859; Baltimore *American and Commercial Advertiser*, Nov. 19 and 21, Dec. 2, 1859.

26. *Ibid.*; Savannah (Ga.) *Daily Morning News*, Nov. 8, 1859; Richmond *Enquirer*, Oct. 25, 1859; Diary of Edmund Ruffin, photostat, Stutler Collection; Barton H. Wise, *Life of Henry A. Wise* (New York, 1899), 256; William Hande Brown, *Maryland, the History of a Palatinate* (Boston, 1904), 349-351; Frederick Bancroft, *Life of William H. Seward* (2 vols., New York, 1900), I, 497-498.

27. See, for example, letters to Wise from J. A. Crook of Allenton, Ala., Dec. 1, 1859; Gustavus A. Northington of Kingston, Ala., Nov. 28, 1859; and W. N. Smith of Centre, N.C., Nov. 21, 1859; in addition to numerous comparable letters, all in the John Brown Papers, Library of Congress.

28. Baltimore *American and Commercial Advertiser*, Oct. 21 and 27, Nov. 2 and 9, 1859; Cynthia (Ky.) *News* as quoted in *ibid.*, Nov. 18, 1859; Baltimore *Sun*, Nov. 19, 1859; *National Intelligencer*, Nov. 16, 1859.

29. John T. Morgan of Cahaba, Ala., to Wise, Dec. 3, 1859; John Summers of Alexandria, Va., to Wise, Nov. 17, 1859; A. B. Moore of Montgomery, Ala., to Wise, Dec. 7, 1859, John Brown Papers, Library of Congress; *The "New Reign of Terror" in the Slaveholding States for 1859-60* (New York, 1860); Baltimore *American and Commercial Advertiser*, Nov. 28, 1859; Woodward, "John Brown's Private War," *Burden of Southern History*, 63-67; Filler, *Crusade Against Slavery*, 272-273; Nevins, *Emergence of Lincoln*, II, 85. Brown was not without supporters in the South. A disturbed citizen of Brandon, Miss., wrote Wise that "Even in the fire-eating state of Mississippi, *in this village*, the miscreant Brown has sympathizers." M. R. Westbrook to Wise, Nov. 28, 1859, John Brown Papers, Library of Congress.

30. Baltimore *American and Commercial Advertiser*, Oct. 27 and 28, Nov. 2, 17-22, 26, 28, and 30, Dec. 1 and 2, 1859; Wise, *Henry A. Wise*, 256; Hinton, *John Brown and His Men*, 334, 384-385; Villard, *John Brown*, 522.

31. *De Bow's Review*, XXVIII (January and May, 1860), 542-549; Woodward, "John Brown's Private War," *Burden of Southern History*, 65-67; Avery Craven, *The Coming of the Civil War* (2nd ed., Chicago, 1957), 409-412.

32. Richmond *Enquirer*, Oct. 25, 1859; Villard, *John Brown*, 566-567.

33. Oct. 26, 1859, copy in Sanborn Folder, Houghton Library of Harvard University; Villard, *John Brown*, 506-507.

34. My account of Brown's trial is based on the Baltimore *American and Commercial Advertiser*, Oct. 25-Nov. 3, 1859; the New York *Herald* and the *New York Times*, Oct. 27-Nov. 3, 1859; *Life, Trial and Execution of Captain John Brown*, 68ff.; Morris, *Fair Trial*, 275-292; and Villard, *John Brown*, 476-507.

35. *New York Times*, Nov. 3-14, 1859; Baltimore *American and Commercial*

Advertiser, Nov. 10-12, 1859; Hinton, *John Brown and His Men*, 341-411.

36. Hoyt to Le Barnes, Nov. 14, 1859, Hinton Papers, Kansas State Historical Society; Villard, *John Brown*, 647.

37. The eighteen affidavits (one of them given jointly by Sylvester and Mills Thompson), along with an earlier petition by Sylvester Thompson regarding Brown's "insanity," are in the John Brown Papers, Library of Congress.

38. Several historians have erroneously cited these affidavits as containing evidence that Brown's mother was "insane" for the last few years of her life and "died insane." Actually the affidavits contain no such statements that Brown's mother was "insane." Those documents that bear on his mother read as follows:

Sylvester Thompson's petition (dated Oct. 31, 1859): "And your petitioner represents [reports?] that Brown's Mother died about fifty-one years ago, a young woman. The Grand-Mother of Brown upon the Mother's side died insane and was insane for many years prior to her death. His Mother's Sisters including the Mother of your Petitioner [Sylvester Thompson], three in all, have all been at times insane."

Ethan Alling's affidavit: "Affiant also says that he is acquainted with the family of Gideon Mills of Hudson [a maternal uncle of Brown's] who is a [brother] of John Brown's Mother and that several of his children have been and some of them now are insane. And was also acquainted with Mrs. Richardson late of [Swinsbough?] who was also a sister of said John Brown's Mother and was reported to be insane for several years before her death."

Gideon Mills's affidavit: "The Mother of this affiant who was a [brother] of the Mother of said John Brown was insane for a number of years before her death and died insane." Internal evidence in Mills's affidavit (as well as statements made in other affidavits that bore on this point) prove that Mills was referring to his own mother—Brown's grandmother—in this passage. He was *not* referring to Brown's mother. The lawyers who assisted in taking such testimony obviously made the language deliberately vague and suggestive, so that Brown and his mother would be judged guilty by association.

George Leach's affidavit: "This affiant also has known several members of said Brown's family in his Mother's side who were insane. To wit Three of the children of Gideon Mills who were the cousins of said John Brown have been so completely insane as to require confinement in Lunatic Asylums." "Another cousin of said Brown, Elizabeth Thompson, now a resident of Hudson, has been for a long time insane."

Joint affidavit of Sylvester and Mills Thompson: "Brown's Mother and ours were sisters. The family name was Mills, and many of the members of this family have at times been insane. Our Grand Mother on the Mother's side was insane for six years, and died insane. Our mother was more or less insane for six years, and died insane as her Mother. We have a sister that has been returned from the Lunatic Asylum incurably insane, and is now living in our neighborhood. One of our maternal uncles has been insane. His name is Oliver Mills. We have [had?] two aunts sisters of the Mother of John Brown, insane." They were "Sarah Woodruff" and "Susan Richardson."

Salmon Thompson's affidavit: "I am well acquainted with many of his [Brown's] relatives in his Mother's side and know many of them to have been insane. . . ."

39. Woodward, "John Brown's Private War," *Burden of Southern History*, 47-48; Villard, *John Brown*, 509. Woodward, Allen Johnson, Allan Nevins, and others have taken these controversial affidavits at their face value. Johnson, in his sketch of Brown in the *Dictionary of American Biography*, III, 131-134, makes a great deal of "the insanity" in Brown's family, asserts erroneously that Brown's mother "died insane," and scolds Villard for dismissing "the question of Brown's insanity" too readily. Allan Nevins wrote a psychoanalytical case study of Brown, included in the *Emergence of Lincoln*, II, 5-27, 70-97, in which he diagnosed Brown's problem as "ambitious paranoia" or "reasoning insanity." Although Nevins' study contains brilliant insights into the Harpers Ferry controversy and reveals more of the contradictions and complexities of Brown's character than anything written before it, the case study nevertheless is flawed by a rash of factual errors and a highly questionable approach. Nevins is no psychiatrist. Yet he borrows the terminology of what is still an imprecise science (presumably on the advice of a psychiatrist in New York and another in Denver, who counseled him) and persists in diagnosing Brown's "mental disease"—his "psychogenic malady"—on the basis of what certain people said about him over a century ago. Before I go on I should like to say that I am *not* arguing that the biographer and the historian have nothing to learn from psychology and what it has discovered about human behavior. On the contrary, as Paul Murray Kendall has said in *The Art of Biography*, 121: "Psychology and psychoanalysis have thrust fingers of light into the cave of the human mind, have deepened our sense of the complexities, the arcane tides, of personality, have enabled us to penetrate some of the dark corners of motive and desire, to detect patterns of action, and sense the symbolic value of word and gesture." It is one thing to learn from what psychology has taught us about human beings. It is quite another for a historian—a layman—to assume the role of the psychiatrist himself, as Nevins did with Brown, and psychoanalyze a historical personality on the basis of controversial evidence. Nevins accepts without question the argument that Brown inherited part of his "mental disease" (repeating the error that his mother "died insane"). Moreover, Nevins uses the affidavits gathered by Hoyt as clinical evidence—and misuses other materials by taking passages of letters out of context—to support his diagnosis that Brown was "a reasoning maniac." Perhaps some day in the future, when the science is more exact, an expert psychiatrist will tell us

what Brown's "mental disorder" was. Or maybe he will conclude, when all the evidence is in, that Brown was no sicker than most of his countrymen, remembering, as one must, the words of Karen Horney that in times of social injustice it may be the passive individual, not the reformer, who is mentally disturbed.

40. Woodward, "John Brown's Private War," *Burden of Southern History*, 47-48.

41. See letters to Wise from Sylvester H. Thompson, Oct. 31, 1859; R. Bethell Clayton, Nov. 2, 1859, the Rev. Edward Brown, Nov. 5, 1859, all in the John Brown Papers, Library of Congress. E. D. Campbell, governor of Wisconsin, and Amos Lawrence also wrote Wise that Brown was a monomaniac; and Aaron Erickson, the New York wool dealer whom I quoted in chap. V of this biography, sent a long letter describing Brown's "monomaniacal" symptoms on the subject of wool.

42. Wise to the superintendent of the state lunatic asylum, Nov. 10, 1859, and the Cincinnati minister to Wise, Nov. 16, 1859, *ibid.*

43. Brown to "Dear Brother" Jeremiah, Nov. 12, 1859, Lawrence *Republican*, Dec. 8, 1859, and reprinted in Ruchames, *A John Brown Reader*, 134.

44. Hoyt to Le Barnes, Oct. 30, 1859, Hinton Papers, Kansas State Historical Society.

45. H. K. Craig to Wise, Nov. 18, 1859; A. L. Harmon to Wise, Nov. 23, 1859; George Weston Jr. to Wise, Nov. 28, 1859; "A Friend" to Wise, Nov. 30, 1859; Davis to Wise, Nov. 2, 1859, John Brown Papers, Library of Congress; photostat of Ruffin's Diary, Stutler Collection.

46. Higginson, *Letters and Journals*, 86-87; Brown to Higginson, Nov. 4, 1859, photograph of original, Stutler Collection; Brown to his wife and children, Nov. 8, 1859, Sanborn, *Life and Letters of John Brown*, 585-587.

XXI. I, JOHN BROWN

1. New York *Herald*, Oct. 31, 1859; New York *Tribune*, Nov. 5, 1859; Hinton, *John Brown and His Men*, 485, 488-490, 496-497, 509; Villard, *John Brown*, 538-539, 651.

2. Brown to his wife and family, Nov. 10, 1859, Villard, *John Brown*, 540-541; Brown to his wife and children, Nov. 8, 1859, Sanborn, *Life and Letters of John Brown*, 585-587.

3. Both letters are in Sanborn, *Life and Letters of John Brown*, 581-583.

4. Nov. 7, 1859, Stutler Collection.

5. Villard, *John Brown*, 540-541.

6. Nov. 12, 1859, Sanborn, *Life and Letters of John Brown*, 588.

7. Brown to Adams, Nov. 15, 1859, Stutler Collection; Brown to Vaill, Ruchames, *A John Brown Reader*, 135-136.

8. Nov. 16, 1859, Villard Collection, Columbia University. Higginson wrote his mother on Nov. 22, 1859, that aid was flowing into the Brown household "from all directions, and that is something, because, besides their

severe bereavements, they greatly need money; though not so totally destitute as many seem to think." Higginson himself had received "some queer
letters about them, one from a man in Winchendon offering to adopt one
of the daughters and teach her telegraphy." Higginson, *Letters and
Journals*, 87-88.

9. Brown to Thomas Musgrave, Nov. 17, 1859, Ruchames, *A John Brown
   Reader*, 139; and Brown to Luther Humphrey, Nov. 19, 1859, John Brown
   Letters, Houghton Library of Harvard University.

10. Brown to his wife, Nov. 21, 1859, to his children, Nov. 22, 1859, and to
    Jason and Ellen, Nov. 22, 1859, Sanborn, *Life and Letters of John Brown*,
    595-598.

11. Nov. 22, 1859, Higginson Papers, Boston Public Library.

12. Interview with Mrs. Thomas Russell, by Katherine Mayo, in the New
    York *Evening Post*, Oct. 23, 1909.

13. Charleston *Mercury* as quoted in the Baltimore *American and Commercial
    Advertiser*, Nov. 10, 1859; Dr. Lewis A. Sayr to Wise, Nov. 30, 1859, John
    Brown Papers, Library of Congress.

14. Nov. 22, 1859, Villard, *John Brown*, 164.

15. Sanborn, *Life and Letters of John Brown*, 622-623; Villard, *John Brown*,
    545.

16. Nov. 22, 1859, "Mason Report," *U.S. Senate Committee Reports*, 1859-
    1860, II, 67-68 (see also 1-12).

17. Nov. 23, 1859, Ruchames, *A John Brown Reader*, 145-146.

18. Sanborn, *Life and Letters of John Brown*, 622-623; Brown to Stearns,
    Nov. 29, 1859, Stutler Collection.

19. Nov. 25, 1859, Sanborn, *Life and Letters of John Brown*, 603-605.

20. Nov. 26, 1859, Villard Collection, Columbia University.

21. Nov. 27, 1859, John Brown Papers, Chicago Historical Society.

22. Ferdinand Julius Dreer Papers, Historical Society of Pennsylvania.

23. New York *Tribune*, Dec. 3, 1859; New York *Herald*, Dec. 5, 1859; *New York
    Times*, Dec. 3, 1859; Villard, *John Brown*, 550-551; Sanborn, *Life and
    Letters of John Brown*, 623-624.

24. Brown to his brother Jeremiah, Nov. 1 [Dec. 1], 1859, Stutler Collection.

25. Brown to his wife, Dec. 2, 1859, Dreer Papers, Historical Society of Penn-
    sylvania; Brown to Lora Case, Dec. 2, 1859, original in the Henry W. and
    Albert A. Berg Collection, New York Public Library. A copy of the
    original is in the John Brown Jr. Papers, Ohio Historical Society.

26. Sanborn, *Life and Letters of John Brown*, 625; Cook's letter of Dec. 7,
    1859, Hinton, *John Brown and His Men*, 484-485; New York *Tribune*,
    Dec. 3, 1859; New York *Herald*, Dec. 3, 1859.

27. John Brown Papers, Chicago Historical Society; Villard, *John Brown*, 554.

28. David Hunter Strother's eyewitness account (ed. by Boyd B. Stutler), "The
    Hanging of John Brown," *American Heritage*, VI (February, 1955), 8-9;
    Thomas J. Jackson to his wife, Dec. 2, 1859, typescript, Stutler Collection;
    Ruffin's Diary, entry of Dec. 2, 1859, *ibid.*; Booth to John Clark, Apr. 20,

1865, *ibid.*; Preston's account of the execution, Dec. 2, 1859, in Elizabeth Preston Allan, *Life and Letters of Margaret Junkin Preston* (Boston, 1903), 111-117.

XXII. BEYOND THE GALLOWS

1. Dec. 3, 1859.
2. Lawrence *Republican*, Dec. 8, 1859. The Lawrence *Herald of Freedom*, Dec. 15 through Dec. 30, 1859, which had taken a very critical editorial view of Brown, unhappily observed that Kansans were now praising the Pottawatomie massacre and calling Brown a hero who had saved the territory for freedom in 1856.
3. Lane, *Fifty Years and Over of Akron*, 591; Samuel P. Orth, *A History of Cleveland* (Cleveland, 1910), 295; *A Tribute of Respect Commemorative of the Worth and Sacrifice of John Brown of Osawatomie: It Being a Full Report of the Speeches Made and Resolutions Adopted by the Citizens of Cleveland* [on Dec. 2, 1859] . . . (Cleveland, 1859); Land, "John Brown's Ohio Environment," *Ohio State Archaeological and Historical Quarterly*, LVII, 42-46.
4. Thomas, *Garrison*, 397-398. For reaction to the execution in Rhode Island, where a commemorative meeting occurred in Providence and an anti-Brown service in South Kingston, see John Michael Ray, "Rhode Island Reacts to John Brown's Raid," *Rhode Island History*, XX (October, 1961), 103-108.
5. Child to "Dear Mary," Dec. 2, 1859, and to Henry Denny, Dec. 20, 1859, Stutler Collection; Lawrence *Republican*, Dec. 22, 1859.
6. Phillips, *Speeches, Lectures, and Letters*, 289-293; receipts and memorandum regarding Brown's coffins in John Brown Papers, Huntington Library, and in Stutler Collection; Obituary of Lyman Epps, Sr., newspaper clipping in W. E. Connelley Scrapbooks, II, Stutler Collection; Villard, *John Brown*, 561-562. The skeleton of Watson Brown was recovered in 1882 and taken to North Elba for permanent burial.
7. Fawn Brodie, *Thaddeus Stevens, Scourge of the South* (New York, 1966 ed.), 135-137.
8. The other members of the Mason Committee were G. N. Fitch, J. Collamer, and J. R. Doolittle. The minority report agreed with the conclusions of the majority led by Senator Mason, but criticized its latitude in probing the witnesses' political views and attitudes on slavery. "Mason Report," *U.S. Senate Committee Reports*, 1859-1860, II, majority report, 1-19; minority report, 21-25.
9. Woodward, "John Brown's Private War," *Burden of Southern History*, 67-68; Nevins, *Emergence of Lincoln*, II, 98ff.
10. There were many John Brown songs composed during the war. The celebrated "John Brown's Body," the most widely sung of the Brown hymns which Union troops always associated with John Brown of Harpers Ferry,

was actually based on a sarcastic tune which men in a Massachusetts outfit made up as "a jibe" against one Sergeant John Brown of Boston. See Boyd B. Stutler, "John Brown's Body," *Civil War History*, IV (September, 1958), 251-260.

MANUSCRIPTS CITED

This list contains only those manuscript sources cited in the preceding pages. It does not include the many other manuscript collections which I examined but did not refer to in the notes. Nor does the list include newspapers and printed sources used in the preparation of this biography. These items can be readily identified in the notes.

ABBOTT, J. B. Papers. Kansas State Historical Society, Topeka.

ADAIR, S. L. "Life of Frederick Brown," Kansas Collection, University of Kansas, Lawrence.

———. "Recollections of some of the events in the years of 1855 and 1856." Miscellaneous Documents, Kansas State Historical Society, Topeka.

BERG, HENRY W. and ALBERT A. Collection. New York Public Library, New York, N.Y.

BLACKMAN, W. I. R. Papers. Kansas State Historical Society, Topeka.

BLOOD, JAMES. Papers. Kansas State Historical Society, Topeka.

BONDI, AUGUST. Papers. Kansas State Historical Society, Topeka.

BROWN, G. W. Papers. Kansas State Historical Society, Topeka.

BROWN, JOHN. "A Brief History of John Brown otherwise (old B, & his family: *as connected with Kansas*; by one who knows," in the Ferdinand Julius Dreer Papers, which see.

———. Collection. John Brown's Farm, Lake Placid, N.Y. This consists of several Brown family letters and documents and numerous printed materials germane to the Brown story.

———. Letterbooks of Perkins & Brown, 1846-1847, 1849-1850. 3 vols. These items are in the Boyd B. Stutler Collection, which see.

———. Letters. Atlanta University Library, Atlanta, Ga. This collection includes 44 letters which Brown wrote to Seth Thompson between 1826 and 1849, one letter Brown composed to David Hudson, and five documents that pertain to Brown.

———. Letters. Houghton Library of Harvard University, Cambridge, Mass.

———. Letters. Illinois State Historical Library, Springfield. Seven very valuable Brown letters comprise this small collection.

———. Letters. Torrington Public Library, Torrington, Conn.

———. Letters. Western Reserve Historical Society, Cleveland, Ohio.

———. Letters. Yale University Library, New Haven, Conn. This collection consists of six letters which Brown wrote to his wife and to Simon Perkins, and another letter which attested to Brown's alleged insanity.

———. Memorandum Book, 1843-1846, in the John Brown Papers, Henry E. Huntington Library, which see.

———. Notebooks, 1838-1845, 1856-1859. 2 vols. Boston Public Library, Boston, Mass. Volume 2 has almost daily entries concerning Brown's Virginia plan, plus those remarkable notes about guerrilla operations, with references to Mina and Wellington, and the list of Southern towns where federal arsenals or forts were located.

———. Papers. Chicago Historical Society, Chicago, Ill.

———. Papers. Henry E. Huntington Library, San Marino, Calif. This collection includes not only the Memorandum Book listed above, but seventeen Brown letters and two boxes of documentary material about Brown. Some 371 additional pieces germane to Brown are scattered about in other collections in the library.

———. Papers. Kansas State Historical Society, Topeka. A rich repository of Brown family correspondence, as well as countless other documentary materials, many relating to the Pottawatomie massacre, such as newspaper clippings and signed testimonies of several of Brown's Kansas contemporaries.

———. Papers. Library of Congress, Washington, D.C. This invaluable collection consists of 75 broadsides and other documents pertaining to Brown and the Harpers Ferry raid; 10 letters in typescript which Brown wrote to Simon Perkins; and some 400 other letters, some written by Brown himself, others written about him concerning the Harpers Ferry attack. The controversial affidavits concerning Brown's alleged insanity are also located here.

———. Papers. Ohio Historical Society, Columbus, Ohio. This includes a number of Brown family letters and documents and other materials that relate to Brown. Additional Brown materials are located in the Charles E. Rice Collection and the Edward C. Lampson Collection, also owned by the Society.

———. Scrapbooks. 16 vols. Kansas State Historical Society, Topeka.

———. "Sambos Mistakes." Maryland Historical Society, Baltimore, Md.

BROWN, JOHN JR. Papers. Ohio Historical Society, Columbus, Ohio. This extremely useful collection includes 382 pieces, most of them letters written by the Brown family, as well as a copy of volume 1 of the Letterbooks of Perkins & Brown and the 2-volume diary of John Brown Jr.

BROWN, O. C. Papers. Kansas State Historical Society, Topeka.

BUTLER-GUNSAULUS. Collection. University of Chicago Library, Chicago, Ill. This contains two letters from Brown and another from Thomas Wentworth Higginson about Brown.

CONNELLEY, WILLIAM E. John Brown Scrapbooks, located in the Boyd B. Stutler Collection, which see.

DANA, RICHARD HENRY JR. Journal. Massachusetts Historical Society, Boston, Mass.

DREER, FERDINAND JULIUS. Papers. Historical Society of Pennsylvania, Philadelphia. A number of letters written by Brown or his contemporaries and other manuscript matter relating to Harpers Ferry are located in this collection.

EVERETT, JOHN and SARAH. Papers. Kansas State Historical Society, Topeka.

FOSTER, C. A. Papers. Kansas State Historical Society, Topeka.

GEE, CLARENCE S. Collection. Lockport, N.Y.

GIDDINGS, JOSHUA R. Papers. Ohio Historical Society, Columbus, Ohio.

HANWAY, JAMES. Papers. Kansas State Historical Society, Topeka.

HIGGINSON, THOMAS WENTWORTH. Papers. Boston Public Library, Boston, Mass. Another indispensable source for the student of Brown, this collection consists of a number of letters written by Brown and the Secret Six, as well as Higginson's memorandums and other documents.

———. Papers. Houghton Library of Harvard University, Cambridge, Massachusetts.

———. Papers. Kansas State Historical Society, Topeka.

HINTON, RICHARD J. Papers. Kansas State Historical Society, Topeka. Not only does this collection contain a number of letters by Brown and his men, James Hanway and C. G. Allen; it also has the reminiscences of George P. Gill and other documentary materials pertaining to the John Brown story.

HOWE, SAMUEL GRIDLEY. Papers. Massachusetts Historical Society, Boston, Mass.

HUTCHINSON, WILLIAM. Scrapbook. Kansas State Historical Society, Topeka.

HYATT, THADDEUS. Papers. Kansas State Historical Society, Topeka.

PATE, H. CLAY. "John Brown." Kansas Collection, University of Kansas, Lawrence.

REED, BYRON. Collection. Omaha Public Library, Omaha, Nebr.

SANBORN, FRANKLIN B. Folder. Houghton Library of Harvard University, Cambridge, Mass. Included here are copies of 82 letters written by Brown and members of his family, plus the agreement between Perkins and Brown signed on Jan. 9, 1844.

SANBORN, FRANKLIN B. Letters. Atlanta University Library, Atlanta, Ga. This collection consists of 17 letters which Sanborn wrote to Brown in 1857 and 1858.

———. Folder. Houghton Library of Harvard University, Cambridge, Mass.

Included here are copies of 82 letters written by Brown and members of his family, plus the agreement between Perkins and Brown signed on Jan. 9, 1844.

——. Papers. Kansas State Historical Society, Topeka.

——. John Brown Scrapbooks, located in the Boyd B. Stutler Collection, which see.

SMITH, GERRIT. Papers. Syracuse University, Syracuse, N.Y.

STEARNS, GEORGE L. Papers. Kansas State Historical Society, Topeka.

STUTLER, BOYD B. Collection. Charleston, W. Va. Consisting in all of "several thousand" pieces, this collection of Brown materials is perhaps the most important one in existence. In it are 104 of Brown's original letters, the Letterbooks of Perkins & Brown, which contain 456 letters written by Brown, a number of original family letters, a score of related letters, newspaper clippings, various unpublished documents that pertain to Brown, broadsides, reprints of speeches, songs, plays, published articles about Brown, and a bibliography of John Brown in periodical literature compiled by Mr. Stutler, as well as the scrapbooks of John Brown matter collected by Franklin B. Sanborn and William E. Connelley.

U.S. DISTRICT COURT, SECOND JUDICIAL DISTRICT, TERRITORY OF KANSAS. Records. Federal Records Center, Kansas City, Mo. On file here is the Journal of the Second District Court, 1855-1860, which contains entries for the April, May, and June, 1856, terms of Judge Sterling G. Cato that are pertinent to Brown. Other records of the Second Judicial District, on file at the Center, are the Attorneys Trial Docket, 1856-1861, the Minute Book of the Second District Court, 1855-1860, and the Final Record Book, vol. C, 1857-1863. In addition, the Center has a number of important records of the First Judicial District, Territory of Kansas.

VILLARD, OSWALD GARRISON. Collection. Columbia University Library, New York, N.Y. This includes numerous source materials, letters, and documents which Villard gathered during his research on Brown.

INDEX

Abbott, J. B., 154

Abolitionists, 27–31, 234–236, 240; in Ohio, 29–30, 39–41, 52–53; gag rule against, 52; in Springfield, Massachusetts, 58–59; Kansas laws against. 100; Southern attitude toward, 235–236, 240; JB regarded as martyr, 318–319

Adair, Florilla Brown (Mrs. Samuel Adair, half-sister of JB), 84; letter quoted, 122

Adair, Samuel: goes to Kansas, 84, 85, 87; in Osawatomie, 106; shelters JB's sons after Pottawatomie massacre, 140; opinion of massacre, 141, 146; house searched, 145; before attack on Osawatomie, 169; JB writes to, 215; sends money to JB, 218; JB ill at his house, 257; approves of JB, 317; mentioned, 118, 122, 332

Adams, George, letter from JB quoted, 340

Adams, John Quincy, 15, 20, 52

Adirondack Mountains, 65, 66

Africa, Negro colonies in, see Colonization of Negroes

Akron *Summit Beacon*, 110, 111

Albany, Georgia, *Patriot*, 320

Alcott, Bronson, 181, 318; praises JB, 269

Allen, C. G, 163–165, 172

Allstadt, John, 291, 299

American Colonization Society, 28, 29

Anderson, Jeremiah Goldsmith: joins JB, 261; goes to Harpers Ferry, 273, 275; at Kennedy's farm, 280; in Harpers Ferry raid, 299; killed, 300; letter to his

brother quoted, 281; mentioned, 268, 269, 271, 272

Anderson, Osborn P.: at Chatham convention, 243, 246; joins JB, 286; in Harpers Ferry raid, 294, 295; escapes, 298, 302, mentioned, 282, 288

Anderson, Samuel, 165, 166

Andrew, John A., 271, 316, 359

Annoyance Associations, 86, 89

Antislavery movement, 27–32; *see also* Abolitionists; Colonization of Negroes

Appeal, David Walker, 27, 61

Ashtabula League of Freedom, 273, 316

Atchison, David R., 84, 89, 106, 109, 123, 168, 176

Atchison *Squatter Sovereign*, 123, 142

Austinburg, Ohio, school, 48, 51, 52

Avis, John, jailer, 337, 343, 348–350

Baldwin, David, 121, 122

Baltimore *American and Commercial Advertiser*, 303, 307

Barber, Thomas, murdered in Kansas, 107–108

Beckham, Fontaine, mayor of Harpers Ferry, killed, 296

Beecher, Henry Ward, sermon on JB, 318–319

Bernard, Joab, 155

Big Springs, Kansas, free-state convention, 101

Black Jack, battle of, 152–154

Blair, Charles: JB orders pikes from, 199, 211, 272, 276, 286, 301; denies knowl-

421